The "Great Satan" vs. the "Mad Mullahs"

The "Great Satan" vs. the "Mad Mullahs"

How the United States and Iran
Demonize Each Other

William O. Beeman

Westport, Connecticut
London

Library of Congress Cataloging-in-Publication Data

Beeman, William O.
   The "great Satan" vs. the "mad mullahs" : how the United States and Iran demonize each other / William O. Beeman.
      p. cm.
   Includes bibliographical references and index.
   ISBN 0–275–98214–9 (alk. paper)
   1. United States—Relations—Iran. 2. Iran—Relations—United States. I.
Title.
  E183.8.I55B43 2005
  327.73055'09'045—dc22   2005003454

British Library Cataloguing in Publication Data is available.

Library of Congress Catalog Card Number: 2005003454
ISBN: 0–275–98214–9

First published in 2005

Praeger Publishers, 88 Post Road West, Westport, CT 06881
An imprint of Greenwood Publishing Group, Inc.
www.praeger.com

Printed in the United States of America

The paper used in this book complies with the
Permanent Paper Standard issued by the National
Information Standards Organization (Z39.48–1984).

10 9 8 7 6 5 4 3 2 1

For Frank

Contents

Preface

This book is a work that has had a long gestation. As a linguistic anthropologist I have had a fascination with understanding the concrete effects of communication in face-to-face interaction. The idea that the dynamics of small-scale interaction might be applied to larger entities was reinforced by the work of several disparate scholars. The first was the great anthropologist Margaret Mead.

She had known the two great wars of the twentieth century—World War I as a child, and World War II as a fully established adult professional. With her strong emphasis on children and the family in her research before 1940, it is not surprising that she would come to focus on the ways that the societies of the world could work toward peace and safety for all. She hoped that a better world would emerge through the process of cultures learning from each other. Above all, Mead was a firm believer in the ability of all human entities to benefit from each other's cultural wisdom.

In this regard, she saw anthropologists as central and essential in this process, since it was uniquely the task of anthropology to make the knowledge of different cultures explicit to all. Mead viewed anthropology as both a *pure science* and an *applied policy science*. Although the academic goals of anthropology were to explicate the cultures of the world, compare them and continue to develop knowledge of the nature of humanity; it was also a sacred goal of anthropology to inform, advise, and persuade those who have the power to change the policies and actions of government for the betterment of humanity.

Mead had a particular interest in war and conflict. She authored more than sixty-five academic papers and countless more informal articles on this subject. She pointed out that the reason for war should be not simply "to bash somebody over the head but to build a better world." Thus, the focus for anthropologically informed policy needed to be not on war itself but rebuilding afterward. During World War II, she wrote that even during the war we needed to make preparations for the postwar period and develop a better world through better understanding, even of our enemies. This is an important message for us today—certainly an important message for the U.S. government, who launched a war in Iraq without giving any thought to the postwar scenario. In reading what she wrote during World War II, I was continually struck by the message she had for Americans, and ultimately for the world—a positive message even during a time of war.

With the purpose of preparing the peoples of the world for life in an internationalized postwar world, she began work on a magnum opus: *Learning to Live in One World*. This book was to have been a "manual" for an international community, in which the cultures of the planet would learn to "cherish" one another, learn from each other, and find ways to live together. The book was a gift to all people everywhere, from one of the few people on the planet who had the breadth of perspective to be able to see the world as a whole, rather than a collection of small factionalized groups continually in conflict with each other.

The book as a whole is an appeal to humanity to work toward a world in which racial, cultural, and economic differences will not be the occasion for prejudice between peoples, but rather a source of pride, appreciation, and wisdom for all. The manuscript is reposited in the Library of Congress, but the following passage may provide sense of the thrust of the book:

> the significant points for a sort of dynamic science of inter-cultural relationships are the whole positions of one group vis-à-vis another. Such positions are not merely international, or inter-racial or inter-religious, but they are also inter-class, and inter-situational. One has only to look at the chasm which yawns between state and federal officials and then realize that two years ago, all of the federal officials in question *were* state officials, to recognize that systematic vis-à-vis attitudes must be taken into account in any discussion of social action.

Mead's book was also to have been a "manual" for anthropologists, showing them how to refocus their work to concentrate on the international community. Her approach was both theoretical and methodological:

> we will assume that the system of relationships which we call nationalism has certain similarities wherever it occurs in the world, that it is in fact a social invention, springing perhaps from multiple sources, but now, since the whole world has come within one system of communications, tending more and more to become a strictly comparable phenomena [*sic*]. This being the case, it is permissible to examine international attitudes of any two countries, vis-à-vis each

other, to describe the regularities in these attitudes, and outline the dynamics of the inter-relationship.

The writing of this book was cruelly interrupted by an event that would leave its mark on Margaret Mead's work for the rest of her life: the dropping of the nuclear bomb on Hiroshima and Nagasaki. Mead was horrified at this act. She wrote about it many times before her death, both in professional, anthropological publications and for the popular press. The prospect of the annihilation of humanity through military technology was a clarion call—an emergency.

At this point Mead abandoned the writing of *Learning to Live in One World*. Indeed, she hinted in her autobiography, *Blackberry Winter: My Earlier Years*,[1] that she had destroyed it. From her correspondence we can discern that she felt that the message of the book was perhaps not strong enough. The idea of a halcyon postwar period, with nations gradually moving toward peaceful coexistence, was shattered for her. With the possibility of the destruction of the peoples of the world now present, a more active stance was needed.

She later expanded her concerns to include concerns about the environment, food supply, race and ethnic relations, and all things relating to the survival of humanity, and she began to push for explicit policies, testifying before congress, serving on national advisory commissions, and always speaking out in every possible public forum. She did a tour with the National Aeronautics and Space Administration with a lecture entitled: "The Next Billion Years: Our Uncertain Future," and many other acts as a public intellectual. Though many anthropologists did not appreciate her work in this arena, she made the voice of anthropologists legitimate in policy circles. To the extent that anthropologists have influence in governmental policy discussions today, we can thank Margaret Mead and her colleagues, including her great mentor and friend, Ruth Benedict.[2]

The idea that anthropological analysis could be applied to the actions of governments acting in a coroporate fashion was not limited to Mead. The late Lloyd Fallers wrote a slim book, *The Social Anthropology of the Nation State*,[3] which articulates approaches to looking at governmental units as whole cultural entities. The notion of "governmentality" as a set of cultural institutions or habits exhibited by the corporate actors of states and other official authorities has slowly gained currency in anthropology, through the inspiration of Michel Foucault, and others who have developed this idea.[4]

With these thoughts in mind, it seemed that an examination of the cultural underpinnings of the long-standing feud between the United States and Iran would prove fruitful. In doing this, I hope to make clear that I am speaking of symbolic communication as it occurs between officials who lay claim to representing the policies of their nations. Readers of this book should never confuse this with the attitudes of individuals. Of course, there are millions of Americans whose attitudes toward Iran and Iranians are vastly different from the official attitudes expressed in Washington, D.C. Many, like myself, in fact, try to put forward our different views of how relations between the two nations should be modified. Similarly, in Iran there is a vast range of attitudes and ideas about the United States. This is complicated by travel, emigration, and the crosscurrents of modern communication.

Nevertheless, official pronouncements between the governments of Iran and the United States and their representatives are made on a regular basis regarding the other nation, and these pronouncements have an astonishing uniformity that has persisted for nearly three decades at this writing. Since the officials making these representations have changed many times during this period, one can only conclude that the mode of communication—which I identify as mutual demonization—is endemic to the "cultural dynamics" of the relations between the two nations. The explication of this dynamic constitutes the bulk of this book.

Acknowledgments

I wish to thank Brown University for the sabbatical leave that allowed me to complete this manuscript, and Stanford University, particularly the Department of Cultural and Social Anthropology, for providing me a congenial and productive home during this period. I also thank Mary Catherine Bateson, Michael M. J. Fischer, Nikki Keddie, James Peacock, Ruhollah K. Ramazani, and Marvin Zonis for suggestions that greatly improved the text. My dear friend Mohammad Bagher Ghaffari, the great actor, director, and theatre scholar, and his wonderful extended family are not only my own Iranian family, but my continual inspiration in understanding Iranian culture. Diana Rosenthal was a great help in editing the final manuscript.

My special thanks to Sandy Close of Pacific News Service and the fine editors there, Andrew Lam, Mary Jo McConahay, and Franz Schurmann, and especially Brian Shott for supporting my career as a writer of public opinion. I also thank Jahan Salehi and Henry Sholar of Agence Global, Robert Whitcomb of the *Providence Journal*, Kim Fararo of the *San Jose Mercury News*, and other news editors too extensive to mention for their support of my public writing.

Thanks, too, to my wonderful family, who support me in all things, even though we don't all agree on political matters. Finally, my everlasting gratitude to my partner, Frank Farris, who makes my life a joy.

A Note on Transcription

The transcription of Persian and Arabic into Roman orthography is a continual problem for scholars and writers. In this book I have chosen to use a simplified method that is geared to be friendly to Western readers, and which also approximates newspaper usage for proper names and geographical locations. The long vowels, ā, ī and ū are transcribed as simply a, i and u, and the Arabic letters "hamza" and "eyn" are both represented by an open single quote. Differentiation between the four Arabic letters pronounced as /z/, the three letters pronounced as /s/ the two letters pronounced as /h/, and the two letters pronounced as /t/ in Persian is not made. Moreover, I have adopted Persian pronunciation conventions for the transcription of short vowels in most cases, so "Mohammad" is used in preference to "Muhammad," and "baten" in preference to "batin." In quoted material, the author's original transliteration is maintained. I have preserved the spelling of proper names (e.g., Mahmoud, not Mahmud) when these spellings have appeared in print in the press and elsewhere. Also, certain common words (e.g., jihad, not jehad) are given their common Western spellings. I apologize in advance to those who appreciate greater exactitude in these matters.

—— 1 ——

Discourse and Demonization

The past three decades marks one of the most remarkable chapters in the history of international foreign relations—the era of troubled and difficult relations between the United States and the Middle East. The period is remarkable first, because of the extraordinary degree to which the nations of the region and America lacked perspective on the cultural basis for each other's political motivations and strategies in the international arena; and second, for the degree to which each side was able to use vilification of the other as a political stratagem for domestic political purposes. The difficulties between the two regions have seemingly reified into the kind of clash between cultural worlds predicted by historian Samuel Huntington.

Yet, the difficulties faced by America and the nations of the Middle East went beyond simple misunderstanding or conflict of interests. Nor was it as simplistic as Huntington's "clash of civilizations." The differences experienced were essentially cultural and communicational. In cultural terms, forces in both the United States and in the Middle East constructed a mythological image that served to "demonize" the other parties in vivid terms, calculated to be immediately understood by the man on the street.[1] Paradoxically, parties on both sides then fulfilled the worst expectations of the other, playing true to these extreme images.

A Brief History of Grievance

Middle Eastern opposition to the West is far from being a phenomenon invented by Iran, Iraq, Osama bin Laden, the Taliban, or the Palestinians. It has grown consistently since the beginning of the nineteenth century as an effective oppositional force, both to the West and to local secular rulers. Western powers were blind to Middle Eastern opposition forces throughout the twentieth century because they were overshadowed by great power rivalry during this period. I will present this history in greater detail below, but a brief summary will serve to set the scene for the arguments to follow.

American citizens have short memories; they believe that events such as the Iranian Hostage Crisis of 1979–81 or the horrendous attacks on New York and Washington on September 11 happened solely as a result of events proximate to these crises. Nothing could be further from the truth. The roots of these and every other modern confrontation between the United States and Middle Eastern states and groups go back more than 150 years. All arise from a single source: the heritage of difficult relations between European colonial powers, with whom the United States is inextricably linked, and the Middle East.

The original leader of the opposition to the West was Jamal ad-Din al-Afghani (1838–97). Called the "Father of Islamic Modernism, al-Afghani was educated in Iran, in Najaf and in the other Shi'a shrine cities of present day Iraq[2] and India.[3] In 1865–66, after a number of years of uncertain residence, he returned to Tehran, then traveled to Mashhad and finally Herat in Afghanistan, where he began his career as a religious political figure.[4] He traveled throughout the Islamic world, promulgating an "Islamic reform movement." His use of an Islamic ideology helped him to transcend ethnic differences in the region, and preach a message all would understand. He sought to mobilize Muslim nations to fight against Western imperialism and to gain military power through modern technology. Al-Afghani claimed that Britain, France, and Russia in particular were operating in collusion with Middle Eastern rulers to rob the people of their patrimony through sweetheart deals for exploitation of natural and commercial resources in the region.

As a direct result of the efforts of al-Afghani and his followers, groups such as the Muslim Brotherhood evolved throughout the region. These groups generally espoused three methods in their political and religious activity: personal piety coupled with evangelism, religious modernization, and political resistance to secular regimes.

According to the Middle Eastern oppositionists, the Western nations have committed a litany of crimes against the Muslim world. After World War I, the Middle Eastern peoples were treated largely as war prizes to be divided and manipulated for the good of the militarily powerful Europeans. The British and the French—without consent or consultation on the part of the residents—created every nation between the Mediterranean Sea and the Persian Gulf for their own benefit. This increased the resentment of the fundamentalists against the West and against the rulers installed by Westerners.

During the cold war conflict following World War II, the United States and the Soviet Union fought over the Middle East nations like children over toys. Governments such as those of Egypt, the Sudan, Iraq, and Syria were constantly pressed to choose between East and West. The choice was often prompted by "gifts" of military support to sitting rulers. With ready sources of money and guns in either Washington or Moscow, Middle Eastern rulers could easily oppress the religious fundamentalists who opposed them. This added still further to the anger of the religious reformers. At this point the oppositionists abandoned political action through conventional political processes and turned to extra-governmental methods—terrorism—to make their dissatisfaction felt.

The United States became the sole representative of the West after 1972, when Great Britain, poor and humbled, could no longer afford to maintain a full military force in the region. Anxious to protect oil supplies from the Soviet Union, Washington propped up the shah of Iran and the Saudi Arabian government in the ill-fated "Twin Pillars" strategy. This ended with the Iranian revolution, leaving America with a messy patchwork of military and political detritus. When Iran went to war with Iraq, the United States supported Saddam Hussein to prevent Iran from winning. Anxious about Soviet incursions into Afghanistan, it propped up the Taliban. These two monstrous forces—Saddam and the Taliban—are very much an American creation.

America finally had to confront its former client, Iraq, in two Gulf Wars. As a consequence of the First Gulf War under President George Herbert Walker Bush, Americans established a military base on Saudi Arabian soil—considered sacred by pious Muslims. Saudi officials had been resisting this move for years, knowing that it would be politically dangerous both for them and for the United States. This action was the basis for Osama bin Laden's opposition to the United States.

The Second Gulf War under President George Walker Bush resulted in the removal of Iraqi dictator Saddam Hussein from power, and an American occupation of Iraq that is still continuing at this writing. The establishment of fourteen permanent military bases on Iraqi soil made it seem as if the United States was not likely to leave the region in the near future.

All of this meddling only confirms the century-old assertion that the West was out to rob the people of the Middle East of their prerogatives and patrimony. The current revolutionaries in the region, including bin Laden, have political pedigrees leading directly back to the original reformer, al-Afghani. Willy-nilly, the United States and the Middle Eastern opposition work together to keep reinforcing these old stereotypes. It is essential that both sides find a way to break this pattern, or we will be mired in these troubled relations forever.

The Cultural Discourse of Conflict

Fifty years ago, the study of culture conflict for anthropologists was limited to peoples who lived in close proximity to each other. The most frequent subjects of study were factions of the same society. Even in more recent times, studies of conflict and violence seem restricted to internal divisiveness within nations rather than between nations.[5] International conflict was largely left to the purview of political scientists.

After World War II, no one could have predicted that the United States would eventually be involved in conflicts in places as remote from North America as Lebanon, Korea, Somalia, and Vietnam. These conflicts were relatively short-lived, and were limited military operations.

One engagement seems to have a different character than all of these others—the American engagement with Iran. It is now the longest standoff the United States has ever had with another nation, with the possible exception of Cuba and North Korea. Even during the cold war era, the United States maintained diplomatic, cultural and economic relations with Russia and other communist states. The engagement with Iran is important and distinctive for another reason—its initial stages arguably constitute the opening volleys in what promises to be an extended conflict with oppositional forces throughout the Islamic world.

Postmodern Conflict

The conflict with Iran as it continues today is a true postmodern culture conflict. It centers not on substantive differences or real conflict, but rather on symbolic discourse: both nations construct the "other" to fit an idealized picture of an enemy. The process is reminiscent of the cold war in its processes of mutual demonization, but it differs from the cold war conflict between the United States and the Soviet Union in a number of significant respects.

First, unlike the situation of the cold war, Iran and the United States hold little or no immediate danger for each other. Both try to emphasize the danger of their opponents, but on close examination, these constructed threats have little or no substance.

Second, the mutual opposition between the two nations exists at an abstract, governmental level, but it is not generally shared by the populations of the two nations. Both nations maintain that their quarrel is not with the people of the other nation, but with the "government."

Third, the demonization of the "government" in both cases is not substantive, but rather symbolic—and shifting. It sometimes applies to individuals, such as Ayatollah Ruhollah Khomeini or President George W. Bush, and sometimes to vague unspecified forces within the two governments. This is revealed in statements such as "Iran supports terrorism," or "America oppresses the Gulf region."

Fourth, officials of the two nations do not talk directly to each other. Most communication is carried out through back channels, or primarily through the media. This process of indirect discourse between nations is endemic in today's world, but it is virtually the only means of communication between the United States and Iran.

Fifth, the relationship between the United States and Iran is unique in the world. Virtually no other pair of nations shares this strange pattern of noncommunication.[6] It is only with each other that they share this unusual disjunction.

Finally, the differences are structurally irresolvable, since both sides demand that the other conform to their cultural sensibilities. The paradox is profound, since both nations operate with a functioning constitution that is assiduously followed by their respective national leaders.

Anthropological Insight

The problem is profoundly in need of anthropological insight, in that an understanding of the dynamics of both cultures is necessary in order to comprehend the nature and persistence of the conflict. One difficulty lies in the ways that both societies deal with dissention.

Laura Nader has been instrumental in pointing out discrepancies between American models of conflict resolution and native models of social justice. In a series of papers exploring this theme, she has shown that "Harmony Coerced is Freedom Denied," to quote the title of one of the more popular renditions of her thesis.[7] Her thesis of coercive harmony suggests that the United States has developed a culture where disharmony is seen as something that needs to be controlled. When there are genuine social injustices, however, "Coercive harmony can stifle dissent for a while. But if dissent is too tightly bottled up, it will explode."[8] Nader's specific critique was developed as a critique of the practice of Alternative Dispute Resolution (ADR), which has become a precondition for receipt of American aid abroad,[9] but it is generalizable to overall American foreign policy practice.

Iran is not free of its own difficulties in conflict resolution. Iranians are adverse to compromise, seeing it as weakness and loss of honor.[10] In a dispute, parties can remain estranged for years until someone mediates the dispute. During this period, the parties remain hostile. This withdrawal, hostility, and need for mediation exists at the interpersonal level, and can extend to international relations.[11] Moreover, in Islamic terms, compromise with evil is not only impossible, but blasphemous. In Islam, sincere believers must "promote the right, and resist the wrong." If a force in the world is identified as corrupting, it must be opposed.

For Iran, Iraq, the Taliban of Afghanistan, and terrorist organizations such as Osama bin Laden's al Qaeda, the United States became the Great Satan, to borrow Iran's epithet. The Middle Eastern oppositionists saw America as an external illegitimate force that continually strove to destroy the pure, internal core of the Islamic World. It was also seen as the inheritor of the mantle of colonialism carried out earlier in the twentieth century by Great Britain, France, and the Soviet Union.

For the United States, the resistant forces of the Middle East took on a demonic form—that of the "crazy outlaw" nations and terrorist groups whose activities were illegal, unpredictable, and irrational. Every president from Ronald Reagan to George W. Bush vilified these forces. In Nader's terminology, they represented disharmony in an extreme form, because they threatened the international social and political order.

Each side's mythology of itself and its role in world affairs complimented this "mythology of the other." All of the Middle Eastern forces counted their efforts against the United States as proof of modern success in confronting a formidable enemy. For Iran this was the revolution of 1978–79 and the subsequent 444-day hostage crisis. For Iraq, it was the Gulf war. For Osama bin Laden and other terrorist leaders, it was a series of aggressive attacks against the United States. These included bombing of the American embassies in Kenya and Tanzania in 1998 and the horrific suicidal attacks on the twin towers of the World Trade Center in New York and the Pentagon in Washington. These groups thus become not just revolutionary oppositionists; they become the guardians of justice and equity for the people of the world.

For the United States, a more complex structure which I term below the "U.S. Foreign Policy Myth," held sway. As I will explain, this myth sees the "normal world" as a body of nation-states arranged in a dichotomous structure—for or against the United States and its interests. The oppositional forces of the Middle East confound this model. The United States therefore places them in a residual category, and tries to eliminate them—to purify the world, as it were. The United States therefore becomes not just the guardian of democracy or freedom, but of world order.

These mythologies became ideological filters for transmission (or, more accurately, nontransmission) of messages between the two cultural worlds. Such filtering might be sufficient to create the kind of abortive understanding that took place between the two nations with such relentless regularity. However, the ideological problems were reinforced by a communicational structure that was equally conducive to reinforcing the mutual negative images both nations held of each other.

A Problem of Discourse

The communication problems can be thought of as problems of mutual discourse that have become increasingly more severe. The United States and all of the Middle Eastern opposition forces mentioned above have operated with different, often contradictory notions of how discourse on an international level should be managed. This often caused drastic misreading of the content of communication between the two cultural worlds, and mutual accusations of deviousness, insincerity and bad faith.

The formal study of discourse has seen considerable growth during the past two decades. Discourse analysts posit a set of implicit contextual agreements between parties that allow face-to-face conversation to take place in an unimpeded manner. Critical theorists such as Bourdieu, Derrida, and Baudrillard have extended the term "discourse" to include the culturally contextualized rhetorical practices of governments, scholarly institutions, and commercial business. The theoretical relevance of discourse studies for this problem will be discussed in greater detail in the following chapter, but I wish to underscore here the need to understand the contextual factors which underlie disturbed discourse as a key to explaining.

The United States government is bureaucratically geared to speaking to foreign powers using a set of communicative routines and principles inherited from eighteenth- and nineteenth-century European diplomatic practice. The practices emphasize face-to-face communication between elite governmental officials at equivalent levels (head of state to head of state, secretary or minister of foreign affairs to secretary or minister of foreign affairs, and so on). Special protocol rules apply for communication between persons who are of nonequivalent hierarchical position. These principles thus imply a universal hierarchy of bureaucracy, and a universal set of understandings about management of discourse parameters within that hierarchy. The routines are widely used because the international community, who learned them from colonial powers, implicitly accepts them.

These traditional practices have been modified by modern technology; there is increasingly greater immediacy of physical and verbal contact every day through electronic communication, worldwide telephone service, courier services and high-speed travel. An additional channel of communication is provided through satellite television transmission, international radio, and electronic transmission of information for publication in newspapers and periodicals.

Much energy has been devoted to protecting the basic structure of the earlier forms of government-to-government communication in the face of this new technology. New technology is often seen as a threat to diplomatic action. Thus, substantive discourse between members of the international foreign policy community must be protected from the corruption of media reporting, and from the threat of fast and easy electronic information gathering and transmission. This perceived threat has given rise to a new profession: that of the media manager who attempts to preserve a controlled construction of events as they are transmitted, reported, and reenacted through these new communication forms. Typically, in most international relations dealings, both parties not only decide substantive issues, but also choose the ideal manner in which their dealings will be transmitted to outsiders. Bad faith is attributed to either party who departs intentionally from the preconceived scenario.

The U.S.-Middle Eastern communication situation was complicated by this set of factors. After the fall of the shah in Iran, for example, the new revolutionary government had no practice in the forms of communication used in international relations by the United States and most of the foreign community. Moreover, it had a highly original view of the ways in which new forms of communications technology could be used in both statecraft and in international relations, not at all in accord with standard U.S. government practice.

Iranian leaders, for their part, saw no reason to accept rules for international diplomacy set down by the United States or by any other nation. Angered by what they perceived as arrogance, and deeply suspicious of American motives, they vigorously asserted that they would pursue an "Islamic response" to international relations, which was "neither East nor West."[12]

Iranian leaders puzzled and frustrated Americans who had to deal with them. They complained bitterly that the Iranians would "not play by the rules." The situation grew especially difficult during the hostage crisis of 1979–81, when American officials *had* to communicate with Iranian leaders in order to secure the release of the American hostages held in Tehran. It was humiliating for them to face the fact that there was often no one in Tehran willing to talk to them under any circumstances. Similar problems arose throughout the course of the lengthy Iran-Iraq conflict.

Saddam Hussein of Iraq had precisely this kind of difficulty in reading American communication structures. Having been supported by the United States in his war with Iran in 1980, he was disposed to read nuanced or equivocal messages in reaction to his inquiries about invading Kuwait as positive responses from an ally. He was as surprised by the American resistance as was the United States by his aggressive action. The result was a debilitating, continued war and a permanent rupture.

Osama bin Laden and his allies, the Taliban of Afghanistan, were openly supported by the United States for almost eleven years, starting in 1979 in their war with the Soviet Union. They were also surprised both by American attacks against Iraq and by the establishment of a United States military presence in Saudi Arabia during the Gulf War. The United States continued to give mixed messages as it provided indirect support for the Taliban while insisting that they betray their ally, Osama bin Laden.

In the discussion below, I take the position that no person or persons can be blamed for the communication difficulties that arose during this difficult period. The problems were *systemic*, and would have been encountered by any persons in power during this period. They were also *dynamic*, in that they reinforced themselves as the two parties tried to struggle with them. They may have been unavoidable given the course of historic events. It is nevertheless my hope that in pointing out those aspects of U.S.-Iranian rhetoric which proved difficult, it may be possible to avoid similar situations in the future, or at least to adopt more productive response patterns when they occur than were adopted by either the United States or Iran.

In the chapters that follow, I hope to present first an American symbolic construction of a thematic topic pertaining to Iran, and then an Iranian construction of the same topic, including an Iranian construction of the American view of that topic. In the end, few of these constructions have much to do with a sober assessment of facts, or of reality, but they do have a great deal to do with fulfillment of image expectations on the part of both parties.

Chapters 2 and 3 deal with what I term the "master myths" of construction of the other for both the United States and for Iran. They represent idealized worlds in which selective views of the "other" have a cosmological significance. In this case, both the United States and Iran play a villain's role in the generalized political world of the other party. These cosmologies are quasi-religious in nature. In the case of the United States, the mythology involves a worldview that is constructed on a model that mirrors the history and idealized governmental structure of the United States itself. In the case of Iran, it involves a model based on themes that predate Islam itself, but which mirror a geography of morality and purity in which outside forces are routinely seen as negative.

Chapter 4 deals with differences in the rhetorical structures that the two nations use to construct dialogue with each other. Frequently it is not so much the imagery of "otherness" that is so powerful in creating hostility between two nations, it is also the disconnect in the discourse that creates impediments to understanding.

Chapters 5 through 9 present the structure of the dynamics of mutual demonization between the United States and Iran. Chapters 5 and 6 deal with the *symbolic* presentation of the two grand images: the Great Satan and the Mad Mullahs. The Iranian Revolution of 1978–79 is a watershed event for U.S.-Iranian relations; therefore the differing constructions of that cataclysmic historical episode become key in developing an understanding about U.S.-Iranian relations. Nevertheless, the symbolic stereotypes that each nation developed for the other preexisted their specific realization in national rhetoric.

In Chapter 7, I try to introduce a reality check into the discourse, exploring as carefully as possible the real events that informed relations between the United States and Iran during the gestational period for these images. One important element is the notion of theocracy and its differing view in Iran and in the United States. Although Iranians may yet create a newer governmental structure to replace that of Khomeini's Islamic Republic, the essential differences about the viability and suitability of an Islamic Republic as the proper ruling structure for Iran or any state continue to divide Iran and the United States.

In this chapter, I also deal with differing views of the United States' history with Iran. From an American standpoint, the United States never did anything but try to help the Iranian people up until the revolution. From an Iranian standpoint, what the United States counted as "help" was exploitation. In this chapter, I show that Iran's desire for modernization is a dominant theme in this relationship.

Chapters 8 and 9 show how both Iran and the United States selectively interpreted events subsequent to the Iranian Revolutionary period to justify their continued demonization. The United States will perhaps never shake off the shocking demonic epithet: Great Satan; the many "sins" of the United States are detailed in Chapter 8. Whereas the bearded, scowling visage of Ayatollah Ruhollah Khomeini serves almost as a visual trope for the negative, devilish view of Iran in the United States—a Mad Mullah among other Mad Mullahs. Although these are symbolically constructed images, and their wellsprings come from the respective cultures of the United States and Iran, rather than from any sober assessment of political or historical events, nevertheless it should be noted that neither the United States nor Iran in recent years has done much to belie these images. It seems that an almost purposeful antagonism on the part of each state toward the other perpetuates them.

The "sins" of Iran are explored in Chapter 9. One important touchstone for Americans is the perceived contrast between the role of women in Iranian and in American life. This has been a subject of continual discussion both in Iran and in the United States. In the United States, the treatment of women under the Islamic Republic has been an index of the worthiness of Iranian civilization. They are frequently seen as oppressed and helpless. In Iran, American women are frequently seen as commodified objects of male desire. Neither view is accurate of course, but it is these images that frequently give the two nations one of the most potent views of the other.[13]

A recent issue that has created new tensions between the United States and Iran revolves around Iranian use of nuclear power, also covered in Chapter 9. A light-water nuclear reactor in the town of Bushehr, and subsequent experimental facilities near the cities of Isfahan and Natanz triggered fears that Iran might be trying to develop nuclear weapons not only in these sites, but in others yet to be discovered. Whether these fears might be justified, or merely be tactics designed to curry support in the United States for some eventual action to overthrow the clerical government of Iran remains unclear at this writing. What is clear is that U.S. citizens have unusual sensitivity to questions of nuclear proliferation, feeling that any state that pursues nuclear power is a potential villain in the world. Iranians for their part feel that they have an absolute right to pursue nuclear energy development if they so choose. For them, it is a hallmark of their membership among the modern states of the world, and a source of pride.

As I have tried to point out in this first introductory chapter, the mass media have been instrumental in promulgating the images that divide these two populations. In Chapter 10, I discuss the cultural conception of the media and their role in social and political life. Because of their importance as the conveyance of imagery, these are especially important in governing the manner in which the two nations characterize each other. These conceptions are also crucial in determining the ways in which the two nations have failed to understand how they are portrayed in the public representations of each society.

Finally, in Chapter 11, I explore a path to a strategy for mutual coexistence between Iran and the United States. The three-decade standoff between the two nations is an impasse that will require time to break down. In both nations, compromise in the face of "evil" is difficult. The United States under the administration of George W. Bush has paradoxically moved toward a hardening of what used to be fairly tolerant principles of dealings with other nations. The Bush doctrine of the Axis of Evil, mentioned in his State of the Union Address in January 2002, and in which Iran was implicated, marked a firmer hardening of the lines between the two states. We can only hope that with the inevitable transitions that come with leaders passing from the scene, either by death or expiration of office, this stance on both sides will soften.

In concluding this introductory chapter, I must confess that I believe that a rapprochement between Iran and the United States is inevitable. The mutual interests of the two countries are too close, and the sensibilities of the two cultures too similar at base, to maintain perpetual hostility. The Archimedean difficulty is to find a fulcrum for the lever of mediation that must be implemented to bring the two states into synchrony once again. It will surely happen, but the dynamics of the occurrence of this inevitable event remain unclear.

2

American Myths

All nations maintain myths both about themselves and about others with whom they have dealings. These myths form part of the repertoire of the cultural dynamics leading to the creation of "imagined communities" as posited by Benedict Anderson (1983). The peoples of the United States and other nations, along with their respective governments all support these myths as working hypotheses for dealing with each other. The hypotheses, in Gadamer-like fashion[1] govern the public discourse of these governments and ultimately their actions. In this chapter I will explore a selection of these myths and show how they function to construct both self-image and images of the "other" for Americans. In the following chapter, I will show how these mythic structures work for three case studies of Middle Eastern opposition to the United States.

American Myths

The "U.S. Foreign Policy Myth"[2] is an extremely powerful and pervasive American belief system about the nature of foreign policy, how it is conducted, and how it affects American life. This belief system is troublesome because of the hold it has in shaping political strategy and defining "normalcy" in foreign affairs, even when it falls far from the mark in reflecting reality. At best foreign policy and military strategy based on this system of belief is ineffective. At worst it is detrimental to American interests.

The United States is not alone in espousing such a system. Indeed, virtually every nation operates in the foreign policy realm from an equally inaccurate base of beliefs. (I will deal with Iranian myths below.) It is natural for this to be so. Nations, like individual human beings, develop habits of thinking, often based on real short-term experience or shaped by a particularly powerful leader, which are difficult to break. When these habits are institutionalized within the bureaucracy they become especially pervasive. In this case, the U.S. foreign policy myth is narrowly applicable. It works fairly well when dealing with Western industrialized nations, including the Soviet Bloc. It may also have been serviceable in dealing with the rest of the world in the immediate post–World War II period. However, it has become woefully outdated for dealings with the global community in the past two decades, and will become even more outdated as mankind moves further into the twenty-first century. As an additional point of contrast, those who have memories of earlier periods in U.S. history will be able to see how the current belief system differs from that of previous periods.

The Five Principles of Belief

The world consists of nation-states. It is not surprising that the United States should come to believe that the world consists entirely of nation-states with basically homogeneous populations whose primary identity (and homogeneity) derives from identification with their common nationhood. The United States was, after all, the first great nation founded on this principle.

Of course, there are very few nation-states in the world. One can think of a few European countries, Japan perhaps, or a few of the relatively new Pacific island states, but that is about the extent of it. The majority of the people of the world do not identify primarily with their nationhood, and certainly not with the central governments that rule the nations in which they happen to live. Americans will regularly declare that they are loyal to their president, even if they didn't vote for him. Some would go so far as to assert that they would sacrifice their own lives to protect him. However, the notion that one would sacrifice one's life for one's president or prime minister is a patent absurdity in virtually every other nation on earth.

A dichotomous power struggle is the most important organizing principle in world politics. All other political relationships must be ranked in terms of it. Before World War II, even the United States accepted the belief in a multipolar world structure. Since that conflict the United States has adopted a bipolar model, and tends to structure the entire world order within this framework. Even after the demise of the Soviet Union, this model has a tenuous hold on the American psyche.

Of course, for most nations on earth, the capitalist-communist struggle during the cold war was very nearly irrelevant for the conduct of everyday life, except as an enormously bothersome obstacle which they had to confront at every turn. Nations that wanted to steer a middle course, such as India, paid for not choosing sides. Washington declared them "unreliable" and withheld both foreign aid and trade benefits.

In the post-Soviet period, the dichotomous polarity shifted to a range of primarily Islamic nations (North Korea and Cuba being the sole exceptions) that would not acquiesce to American policy. Washington sometimes identified these as "rogue nations," or "supporters of terrorism." Curiously, nations that give the United States trouble in other ways, such as those that have significant drug trafficking, do not get included in this diametric opposition.

The Islamic nations in this rogue's gallery have included Lybia, Syria, Iran, Iraq, the Palestinian Authority, and more recently, Afghanistan. There is a curious quality about the opposition itself, however. Although it only includes a small sampling of nations in the Middle East, all Islamic nations in the region tend to get included by association in the American popular consciousness, and the American government does little or nothing to counteract this unfortunate association.

The tendency to demonize these nations and their citizens is very strong. The American government gives the impression that support for terrorists is a principal function of these governments. Moreover, they have been accused without strong evidence of developing "weapons of mass destruction," including nuclear weaponry. The possibility of nuclear destruction is of course a paramount concern for thinking people everywhere. However, it is the height of bitter irony that the mass of nuclear weaponry is held by Western European and North American nations. Further, it is clear that the bulk of the people who will be destroyed and suffer in a nuclear holocaust have absolutely no interest in the imagined dichotomous ideological struggle that the United States envisions.

In the end, few nations would accept the American belief that all nations must eventually assign themselves to one ideological camp or another—whatever its construction. Most are already well in advance of American thinking. Rejecting this bipolar model, they envision a multipolar world with a variety of ideological, religious, and political shadings, and mutual respect for human difference.

Economics and power are the bases of relations between nations. Power politics as a philosophy has been with the United States only a short time. It was articulated in an effective manner by Hans Morganthau, perhaps the principal teacher of the current crop of U.S. politicians exercising executive power in the U.S. foreign policy community. Former Secretary of State and National Security Advisor Henry Kissinger was perhaps its most celebrated practitioner. Another source for this ideological disposition was the late Charles Strauss of the University of Chicago.

For anthropologists of all shades it is particularly galling to see that in the United States' conduct of foreign policy, almost no attention is paid to cultural differences between nations. It is assumed that wealth and military might are universal levelers, and that little else matters. Occasionally it is recognized that religious feeling, ideology, pride, greed, or altruism may be factors in the course of human events, but such matters are often dismissed as unpredictable factors.[3]

The shortcomings of this policy have devastated the United States in the post-Soviet period. Nowhere has this been more evident than in the Middle East. Islam has served as a master symbolic rubric under which individuals from many nations have been able to group themselves and their concerns. Thus, Islam becomes both a symbolic statement of identity, and a basis for spiritual legitimization of that identity for people of the region, who in fact have distinctive histories and folkways.

The willingness of people throughout the Middle East to make enormous sacrifices for cultural and religious causes has been enormously frustrating for the United States and its allies. Suicide bombings have been particularly upsetting and incomprehensible. On September 11, 2001, nineteen Middle Eastern individuals from a variety of nations hijacked four airliners, and crashed them into the World Trade Center in New York City and the Pentagon building in Washington, D.C.[4] The destruction and loss of life in these incidents had an astonishing effect on the people of the United States—something akin to culture shock. This was heightened when it was realized that the hijackers were materially relatively well-off, well-educated, had families and other ties to the community, and had lived in the United States or other Western countries. Apparently, their motives were entirely ideological.

Nations are ruled by small groups of elite individuals. It is difficult to understand why the United States, with a strong internal ethic supporting democracy and broad-based, grass roots participation in public affairs finds it so difficult to take these same broad-based processes seriously in other nations.

Yet, again and again, one finds that the conduct of United States foreign policy is based on identification and support of narrow elite political structures: elite elected officials, elite dictators, elite religious officials.

Clearly, American government officials believe that power inheres in these narrow structures. An office is the chief sign of this power, perhaps reflecting the earlier stated belief that the world consists of nation-states. Thus, the United States cannot easily see underlying cultural processes which contribute to social change, or, seeing such processes, feels them to be automatically negative in nature because they threaten the established order.[5]

Even in dealing with "enemies" it is difficult for Americans to break out of this thought pattern. Yasser Arafat, former leader of the Palestinian Authority, was presumed to have control over all Palestinian political groups. In fact, there were a large number of groups opposing Arafat, who carried out independent political and military actions against Israeli authorities in the West Bank territories. Railing against Arafat for the actions of these groups was a largely useless exercise. Largely based on the myth of the single leader, this continued until his death in 2004.

As will be seen below, the terrorist organizations attached to Osama bin Laden have been equally diffuse and not necessarily under his direct control. Nevertheless, the United States has targeted bin Laden specifically, under the mistaken assumption that eliminating or controlling him will eliminate or control the action of these groups.

The normal conduct of foreign policy thus consists of the elite leaders of nation-states meeting in seclusion, discussing matters of power and economics presumably in the context of a dichotomous world conflict. This final point is not a separate belief, but rather the congruence of the preceding beliefs into an image—a scenario which in fact, describes much of the conduct of foreign policy carried out by the United States in recent years.

The assumption is made that if one can approach national leaders under these circumstances, all problems of foreign relations can be resolved. Since money and guns don't mean much in many contemporary conflicts, and national leaders often do not control the social and political processes in their non-nation-states, this is a somewhat foolish operating practice. Nevertheless it persists, causing the United States to lurch from clumsy mistake to clumsy mistake.

Normalcy

As mentioned above, the U.S. foreign policy myth is a definition of normalcy—of expectations about how actors in the world behave and are motivated to act. Nations and actors that do not fit this mold are relegated to residual cognitive categories: "irrational," "crazy," "criminal," "unpredictable," and "deviant."

The United States had indeed become accustomed to pursuing serious foreign policy negotiations over economic and military conflict exclusively with other Western industrialized nation-states. "Third world" and "developing" nations were traditionally dealt with in offhand, summary fashion. The legitimate needs and desires of the peoples of these countries, especially when they were in conflict with the recognized elite leadership structures, were never a part of U.S. foreign policy considerations. Indeed, such factors were regularly ignored or seen as directly opposed to U.S. strategic interests since they were viewed as "destabilizing forces."

The "Kissinger doctrine" in U.S. foreign policy, which still pervaded the policy community, was opposed to attempts to understand the needs of other nations, feeling that it was their job to represent their own needs to the United States. Policy was often carried out with the aid of elite leaders—plumbers—who had been co-opted through a combination of economic and military force.[6] Indeed, until the conflict in Vietnam in the 1960s and early 1970s, it had been possible to deal with conflict in these nations almost exclusively through co-optation, military threat or economic pressure.

The Vietnam conflict should have been a warning to Americans that the basis for international relations in the world was changing. Unfortunately,

Vietnam was treated as an aberration—a defeat to be ignored and forgotten as soon as possible. The basis for U.S. involvement in the conflict was unqualified U.S. support of a dictatorial regime that was out of contact and out of favor with its own population. That support arose from U.S. need to carry out its own foreign military strategies, based on a popular domestic political posture of containment of communism.

Iran filled a similar role in U.S. foreign policy sphere to that of preconflict Vietnam. It was one of the "twin pillars" of U.S. Defense in the Persian Gulf region (the other being Saudi Arabia). In the immediate postwar period, oil supplies from the Gulf region were critical for the United States, and the specter of Gulf oil falling under the domination of the Soviet Union, however unrealistic that scenario might have been, was enough to justify a massive foreign policy effort aimed at shoring up friendly rulers in the region—more plumbers—who could be counted upon to carry out U.S. foreign policy with little need for U.S. officials to involve themselves in great depth with the nations in question.

The Shah of Iran, Mohammad Reza Pahlavi, was an ideal plumber in U.S. eyes. He was restored to his throne in 1953 through the efforts of the U.S. Central Intelligence Agency after a coup d'etat engineered by Prime Minister Mohammad Mossadeq, which American officials feared would allow greater Soviet influence in Iran. Thereafter the shah became one of the United States' chief political and military clients. He purchased billions of dollars of advanced military equipment from the United States and provided a fertile economic climate for Western investment in the Iranian economy.

The shah was an extremely clever client. The money for all of his purchases and economic improvements came from the sale of oil to Western nations, the price of which was jacked up some 400 percent in 1973 by the Organization of Petroleum Exporting Countries (OPEC) largely due to the shah's influence. Thus, the United States and its allies were actually paying for economic improvement and arms purchases by Iran through the increased price of oil.

Iran's pattern of dealing with the United States during the postwar period was a continuation of a century of similar dealings with other great powers. Iran had been in conflict with other industrialized nations—Great Britain and Imperial Russia in the nineteenth century and the Great European Powers in this century. However, it had always been powerless to resist—either militarily or economically—in any significant way. The Pahlavi shahs, like the Qajar shahs before them were alienated from their own populations. Strapped for ready cash, they cleverly decided that cooperation with Western powers and Russia in economic and military matters was far more prudent—and profitable—than defiance. They sold concessions to foreigners on almost every national resource: agricultural, industrial, mineral, commercial, and transportation. In the process they became wealthy themselves.

It was possible for them to do this by establishing a very special kind of foreign relationship with the United States and other Western nations—a state of cultural insulation whereby the West was largely prevented from coming into close contact with Iranian culture and civilization. The United States, being Iran's chief ally in the West, was most affected by this policy in the post–World War II years. Mohammad Reza Pahlavi insisted that all U.S. military and commercial dealings with Iran be passed through Iranian government channels. The CIA was active in Iran, but could not pass reports on Iranian internal affairs back to the U.S. government of which the shah did not approve. With few exceptions, embassy staff members did not speak Persian until the period immediately following the revolution, and were, in any case, kept from meeting with the bulk of the Iranian population.[7]

The Iranian Revolution marked a dramatic watershed in this state of affairs. After a brief six-month period of secular nationalism, the government was taken over by religious forces. The secular nationalists were out of power and Iran became an Islamic republic. Suddenly the rules for interaction between Iran and the United States changed. Iran's leaders adopted an independent set of international relations goals, summed up in the phrase "neither East nor West." They expressed the desire to establish a true Islamic Republic based on religious law.[8] They became deeply suspicious of U.S. motives, fearing that, as in 1953, the United States would attempt to reinstate the monarchy in order to regain the economic benefits enjoyed during the reign of the shah.

More disturbing for American politicians was the attitude of the new Iranian leaders. They assumed an air of moral superiority, and were not interested in cooperation with Western nations on Western terms. Moreover, they seemed comfortable committing acts, which outraged the United States with no apparent thought as to the possible consequences. This kind of behavior was inexplicable for most Americans.

To add to the difficulty, in the immediate postrevolutionary period, the Iranian leaders were not in full control of their own nation.[9] Though identified by U.S. policy makers as elites, they had very little capacity for independent action on the foreign policy scene. As will be seen below, their ability to act vis-à-vis the United States was especially limited.

In short, post-Revolutionary Iran violated every tenet of the U.S. policy myth. Iran looked like a nation-state, but its political structure was, both under the shah, and today, far more tenuous than that of any Western nation. After the revolution it was not concerned with the East–West struggle, preferring to reject both sides. Its national concerns transcended matters of military and economic power; it was often far more concerned about questions of ideology, morality, and religious sensibility. Its elites were and continue to be informal power brokers and balancers of opinion rather than powerful actors able to enforce their will directly on the population. Moreover, they have had to be extremely careful about contact with foreign powers, since their offices do not protect them from political attack as a result of such contact.

The United States was doomed to be disappointed with other nations in the region as well for much the same reasons. Iraq was a quintessential non-nation-state. A kingdom cobbled together by the British at the end of World War I, it combined a large Iranian-origin Shi'ite Muslim population with an Arab Sunni Muslim population and a large Sunni Kurdish population. To make matters worse, the Kurdish population sat on a large proportion of the income-producing oil reserves in the nation.

The country was held together for years by the British army. After World War II when the army withdrew, the nation devolved into a revolutionary state with a series of coups and countercoups culminating in the ascendancy of Saddam Hussein. He was decidedly a head of state, but in order to rule over such a disparate population he had to exercise the most ruthless methods possible. He was an effective plumber when fighting Iran, but an equally formidable enemy when fighting the United States. Saddam Hussein operated on principles of self- and national aggrandizement. Well aware of the fragility of his own rule, he shored up his authority by making the United States a bigger enemy to his people than he himself was.

Like Iran, Iraq frustrated the American foreign policy myth. The nation looked like a nation-state, but it was not.[10] Saddam Hussein looked like a head of state, but could only hold his office by the exercise of force. Saddam and his nation did not respond to appeals—even coercive ones—to national self-interest, but rather to pride, and defiance.

Finally, terrorist groups such as those led by Osama bin Laden fall totally outside of any model the United States ever had concerning international politics. They are diffuse in the extreme, not conforming to any political borders. They have a head, but not one that can effectively command the actions of the group or even the loyalty of followers within the group. Finally, they have no economic or political self-interest at all. Their motivations seem totally ideological, unaffected by either guns or money.

All of this has given U.S. leaders fits. None of the opponents to the United States conform to the set model of international behavior with which the foreign policy community is prepared to operate. As a result all are "crazy outlaws" who deserve to be attacked, using methods that fall outside international standards of engagement.

American Archetypes—George Washington and Abraham Lincoln

Americans not only have mythic models about the world, they also have mythic formulations for their own identity. The mythic archetype that best conforms to this model in the current struggle with the Middle East is an amalgam of the greatest American national heroes, George Washington and Abraham Lincoln.

George Washington is seen in the American myth as the fearless warrior liberating the nation from tyrannical rule, and establishing democratic institutions for the people. Washington's legacy is also one of isolationism—America for Americans.

Lincoln is seen as protector of the integrity of the nation-state. Having liberated the nation from incorrect thinking about oppression of other human beings, he has become the arch protector of freedom. He was also willing and able to wage war in defense of these ideals.

Extensions of both the Washingtonian and Linconian ideals are seen in other presidents who have been established as models for American leadership. James Monroe and the Monroe doctrine, Theodore Roosevelt, Woodrow Wilson, Franklin Roosevelt, Harry Truman, and Ronald Reagan—all have been invoked as having many of the same mythic qualities of American leadership—willingness to confront evil, to have America "go it alone" and serve as protector not only of the United States itself, but of American ideals wherever they can be detected.

The Washington and Lincoln ideals are powerful models for Americans in their struggles in the Middle East. As historic models for behavior they are beyond reproach. Americans see Middle Eastern oppositionists as destructive of social order, as oppressive to women and minority religious groups, and as hostile to democratic ideals. Liberating the world from their tyranny is clearly a job for a Washington. Protecting their freedom is a job for a Lincoln, who will wage war to counter these forces, singing the "Battle Hymn of the Republic" as he goes.

— 3 —

Middle Eastern Myths

For American citizens, one of the most difficult aspects of relations with the Middle East is the task of comprehending the blanket condemnation leveled against the United States by everyone from the leaders of the Iranian Revolution to Osama bin Laden. The vituperative, accusatory rhetoric seems to be aimed at indicting all U.S. leaders—and by extension American citizens since World War II—for unacceptable interference in Middle Eastern internal affairs, and for the destruction of the culture and economy of the region.

Equally incomprehensible was the violence with which the United States was attacked or resisted in its dealings with the opposition forces. Again and again Americans asked themselves: "Why do these people seemingly hate us so much that they commit these incredibly violent acts against us?"

For most Americans it seems incredible that such a blanket condemnation of the United States could have any substance in fact. Didn't the United States want to help the Middle East develop in the 1960s and 1970s? Weren't American industrial firms invited by the governments of the region to engage in joint economic ventures for the ostensible benefit of the people? Wasn't the U.S. interest in developing regional military strength during this period also in the best interests of the citizens? From an American standpoint it seems that the United States could be accused of no worse than wanting to make an honest dollar in a fertile market.

In the light of disinterested hindsight, however, it seems that there was indeed real justification for the complaints of the opposition forces in the region. However, even in situations of oppression and anger, violent resistance is not always the path chosen by those who feel themselves wronged. The peoples of the region had a style and a substance to their resistance, formulating their opposition according to their own set of mythic structures.

In the following discussion I characterize three of these mythic structures in terms of the archetypal Islamic heroes they most closely resemble. The Iranian myth is centered on Imam Hossein, grandson of the prophet. The Iraqi myth resembles Omar, third Caliph of Islam. Osama bin Laden's mythic structure is based on Saladin, the Kurdish defender of Islam against the Crusaders.

Iran—Imam Hossein: The Purifying Martyr

Religious systems, like all systems of patterned symbolic elements, are not merely static arrangements of idealizations—they are dynamic, and occasionally make their dynamic nature explicit. Such is the case with Iran.[1]

The central symbolic pattern in Iran, which renders human actions both great and small as meaningful for Iranians, is the struggle between the inside (the internal, the core) to conquer the outside (the external, the periphery).[2]

The struggle between inside (*baten/anderun*) and outside (*zaher/birun*)[3] has been encapsulated in the central myth of Shi'a Islam—the martyrdom of Imam Hossein, third Imam of Shi'a Muslims, and significantly, grandson of the Prophet Mohammad.

Hossein's father, Ali, was the only caliph to be recognized by both Shi'ites and Sunnis. Following his death, his son Hasan was convinced to resign his claim to leadership by Sunni partisans, who then usurped the caliphate, bestowing it on the ruler of Damascus, Mo'awiyeh. On his death, it passed to his son, Yazid.

Hossein was called upon to recognize the leadership of both caliphs of Damascus, but he refused—and this act set the stage for his subsequent martyrdom. In this legendary act of refusal, Hossein came to represent for Shi'a Muslims the verification of the truth of the spiritual leadership of Ali and his bloodline (also the bloodline of Mohammad), through his willingness to be martyred when his own right to succession to leadership of the faithful was challenged.

Thus, Hossein has continued to provide Iranians with a concretization of the struggle between internal and external forces. In death, he became an eternal symbol of the uncompromising struggler against external forces of tyranny, the defender of the faith, the possessor of inner purity and strength, the great martyr in the name of truth.[4]

Yazid and his henchmen, on the other hand, have become the supreme symbols of corruption. Not only are they murderers, but they also represent false doctrine—imposed from without. The sufferings of the family of Hossein, who survived the slaughter of their patriarch, are laid to Yazid's account, as are by extension, the sufferings of all Shi'ite followers in subsequent history. To this day, a cruel, corrupt individual who brings ruin to another is labeled "Yazid."

Opposition

The leaders of Iran's revolution were in the forefront in their opposition to America. At the time of the revolution, Iran was in a terrible state. It had a demoralized population, an economy sprawling and out of control, and a repressive, autocratic government that allowed its citizens no influence whatsoever in policies that affected them directly—not even the right to complain.

But, by the assessment of its own members, a far more serious development had taken place in Iranian society: the civilization had lost its spiritual core. It had become poisoned—obsessed with materialism and the acquisition of money and consumer goods. For pious Iranians, hardships can be endured with the help of one's family and social network; and through faith, *tavakkol*, ultimate reliance on the will of God. But to lose one's own sense of inner self—to be a slave to the material world—is to be utterly lost.

Understanding why Iranians came to feel this way about themselves, and why the United States came to be blamed for causing this state requires a close analysis of Iranian cultural and ideological structures. Iranian ideology was expressed during the revolution—and after—in religious terms.[5]

However, using "religion" or "religious fervor" as a label for Iranian opposition to the United States is far too simplistic. Anti-American feeling was widespread during and after the revolution, and was not confined to people who followed the clergy. It was also acutely felt among secularized members of the middle and upper classes, who cared not a fig for the mullahs and ayatollahs.[6] More significantly, it was expressed by many highly religious persons who actually opposed the clerical leadership of Iran, and who were convinced that the United States was supporting that leadership.

The reason for the violent expression of anti-American sentiment which wreaked havoc on relations between the two countries and eventually led to the taking of a whole embassy full of American hostages in November 1979 lies in the symbolic role which the United States played vis-à-vis the Iranian nation in Iranian eyes.

Taking their clue from Ayatollah Ruhollah Khomeini, the Iranian revolutionaries delighted in referring to the United States as the Great Satan in public street demonstrations. Although this epithet seems to be hyperbole on the part of the mob, such names give important clues to the symbolic conceptions being invoked. In this case it is significant that the term Great Satan was used, and not another.

In order to understand the full significance of this seemingly straightforward linguistic usage, it is necessary to look at Iranian inner symbolic life.

Internal and External—the Moral Dimension

Religious doctrine often serves as the most tangible concretization of the core symbols of society. In so doing, religion both makes statements about the truth of the conceptual world in which society exists; it prescribes for society's members what they should do, and what they should avoid doing. Furthermore, religion serves as a formal statement of symbolic categorizations in cultural life. It helps man regulate his life by placing certain aspects of it at the core of his value and action systems, and relegating other aspects to the periphery.

The contrast between the pure inner core and the corrupt external sphere in Iranian ideology is explored in depth in a study by M. C. Bateson and others.[7] This paper discusses the differences between the exemplary traits of *safa-yi batin,* "inner purity" and the bad traits of the external world which lead one to become *bad-bin,* "suspicious, cynical, pessimistic." The bad external traits, epitomized in adjectives such as: *zerang* "shrewd," *forsattalab* "opportunistic," *motazaher* or *do-rou* "hypocritical," *hesabgar* "calculating," and *charbzaban* "obsequious," "insincere," are qualities which Iranians feel they must combat in themselves as well as in the external world.

Iranians during the Pahlavi era, especially during the final ten years, would often express regret at behavior which they felt was unduly at odds with the good qualities desirable for one with a pure and uncorrupted inner core. A doctor of the author's acquaintance in a village outside of the city of Shiraz once went into a long disquisition on the difficulties of living in what he assessed as a corrupt world:

> They are all corrupt, all of my superiors. They are stealing all the time, and not just from the government—they also steal from the poor people who come to them for medicine and treatment. God help me, in this system they *force* me to be dishonest as well. They will give me medical supplies, but only if I pay them some bribe. When I ask them how I am to get the money, they tell me to charge the patients. So you see I have no choice, I must steal, too, if I want to carry out this job. I hate myself every day of my life for being dishonest, and I wish I didn't have to be, but I can't help it.

Iranian concern with this problem is reflected extensively in expressive culture. One of the principal themes of Iranian literature, films, and popular drama shows characters caught between the drive toward internal morality and the external pull of the corrupting world. This is, in fact, one of the central concerns in the doctrine and practice of Sufism, where the killing of one's "passions" (*nafs*), is one of the prerequisites to achieving mystic enlightenment. Display of one's concern for the depth of feeling that accompanies the drive toward the pure inner life is highly valued throughout Iranian society. This leads individuals to disdain that which is superficial or hypocritical. A tension exists between the internal drive toward morality, and one of the highest compliments one can pay another person is to say: "his/her inside and outside are the same."[8]

The Iranian ideal type is described in other terms by Fariba Adelkhah in her recent study, *Being Modern in Iran*. Adelkhah describes the virtues of such figures as Imam Hossein as embodying the quality of *javānmardi*. A good part of her study is devoted to unpacking this term, which embodies much of the virtues of the *bāten* orientation specified above, but it also describes heroes such as Imam Hossein and others. She describes it in the following way:

> The word javanmardi, which thus defines an existential ethic—that is a lifestyle—comes from the idea of youth (*javan*, young; *mard*, man). It is the Persian translation of the Arabic word *futuwwa* (pronounced *fotowwat* in Persian), which in turn comes from the root *fati* (young). Those who act in accordance with this code of ethics are called javanmardi or *fati*. They are distinguished by two essentials: the spirit of generosity (*sekhavat*) and courage (*shoja'at*)[9]. . . . The *javanmard's* purity of heart (*cheshm-o del pak*), which is part of the baten side of life, is shown in the externalized practice of giving which, being a material action, belongs to the *zaher* category, but is conceived as above all giving of oneself: 'the man with full eyes and mouth' (*cheshm-o del sir*) is not overwhelmed by the good things of this world, he can give up his interests, he willingly 'does without' his wealth by letting others benefit by it.[10]

Internal and External—the Legacy of History

The struggle between the pure forces of the inside and the corruption of the external exists not only in the idealization of individual morality; it also is a principal theme in the popular view of the history of Iranian civilization.

For ordinary Iranians, the waves of external conquest which have buried their land over the centuries: Alexander and the Greeks, the Arabs, Ghengis Khan and the Mongols—are as alive as if they happened yesterday. The British/Russian partition of the country into two spheres of influence in 1907 continued the pattern of cycles of conquest. Finally, as will be argued below, the economic domination of Iran by the United States in the post–World War II period seemed to extend the age-old pattern into the modern period.

Nevertheless, every time Iran was conquered by one of these great external powers, the nation subsequently rose like a phoenix from the ashes and reestablished itself. The times between these conquests were peak periods in Iranian culture. They were the periods of the flowering of the greatest literature, art, philosophy, mathematics, artisanry, and architecture.

Thus, the struggle between inside and outside, when painted on the canvas of Iranian history, is seen as a struggle between the destructive forces of external invading conquerors and the reproductive growing forces of the internal core of Iranian civilization. The internal core has thus far been the victor.

From this exposition, it should be clear that in Iranian society the source of corruption is external to the individual, and to society itself. If civilization or individuals become corrupt, it is because they do not have the strength to resist forces from without that are impinging on them at all times. This particular directionality gives a specific bias to Iranian political psychology. As internal conditions within the country become more and more difficult, the tendency on the part of the population is to search for conspiracy from an external source. This was a distinct feature of the Pahlavi regime, which saw opposition to the central government as a Marxist-inspired plot. The same bias inspired the efforts of the oppositionist forces, who saw the central government policies as inspired by non-Iranian considerations. The confrontations which led to the revolutionary events of 1978–79 and the ouster of the shah took place in an ironic context: both the shah and his opposition viewed themselves as defending the inner core of the civilization against the external forces of corruption and destruction. Thus, the battle of the Revolution can be seen as a battle of definitions: he who could make his vision of the inner core valid for the population as a whole, could control the nation.

The duty of a righteous Muslim is to resist corruption and promote the good. Any action is justified against a corrupting force. Thus, the ouster of the shah was presented as a religiously justified action, and persecution of those who supported the shah was likewise seen as justified.

The United States for postrevolutionary Iran fit perfectly into the cultural mold reserved for corrupt forces. It was an external, powerful, secular force. It supported a regime that Revolutionary leaders designated as corrupt. It gave the shah refuge and refused to allow verification of his claim of illness, thus raising the possibility that it was plotting against the Revolution.[11] When the Iran–Iraq war began, the United States seemed to "tilt" toward Iraq, a second corrupt external force, and demonstrated again and again in its actions in the Persian Gulf region that it was working against Iran's interests in the course of the war. It was thus easy for Iran's leaders to apply the epithet Great Satan to the United States and make it stick.[12] I will explore the power of this symbol in greater depth in Chapter 5.

Sincerity, Political Rhetoric, and Cultural Impedance

Iranian and U.S. leaders have accused each other of manipulative and insincere dealings with each other. Such accusations are extremely difficult to evaluate in a multi-cultural context.

First, it must be understood that both U.S. and Iranian leaders, in their foreign relations decisions and pronouncements are appealing primarily to their domestic constituencies. Thus, they attempt to say and do things that make themselves look good, whatever they may actually believe about a particular situation.

American leaders, for example, were opposed to negotiations with Iran over the release of the embassy hostages held in 1979–81 for nearly a year partly because they did not want to set Iran, an "outlaw nation," in a relationship of seeming equality with the United States. They also wanted to look for more traditional solutions through economic and military threats, and searching for plumbers to effect the hostage release. It is somewhat ironic that the hostages were released in the end through a mediated negotiation.[13]

Iranian leaders have had difficulties dealing directly with American officials since the revolution because of the taint such relationships carried. Through their vilification of the United States they effectively denied themselves any access to these officials, even though such access might have been important for the ongoing progress of the Revolution. The threat to their careers, indeed, their lives, was very real. In the first three years of the revolution they could not be known to be talking to or receiving messages from Americans. Indeed, to avoid accusations of collusion with the United States during the hostage crisis, "secret" messages from U.S. officials would be opened and read in public by nervous Iranian leaders.

The fact that Iranian and U.S. leaders *do* talk on occasion when necessary shows that at some level officials in both nations understand the difference between pragmatic dealings and public symbolism. Even so, this does not eliminate the cultural impedance which prevents full understanding by one side of the actions of the other.[14]

It has taken Iranian leaders, most of whom had no experience in dealing with international politics prior to assuming power, some time to understand how to behave in a way that the Western world will find comprehensible. The United States did not crumple at being called the Great Satan, nor did it cease pursuing what it considered its own strategic interests even in the face of curses and gadfly tactics by the Iranian regime.

An important change in Tehran, already starting with the cease-fire in the Iran–Iraq war, has been the search for an international voice for the Islamic Republic. This may mean projecting an image of Iran as more of a nation-state than it really is (certainly not an uncommon strategy among newer nations), or stressing issues, such as economics, which are easier for the United States and its allies to deal with, over ideology and religious sensibility. The Great Satan epithet seems to have been laid to rest at this point except when needed for staged symbolic public demonstrations. If this process continues, it may constitute a kind of Pahlavization of the Revolution as Iran once more insulates its true cultural feelings behind a patina of Western-oriented international communication strategies.

The Iranian myth of the West is not the only one that holds sway in the

Middle East today. To point up the strength of the Iranian myth, we can consider two other important scenarios that also govern behavior throughout the region—those of Iraq, and of the al Qaeda movement led by American arch enemy, Osama bin Laden.

Arab Myths—Omar the Caliph and Saladin: Defenders of the Civilization

Raiding was important in the first decades of Islam. Following the death of the Prophet Mohammad in the seventh century A.D., the Arabian tribes, united under the banner of the new religion, supported themselves in part through conquest of neighboring tribes.

They had two powerful neighbors to the north: Sassanian Iran and the Christian Byzantine Empire. These two great empires had been fighting each other for centuries, but they still had a reputation for ruthless militarism.

Under the third Caliph of Islam, Omar, the Muslim raiders reached the northernmost reaches of the peninsula—near present-day Kuwait. They made a few test raids on the borders of the two empires. To their amazement, there was no retaliation. Emboldened, they moved further north. A few army units met them, but they were easily defeated. To their great surprise, the great powers to the north had exhausted themselves fighting each other.

Meeting no resistance to speak of, the Islamic forces moved forth, and within ten years had conquered and consolidated all of the land from present-day Morocco to Afghanistan, including all of Iran. Damascus, and then Baghdad became the Moslem capital, and for four centuries the Arab capital was the center of all important civilization in the Middle East. It was a fabulous center of science, mathematics, poetry, literature, and also Judaic studies.

The Iraqi conquest of Kuwait bore an eerie similarity to the first Muslim conquests in the region. The armies of Saddam Hussein, bent on creating a new sphere of Arab interest in the region centered in Baghdad, first fought Iran to a standstill.

They then swept into Kuwait in the wake of the end of the cold war—a debilitating three decades of economic and military expenditure on the part of the Soviet Union and the United States. The cold war left both powers exhausted and unable or unwilling to defend their prime spheres of influence. If the two great powers had still been engaged with each other, Saddam would never have been able to make his move. Like the conquerors of twelve centuries ago, he threatened to eclipse a good part of the Middle East.

Americans, aghast at the boldness of this move, wondered if it was possible for Saddam to succeed. The chances were surprisingly good at the time. George H. W. Bush, after 100 days of engagement, declared an American victory in Iraq, but the Iraqis never stopped fighting, and they never surrendered. It took the forcible ouster of Saddam Hussein in the U.S. invasion of Iraq in 2003 to end this scenario.

Saddam was a man with a vision. Like the caliph Omar, and other conquerors of old, he saw a renewed Arab empire, built on oil wealth, centered once again in Baghdad, with himself as the *faqih* and guide. He had no use for the soft, corrupt sheiks of the Gulf, squandering their oil wealth on cars, jewels, and mansions throughout the world. Saddam saw them as irrevocably tied to Western economic influences who were hostile to Islam and Arab civilization. He knew that the sheiks have no real constituency among their people, and no way to defend themselves.

He felt that the United States and the Soviet Union were, in this regard, mere paper tigers—unable to make a military move because of lack of will. They also could not operate because of the difficult logistics involved in moving in and out of the Gulf, which lacked local land-based staging areas. Saddam saw the ineffectiveness of U.S. economic and arms embargoes against Iran. He was betting that cooperation on the part of the world community to blockade him would die as people everywhere realized there was money to be made by ignoring sanctions against him.

His mythology was supported by many in the rest of the Arab world. He had a surprising number of supporters—both out of fear and admiration. His battle against Iran was financed and applauded by almost every Arab state. The Palestinian Authority expected him to help them directly in their struggle with Israel. Many of the same people who were inspired at Ayatollah Khomeini's confrontation with the West had equal admiration for Saddam's Arab nationalism, sharing his dream of the renewal of a great Arab Islamic civilization in the Middle East.

However, as Saddam's hubris and paranoia increased following the long war with Iran in the 1980s, his behavior blunted the enthusiasm of other Arab nations. His invasion of Kuwait in 1981, based on claims dating back to the construction of old Ottoman provinces enhanced by anger at alleged Kuwaiti poaching of Iraqi oil, further increased regional discomfort with his rule. Finally, as religious sentiment took over militant movements in the Middle East, his adherence to secular rule made him anathema to religious zealots such as Osama bin Laden. Nevertheless, his basic message of opposition to Western hegemony resonated strongly throughout the Middle East, transcending his removal from power. The widespread, violent resistance to the post–2003 American invasion was largely inspired by this stance.

Osama bin Laden—Saladin for a Modern Age: The Resolute Protector

Osama bin Laden is the quintessential Islamic revolutionary. He has mythologized his own existence. He wishes to be thought of not as an anti-American terrorist, as he has been characterized, but rather as someone who would do anything to protect Islam, and the people of the Middle East. This is very much in the style of Saladin, the Kurdish general who defended Islamic lands from the Crusaders in the twelfth century, and Jamal ad-Din al-Afghani, the nineteenth-century protector of Islam, after whom Osama models his philosophy and his movement.

Bin Laden began his career fighting the Soviet occupation of Afghanistan in 1979 when he was twenty-two years old. He not only resisted the Soviets but also the Serbians in Yugoslavia. His anger was directed against the United States primarily because of the U.S. presence in the Gulf region—more particularly Saudi Arabia itself—the site of the most sacred Islamic religious sites.

According to bin Laden, during the Gulf War, America co-opted the rulers of Saudi Arabia to establish a military presence in order to kill Muslims in Iraq. In a *fatwa*, a religious decree, issued in 1998, he gave religious legitimacy to attacks on Americans in order to stop the United States from "occupying the lands of Islam in the holiest of places."[15] His decree also extends to Jerusalem, where the second most sacred Muslim site—the al-Aqsa Mosque—is located. The depth of his historical vision is clear when, in his decree, he characterizes Americans as "crusaders" harkening back to the Medieval Crusades in which the Holy Lands, then occupied by Muslims, were captured by European Christians.

He will not cease his opposition until the United States leaves the region. Paradoxically, his strategy for convincing the United States to do so seems drawn from the American foreign policy playbook. When the United States disapproves of the behavior of another nation, it "turns up the heat" on that nation through embargoes, economic sanctions or withdrawal of diplomatic representation. In the case of Iraq following the Gulf War, and again in the second Iraq war, America employed military action, resulting in the loss of civilian life. The State Department has theorized that if the people of a rogue nation experience enough suffering, they will overthrow their rulers, or compel them to adopt more sensible behavior. The terrorist actions of September 11, 2001, are a clear and ironic implementation of this strategy against the United States.

Bin Laden takes no credit for actions emanating from his training camps in Afghanistan. He has no desire for self-aggrandizement. A true ideologue, he believes that his mission is sacred, and he wants only to see clear results. For this reason, the structure of his organization is essentially tribal—cellular in modern political terms. His followers are as fervent and intense in their belief as he is. They carry out their actions because they believe in the rightness of their cause, not because of bin Laden's orders or approval. Groups were initially trained in Afghanistan, and then established their own centers in places as far-flung as Canada, Africa and Europe. Each cell is technologically sophisticated, and may have a different set of motivations for attacking the United States.

Palestinian members of his group see Americans as supporters of Israel in the current conflict between the two nations. In the Palestinian view, Ariel Sharon's ascendancy to leadership of Israel triggered a new era, with U.S. government officials failing to pressure the Israeli government to end violence against Palestinians. Palestinian cell members will not cease their opposition until the United States changes its relationship with the Israeli state.

Bin Laden's mythic view of the United States is clearly the image of the crusaders of the twelfth century, evolved into the colonialists of the nineteenth and twentieth centuries, combined with the opressive regimes of today. His struggle is the struggle of Saladin, Jamal ad-Din, the Muslim Brotherhood and Khomeini all rolled into one ferocious, ideological fighter willing to sacrifice all for an ideology.

Conclusion—Mythic Types

These mythic archetypes are presented here not because figures like Ayatollah Khomeini, Saddam Hussein, and Osama bin Laden really think of themselves as embodiments of these historic figures, but rather because these figures represent positive heroic archetypes. Behavior emulating these figures is admired.

One can see the working of this process in nation building throughout the world. The new nation of Tajikistan, following the breakup of the Soviet Union adopted as a national hero Isma'il Samani, the eleventh-century ruler of the Samanid Empire based in Samarqand. His era was unprecedented for its peace and its cultural growth. The Kyrgyz chose Manas, the medieval warrior-poet whose epic story even inspired the Kyrgyz constitution. Uzbekistan made another interesting choice for its national hero. Timur Lang, known in the West as Tamerlane, became the national hero. His choice seems odd, since he had a reputation for being a ruthless warrior and an authoritarian ruler. However, for the Uzbeks, the fact that he established a great Turkic Empire in place of a Persian one in a city the Persian rulers of the region had built and held for many centuries qualifies him as a Turkic hero.

These sources of inspiration live on, as they are held up to children as people worthy of emulation. In this manner, the highest ideals of one culture may be ignored or even disdained by another. When nations wish to understand each other, it is always wise to look to the myths and heroic figures. Overdrawn though they may be, they will always be a source of metaphor, myth, and inspiration for the people.

Discourse and Rhetoric

Dysfunctional Discourse

The United States gradually became locked into its unusual, dysfunctional discourse situation with Iran in the post–World War II period. The communication difficulties increased immediately following the Iranian Revolution of 1978–79.[1]

The Structure of Discourse—Implicit Models of Communication

One way to analyze the dysfunctional discourse during this period is to compare it with the processes of face-to-face communication. The formal study of face-to-face communication has been an important development in several fields in the social sciences and humanities in recent years. Pioneers include Charles Fillmore, Paul Friedrich,[2] H.P. Grice,[3] John Gumperz,[4] Dell Hymes,[5] Harvey Sacks,[6] and Emmanuel Schegloff.[7] In general, interpersonal communication is seen to be a series of *speech acts* situated within a broader context of *speech events*, which constitute occasions for communication. Speech acts and speech events are culturally constituted; that is, there are distinct, identifiable forms of discourse within every culture which have their own unique shape and form.

In describing components of discourse, a number of analytic schemas have been adopted by researchers in linguistics and anthropology. Most of these schemas contain a checklist of components or factors which must be attended to in order to describe the unique properties of each particular speech situation. One common set of factors enumerated and discussed by Hymes,[8] Jakobson,[9] and others consists of participants—addressors, addressees, auditors; codes—languages or varieties used; contact or channels—verbal, written, broadcast; context and setting; and message.

Other factors may be adduced, including topic, event, style, settings (physical and psychological), outcomes (intended and actual), and key, the manner or spirit in which a communications is given, but the above are in common use by communication analysts. They provide a means of describing particular communication situations and comparing communication styles across cultural boundaries. These checklists imply that participants in communication belong to the same *speech community* and thus share a sense of common principles of *appropriateness* in their speech, and the ability to judge *effectiveness* in communication.[10]

This schema is fine for the study of normal communication within a single cultural tradition. However, it must be modified when trying to analyze the impedance in communication that occurs in cross-cultural settings. Where there are conflicting assumptions about the parameters of communication, no assumptions can be made concerning normalcy. The "message" produced by an initiating party may appear as something quite different to the receiving party.

Taking the checklist of communication elements cited above, it is possible to show how each element may have one meaning for a speaker and another very different meaning for a hearer. In the following sections I will present a model for describing dysfunctional communication in an international setting, which will then be used in subsequent chapters to analyze and explain some of the difficulties obtaining between the United States and Iran, the subject of this study.

Communication Dysfunctions

Four areas of dysfunction, listed below, are especially destructive of cross-cultural discourse:

Differences in identification of elements. An element of behavior that is recognizable as an element of communication in one cultural setting may not exist as a recognizable element in another cultural setting. For example, many forms of nonverbal communication may be important as channels of communication in some cultures, but are unrecognizable in others. Verbal silence in discourse is one such example. It can be both expected and positive or unexpected and negative. Special keyings or genres in one society have no correlate in others. Even defining who may be a participant in communication may be variant in different cultural settings. Addressing deities in public, a potent form of social control in some societies, depends on a separation of "addressees" from "hearers" for the desired rhetorical effect. This separation may be hard to comprehend for persons in societies used to fusion of these two elements.

Differences in the "grammar" or acceptable co-occurrence of different elements. Just as phonemes can be combined to make proper words in a given language, or different food items can be combined to make a recognizable kind of meal (e.g., breakfast), so can specific communication elements be combined to construct recognizable, legitimate speech acts and speech events. These constructions may differ considerably across cultures.

Perhaps the simplest communication dysfunction consists of disparate identification of communication elements on the part of communicating parties. For example, party A sees a channel of communication (e.g., a telephone) as a proper channel for delivering a particular kind of message (e.g., an invitation). Party B sees such messages as only being legitimate when delivered through another channel (e.g., in writing, delivered through the mail or in person).

Differences in assessment of expertise in communication. Every society has a clear sense of both appropriateness and effectiveness in communication. Expertise in communication involves handling communicative elements in such a way that they are appropriately used, not causing unintended social disruption, and effectively used, accomplishing the goals of the speaker. What counts as commuicative expertise in one culture may be unrecognizable as such in another. For example, silence on the part of a political leader may be a highly effective communicative device in some cultures, but others may take it as a sign of weakness. In 1951 and 1952, for example, the frequent public weeping of Iranian prime minister Mossadeq was highly effective in mobilizing Iranian public support for his political program, but Americans saw this communicative device as a sign of incompetence (or worse). U.S. presidential candidate Edmund Muskie was virtually eliminated from the presidential race after weeping in public as the result of an unkind remark about his wife.

Differences in the ongoing evaluation of the course of communication. When dealing with any interpersonal communication, the expectations of communicating parties about the predicted course of the interaction is always a factor. Every communication event has a set of stages which may be rigidly prescribed (as in a religious ceremony) or which may have a number of junctures with optional directions for action, as in a seduction, or an encounter between a buyer and a seller. In cross-cultural situations there are almost always significant differences in these expectations which can cause well-intentioned communication to go awry.

The Structure of U.S.-Iranian Discourse

American-Iranian communication difficulties can be inventoried using a well-known schema developed by linguist Roman Jackobson, listing the basic elements of communication as addresser, addressee, code, contact or channel, context and message mentioned above.

Addressers and addressees. Both Iran and the United States began talking with each other, using different implicit models of how international communication should take place. The United States, wedded to a model of the world consisting of nation-states, insisted on finding persons of authority with whom to talk. Iranian opposition groups during the period of the shah functioned at a substate level. Even after the revolution of 1978–79, official leaders, as I note below, were talking as much *to* their own populations as *for* them, in international dealings.

Thus, both the United States and Iran have addressed each other for years with the specific intention of addressing someone else. The results have been disastrous. After nearly three decades following the Iranian Revolution of 1978–79, the two nations had not established diplomatic relations, and continued to refuse to address each other publicly. Most often, difficulties in communication arose when there was a disparity between the actual and intended addressee. The most common dysfunctional communication occurred when both sides were ostensibly addressing each other, but were in fact addressing their own constituencies.

For Americans, the most difficult communication to understand were public demonstrations in which large crowds chanted "Death to America!" American reporters on the scene were astonished when individuals who were engaged in these demonstrations treated them with friendliness and respect. They were regularly told "Oh, we like Americans. We don't like the American government." Given the penchant of Americans to see the world in terms of nation-states (see Chapter 2), this distinction was difficult for many to fathom.

In fact, the demonstrators were doubly puzzling to American observers. First of all, they were not speaking on their own behalf. Although some may have come to these demonstrations on their own recognizance, for the most part they were organized by the government, and frequently paid. Thus, they were the "speakers" but not the "addressers" of the message they were conveying. Further, the "hearers" may have been Americans, and indeed the entire world community, but the addressees were for the most part the most conservative elements of the Iranian population.

The demonstrations were undertaken at a time when the new government of the Islamic Republic of Iran was at its most fragile stage. The period from February to November 1979 was a transitional period in which the religious leaders fully established themselves in power in Iran. The Provisional Government established by Khomeini consisted largely of noncleric National Front Leaders. These leaders envisioned the successor government as a secular democracy based on European models. However, hard-line religionists had a different vision. They favored an outright theocracy based on Islamic law.

On March 30–31, 1979, the Provisional Government held a national referendum on the form the new government would take. At Khomeini's insistence, the public was asked to vote whether Iran should become an Islamic republic: "yes" or "no." Official tallies placed the "yes" vote at 98 percent.

Next, the nation decided on a constitution for the new government. In the summer of 1979, two drafts of a constitution were put forth, neither giving power to Khomeini nor to the clerical leaders. There was great debate between hard-line Islamicists and secular nationalists. Eventually, as a compromise an Assembly of Experts was elected to draft a third constitution. The Assembly had heavy representation from religious hardliners. This third draft invested ultimate power in a faqih (Chief Jurisprudent) along with a five-man religious Council of Guardians. Great dissent over this document raged in Iran throughout the Fall. The secular National Front leaders were chief in their opposition, fearing, as secular nationalist leader Mehdi Bazargan asserted, a new "dictatorship of the clergy."

Fate intervened in the ratification process to sway public opinion in favor of the hard-line religious leaders. The former shah, who was now deathly ill, had been traveling from nation to nation looking for a place to live. He appealed to the United States for medical treatment. Despite dire warnings from the U.S. Embassy in Tehran of the dangerous consequences of admitting him to America, the Carter administration allowed him to fly to New York on October 22, 1979.

The reaction in Tehran was immediate. On November 4, a group of students took over the U.S. Embassy and held all personnel hostage. The Americans remained captive for 444 days. The capture of the Embassy touched off a huge anti-American reaction in Tehran which lasted for months. Khomeini was genuinely worried about losing control of the government to these radical forces. The demonstrations solidified the image of the United States as an outside enemy helping to shore up the need to ratify the new government and helped the clerics to establish their credentials with the most radical forces in country.

As a result, officials of the Provisional Government, notably Bazargan, were implicated in the decision to give refuge to the shah, and were forced to resign. These events effectively blunted all secular nationalist opposition to the establishment of a theocratic government with Khomeini at its head. On December 2–3, 1979, the nation accepted the new constitution with a 99 percent approval vote.

These protests against the United States continued for years—indeed, until well after Khomeini's death. They became a kind of modern ritual. In the ten years from the onset of the revolution until Khomeini's death on June 3, 1989, the new government groped toward stability. Despite continued infighting between political factions, internal political transitions were generally peaceful. A debilitating war initiated by Iraq in November 1980 was fought to a standstill by July 1988. The continued power of the vigilante komitehs and their successors, the para-military Pasdaran, were cause for public alarm. These groups continued to enforce a rough-and-ready Islamic morality along with keeping the peace. Those seen as offenders of Islamic codes of modesty and morality, as well as adherents of the former regime were accosted on the streets and summarily presented before Islamic judges. Many were executed or imprisoned. Eventually the actions of these vigilante groups were curtailed, as they were redirected to fight the war with Iraq. The new government continued to be hostile toward the United States, but it improved relations with most other nations.

Codes. It is impossible for nations engaged in communication with each other not to engage in the use of tropes and figures of speech to characterize themselves and others. Both metaphors and euphemism are part of the codes of communication used by political leaders to speak both to each other and to their own constituents. The codes may differ significantly depending on the audience.

Such differences in codes can also imply a difference in the *key* of the message—the manner in which the statement is to be taken. One code may put a positive spin on an attribute or action. A virtual synonym with a negative connotation creates a slur.

Perhaps the most frequently used epithet to denigrate Iran is the term "terrorist." As Geoffrey Nunberg points out in his book, *Going Nucular: Language, Politics, and Culture in Confrontational Times*, "for the press and most of the public, *terrorist* connoted bomb-throwing madmen. Politicians weren't above using the word as a brush to tar socialists and radicals of all stripes, whatever their views of violence."[11] He goes on to point out that:

> By the 1980's, *terrorism* was being applied to all manner of political violence. There was a flap over the word in 1989 when the *New York Times* editor A. M. Rosenthal attacked Christopher Hitchens for refusing to describe the fatwah against Salman Rushdie[12] as terrorism. Hitchens had a good point. The fatwah may have been repugnant, but it was far from an act of indiscriminate violence—more like state-sponsored contract killing. But by then the word had acquired a kind of talismanic force—as if refusing to describe something as terrorism was the next thing to apologizing for it. By the 1990's people were crying terrorism whenever they discerned an attempt at intimidation or disruption.[13]

Beyond the use of loaded words like *terrorism*, linguist George Lakoff, in a series of articles and books has tried to show how the use of the processes of "framing" and skillful use of metaphor can bias the perceptions of an audience toward any topic. These linguistic "spins" have been used in a particularly skillful way by Western politicians with regard to Middle Eastern peoples, and more particularly with regard to Iran and Iraq.

In an influential paper written in 1990, "Metaphor and War,"[14] Lakoff placed these kind of anecdotal observations in a wider frame. He later re-iterated many of these points in his book, *Don't Think of an Elephant: Know Your Values and Frame the Debate.*[15] Lakoff's first observation is that U.S. foreign policy uses, as a central metaphor, the idea that *a nation is a person.* He writes: "The nation as a person metaphor is pervasive, powerful, and part of an elaborate metaphor system. It is part of an international community metaphor, in which there are friendly nation, hostile nations, rogue states, and so on."[16]

American politicians have used this device particularly well, being particularly skillful in portraying Iran as a rogue nation, hostile to the United States.

On April 27, 2004, Under Secretary of State for Arms Control and International Security John Bolton issued the following statement: "Iran's oil-rich environment, grudging cooperation with the IAEA, its deception, and its 18 year record of clandestine activity leads us to the inevitable conclusion that Iran is lying."[17] This is illustrative of many hundreds of similar statements from Bolton and other U.S. officials constituting an almost perfect illustration of Lakoff's metaphorical rhetoric, personalizing the nation of Iran as an actor, and showing its misdeeds.

Lakoff goes on to point out that one important addition to this metaphor is a "rational actor model." In this model, it is presumed that nations behave according to rational self interest, and these self interests include preserving material assets such as wealth, natural resources and military assets. Iran and Iraq are portrayed as motivated by other factors entirely, such as religious fervor, honor and other intangibles. Thus they could be portrayed as "irrational."[18]

Jerome Corsi, a Bush administration supporter, co-author of the book-length attack on 2004 Democratic Presidential Candidate Senator John Kerry, *Unfit for Command*, penned a new book attacking Iran for the nuclear policies of that nation. Titled *Atomic Iran*,[19] the book presents cataclysmic scenarios of atomic attacks on the United States and Israel from Iran's government.

Corsi writes in the book: "What has emerged as a more serious threat, especially with the mad mullahs going nuclear, is what is known as the improvised nuclear device (IND). The IND has become the preferred choice of serious terrorists." He goes on to describe a fantasy atomic explosion in New York: "A mushroom cloud and fireball expand upward. Instantly, all communications that depend on this area for broadcast stop. National television stations and hundreds of radio channels are instantly off the air. Cell phones throughout the region malfunction. New York City drops off the world communication map. It is not like 9/11, where the rest of the world could switch on their televisions and watch live what is happening."

In one fell swoop, Corsi thus creates a narrative where irrational Iranians are accused of being terrorists and creating mayhem that has never actually occurred. The book sold 150,000 copies in advance of its release in March 2005.

Finally, the "nation as person" strategy is used to construct scenarios where there are victims and heroes. Iran has been continually placed in the villain's role. Typical were the remarks of Secretary of State Condoleezza Rice during the confirmation hearings for her post, where she classified Iran under a group of nations that she called "outposts of tyranny."[20] On March 8, 2005, President George W. Bush reinforced this picture of tyranny and oppression in an address at the National Defense University, where he said: "The Iranian regime should listen to the concerns of the world, and listen to the voice of the Iranian people, who long for their liberty and want their country to be a respected member of the international community. We look forward to the day when Iran joins in the hopeful changes taking place across the region. We look forward to the day when the Iranian people are free."[21] President Bush continues by associating the United States with the forces of freedom. The assumption is that the Iranian people are not free, because of their leaders, but that the United States serves as a liberating inspiration, if not a direct liberator of the Iranian people.

The depiction of enemies such as Iran and Iraq as villains, and Western powers as heroes has a long pedigree. On February 3, 1991, *The Guardian* newspaper gave a report on vocabulary that had been used by the British press in describing the West and the Iraqis in the first Gulf conflict. Among the comparisons brought up by *The Guardian* were items such as:

- *We have* reporting guidelines. *They have* censorship.
- *We suppress. They* destroy.
- *We launch* first strikes. *They launch* sneak missile attacks.
- *Our boys are* cautious. *Theirs are* cowardly.
- *Our boys are* brave. *Theirs are* fanatical.
- *Our missiles cause* collateral damage. *Their missiles cause* civilian casualties.
- *Our planes* fail to return from missions. *Their planes* are zapped.

One would expect the enemy in a conflict to be described in negative terms. Therefore, the differences in code are perhaps not surprising. However, it is interesting to note the specific qualitative dimensions that govern the dichotomy between the descriptive terms, in the case of Iraq. The enemy is portrayed as weak, irrational, childlike, and cowardly. The Americans, and by extension the British, are seen as strong, rational, mature, and brave. The characterization of the Iraqis constitutes an almost perfect paraphrase of Edward Said's description of Western Orientalist attitudes toward Middle Easterners in his famous study, *Orientalism*.[22] It is as if, having a

Middle Eastern enemy, the West had a ready-made code of invective that could be invoked. The code itself is not descriptive; it is evocative of emotional and prejudicial overtones that go back centuries.

The United States is the subject of invective as well, conforming to Middle Eastern structures of negative characterization. No image could be more deeply evocative than the characterization of the United States as The Great Satan by Iran. However, even this is subject to misunderstanding. Satan is not merely a figure of evil in Islam. He is a fallen angel—bright and beautiful, and jealous of humanity. Therefore, he tempts humankind to stray from God's path. In characterizing the United States in this way, Iranian revolutionaries were trying to emphasize the fact that America led Iran astray from its correct religious and spiritual path.

Channels and contact. Communication between Americans and Iranians has been multichanneled, and indirect. Very little nonmediated communication took place between U.S. leaders and Middle Eastern political and social bodies for many years following the Revolution. Intermediaries handled most messages. Alternatively, communications were delivered through public speeches as "signals" to the other party. The diffuseness of this kind of communication created enormous confusion. Since official communiqués were sparse, literally *anything* could be treated as a significant message by observers of the other nation. Added to this was the disinclination of Americans to speak directly to Middle Eastern leaders without some guarantee that such talks would be productive. Regional leaders were likewise afraid to talk to Americans for fear of being "tainted" by the contact, and losing their office, or even their life, or being jailed for collusion.

Context. Finally, the basic styles of communication were predicated on different theories of what the audience for communication was like. The United States largely assumes *egalitarian* communication structures within communities, and *hierarchical* structures between the two communities. The Iranian model was precisely the opposite. They assume *hierarchical* structures within their own community and *egalitarian* structures between the two communities.

In Iran, as I have shown in a number of other publications,[23] communication tends toward hierarchical skewing.[24] It is frequently difficult for Iranians to maintain egalitarian discourse, particularly in the public arena. Therefore, speakers adopt the somewhat unusual strategy of using self-lowering forms in conjunction with other-raising forms, denigrating one's self while elevating one's interaction partner. When both parties do this simultaneously, the communication takes on a flavor highly characteristic of Iranian life. In the internal political arena, hierarchy is largely assumed. However, in dealing with foreign powers, such as the United States, Iran expects to be treated as an equal.

In the United States, hierarchy in interpersonal relations is frequently suppressed. Everyone calls everyone else by their first names, and overt assertion of superiority is frowned upon. However, in the international arena, the United States assumes that other states will subordinate themselves to superior American power.

Iranians frequently express puzzlement at this difference in communicational attitude. They note that Americans are friendly on an interpersonal level, but that the U.S. government is frequently haughty and hostile, demanding obeisance and acknowledgment of U.S. superiority. Iranians are ready to grant deference to interaction partners, but they are not ready to have it demanded of them. Under such circumstances they bristle and resist.

Clearly, the Iranian and the U.S. assumptions about the context of communication cannot coexist in the same discourse sphere with ease, and indeed they do not. When the United States tried to bully Iran starting in 2003 over the development of nuclear weapons, Iran resisted tooth and nail. Eventually, they agreed to begin inspections, once the foreign ministers of Great Britain, France, and Germany sat down and negotiated with them face-to-face in a dignified, egalitarian manner.[25]

Message. Both the United States and Iran have been extraordinarily inept at getting their messages across to each other. Jakobson pointed out that in any communication, the message is conveyed through what he called the "poetic function." In real poetry, this function embodies such techniques as rhyme, alliteration, onomatopoeia, and choice of unusual or colorful words. In other forms of discourse this means choosing forms of discourse that are less predictable or probable to draw attention to, and underscore the message.

Since neither Iran nor the United States has a good idea about the communication systems of the other, adopting a "poetic" strategy was impossible. The communications misfired again and again. The United States was particularly inept, since it had so few people who knew Persian, or knew anything about Iranian communication structures. The Iran-Contra Affair, in which U.S. arms were sold to Iran in exchange for cash used to support Latin American guerrilla groups "off the books" is a case in point. The American perpetrators of these dealings brought their Iranian hosts a cake in the shape of a key to symbolize the cooperation between the United States and Iran in this matter. The cake simply puzzled the Iranians, and appeared slightly ridiculous. Since the gesture was improbable, it did get the Iranian officials' attention, but they were unable to interpret it.

One of the most difficult limitations in communication between nations is the necessity for translation. The difficulty arises not just in the rendering of equivalent vocabulary between languages, but in the establishment of equivalent contexts of interpretation. In translation, the poetic functions used in the original message frequently are impossible to replicate. A vivid word in one language may have no equivalent in the other language. Thus, in diplomatic negotiations one must translate more than words; one must also translate intentions.

The inability of U.S. officials to understand messages is not limited to Iran. At one point in the Gulf conflict, Saddam Hussein offered to withdraw from Kuwait as part of a plan for settlement of the Gulf conflict. His offer was dismissed out of hand by President George H. W. Bush as "a cruel hoax." President Bush based his objection was the claim that "conditions" attended Saddam's offer.

The "conditions" for withdrawal which Bush condemned were a list of Middle Eastern political issues which Saddam supplied as an agenda for the postwar period. The Bush administration chose to interpret Saddam's statement as implying "linkage" between things such as negotiation of the Palestinian issue and Iraq's pullout from Kuwait.

However, President Bush was wrong. The postwar agenda was appended to the pullout offer using the Arabic term *al-rubat*. This literally means "relationship." Forms of the word are used in common parlance to say things like: "with regard to," "relevant to," and "pertaining to."

In short, Saddam's offer was genuinely different from his earlier proposals. He was not establishing conditions for withdrawal from Kuwait, but only listing the issues which were "related" to settling of the Gulf issue.

Bush's councilors surely presented a range of possibilities for interpretation of Saddam's offer, and one can always quibble over the meaning of a single word. But in purposely choosing to treat the Iraqi language in the most negative light, the Bush administration also missed the significance of the proposal as a signal. Far from being a "cruel hoax," the more important message Saddam was providing in altering his language from previous formulations was that he was willing to negotiate the withdrawal.

Bush's recalcitrance at even addressing this proposal opens the question as to whether the United States really wanted Saddam to withdraw or not. Washington's official position had been that there was nothing to negotiate—Saddam must simply leave Kuwait, and that was all. However, the Bush administration treated Saddam's simple withdrawal offer as a "nightmare solution" because it would preclude the United States from destroying Saddam's government and military machinery. The mood in Washington seemed to be: "No matter what Saddam says or does at this point, we are going to destroy Iraq."

It is my opinion that Saddam at that point was attempting to end the conflict with a modicum of Middle Eastern honor intact. Since war is a dynamic process, the events which would have allowed him to retain honor in Middle Eastern terms varied over time. At the point he made his offer, keeping Iraq intact, and being the prime mover in prompting attention to a wider Middle Eastern peace would have been enough to entice him to leave.

The consequences of the American treatment of Iraq proved cataclysmic for the region, creating turmoil which spread without end, lasting more than a decade at this writing and threatening to extend many years into the future. Saddam had already paid dearly for his adventure in Kuwait. His nation was crippled. Saddam's own behavior toward his own nation worsened as he sought revenge against the United States.

We will never know if President Bush's interpretation of Saddam's offer was a misunderstanding or a willful misinterpretation. There is no question, however, that following this interchange, the war moved to a new level of intensity.

It was at this point that Saddam Hussein became a "marked man." A group of civilian politicians, the "neoconservatives," began in 1992 to plan for Saddam's eventual removal from power. They lobbied President Clinton and leaders of Congress to attack Iraq. Finally, following the election of President George Herbert Walker Bush in 2000, many of these individuals were elected or appointed to national office. These included Secretary of Defense Donald Rumsfeld and Vice President Dick Cheney. The terrible tragedy of the destruction of the World Trade Towers in New York and the attack on the Pentagon in Washington on September 11, 2001, gave them the public support they needed to attack Iraq, although it was later definitively proven that Saddam had nothing to do with the September 11 attacks, and that he posed no military threat to the United States.

Iran, for its part, looked on the 2003 invasion of Iraq with enormous trepidation. The United States seemed to be establishing a bulwark on both their Eastern border in Afghanistan, and their Western border in Iraq. However, the Iranians had no way to effectively express their dismay, except to repeat the same rhetoric they had used since the revolution. The United States had no way of dealing with Iran except to implicate them in the attacks against the United States.

Conclusion—The Structure of Miscommunication

It seems clear that tremendous difficulties attend communication between the United States and Iran, but given difficulties that have also attended U.S. communication with Iraq and other nations in the Middle East, it would seem that Iran is not the only nation with which the United States has difficulty communicating.

For their part, Iranians also have trouble understanding the United States. Viewing Americans as powerful actors, but puzzling communicators, Iranians frequently mistake clumsiness in discourse for arrogance. Americans have trouble allowing Iranians equality in dealings with officials in the U.S. government, while puzzling over their excessively polite manner in interpersonal relations.

Almost every communication element is misunderstood in communications between the two nations. This could be remedied with increased contact and interpretation not just of words, but of context, code, and channels. Total translation is an elusive and difficult goal, but it is absolutely necessary if Iran and the United States are ever to develop rapport with each other.

— 5 —

Images of the Great Satan

The Great Satan, as a symbolic construction of the United States is symbol that is likely to endure for all time. It is so evocative, so powerful, that it dominated the rhetoric of the Iranian revolution. For Muslims, the term is a literal translation of the Arabic "shaitan ar-rajim" that is invoked at every prayer, in which God is entreated to protect the believer from evil. The image has a double meaning for Iranians, because of Iran's Zoroastrian past. Some Shi'a theologians vehemently deny the connection between the Zoroastrian force for evil, Ahriman, and *Shaitan* as specified in the Qur'an, though the parallels are palpable and clear.[1] However, such denials only testify to the salience of the comparison between the two religious traditions.

The matter is further enhanced by nonreligious legend and myth. The apical evil force is the White Div,[2] presented in its most fearsome form in Ferdowsi's *Shahnameh* (Book of Kings), the Iranian national epic. The White Div was defeated by the Iranian national hero, Rustam, in a great battle depicted in the *Shahnameh* in exciting detail. The White Div as a symbol of evil for Iranians has a triple resonance. First, it is a force coming from outside Iran. Second, it was defeated by an internal, supremely good Iranian hero, and finally, it is clearly associated in Islamic times with *shaitan* or the Satan of the Qur'an.

Drawing upon the imagery of the United States as the Great Satan should have somehow alerted American analysts that the epithet was not being directed at the United States or its citizenry, but rather at Iran and its citizens. It was an attempt to show Iranians that the United States and all it supported, principally Shah Mohammad Reza Pahlavi, was a force alien to Iran and its civilization—a force that was attempting to corrupt the Iranian people.[3]

This made the analyses of most American commentators somewhat irrelevant to Iranians, as true and accurate as many of them were. Barry-

Rubin, in his study of the U.S.–Iranian relationship, *Paved with Good Intentions*,[4] tried hard to counter the idea that the United States' operations in Iran were intended to be damaging to Iran. The superb work of Marvin Zonis,[5] Gary Sick,[6] and James Bill[7] went even further, showing that the United States was actively deceived by the shah and his secret police, SAVAK (Sazeman-e Amniyat va Ettela'at-e Keshvar), or organization for national security and intelligence. Kenneth Pollack, in his recent book,[8] fairly rails at the Iranians' charges against the United States, showing them with some accuracy, to be wrong or unjustified. Ruhollah Ramazani explores the pattern of relationships that sustained the United States and Iran in symbiosis during the years preceding the revolution.[9] All of these works are essential reading, and they are all great in their own way, but they frequently miss seeing Iran from the perspective of its cultural core. Anthropologist Michael M. J. Fischer[10] and historian Roy Mottaheddeh[11] come much closer to understanding Iran on its own terms.

However, as I have argued in encapsulated form already in this discussion, and will elaborate below, cultural logic, especially when it embodies powerful symbols, is far more effective in shaping public attitudes than mere facts. Nowhere is this more true than in Iran, where there is a powerful culture of imagery and symbolism already part of the national heritage. Nor should this idea be odd for Americans. Denizens of Washington, who have ever conducted a political campaign know that symbols and slogans that hit cultural nerves matter to citizens in a profound way. It is therefore surprising that some of America's finest political minds would fail to understand this basic fact with regard to Iran.

However, the tension between this symbolic view of the world and the realities of international politics has been profound since the Revolution. This fact has been commented on extensively since that time—not always with much understanding, however.[12]

In order to fully understand the invocation of the Great Statan image, it is necessary to revisit some of the earlier concepts in this discussion. In Chapter 3 above, I introduced the central symbolic pattern in Iran—the struggle between the inside, the internal, the core, to conquer the outside, the external, the periphery.[13] The contrast between the pure inner core and the corrupt external sphere in Iranian ideology is, as I have mentioned previously, explored in depth in a now classic study by M. C. Bateson and others.[14] It should once again be noted that in light of the tension between the pure internal and the corrupt external, one of the highest compliments one can pay another person is to say: "his/her insides and outsides are the same."[15]

It is also useful once again to be reminded that Iran, having been conquered from the outside so many times, was able to recover (according to the historical view of its citizens). This was because the inner core of the civilization was seen as much more worthy and powerful than the external forces that would destroy it. The periods of conquest were, in retrospect, seen as periods of nascent cultural triumph. As the conquerers themselves were conquered by Iranian civilization, these were, paradoxically, the periods of the flowering of the greatest literature, art, philosophy, mathematics, artisanry, and architecture.[16]

And, as we saw above, the image of Imam Hossein looms as a synchretic religious realization of the clear triumph of inside over outside. In his martyr's death, he became the ideal symbol of the uncompromising struggler against external forces of corruption.[17]

Superiors and Inferiors

Another dimension of everyday life, relevant to understanding the Iranian conception of the role of the United States in Iranian affairs, during the decades following World War II is the dimension of superiority vs. inferiority in human social relations. I have dealt with this in previous publications, and have alluded to it earlier in this discussion.[18]

Status in Iran is largely a relative matter. One who can claim higher status, superior wisdom, or greater acclaim from those surrounding him or her may by his or her mere presence convince even the highest official to accept an inferior position in a social encounter. Even the lowest street sweeper is, in contrary fashion, able to claim superiority to younger street sweepers. Consequently, adroit individuals in society must be capable of operating at different levels at all times, knowing both the proper and effective ways that their actions should be taken. It may be this quality of the way in which behavior is both projected and interpreted in Iran that has prompted some foreign visitors, like Lord Curzon, to observe that in Iran: "The same individual is at different moments haughty and cringing."[19]

Status positions within the stream of social life are likewise strategic positions with complementary rights and duties. Persons in a "high" status position are expected to dispense favors, dispense rewards, and give orders. This can easily be seen as a set of obligations that involve taking action on another's behalf, dispensing material goods, and issuing a stimulus for either action or goods. In a pure state, these expectations are an absolute characteristic of the high status position, and are obligatory. The implied ethic in this case is one of *noblesse oblige*.

Low to high status is likewise defined by orientation to action, goods, and stimulus for both, in a fashion complimentary to the ethic of noblesse oblige above. Low status persons are expected to render service, pay tribute, and make petitions. The ethic implied here is one of *duty*.

It can easily be seen that the status obligations incumbent on social actors within Iran may in many cases be differentiated only in symbolic terms. A person defined as taking an inferior role may pay rent to a landlord, or bribe an official. The landlord may give his tenant a present at the New Year, and officials may reward their retainers and dependents with money or privileges. The absolute value of the goods exchanging hands in both downward and upward directions in either case may be the same, but the meaning attached to the exchange is different.

Much of this exchange involves intangible dealings. Inferiors are expected to praise and defer to superiors. Superiors are allowed to make grand gestures, and be identified as benefactors of others through their actions.

It is important to understand here that both inferior and superior parties in social relations retain social and personal respect within the bonds of inequality. Respect, in part, lies in knowing one's obligations and fulfilling them correctly and carefully. There is, thus, a hidden agenda in this kind of social relationship—both parties must agree to preserve the respect of the other by not misusing the relationship. The bond endures as long as reciprocity is maintained, and each party is confident that he or she is not being manipulated or abused by the other person.

It is not surprising, then, that some of the strongest social and emotional bonds in Iranian society obtain between superior and inferior actors in social interaction. Affective psychological testing seems to bear this observation out: great affection is seen to be expressed by Iranians toward figures whom they revere and respect.[20]

Relations of equality are no less complex in Iranian social life. Equality relationships are highly unstable, and supremely demanding. Parties in equal status relations must adhere to a bond of absolute reciprocity and unquestioned loyalty. For this reason, one is able to achieve this sort of understanding with another person only rarely, and usually only for short periods of time. It is thus not surprising that, one's best friends are often family members. Same-age, same-sex cousins are likely candidates for equality relationships, as well as schoolmates and childhood playmates.[21]

The relationship between respect and affection is highly complex in Iran. In a real sense one cannot really exist without the other. Relationships of equality as well as inequality are continually tested for sincerity, and are often rent asunder after years of endurance on the basis of a single small incident.

Similarly, a relationship of equality or inequality may be forced upon a person, but if the rights and obligations of the position are not observed with sincerity, the respect that is necessary to cement the relationship into place cannot be established. An illegitimate claimant to a position of superiority will soon be completely undermined by those whom he expects to serve him or her. Likewise, a person not accepted as worthy to serve in an inferior position will be betrayed, cast off, or sacrificed.[22]

The External Seduces the Internal—Submitting to Inferiority

Many have commented on the economic difficulties that proceeded the revolutionary events of 1978–79 leading to the downfall of the former shah. As serious as these difficulties were, however, they could never have translated into the complete rupture between the monarchy and the people which led to the enormously rapid destruction of the Pahlavi regime, if they had not occurred in such a way that they could be defined as a betrayal of the basic ideals that govern Iranian social ideology and morality. The reaction against the shah was not calculated political strategy—it was outrage. The same outrage was directed against the United States, both at the time of the fall of the shah, and later during the fourteen-month hostage crisis from 1979–81.

The outrage felt by the Iranian people was heightened by the knowledge, rarely acceded to after the revolution, that the Iranian people in some way knew that they themselves had been largely to blame for the economic and social difficulties that beset them during the years of Pahlavi rule. Here again, the eternal war between the lure of the external, material, world as represented by the West and its attractions, and the internal spiritual world, as represented by Iranian religious and cultural values, raged unabated. As one social scientist in Tehran remarked woefully, up to me on surveying one area of the city left in rubble after a confrontation between the people and the army at the beginning of the revolution in October 1978: "The Iranian people have done this to themselves. We thought it would be enough to be rich, buy clothes in Paris, and travel to London every year for a good time. In the end we ended up selling our souls for a few rags and a couple of nights in a cabaret."

The Pahlavi regime wanted to be very strong both militarily and economically, with little serious concern for the common people. The desire for immediate economic development on a massive scale led the regime to a misguided and simplistic reading of the leading growth theory of the 1960s, as promulgated by economists like Walt Rostow and Barbara Ward. Roughly stated, it promised "economic takeoff" if a nation could increase its productivity by a fixed amount for a sustained period. But simple increases in the Gross National Product, which for Iran actually exceeded 20 percent in some of the years in the decade before the revolution—without correcting for inflation—only blinded the prerevolutionary regime to the folly of its superficial planning.

Actual growth in the Iranian economy was, of course, dependent on the measure one wished to use at the time. Annual rate of GNP growth averaged 23.55 percent from 1965–74 without adjustment for inflation. Adjusted to 1972 prices, annual rate of GNP growth was 17.45 percent for the same period. The principal stimulus to GNP growth was the massive oil price increase imposed by OPEC in 1973, which created a massive increase in GNP (49 percent in 1973 and 71.3 percent in 1974; 34.2 percent and 43 percent respectively at 1972 prices). The oil price increase caused a drastic change in the contribution of the oil sector to the economy in general. In 1959, the oil sector contributed 9.7 percent of the total GNP, by 1974 it contributed 47 percent.[23]

The role of the United States throughout this period was all too clear. Iran, as an oil-producing country was a prime market for the sale of U.S. technology and services. Iran wanted instant development; the United States was only too happy to oblige. Iran wanted to become the chief military power in the region; so much the better for the United States. Peacekeeping in this volatile area could be left in the hands of a friendly ally, and that ally would even be paying for the privilege in enormous purchases of arms, albeit with the help of oil consumer in western nations paying higher prices at the gas pump after the oil price increase in 1973. Americans looked upon Iran as an economic gold mine. At the time of the oil price increase, seat-of-the-pants entrepreneurs were descending on the country in droves with no clear business—they just wanted to hang around and see if they couldn't hustle a few million (and many did).

During this period, the U.S. Embassy was much less a spy mission, as claimed by the government of the Islamic Republic as a justification for the holding of the fifty-two American hostages, than a kind of industrial brokerage firm. Hardly a day passed when the ambassador did not have important business with one or another American industrial concern. One of the embassy's principal activities during this period was to put wealthy Americans in contact with wealthy Iranians for their mutual benefit. The embassy cocktail party circuit was a virtual bazaar for business dealings.

Iranian law required that all business operations be 51 percent Iranian owned. Even with those restrictions, Americans could make big money just in the founding of industries. Though Iranians would own 51 percent of the concern, they would also provide 51 percent of the financing through government loans.

The very best people for American investors to do business with were, of course, the royal family and other high government officials, who would meet no bureaucratic opposition in their financial ventures. They could easily obtain millions from government-controlled banks on their signature alone, and no one dared question construction standards or business practices of concerns that had connections with the court. Soon Iran was not only awash in money, it was awash in new industry. The country seemed to be booming.

The view that Iran could be persuaded to bankroll the United States for any purpose extended to all sectors of U.S. society. Even universities were included. Over two hundred institutions in the United States had cooperative arrangements with Iranian institutions. Most of these educational cooperative ventures provided little benefit for Iran, but great financial advantages for beleaguered American colleges facing rising costs and shrinking enrollments in the early 1970s. One notorious educational exchange program between a major American university and an Iranian institution was funded entirely from Iran, and was designed to provide U.S. faculty help to improve and strengthen the teaching at the Iranian University. In practice, the American university used the program as a cheap way to reduce their teaching rolls. The faculty members involved in the program were given full teaching credit toward sabbatical leave for the year spent in Iran, and they tended to treat their tour there as something between a research leave and a vacation. They were often absent from their classes without notice (usually touring archaeological sites in the area) and were lax in classroom preparation and evaluation of student assignments. After 1973, the Iranian university finally terminated the agreement after enduring several years of this abuse.

Americans working in Iran were generally paid at rates far exceeding those paid to Iranian workers. American industrial concerns often had multiple pay scales: U.S. citizens received the highest wages, followed by Europeans and Japanese; Asians (Indians, Pakistanis, South Koreans, and Filipinos) came next. Only one group fell below native Iranians on the wage scale—Afghan unskilled laborers. One oil company paid its American staff up to seven times what it paid its Iranian staff, even though in some cases the Iranian technicians had received precisely the same educational training as their American counterparts, and carried out equivalent duties. Some Iranians had even been classmates of their American coworkers at the same U.S. universities! American salaries for low-level management positions ranged to $50,000 per year, a handsome sum in the 1970s, and middle management could count on scales reaching up to twice that amount. One can only imagine what top executives were being paid.

Inequalities were not limited to pay, however. In the oil fields and other "camp" situations controlled by foreign firms, Iranian technicians were often housed in quarters which were separate from and decidedly inferior to those of Americans with equivalent training and experience. The refinery city of Abadan was divided between luxurious air-conditioned housing with manicured lawns for Westerners, and two-room mud-brick dwellings for Iranian workers.

Personal relations between Americans and Iranians were not especially cordial during this period. The vast bulk of Americans living and working in Iran were essentially technicians, often with no experience in living abroad, who were blatantly living and working in Iran "for the money." The second largest group was the American military that likewise had very little interest in Iran or the Iranians.[24]

Perhaps the greatest source of tension between Americans and Iranians on a day-to-day basis was housing. American companies in Iran, such as Haliburton Corporation and then-independent Brown and Root Corporation (later Kellogg, Brown, and Root) worked under Iranian government contracts on a "cost-plus" basis. That is, the Iranian government agreed to pay the company a certain percentage (usually 10 percent) over its fixed costs if the project was completed.[25] These companies often would move thousands of employees into a city in the space of a month, all of whom would have to find housing immediately. Working through brokers, the Americans would swoop down and rent up every available apartment or house in an area at whatever price was asked. Since housing costs were "fixed costs," they literally didn't care how much they paid—the Iranian government would pick up the bill in any case. Naturally, after a short time, rental costs were driven up throughout the country. In the period from 1972 to 1974 they had roughly quadrupled on every class of property. By 1976 they had doubled again. Although the general inflation in the country can be cited as a contributing factor to the rise in rents, they would never have increased to the extent they did if American business had acted more responsibly.

Oppositionist leaders seized on yet another aspect of the special relationship between Iran and the United States—the right of extraterritoriality granted to many American citizens living and working in Iran. The Vienna Convention of 1961 is the major international legal agreement defining the rights of diplomatic personnel stationed in foreign posts.

Article I of that convention basically assures rights of extraterritoriality—diplomatic immunity in common parlance—to all accredited diplomats serving on foreign soil.

The United States, in that same year, before Iran had actually ratified the Vienna convention, concluded an agreement for economic assistance signed by both nations, which provided that U.S. members of technical assistance missions would be treated "as part of the diplomatic mission of the United States of America in Iran for the purpose of enjoying the privileges and immunities accorded to that diplomatic mission."[26] This essentially guaranteed extraterritoriality for most Americans living in Iran.

When the question of ratification of the Vienna Convention finally came before the Majles (parliament)[27] in 1963, it sparked a lively debate, since the United States had made it clear the year before that it would consider the terms of the Vienna Convention, applicable to the 1961 agreement of economic assistance. Thus, the rights of extraterritoriality were potentially extended to many individuals outside of the embassy staff. The Iranian parliament was clearly caught in a bind. In joining the international community in ratifying the Convention, they would de facto be granting special privileges to American citizens.

Although the ratification passed, one deputy remarked sourly that he would have a hard time replying to someone who said that even a foreign refrigerator repairman or an apprentice mechanic in Iran enjoyed the immunity that Iran's ambassador enjoyed abroad.[28]

The historical significance of the Majles ratification was not lost on Ayatollah Ruhollah Khomeini, already a major oppositionist figure in Iran. The extraterritorial rights granted Americans harkened back to the nineteenth century, when Great Britain and Tsarist Russia had been able to force Iran to grant them the right to try their citizens resident in Iran in special consular courts. Khomeini issued a violent proclamation condemning the Majles action ending with the judgment: "If the foreigners wish to misuse this filthy vote, the nation's duty will be clearly specified. . . . The misfortunes of Islamic governments have come from the interference by foreigners in their destinies. . . . It is America that considers the Koran and Islam to be harmful to itself and wishes to remove them from·its way; it is America that considers Moslem men of religion a thorn in its path."[29]

In October of that same year, Khomeini preached the sermon that would cause him to be exiled from Iran. In this sermon, condemning the right of extraterritoriality once again he said: "If the shah should run over an American dog, he would be called to account, but if an American cook should run over the shah . . . no one has any claim against him. . . . If the men of religion had influence it would not be possible for the nation to be at one moment the prisoner of England, at the next the prisoner of America."[30]

Khomeini's sermon not only condemned the United States, it made an explicit connection between the colonial policies of Great Britain and the subsequent economic and political activities of the United States. In essence, he invited Iranians to equate one hated foreign power with a hated direct successor.

Few Americans living in Iran were prepared to understand these undercurrents, for most lived in almost total isolation from Iranian society and culture. American academics concerned with Iran approached large industrial concerns repeatedly with offers to set up language and cultural training programs for American expatriate employees in Iran, but these offers were never taken seriously. At best they were considered, as one executive put it to me, as "a nice way to keep the wives from getting bored."

Internal Culture Shock

Americans also had little perspective on what Western technology and cultural institutions were doing to traditional Iranian patterns of social life. Tehran, even as late as 1960, was a sleepy, comfortable city where citizens pursued a leisurely, highly interpersonal social life. Visiting friends and relatives was the principal social activity, and few people worried about the outside world.

By 1978, the population of the city had quadrupled. Automobiles glutted the streets everywhere; smog hung ominously in the formerly clean mountain air; and the leisurely pace of life of earlier years had turned into a frantic struggle for most citizens. It took at least an hour to travel anywhere in the city, as traffic jams were totally debilitating. As the urban sprawl spread east and west, family members became widely separated, and could see each other with far less frequency than before. The gap in human contact could be bridged to a limited extent by the telephone, but obtaining this magical device was a lifetime operation. Humorous writers commented that if one signed up for a telephone at birth, it might be delivered at last on the day of one's funeral.[31]

Besides telephones, radios (with built-in tape cassette recorders), cars, and televisions became the new necessities for the modern Iranian family. Even in rural areas one might possess these things and enter the modern age—even if one's village lacked other necessities, such as electricity or piped water. The rural landscape was dotted with television aerials, and the "putt-putt" of the gasoline generators purchased to make the televisions run, filled the air.

In this way, Iran was plunged directly into the age of sound and visual media without ever achieving literacy for the majority of the population. Although National Iranian Radio–Television attempted to support traditional culture through the revival of classical music and traditional cultural forms, it probably did far more to erode cultural life in the provinces than to encourage it. Traditional storytellers, the chief source of entertainment in provincial teahouses, were replaced by the television. Music for weddings was purchased on tape cassettes rather than commissioned from traditional musicians. Young men and women were introduced to styles of life that were completely foreign to them, as Western programming was used to close gaps in a television schedule that Iranian production crews, lacking well-trained technical personnel and a sufficient number of talented artists, could not fill.[32]

Filmgoing became the chief pasttime of the youth of the cities, despite being frowned upon by conservative religious officials. An average of seventy Iranian films were produced annually, most being of a low-budget, highly popular variety emphasizing melodrama, song and dance, and soap opera morality. The public loved them.

Paradoxically, as economic conditions improved for business and government, the Iranian commercial film industry began to suffer a real decline. Foreign films began to drive the popular Iranian commercial productions off the market, partly due to favorable import laws. Inflation increased production costs considerably, making it more profitable for investors in the film industry to import their products rather than manufacture them locally. In the highly inflationary, overheated economy, film production offered too great a risk, and too low a return for most investors—office buildings and apartments were more solid than cellulose.

From 1973 on, the end result was that the proportion of Iranian films seen by the public dwindled to a small percentage of the foreign films on the Iranian screen. However low their quality, the Iranian films reflected Iranian cultural values and aesthetic sensibilities. Foreign films were often disturbing and shocking for traditional classes, who opposed them more strenuously than ever.[33]

Education was one of the chief priorities of the Iranian government under the Pahlavi regime. University education in particular increased tremendously during the post–World War II years. Nevertheless, the ambitious development plans of the shah outstripped the ability of the educational system to produce the expertise needed for the expansion of industry, medicine, construction, and the educational system itself. The public viewed education as a sure stepping-stone to success, and insisted that their children enter some program of higher education following high school. The end result was that nine times as many high school graduates took university entrance examinations each year, as there were places for entering students.

With a burgeoning need for expertise at the postgraduate level and inadequate training programs to produce that expertise, as well as an insatiable public demand for undergraduate education, the only solution for Iran was to export its student population for training abroad.

The Iranian student population in the United States alone grew to 35,000 by 1976—the largest foreign student population of all. Many smaller United States universities, in deep trouble due to shrinking enrollments in the wane of the post–World War II baby boom, became almost dependent on Iranian students to keep them afloat. France and Great Britain experienced similar influxes of Iranian students; even the Philippines and India offered an important educational resource for lower-middle-class Iranians who could not afford the increasingly high cost of Western education.

The return of these students to Iran after years of foreign education had a massive impact on Iranian society. By 1976, there was probably no family anywhere in the country that did not have at least one member who had studied or was studying at a foreign university. Returning students, some of whom who had left home at seventeen or eighteen years old, had developed attitudes toward male-female relations which severely disturbed their elders. Moreover, they seemed often to be impervious to the old codes of respect and deference that formed the backbone of Iranian family life. Young Iranian women defied traditional codes of modesty, and often insisted on living apart from their families in their own apartments while pursuing careers as modern middle-class professionals.

Returning foreign-educated students were not only causing consternation at home. They also were proving to be increasingly unsuited for the development and social needs of the Iranian people. It would be too harsh to put the blame on the shoulders of these individuals directly. Many, if not most, went abroad hoping to acquire the skills necessary to help their advance. Unfortunately, foreign universities emphasized skills that often had nothing to do with Iran. The problems of transforming a bazaar economy into an investment capital network were ill served by American graduate student-level econometrics. The difficulty of working with small agriculturalists in increasing national grain production had little to do with techniques of Western-style agribusiness. Urban and rural housing construction on the dry and mountainous Iranian plateau was not helped through studying architecture at the Sorbonne. German labor management could not aid in modernizing traditional handicraft industries. The returning graduates came back with titles, but with few usable skills. They were increasingly shunted off into bureaucratic caves like the Iranian Plan Organization, never to emerge again.

Thus, despite all their training and living abroad, this group of young Iranians felt both alienated and useless. The high hopes of the 1960s, when the first large wave of Iranian students surged abroad, turned to cynicism and a bitter feeling of helplessness by the 1970s. Many of these students left Iran to take up permanent residence abroad; others stayed and made the best of their condition in Iran. Most, however, harbored a lingering resentment against the United States and the other Western nations that had hosted them—not for anything that had been done to them—but because their education, which was to be their salvation, turned out to be a hollow fulfillment of the promise it had offered beforehand.

The upper middle and upper classes, growing ever larger, began to frequent Europe and the United States in increasing numbers every year. By the mid-1970s, flights between Tehran and the West were solidly booked at all times. Many of the trips were simply for shopping. Tehran matrons bragged that they bought all of their wardrobe in Paris or London—down to the underwear. Boutiques began to open in Tehran and other cities which specialized in Western luxury items, and even advertised: "Did you miss something on your last trip to Paris—then buy it at our boutique!" Young children from these families began to summer at camps in Switzerland. Many could boast that they had never seen the classical Iranian cities of Isfahan or Shiraz, but they had toured all the capitals of Europe.

For the bulk of the population, the foreign orientation of everything around them—television, architecture, film, clothing, social attitudes, educational goals, and economic development aims, seemed to resemble a strange, alien growth on the society that was sapping it of all its former values and worth. Middle-aged people bemoaned the crassness and bustle of modern life, and openly longed for older, quieter times when life was harder, but stability reigned, where one could count on other people's attitudes, and not expect to be shocked, outraged, or disoriented every time one went out of doors, or read a newspaper.

The Internal Rises Up

A series of altercations involving Americans began to clue U.S. embassy staff members and private, commercial-sector, American business personnel that something was dreadfully wrong. Well-publicized street brawls in 1975 between American and Iranian workers in the city of Isfahan caused alarm among expatriate companies working there. These altercations were indicative of "adjustment" problems for U.S. workers. The problems culminated in a dispute between Bell Helicopter and its pilots in Isfahan protesting living conditions in September 1975. The response was to create an American compound called Shain Shahr ("Eagle City") far removed from the city, where American workers could live in splendid isolation. Far from helping the situation, this compound became a local symbol of American imperiousness.[34]

Sadly, even Americans who were aware of these problems tended to take a sanguine view of them. American presence and profits were rationalized by thoughts such as: "Really, Iranians are benefiting from our presence here—they now have cars, televisions and refrigerators and a better telephone system than they did before." Buoyed by the 19 percent GNP growth figures,[35] American officials pointed with pride to the economic boom they had helped to create.

The boom was only superficial, however. The quickest way to create instant industrialization is to set up manufacturing operations for which the basic parts are fabricated elsewhere, and only assembled in the country of sale. Thus, the only thing actually bought when the product eventually is sold is the assembly labor. Virtually every new industry in Iran after 1965 was this type of an assembly industry, and many firms concentrated on consumer goods.

Near-exclusive emphasis on the assembly of consumer goods, the basic elements of which were produced elsewhere, created a bottleneck for investment. Iranian entrepreneurs, finding saturated consumer markets within Iran and no real export markets, faced limited outlets for their money. They could either work backwards from the assembly industries toward establishing basic industries, which would not yield income for a decade if, indeed, they would ever be profitable, or they could put their money into shorter-term investments.

Large-scale industrial investment became impossible for all but the very wealthy, or the very well-connected. Bazaar merchants and middle-class citizens found that they had no access whatsoever to investment capital through normal channels. The development loans available to industrialists at 6 percent interest were a far cry from the rates offered by private moneylenders to small merchants—around 20–30 percent.[36] Small merchants had another problem to face in government-subsidized department stores, which severely challenged both their livelihood and the normal pricing structure of the free bazaar.

Nevertheless, bazaar merchants and middle-class citizens were able to find two areas where they too could make a great deal of money rather quickly. Those areas were land speculation and construction, and the distribution of foodstuffs, both imported and locally produced.

Land speculation and construction could be financed on the basis of capital raised by using an existing business as collateral, or through a system of discounted promissory notes, which constitute the chief form of credit transaction used in the bazaar. When housing prices were doubling in a year, the 20 percent interest rates didn't matter very much. Holding goods off the market until the price rose, and then flooding the market at the higher price could manipulate the sale of foodstuffs.

The central government was outraged at both of these developments because they could not be controlled easily. Government officials were cut in quickly on the most lucrative schemes, and the speculation continued unabated. Of course, the sector of the public that suffered the most were those with no investment capital and no access to any. For these hapless people, life became unbearable as the cost of food and housing soared to astronomical heights.

Following the oil price increase in 1973–74, the country was awash in money with no place for the cash to go. The natural result was tremendous inflation, reaching 50 percent per annum by 1976. By 1977, inflation had begun to affect even the wealthy of the country. Complaints about prices were the chief source of public discontent, and soon the shah moved to gain control over the economy. In a dramatic change of government, Jamshid Amuzegar, the former oil minister and OPEC representative was made prime minister in August 1977. His actions to control the economy were sudden and swift: Tight new regulations and high taxes were imposed on the transfer of land. The government established draconian price controls for foodstuffs, along with strict penalties for violators, including the jailing of neighborhood greengrocers who overcharged or undercut the government price standards.

Ten thousand inspectors were sent to examine store accounts. Guild courts eventually imprisoned 8,000 merchants, exiled 23,000 from their hometowns and fined as many as 200,000 more.[37]

As a final blow, the new government of Amuzegar cut off substantial subsidies to the clergy and religious institutions that had been instituted by the former prime minister, Amir Abbas Hoveyda. It is noteworthy that the shah in exile identified this act as the mistake that caused his downfall.

The results of these policies were immediate and dramatic. The land market collapsed overnight, and with it the construction industry. In the space of less than a month, virtually the entire force of unskilled construction labor was laid off. Although figures during this confused period are inexact, the number thrown out of work numbered in the hundreds of thousands. The government matched the jailing of small merchants for overcharging by importing food from abroad at approximately twice the domestic wholesale cost to make up for the shortfalls. Through all of the economic chaos that resulted, factory owners and manufacturers of assembly-line goods were largely untouched. Prices for their goods actually rose during this period, unchecked by the government. Prices for kerosene and gasoline—a government monopoly—also increased.

To the man on the street, the message was clear—the government was going to control inflation by cracking down on those few areas of the economy in which government officials, the royal family, and foreign investors had little financial interest. The few ventures that had allowed ordinary citizens to participate in the vast wealth of the country would be wiped out.

Frustration yielded to outright protest. Merchants began refusing to pay bank loans and promissory notes, and the banking system began to feel the pinch. Ringleaders of the financial protest and other prominent merchants in the bazaar began to be harassed and jailed. Unemployed construction workers, largely country residents attracted to the cities by wages which seemed high, but which were eroded by inflation, also were restive. After the collapse of the construction industry, they were literally trapped in the cities with no place to turn.

The Internal Conquers the External—The Spreading Revolution

In this climate of discontent, the incendiary exhortations of Ayatollah Khomeini finally began to fall on fertile ground. Opposition to the shah's regime had been increasing for years, but in 1975 the presence of the United States had reached a critical level. Assassinations of American military personnel and advisors had taken place in 1973 and in 1975. In August 1976, just three months before the election of Jimmy Carter, three employees of Rockwell International were waylaid in Tehran and killed by a terrorist group. The police and SAVAK[38] stepped up their efforts against the guerillas, which only caused them to redouble their efforts. The guerrillas were giving a clear message: from their standpoint, the United States was clearly implicated in the domestic policy of the shah's government, and would be subject to further attacks because of it.

With Jimmy Carter's accession to the presidency, the United States began to preach its policy of human rights. Although the principal thrust of the policy was aimed at communist states, Carter felt that he had to concomitantly encourage authoritarian ally states to liberalize their policies toward dissident political expression. The shah complied, and announced a new policy of liberalization, but as James Bill describes it, it seemed to be entirely hollow: "[W]ith the beginning of Jimmy Carter's presidency, the shah set forth a new policy, a program of liberalization that was to include an end to torture, a selective release of political prisoners, an attempt to introduce legal reform, and a loosening of tight censorship controls. As 1977 moved into 1978, the people of Iran quietly watched the exchange of visits between President Carter and the Shah. When no new policies finally emerged, the violence began."[39]

The beginning of the end came on January 9, 1978, when theology students in the city of Qom began a protest against an article authored under a pseudonym by Minister of Information Dariush Foruhar, accusing Ayatollah Khomeini of licentious behavior and other crimes against the state published in the newspaper *Ettela'at*. The demonstration met with violent confrontation by the police, and thereby started the cycle of violence and death that lead to the shah's departure approximately a year later. Quite predictably the bulk of the protesters were drawn from the young unemployed males in the large cities, the protests were underwritten, and financed from the bazaar.

At first, even the hardest of the hard-line oppositionists to the United States could not believe that the American president would support the Iranian government's violence against the people. Ayatollah Hossein-Ali Montazeri was quoted as saying, "We didn't expect Carter to defend the Shah, for he is a religious man who has raised the slogan of defending human rights. How can Carter, the devout Christian, defend the Shah?"[40]

Nevertheless, as the protests continued, President Carter's support for the shah continued unabated. To an Iranian public, already bitter about U.S. economic activity in their country, the Carter human rights doctrine seemed to be yet another form of cruel exploitation: a ploy designed to encourage popular dissent, only to set the protesters up for massacre.

The Great Satan

Iranian rejection of the United States and the former shah is perhaps too easy to understand in material terms alone. The protests that toppled the Pahalvi regime touched every stratum of society in the end, and spread throughout all regions of the country. The rage that caused thousands to burn public buildings, topple statues and march into live rounds of ammunition touched something far deeper than a mere desire for a larger piece of Iran's economic wealth.

As presented at the beginning of this chapter, the Great Satan, the *Shaitan-e Rajim*, corrupts mankind primarily by leading mankind astray. Those believers who existed within the embrace of the Islamic community and followed God's prescriptions for mankind were immune from his wiles. The Shaitan thus performed his actions from outside of the community. If he could make inroads into the Islamic community by corrupting individuals, he could be successful in wreaking destruction in two principal areas: social institutions and human relations.

In the area of social institutions, the principal issue for society is the question of authority. Within Islam, supreme authority comes only from God. This authority is transmitted to his representatives on earth. In Shi'a theology, this line of authority, as has been shown above, becomes invested in the Imamate; it parallels the Sunni doctrine of the Caliphate. Anything that disturbs the legitimate exercise of authority can, by the exercise of religious doctrine be declared to constitute corruption.

Even outside of formal religious doctrine, as mentioned above, the question of authority is associated intrinsically with the symbolic and symbiotic interrelationships between superiors and inferiors, and has always been important in Iranian life. The secular rulers of Iran always served, more or less, at the sufferance of the people they govern. The bazaar, the tribal populations, even the rural farmers of the country have opposed the central rule of the state when they felt too oppressed, or when they felt it would be in their interest to do so. Indeed, the Palhavi era was noteworthy as perhaps the first time in Iranian history when central authority has been extended to the entire Iranian nation; it is also ironic that just as this control was finally complete, the revolution was fomented. Thus, authority is tolerated, as long as it was given legitimacy by the population. Any force that preserves an illegitimate authority is thus seen as corrupting by both religious and secular standards.

In the area of human relations, the rights and obligations obtaining between members of society become the paramount issue. Family members should exercise their duty toward each other; friends should preserve the absolute reciprocity obligatory in their relationship; and superiors and inferiors must likewise fulfill their roles in their social relationship while maintaining mutual respect, and not misuse the power residing in the ethics of noblesse oblige and duty. Any force that can severely disrupt these human relationships is likewise identifiable as one that corrupts society as a whole.

The United States was situated to play the role of an outside corrupting force. It shared an historical legacy with Iran's old nemesis, Great Britain. More importantly, the United States repeated all of the old political patterns that the British had employed: strong-arm tactics in the oil market, demands for diplomatic immunity, undue influence on the throne, monopolistic trade concessions and an imperious attitude toward Iranians and Iranian institutions.[41]

Individual Americans were isolated from the Iranian public, and so it was easy to associate them with the imperial power of the shah. Since most Americans were also working in Iran under contracts associated with the throne, impressions like that of Reza Baraheni, a prominent anti-shah protest writer, were easily formed: "I simply had every bad notion of the Americans before coming to the United States because the only Americans Iranians ever saw were 'working for' the Shah."[42]

Subsequent revolutionary symbolism bears out the thesis that the United States had indeed become associated with external forces of corruption. Carter was referred to as Yazid (the Caliph responsible for the death of Imam Hossein). In this formulation, the shah is depicted as Shemr, the general of Yazid. Another series of street drawings from the revolution shows the shah in the role of the pharaoh of Egypt, with Ayatollah Khomeini as Moses. Jimmy Carter is depicted as the false idol worshiped by the pharaoh/shah.

From these depictions and others, the symbolic position of the United States vis-à-vis the Iranian people in the context of the revolution becomes clear. The United States is the ultimate supporter of illegitimate authority—in this case the shah. In this it joins the other forces and individuals in history that have supported illegitimate rule. In the Iranian symbolic universe, this is the ultimate external corrupting force, and it must be resisted at all costs.

Within the writings of Ayatollah Khomeini, colonial Western powers are treated as projections of a single force opposed to Islam. Facing this force are the Islamic *ulama* who are projections of the legitimate rulers, the Imams. The jurisprudents, faqih, derive their charge from the Prophet himself: His words, "Because the faithful jurisprudents are the strongholds of Islam . . . is an assignment to the jurisprudents to preserve Islam with its creeds, laws and systems."[43]

The colonial powers are seen to be the enemies of this legitimate system:

> The colonialists have spread in school curricula the need to separate church from the state and have deluded people into believing that the ulama of Islam are not qualified to interfere in the political and social affairs. . . . The colonialists and their lackeys have made these statements to isolate religion from the affairs of life and society and to tacitly keep the ulama of Islam away from the people and drive people away from the ulama because the ulama struggle for the liberation and independence of the Moslems. When their wish of separation is realized, the colonialists and their lackeys can take away our resources and rule.[44]

In this way, the United States is only the latest representative of the foreign forces that destroyed the Ottoman Sultanate, divided up the area between the Mediterranean and the Persian Gulf into "illegitimate states," and installed puppet rulers to do their bidding. Thus, all of the great external usurpers of history are linked, and opposed in a single process to the representatives of inner truth.

Both the former shah and the United States were linked to the Iranian people in a special relationship that demanded trust. The great surprise of the Iranian revolution was the rapidity with which it was realized. Even the shah was startled: "Driving through the city of Meshed in an open car only four months before the situation became desperate, I was acclaimed by 300,000 people. Just after the troubles in Tabriz [in February 1978], my prime minister went there and had an overwhelming reception. I can recall nothing in the history of the world—not even the French revolution—to compare with what happened subsequently."[45]

The Iranian public already felt that it was being exploited in its relationship with the United States throughout the first half of the 1970s. Still, as long as the economy continued to expand, the public was willing to put up with the relationship.

The economic difficulties of 1974–77 began to change the picture. Expectations continued to rise, and economic benefits began to fall. The stern economic measures imposed by the Amuzegar prime ministry made it clear that the mass population of Iran was no longer privy to the relationship that had bound them to the government for most of the post–World War II years.[46] Once the breach had occurred, relations deteriorated quickly. The first protests drew fire from the government, and it became clear that there was no longer any relationship between shah and people: a person in a superior position is bound to protect those he shares a relationship with from harm; if he kills them, he is misusing the relationship, and the rupture is sudden and total between the parties.

Here the United States could have retained *its* tacit relationship with the Iranian people, if only it had abandoned the shah at the point when the shooting began.

Thus, the history of the United States and Iran during the years leading up to the revolution is a sad chronicle of misunderstanding and cultural misperception. The United States became the Great Satan, not in a sudden stroke at the taking of the hostages, but through a slow and steady process. In a myopic, almost dogged manner, the United States persisted in digging itself into a ready-made villain's role within the symbolic structure of Iranian society. The great external corrupter of culture and morality, supporter of illegitimate power, and destroyer of the natural bonds that bind men to each other in relationships of mutual benefit; such is the nature of the beast.

━━ 6 ━━

Images of the Mad Mullah

The Islamic Republic, which replaced the shah's regime, has proved to be a terrifyingly puzzling phenomenon for most of the rest of the world. Suddenly, in 1979 Tehran seemed filled with turbaned, bearded, old men espousing a combination of religious and political philosophy that was strange to Westernized ears. When confronted with individuals whose actions are incomprehensible, the natural human tendency is to assign them to a "residual" category within the culture. "Crazy," "irrational," "evil," "incompetent," "moronic," and "incomprehensible" are just a few of these categorizations.

Of course, the incomprehensible actions of any person or group can be made comprehensible with the right information and conceptual tools for understanding. What seems crazy becomes rational in light of historical circumstance, medical history, cultural practice, or individual motive. One must only search for the correct logical framework among many to give clarity to a murky situation.

All too often in international dealings, even sophisticated people are unwilling to do the intellectual work necessary to understand difficult cultural phenomena, and relegate that which they cannot understand to residual categories. What may be more pernicious is the tendency to use this kind of rhetorical categorization strategically to demonize the other—even when comprehensible explanations for difficult actions are forthcoming. In both the Iranian case toward the United States, as I have shown above, and in the United States' case toward Iran, this has been largely the case. Thus, just as the Great Satan was born, so was the Mad Mullah, whose crazed and wild-eyed image became the stuff of editorial cartoons.[1]

However, just as United States' administrations since the revolution of 1978–79 continued to lend fuel to the Great Satan image through their frequently unwitting actions, so has the Iranian leadership contributed to the Mad Mullah image through its actions.

What has been frustrating for the United States is that despite the many predictions that Iran's clerical regime must eventually collapse as a result of its own anachronisms and lack of popular support, and despite crises that would have long since destroyed most European-style governments, it has lasted nearly thirty years, proving sturdier than anyone had predicted. Even though a reform movement has arisen, and Iran's young population continues to be discontented with the religious leadership, it shows no sign of an early demise. Forces within the United States consider its continuation anathema. Neoconservatives within and hovering around the George W. Bush presidential administration have plotted and planned schemes to topple the clerics to no avail.

Clearly there is much that the outside world does not understand about Iran's current regime, its historical background, its political philosophy, and its directions for the future. These are things that no government can afford to ignore, for Iran remains as strategically important a nation today as it ever was in the past. It is the quintessential buffer state standing between the nations of the former Soviet Union and the oil-producing states of the Persian Gulf; between Europeanized Turkey and the nations of Asia; straddling the principal route for the world's principal energy resource—oil. It is Iran's very strategic importance that galls American officials.

The United States was founded on the principle of separation of church and state. The Islamic Republic was founded on the principle of the unity of religion and the state. The two could be no more diametrically opposed. The Islamic Republic of Iran is the only modern example of a working theocracy in the world (with the possible technical exception of the Vatican). In this regard, it is important to understand why the present government continually insists that the mullahs will never willingly step down from power, why their continued role in political life is seen as essential, even when they seem to Americans to be totally inept at governing their nation successfully.

It is also important to understand the mentality of U.S. officials who persist in labeling Iran's leaders as Mad Mullahs to virtually no avail, since Iran has managed to confound five presidential administrations. In the discussion below, I hope to show why Americans have such trouble establishing a basis for understanding the actions of the Iranian government, and also to show how Iranian leaders continue to provide grist for the American mill of name-calling and demonization.

A History of Spiritual Leadership

Shi'a Islam, as opposed to the majority Sunni sect, has been the state religion in Iran since the seventeenth century. Even at the time of its establishment as the official creed, however, the clergy were counseling the population not to obey their secular rulers, who were characterized as impious and anti-Islamic in their conduct.[2] Shi'a doctrine differs very little from that of Sunni Islam in most respects.[3] The principal difference lies in determining the succession of leadership to the faith. For Sunni Muslims, leadership was thought of as proceeding through a line of officials elected by the community of believers following the death of the prophet, Muhammad.

Eventually, leadership of Sunni Muslims was institutionalized in the Caliphate, which passed into the hands of essentially secular rulers. The sultan of the Ottoman Empire was simultaneously caliph of Sunni Muslims until the elimination of the caliphate by Kemal Attatürk in 1926.

Shi'a Muslims adopted a doctrine of leadership succession passing through the direct bloodline of the prophet through a series of spiritual leaders, called Imams. Different readings of lines of blood succession have produced various sects and offshoots of Shi'ism, including the Alawites of Syria, the Druze of Lebanon, Israel, and Syria, and the Isma'ilis whose head, the Agha Khan, rules a large worldwide community.

The largest community of Shi'ite believers are the Ithna'Ashara, or "twelver" community of believers, so named because there are twelve Imams recognized by the community. In this community of believers, three of the Imams hold special significance.[4]

The first important Imam is Ali, cousin and son-in-law of Mohammad (Mohammad had no male heirs). Ali was the only leader to be accepted by both Shi'a and Sunni factions in the early days of Islam. Therefore, in current Iranian political belief, Ali's rule was the most perfect in history. It was a unified rule of all Muslims, sanctioned by the prophet, combining the functions of temporal and spiritual power in one leader.

The second important imam is Ali's second son, Hossein. The caliph of Damascus, Yazid, challenged Hossein's claim to leadership of the faith. Rather than concede leadership to an illegitimate individual, Hossein chose martyrdom on the plains of Kerbala near present-day Baghdad, where he and his followers were slaughtered by Yazid's troops in a particularly brutal fashion, having been held without food and water for ten days.

Imam Hossein's death has been commemorated continually in Iran since at least the ninth century. Every religious occasion is a potential setting for the retelling of the story of his death. He is the prototype for all martyrs, and all those who struggle and sacrifice themselves for the legitimate faith. In this Hossein occupies a place within Shi'ite religious and political life roughly equivalent to Jesus in Christianity.[5]

The third of the great Imams is the twelfth Imam, the Mahdi. Twelver Shi'is believe that the child of the eleventh Imam went into hiding or "occultation," and is expected to return at the day of judgment. Following his disappearance, there were four interpreters of the will of the Mahdi. When the fourth died, there was no one left alive who had religious "infallibility."[6]

The basic premise of governance in the Islamic Republic rests on the principle of restoration of the leadership of the Imams over men's affairs. The current government is seen as ruling in place of the Mahdi, and will continue to do so until he returns to earth. Ayatollah (a religious title meaning "image" or "reflection" of God) Ruhollah Khomeini was often called "Imam Khomeini" by the population, but his correct title was Nayyeb ol-Imam, literally "Imam's representative" or more colloquially "vice Imam." He bears another title: faqih, or "chief jurisprudent," indicating his superiority in religious and legal judgment.

The move to establish a state ruled in principle by the Imams or their representatives has been an historical movement with considerable background. In the seventeenth century, the clerical leaders began to withdraw support from the secular rulers of the Safavid dynasty, and urged the population to follow their guidance instead. Gradually the doctrine developed which urged men to consider the Mahdi as the only legitimate representative of God's law. This quickly led to the conclusion that no temporal ruler could have any authority over man. The only true authority was that of the Mahdi himself, or failing that, the best representative that could be found. It was Ayatollah Khomeini himself, however, who first extended this doctrine to insist on direct rule by the chief religious jurisprudent faqih as the only proper representation of the Mahdi on earth.[7]

This sort of preaching did not make the clergy popular with Iran's rulers, and many religious leaders throughout history were forced to exile themselves to the great Shi'a shrine cities near Kerbala. Sunni rulers—first the Ottoman Sultans, then Iraqi rulers—who were never much threatened by the presence of the Shi'a clergy—always governed these cities. Thus, the Shi'a religious leaders could, for fully three centuries, keep up the attack against secular rulers in Iran in comparative safety. They could also continue to press for establishment of a religious state.

It may seem to some in the West that concern with Imams and religious legitimacy is somewhat esoteric and unrelated to bombings, war, and internal executions in Iran today. Vulgar commentaries, such as recent accounts by the erstwhile eminent historian Bernard Lewis,[8] try and make the case that Shi'a history is fraught with violence. Although there is violence in the Shi'a past, it usually stems from questions of political legitimacy in the Imamate, not unlike European wars in an earlier age.

Early Shi'a struggles against the more powerful Sunni rulers gave the world the term assassin. The term comes from "hashish." The "hashishin," Isma'ili Shi'a—a different branch of Shi'ism from the Ithna'Ashara (twelver) Shi'a of Iran—oppositionists to Islamic governments from Iran to Egypt in the eleventh century, used assassination as one of their chief tactics for gaining power. According to dubious legend, they would use hashish to provide themselves with the courage to carry out their exploits.[9] The martyrdom of Imam Hossein is another tragic episode, very much alive in the minds of the people. The clergy has never shirked from exhorting the population to resist their temporal rulers in political struggle. Several violent clashes with the secular government took place in the twentieth century, the revolution against the shah being only the most recent example.

In a more important sense, however, the question of legitimacy of the government is one of the greatest sources of support for the current regime. The rulers of the Islamic Republic sanction unforgiving clergymen conducting mock trials leading to mass executions. Still the public is presented with a government that claims to be sanctioned by God.[10]

The twelver Shi'a doctrine declares the only legitimate rule to be that of the Mahdi and his representatives—the active, systematic, millenarian scenario in Iran since the establishment of the Safavid Empire in the seventeenth century. Now that the establishment of Islamic rule has actually come to pass, the Iranian population has been extremely uncomfortable in opposing it, since it seems to fulfill prophecy for many fervent believers. To move to delegitimize Ayatollah Khomeini and the Islamic republic would raise the question of whether one might not be warring with God himself in the eyes of many people. In the case of the shah, no such question had to be asked. Because he was a temporal ruler, Mohammad Reza Shah Pahlavi was automatically illegitimate in the eyes of religious authority. The population had only to be convinced that he was corrupt as well, and that he could be overthrown in order for their support to be enlisted in the revolution.[11]

The Materialistic Clergy

There is another face to the Iranian clergy, however, one which helps to explain why resistance to their rule has continued even in the face of their superior claims to legitimacy in establishing the Islamic Republic, adding to their negative reputation. This is the widespread belief that they misuse the enormous wealth at their disposal as a result of their management of religious funds. This suspicion created a predelection to accuse them of misusing state funds in the Islamic Republic.

In 1926, before the advent of the Pahlavi regime with Reza Shah, father of the recently deposed shah, the clergy as a body enjoyed enormous wealth and power within Iran itself. Many were wealthy landholders in their own right. Additionally, the management of religious bequests (*waqf*), much of which was in the form of landholdings, was in their hands. Other monies in the form of charitable giving—the "*khoms*" or tithe and the "*zakat*" or charitable offering—considered to be cardinal religious duties in Islam, were paid directly to the clergy for distribution to worthy institutions, and gave them great power.

More importantly, the entire court system was in the hands of the clergy, as was the educational system before 1926. When added to the control exercised over the economic system through the control of bequests, tithing, and charitable giving, it can be seen that the clergy were very powerful forces in society in every way.

Reza Shah realized that if he were to consolidate his rule, he would have to break the back of the clergy, and he worked steadily at doing this.[12] He built up the secular Iranian army as a source of military control from the throne, independent of other sectors in society. With that military force to back him up, he then proceeded to secularize the courts and the school, building large new secular universities as a counter to theological schools. Eventually, under his son Mohammad Reza, the religious bequests were taken out of clerical hands and administered by the state. Finally, the large landholdings of some clergy were eliminated during land reform in 1963.[13] Land reform hit clergymen particularly hard. Other large land owners could take their capital and establish industrial and business concerns. The clergy would have to give up their profession to take advantage of the new industrial climate in the land. Absentee landholding was ideal for them, because it provided an income with little work on their part. Capital investment required real commitments of time and labor, which was not compatible with a full-time religious life.

Therefore, at least one aspect of the present Islamic regime in Iran involves a feeling on the part of the clergy that their takeover of power amounts to the legitimate act of regaining right and privilege, which had been illegitimately seized from their hands during the Pahlavi era. In reestablishing what they consider to be their proper place in society they may have overreacted. Tales of clergymen, somewhat poor before the revolution, but now living in luxurious houses and driving Mercedes Benz automobiles are told everywhere in Iran. Because almost nothing can be accomplished without the permission of a cleric, the possibilities for bribery are enormous. Not surprisingly, many young men who might have thought of engineering or medicine as a profession decided that theology was not such a bad line of work after all after the revolution, and filled the theological schools in droves. This new educational movement was aided by the fact that the nation's secular universities were closed for two years following the revolution. Another route for joining the clerical establishment was in attaching oneself to the new religious army, the Islamic Guard. This organization was clearly conceived as an alternative to the secular army of the Pahlavis. Indeed, if the war with Iraq had not continued to rage throughout the 1980s, the regular army might long since have been totally eliminated. In the end, all military forces, both the regular army and the Islamic guard were placed under the direction of the faqih.

Opposition to the Clergy

It is this materialistic and overtly political aspect of the role of the clergy in Iranian life that has provided the strongest basis for opposition to them, both inside and outside Iran. Because the ruling clergy were primarily addressing internal Iranian cultural concerns, particularly during the early years of the Islamic Republic, they could have no serious interaction with the United States or its officials. This reinforced the Mad Mullah image for the United States.

The common citizen of Iran has a two-pronged view of the morality of the clergy. On the one hand, children are reared to respect the clergy, and to seek, revere, and emulate them. There is a popular view that is 180 degrees to the contrary. In fiction and folklore, Iranians have long characterized the clergy as having a tendency to let dishonesty and hypocrisy slip into their day-to-day social and religious practice. In a much earlier time—before the Pahlavi dynasty came to power—when day-to-day legal authority in the nation was largely in religious hands, complaints about dishonest judicial practice were often channeled into humorous stories. The rural comic theater and puppet drama are full of stories structured around dishonest clerics.

Such humorous characterizations are probably unfair reflections of the actual practice of most members of the clergy, but the popular stereotype of the greedy, flea-ridden, *mullah* still remains alive in the eyes of many individuals. The influence of these men at the village level was doubly pernicious, for not only did they speak with legal authority, but also with the "authority of God." From such judgment there was no appeal, for who would appeal the word of God? Parenthetically, postrevolutionary legal practice tended to follow this line. In trying "antistate" elements, Ayatollah Khomeini specifically called for the elimination of any appeal process. A judgment once rendered under proper practice of religious law was to be considered inviolate, for it reflected divine authority. The widely noted fatwa issued by Ayatollah Khomeini, calling for the death of author Salman Rushdie for his "impious" portrayal of the Prophet Mohammad in his novel *The Satanic Verses* is an example of such a decree. It has never been lifted.[14]

This history of heavy-handed practice, combined with the enormous influence of the clergy on the thought of the Iranian masses led, in the twentieth century, to overt expressions of anticlericism by the newly emerging secular intelligentsia. Important intellectual figures such as literary and language scholar, Ali Akbar Dehkhoda, denounced the clerics as a body. The most outspoken of these writers was historian Ahmad Kasravi, the principal authority on the constitutional revolution of 1906. Kasravi was assassinated in 1946 by a Muslim activist because of his anticlerical writing, and his books were symbolically burned in public.[15]

Far more serious a challenge to clerical authority has been mounted in recent years by persons working for reform within Islam itself. The most influential of these reformers is the late Ali Shari'ati, who died under mysterious circumstances in England in 1977. Shari'ati's writings have inspired a whole generation of young Iranians, and are as alive today as an intellectual force as they were during his lifetime.[16]

Shari'ati was trained as a sociologist at the Sorbonne in Paris. His vision of Islam sees the religon not merely as a set of religious doctrines, but rather as a total social ideology. His philosophy envisions Shi'ism as a source for the betterment of all aspects of human life, and a source for an all encompassing revolution of thought, word, and deed—an Islamic "protestantism" with an emphasis on "protest." Religion, he believed, should be a process which touches on all areas of knowledge. In this regard, he denounced the clerical establishment for restricting their focus to one narrow activity—the conduct of jurisprudence. By taking refuge in legalisms and judicial acts, the clerics were seen by Shari'ati as neglecting their true duty as Islamic leaders: to enlighten the public and lead them to a greater sense of their social responsibility as Muslims. Instead, he claimed that they merely snare the people in an encircling web of legalism and prohibition. Thus, he pointed out that under the traditional clergy, Islamic philosophy, which should serve to free the mind for meaningful humanitarian action, becomes reduced to a sterile code of rules applied in an automatic fashion.

Shari'ati's writings seem at times somewhat lightweight and oratorical. Nevertheless, their impact on young men and women continues to be tremendous. Indeed, Shari'ati was described as the principal theoretician of the Revolution of 1978–79—especially by those who were anxious to find inspiration in other than clerical sources. Significantly, Ayatollah Khomeini never once acknowledged Shari'ati or his writing, despite their obvious importance in inspiring young "revolutionaries."[17]

Shari'ati's influence was not limited exclusively to the young. Respected members of the clerical establishment itself supported many of his principal ideas wholeheartedly. Not surprisingly, these clerics found themselves in severe opposition to the government of the Islamic Republic.

Ayatollah Sayyid Mahmud Taleghani, a progressive theologian teaching at the University of Tehran, espoused Shari'ati's view of the need for Shi'a Islam to provide the basis for revolutionary change. Indeed, this was the basis on which Taleghani himself supported the revolution to overthrow the shah. Nevertheless, Taleghani quickly became disenchanted with the leadership of Ayatollah Khomeini. When Khomeini moved to establish a new constitution of the Islamic Republic—a constitution that formalized the direct rule of the chief jurisprudent (*faqih*), Taleghani turned in full revolt, publicly denouncing Khomeini's position. He was placed under virtual house arrest, his family was molested, and he died a few months later (in 1979) under highly suspicious circumstances. Later his religious writings were banned by the Islamic courts.[18]

A similar fate befell Ayatollah Sayyid Kazem Shariat-Madari. Ayatollah Shariat-Madari was acknowledged to be the chief clerical leader of the revolution residing within Iran during the events leading to the fall of the shah.

His support was strongest among the Turkish population of Azerbaijan, which make up perhaps 30 percent of the total Iranian population. Indeed, during the Revolution, when the picture of Ayatollah Khomeini was hung in every store window throughout Iran, in Azerbaijan it was Shariat-Madari's picture that was seen. Shariat-Madari, like Taleghani, opposed Khomeini's doctrine of rule by the chief jurisprudent, spoke out against the war being waged against the Kurds, and in general served to embarrass the new regime. He was implicated (falsely) in a plot to overthrow Ayatollah Khomeini, and was stripped of his religious titles. He was placed under house arrest and effectively silenced.[19] Grand Ayatollah Shariat-Madari died in June 1986. His supporters were prevented from holding a public funeral and he was buried secretly in the middle of the night in a remote place.

Shi'a Islam had four other grand ayatollahs besides Khomeini at the time of the Islamic Revolution. These are men who by consensus are given the greatest authority to determine the interpretation of Islamic law. All four of these authorities privately denounced Khomeini's view of Islamic government. One, Grand Ayatollah Mohammad Hosseini Shirazi, made strong attacks in European publications. All of these religious figures were silenced through threats to themselves or to their families.

One worrisome matter for the clerical establishment is that the younger generation is increasingly being "turned off" by the bureaucratic wrangling and positioning for power taking place among religious leaders. Those with secular tendencies are becoming bolder and more defiant. Those with religious tendencies are turning inward rather than paying attention to outward religious practice. In a study carried out recently,[20] researchers Abdolmohammad Kazemipur and Ali Rezaei demonstrated that the establishment of a theocratic regime in Iran has led to the transformation of the nature of faith itself. Through systematic interviews and surveys, they noted that a noticeable shift from "organized" to a more "personalized" religion has taken place, in which the emphasis is placed on beliefs rather than on practices. Greater emphasis is also placed on beliefs that are of a purely individual nature, or with a social nature but organized through civic and nongovernmental bodies, as opposed to those commanded by the government. These results are hardly surprising, and reflect a turning away from the official government sponsorship of religion.

Aside from disorganization and public disaffection, there is also active resistance to the clerical regime. One group that has not been silenced is the Mojaheddin-e Khalq, the "People's Crusaders" (frequently known as the MEK or MKO in the West). This group has been in existence in one form or another for decades, but it gained strength during the 1960s when it emerged as a major force confronting the shah's government. The Mojaheddin is actually a confederation of smaller groups with slightly differing philosophies. All have been heavily influenced by the writing of Shari'ati, and are deeply committed to Islam. They have also been influenced by leftist and Marxist philosophies, especially those which support the idea of revolutionary liberation movements. Shari'ati himself was deeply influenced by the writings of Franz Fanon, and that writer remains an important influence among the Mojaheddin.

There is now excellent evidence to show that the Mojaheddin were the actual effective forces in bringing down the last vestiges of the shah's government. Following the establishment of the Islamic Republic, they demanded a role in the new government. Their request was flatly turned down by the leaders then in power, and their war with the clerical establishment began in earnest.

It has been primarily the Mojaheddin that have borne the brunt of the massive executions that took place in Iran after the ouster of former President Abol-Hassan Bani-Sadr. Their principal leader, Massoud Rajavi fled with Bani-Sadr to Paris where he served as a self-declared prime minister of a government in exile. Despite brave words and assertions that Khomeini's regime was about to fall and give way to a "New Islamic Order" where democracy would prevail, the efforts of the Mojaheddin and other oppositionist groups have not been able to succeed in weakening the existing political power structure. Indeed, bombings, assassinations, and other violent acts against the clerics seemed to do little more than cement the political structure into an even tighter and more rigid structure than before. As one cleric was eliminated, others quickly moved to fill his place.

During and following the second Gulf War in 2003, the United States viewed the Mojaheddin-e Khlaq (MEK), who had been stationed in Iraq and supported by Saddam Hussein since their exile from Iran after the Revolution, as a possible vanguard to topple the clerical regime in Tehran. Neoconservatives Daniel Pipes and Patrick Clawson, influential with the George W. Bush administration, were among those who advocated U.S. support of the group to battle the clerics: ". . . because Iran's mullahs irrationally fear the MEK (as shown by their 1988 massacre in the jails of Iran of 10,000 long-imprisoned MEK members and supporters), maintaining the MEK as an organized group in separate camps in Iraq offers an excellent way to intimidate and gain leverage over Tehran."[21]

It has been unfortunate for the George W. Bush administration that the MEK is also intensely disliked by the Iranian population, largely because of their residence in Iraq during the Iran–Iraq war when they fought against Iranian troops and were supported by Saddam Hussein. Today they are seen as traitors by much of the Iranian public.

The Bush administration, and commentators like Pipes and Clawson misunderstand the anger the clerics feel toward the MEK, because they fail to read the history of the Iranian Revolution from the perspective of the current leadership. It is important that the religious establishment in Iran "own" the revolution. The revolution was effected by a coalition of forces:

secular nationalists, "Marxist-Muslims" (as they were termed by the shah and religious forces). The MEK was active in Iran long before the revolution, and they were part of that original coalition. During the purge of the nonreligious forces—which took place during the hostage crisis, the MEK were forced out along with the secularists.

The MEK continues to claim that they were the ones who made the revolution, and that they were deceived and cheated of a place in the government during the "second phase" of the revolution.[22] The current religious regime wants to supress this part of the revolution narrative, and they view the MEK as counterrevolutionaries—especially because they now seem to be allied with the United States. The religious leadership knows to a certainty that the MEK wants to reinstate secular—perhaps even neo–Marxist—government, since that was the "platform" on which they supported the original revolution. So, there is old enmity between the MEK and the regime dating from the revolution, and the public hates them because they seem to have been traitors during the Iran–Iraq war.

Finally, the United States should clearly understand that the MEK would be happy to let the United States give it a free monetary and logistic ride, but they have no use for America—any more than they did during the shah's regime. If through some miracle they got into power in Iran, they would turn the United States out in a second.

Thus, it seems that for the time being, assaults on the political order of the Islamic Republic from without will not be successful in eliminating the clerical regime. The Iraqi assault on Iranian territory, which was designed to topple the Tehran regime, was a miserable failure; the urban guerrilla warfare of the Mojaheddin and other groups have not succeeded either. International censure of the extreme actions of the government has only served to strengthen government claims that they are under siege from external corrupt forces.

Even less effective are characterizations of the Iranian regime as mad or crazy mullahs. At 6:20 P.M. on February 7, 2005, former CIA director James Woolsey gave an interview to journalist Britt Hume on the Fox News program *Special Report*, in which he once again opined that Iran "was a paradox" because, while the people loved the United States, the state had been taken over by "crazy mullahs." He then said that the United States is "taking a firm stand" against those "crazy mullahs." When Hume asked if the Iranians would eventually rise up against their government, Woolsey cited, "general strikes in the twentieth century" to claim that the Iranians might indeed act. In subsequent days, Condoleezza Rice, newly appointed secretary of state, once again hinted that the United States might attack Iran if it did not reduce its nuclear program. Woolsey was right, in a sense; Iranians did foment demonstrations—but against the United States. On February 9, 2005, Iranian demonstrators took to the streets condemning the United States and showing slogans and pictures implicating the United

States in the original revolution of 1978–79—the better to convince commentators like Woolsey of their "madness."

The Principal Source for Change—Internal Decay

The Mad Mullah epithet may also be in the end a self-fulfilling prophecy, since sources for governmental change seem to lie within Iran itself. Several possibilities present themselves. The death of Ayatollah Khomeini was an obvious turning point in Iranian affairs. Former Prime Minister Mehdi Bazargan, who was forced to resign because of his inability to control events surrounding the taking of the U.S. hostages in 1979, once warned Khomeini, "The Constitution of the Islamic Republic will not outlive you." Bazargan was wrong, but this feeling must have been shared by many in Iran, who hoped to replace the Islamic Republic with something more to their own liking as soon as Khomeini died. For their part, the clerics first moved to groom Khomeini's handpicked successor, Ayatollah Hossein-Ali Montazeri for his job. Ayatollah Montazeri, who was one of Khomeini's students, might himself have been the source for change—because of his initial weakness and lack of public standing. Most observers acknowledged at the time that he never would be able to fill Khomeini's shoes adequately. This would have led to an almost automatic downgrading of the entire clerical establishment in the eyes of the Iranian public.

Montazeri proved to be a surprise. An initial strong supporter of Khomeini, he grew more and more disenchanted with the Islamic Republic, finally disagreeing openly with Khomeini over treatment of prisoners in the Iran–Iraq war. He finally published a criticism of the Islamic Republic in 1989 in the newspaper *Kayhan*. Khomeini stripped him of his religious titles, and launched a propaganda campaign against him. He later chose President Ali Khamene'i, another of his former students, to succeed him, in what one commentator called a "battlefield promotion," since Khamene'i was only a mid-ranking cleric with inadequate religious credentials to be declared a Grand Ayatollah.[23]

Later, when President Mohammad Khatami, a reformer, was elected, Montazeri gave another highly critical public speech in which he said, "If two or three people sit and make all the decisions for the country, it will not progress in the contemporary world. 'Republic' means 'government of the people.' "[24] Another speech attacking Khamene'i resulted in a crowd rioting and destroying his home. He was confined permanently to his home in 1997.[25]

Early signs in the post–Khomeini government showed that other dissenting movements were beginning to surface within the ranks of the Islamic Republic Party itself. When he was newly elected as president in 1981, then Hojjatoleslam (a title one degree lower than Ayatollah) Ali Khamene'i had some difficulty in selecting a prime minister. Ayatollah Mohammad Reza

Mahdavi-Kani, the provisional prime minister, had resigned to give the new president a free choice in selecting his new government. But Mahdavi-Kani fully expected to be reappointed. For whatever reason, Khamene'i chose his own candidate, Ali-Akbar Velayati, a western trained physician, as prime minister. Ayatollah Khomeini refused to endorse Velayati, and as a result he failed to gain parliamentary approval. Subsequently, Mir-Hussein Mussavi, the former foreign minister, was selected. This kind of juggling has been common throughout the history of the Islamic republic. However, though shaky, the solidarity of the clerical establishment has held.

In an article for Pacific News Service of San Francisco, Mansur Farhang, first Iranian Ambassador to the United Nations appointed by the Khomeini regime, suggested that wrangling over selection of the prime minister showed the first factional cracks in the organization of the Islamic Republican Party itself. Claimed Farhang, one faction was led by Khamene'i, and another by Parliament Speaker Ayatollah Ali Akbar Hashemi-Rafsanjani. Later, of course, the reform movement, led by Mohammad Khatami caused yet another realignment of political loyalty. It is likely that as outside opposition to the Islamic Republican party was driven further underground by its somewhat ruthless persecution by the government leaders, that the internal factions started a process that would lead them to make themselves felt to a much greater extent.

The principal danger to the current order, however, comes from another source altogether: from that of the clerics. They have succeeded in establishing themselves in power, and defending themselves from usurpers. However, Ali Shari'ati's critique of the clergy as too narrow and solipsistic in their approach to religion and government has shown itself to be all too true. Iran has suffered mightily on the economic front, and the prognosis for recovery is not good at present, even after twenty-five years of relative governmental stability.[26]

The clerical attitude to the economy seems to have been: attend to the implementation of Islamic law, and the economy will take care of itself. This may have been a reasonable philosophy in the day of Imam Ali, but in today's world Iran is intimately tied to an international economic network without which it will literally perish.

From 1974 through 1978, oil was in short supply, and Iranian revolutionary leaders felt that the world would continue to beat a path to Iran's door to buy petroleum products no matter what the internal conditions of the country were like. The world supply of oil is highly volatile. In glut conditions, no one is interested in Iranian oil products at all, if they can avoid buying them. Indeed, Japanese oil contracts with Iran, the most reliable source of oil income for the Islamic Republic, have been frequently renegotiated downward in times of high supplies. Internal political conditions in Iran seem so unstable to the outside world that no reasonable business concern wants to commit itself to long-term arrangements. Massoud

Rajavi, leader of the Mujaheddin-e Khalq (MEK, MKO), added an ominous note to this situation before the fall of the Saddam Hussein government, which gave the MEK safe harbor, warning international business that anyone dealing with the Khomeini regime would undergo sanctions by any government that would replace it in the future. He continued these threats down to the present day, even after the United States deposed Saddam Hussein and negotiated an agreement with the MEK to allow it to continue its existence.

Iranians have had great difficulty presenting any kind of reasonable climate for international investment throughout the years since the revolution. The war with Iraq has not helped. In 1994, Iran was rated at the bottom in one influential article comparing the investment climate for a number of world nations.[27]

One extended controversy over a joint Iran–Japanese petrochemical plant constructed in Bandar Khomeini in southern Iran is a case in point. When the project was 85 percent complete at the time of the revolution, the giant Mitsui Corporation, partners in the venture, understandably refused to invest any more capital in an operation that would never provide any profit whatsoever for the partners. After all, Mitsui reasoned, once the Iranian plant begins operations, who will the product be sold to? Iranian internal industry is at a complete standstill, so no market will exist within Iran. Moreover, the plant was not likely to be able to produce products of export quality at competitive international prices.

In the shah's Iran, where even inefficient industry made money through protectionist tariffs, guaranteed purchase by government controlled industry and heavy subsidies, this investment seemed to be a good thing. In postrevolutionary Iran, it became a giant white elephant. The *Japan Times* printed a plaintive editorial urging Mitsui indirectly to find some way to continue the operation so as not to sever the last major commercial tie between Iran and Japan; but however inconvenient it might have been politically for Japan and Iran, Mitsui's stand was a correct business decision. Either the new rulers had to find some way to guarantee the investment climate of their country, or they just simply contract with outsiders—cash on the line—for construction of the facilities they felt they needed.[28]

This raised another question—where the cash was going to come from. Iran continued to be dependent on the vagaries of oil price fluxuations. Shortly after the revolution in 1982, Ali Reza Nobari, head of Iran's Central Bank under former President Bani-Sadr, revealed that the nation was virtually bankrupt. The reduced oil exports only attracted enough cash to keep the import of consumer goods and food operating—an operation which was probably essential to avoid massive public protests. Most importantly, the country was not able to get the sophisticated spare parts it needed to rebuild its oil industry. Aid promised from East Bloc nations, such as Romania, proved not to be of much help in rebuilding the largely

American-made facilities, and in any case was disrupted by the fall of the Soviet Union. Moreover, Iran became crippled in its ability to borrow funds on the International market. "Their credibility for borrowing from banks is zero, even from the World Bank or the IMF (International Monetary Fund)," claimed Nobari in an interview with Reuters News Service in November of 1982.

These conditions presented the clerics in Tehran with a difficult set of dilemmas that political solidarity, executions, and moral posturing could not solve. Simple lack of the necessities of life and declining living conditions threatened the religious support of the masses for the regime. At the time, in the years immediately following the revolution, the government looked as if it might well collapse internally under the weight of its own problems.

The war with Iraq was both the greatest asset and the greatest liability for the Iranian government. This war, which lasted longer than World War I, maintained the clerics in power while creating growing discontent on the part of families whose children had died. War casualties numbered over 100,000 at the end of the war.

It became quite clear that the shallow economic and industrial policies of Mohammad Reza Pahlavi had not resulted in the industrial transformation that would stabilize Iran's economy, and move it beyond reliance on the sale of crude oil and natural gas. What was needed, according to many was a thorough transformation of economic relations.[29] However, the clerics were largely not economists. The overall standard of living in Iran for the urbanized classes dropped (although some improvements were seen in the lives of rural residents). Unemployment in particular was a burning social issue.

During his presidency (1989–97) Ali Akbar Hashemi-Rafsanjani, who came from a mercantile family, made a priority of trying to modernize the economy, but left some 11,500 uncompleted projects due to poor management and lack of funds. Private investment, essential for a modernizing economy was only at about 15 percent of GDP—compared to 30 percent as the average for developing nations. Inflation was reported at 16.9 percent, which was generally acknowledged to be an underestimate.[30] Rafsanjani's effectiveness as a spur to economic development was somewhat blunted by the widespread knowledge of the growth of his personal wealth.

Mohammad Khatami, after his election as president in 1997, tried to effect some economic reforms, but the political will of the ruling clerics was weak. In a long exortation to the public on television shortly after his election, he candidly acknowledged the economic problems of the regime with the approval of Ayatollah Khamene'i and called for an increase in private investment, as well as a frontal attack on the endemic unemployment problem.[31] Although it was clear that he knew that the regime had problems in moving the economy forward, he was clearly unable to lead an effective plan. Ironically, Iran's one great technological success was in the development of its nuclear industry—a development that attracted the ire of the United States because of its supposed potential for the development of nuclear weaponry. The George W. Bush administration made it a priority to shut the development of nuclear power down.

Former East Bloc nations continued to be helpful partners. As Iran continued to be estranged from foreign currency markets (thanks to the American embargo), resulting in a lack of foreign exchange, and exacerbated by an inability to provide an adequate business climate, the temptation to turn to Eastern Bloc countries to fill industrial and consumer needs grew steadily. Post–Soviet Russia allowed Iran to ride along for a few years on credit in hopes of cementing a more permanent relationship in the future. Such a relationship would not be an unmixed blessing for the Russians. Iran proved to be just as sticky in dealing with them as with the West—especially considering Iran's support of the Afghan resistance during the Soviet period.

Iran's one big play for international respectability in postrevolutionary years was the small initiative on a peace settlement for Afghanistan. Iran's plans were not unreasonable, and were likely workable, but they were rejected out of hand by the "Afghan government." This and a purge of the pro-Moscow Tudeh party in 1982 and 1983 put a chill on Soviet-Iranian relations, which carried over briefly into the post-Soviet period. Iran continued to be deeply interested in Afghanistan when the United States invaded that nation in 2002.[32]

Following the election of Vladimir Putin as Russian president, economic relations improved. Iranian nuclear development, particularly the completion of a nuclear power plant at Bushehr (Bushire), was directly dependent on Russian technological aid.

The Reform Movement

The great hope of many Iranians, especially younger citizens, was the so-called "reform" movement of President Mohammad Khatami beginning with his presidency in 1997. The Iranian government seemed to be changing. Ali Akbar Hashemi-Rafsanjani had completed two terms as president before the elections of May 1997. He was considering trying to change the election laws and run for a third term, but in the end, the idea that he might run was opposed by Khamene'i.

President Khatami was nominated by the Militant Clerics Society (Majma'-e Rohaniyan-e Mobarez [MRM]), the most extreme left of all the political organizations. He had impeccable clerical credentials, and so survived the vetting process by which candidates are eliminated if the Council of Guardians considers them to be unsuitable.[33] No one thought that Khatami, a relative lightweight, had a chance. He was able to win the election on the basis of support from Iranian women and the many student organizations in the country.

In retrospect, Khatami's election is not surprising when one considers Iran's demographics. The majority of Iran's young population had no personal knowledge of the revolution that brought Ayatollah Ruhollah Khomeini to power. Indeed, few of them even remember Khomeni himself.

Khomeini's successor, "chief jurisprudent" Ali Khamene'i had a fatal illness, and at this writing is still not in the best of health. Hard-liners have been seeking someone with sufficient religious scholarly stature to succeed him. Such a person would need to be both respected and committed to the revolutionary goals of Khomeini. Thus far no such person has been found. The simple reason for this is that among Shi'a Muslims, individual leaders collect their own followings. At the time of the revolution it was estimated that 60 percent of all religious Iranians acknowledged Khomeini as their spiritual leader. At his death, this support both dissipated and was diluted by the astonishing rise in the population of citizens younger than twenty-five. It is likely that the role of spiritual leader will either disappear or be greatly reduced at the death of Khamene'i. The removal of Saddam Hussein from power in Iraq also resulted in the rise of the profile of the grand ayatollahs resident there, particularly in Najaf. In particular, the stock of the Iranian Grand Ayatollah Sayyid Ali al-Hosseini al-Sistani[34] rose tremendously in the wake of Saddam's demise. Since Ayatollah al-Sistani's rise in prominence his following in Iran has increased. He may be the Shi'a leader with the largest following in the world in the near future. This will further undercut the authority of Khamene'i and his successor.

Parliamentary elections in 2000 further concretized the reformer's hold on government. President Khatami's reform-minded supporters were able to seize the upper hand from the hard-line revolutionaries. The difficulty that eventually emerged had to do with Iran's constitution. All judiciary power and control of the military reside under the chief jurisprudent, Khamene'i, and the council of Guardians that pass on every piece of legislation. The executive branch under President Khatami and the legislative branch under the Iranian parliament have no effective power when they must face a potential veto from the Guardians. Nor do they have real power when judges and military forces are under control of the hard-liners controlled by Khamene'i.

The public grew frustrated with President Khatami when he could not deliver on promised reforms. By the end of his presidency in 2005, his supporters were disillusioned and unhappy.[35]

Internal debates continue as the two government factions remain at loggerheads. Struggles over curtailment of repressive measures against dissidents, support of Islamic movements outside of Iran, and questions about relations with the United States remain as the political scene in Iran continues to evolve. Dissident Iranians, mostly outside of Iran, continue with legitimacy to protest human rights' abuses within the country.

The course of Iranian governmental reform is very crooked. Former president Ali Akbar Hashemi-Rafsanjani has emerged as an amazingly resilient figure, heading up the "Expediency Council," a nonelected body created by Ayatollah Khomeini to mediate between the president and the parliament. The Expediency Council evolved in a way that had it mediating more between the faqih, Khamene'i and both the parliament and president.[36] Clever Rafsanjani used his position as mediator to wield considerably more power than he otherwise might ever have had under Khatami's government.[37] In early 2005, Rafsanjani announced that he would run for another term for president, since Khatami could not succeed himself after two terms in office.

Time is on the side of the reformers, however. The ever more youthful Iranian population is growing restive and by 2010 the post-revolutionary youth will be the majority among the voting public. Dissatisfied with the ineffectiveness of the reformers, and tiring of the heavy-handedness of the conservative clerics surrounding Khamene'i, they will eventually effect their own change in government if the United States will be patient and let things take their normal course. Former Iranian Finance Minister, Jamshid Amuzegar concurs with this assessment. In an article for *Foreign Affairs* in 2003 he wrote:

> If the United States truly wishes to see a modern, democratic, and peaceful Iran, Washington must follow a calculated "wait and see" policy. Neither Bush's anger, nor his empathy, nor even his promise of friendship with democratic forces will be enough to change Iran. Thus as long as U.S. vital national interests are not seriously threatened and Iran is not clearly implicated in anti-American terrorist acts, the United States should refrain from both unsubstantiated accusations and implied threats against the Islamic Republic. Washington would be best served by letting the currently accelerating process of democratization run its course. The theocracy's days are numbered—Iran's own internal currents assure this.[38]

Impatience in Washington

The United States has been curiously passive-aggressive in the face of these changes. Despite feints at improving relations, American foreign policy toward Iran remains lodged in the vengeance politics of the post-hostage crisis era. Iran continues to be demonized and despised in legislative halls—and the Mad Mullah image provides an overly fascile, dismissive argument to anyone in government who suggests that meaningful negotiations with Iran on matters of mutual interest might be pursued. The foolish attempt to isolate Iran economically—although contributing to an economy already weakened by the war with Iraq—has failed, leaving America's European allies shaking their heads in puzzlement at Washington's quirkiness.

What seems stranger still is Washington's toying with the idea of effecting regime change in Iran, much as the Bush administration tried to do by invading Iraq in 2003. The plans were clearly in place long before the Iraqi invasion, showing that the Bush administration had Iran in its sights before getting rid of Saddam Hussein.[39] In order to justify this action, the United States accused Iran of harboring al Qaeda leaders in May 2003. There was not a shred of evidence that this was true. The accusation is so insubstantial that it leads one to believe that the accusation was designed to be a prelude to some dramatic political or military move, such as an attempt at forced regime change in Iran.

This kind of accusation was, of course, nothing new. The Bush administration had a long list of unsubstantiated accusations against Iran, falling into several categories of supposition: Forward accusations about what Iran is likely to do in the future, such as to develop nuclear weapons; unproven suspicions of Iranian involvement in past attacks against the United States, such as the 1996 attacks on the Al Khobar Towers in Saudi Arabia; and complicity with American enemies, such as the accusation that Iran is harboring al Qaeda leaders. All these charges fall apart upon closer examination.

Iran's nuclear program will be covered in greater length in later chapters below. However, it is important to understand that the program was advised and engineered by the United States. In the 1960s, before North Sea and Alaskan oil had been developed, the United States urged Iran to develop nuclear power, as a way of saving its oil reserves for high-value uses such as petrochemical and pharmaceutical production. In reality, America wanted Iran to save its oil for the use of the West. The United States never helped Iran to develop anything more sophisticated than laundry powder and fertilizer.

The nuclear plant recently opened in Bushehr, which was denounced as an incubator for nuclear weapons, was actually started with America's blessing under the regime of the shah in the 1970s.

An Iranian connection with the Al-Khobar Towers attack is equally unproven. Despite years of investigation, this attack, like an attack on a Vinnell Corporation compound in Riyadh the year before, and the recent bombings in Riyadh, seem to have been carried out by indigenous Saudi groups that oppose the royal family. When examined closely, the grand conspiracy that would tie Iran and al Qaeda to these attacks fell apart like a house of cards. A Justice Department indictment issued by a Grand Jury in Alexandria, Virginia, on June 21, 2001, could do no more than claim that "Since the group was outlawed in Saudi Arabia, its members frequently met in neighboring countries such as Lebanon, Syria or Iran."

This resulted in the third charge—that Iran was harboring operatives of the al Qaeda organization responsible for the destruction of the World Trade Center and attack on the Pentagon on September 11, 2001. This accusation seemed to hinge on the possible presence of Saif al Adel, an Egyptian who might or might not have been hiding out in northern Iran, having possibly sneaked over the border from Northern Iraq during the American invasion. Adel had been accused of masterminding the recent Saudi attacks.[40]

Despite a flurry of false reports claiming that al Adel was in Iran, no one has demonstrated whether Adel was actually there, whether he really is an al Qaeda operative, or whether he really had anything to do with the Saudi attack. The accusation seems to stem from the opinion of a lone expert: Rohan Gunaratna, a former U.N. terrorist specialist and author of the book *Inside al Qaeda*.[41]

Even if evidence had been revealed that Adel had been in Iran and had, in fact masterminded the attacks, there was never any proof of Iranian complicity in any of this. In fact, the Iranian regime had been opposed to Osama bin Laden and to his hosts in Afghanistan, the Taliban, since the early 1990s. In 2002, Iranian officials repatriated Saudi al Qaeda members to Saudi Arabia almost as soon as they crossed the Iranian border.

So what kind of a game was the Bush administration playing? The only reasonable conclusion is that this volley of accusations was a pre-emptive justification for some political or military action against Iran. However, this strategy was based on a bad misreading of the mood of the Iranian public, and their attitude toward their own government.

Washington is naturally antipathetic to the idea of religious rule in any nation, and Iran wears this feature of its government like a badge of honor. The Iranian clerical leadership has repressed freedom of expression and controlled the public behavior of its citizenry. On this basis alone, Washington insiders are convinced that regime change in Iran would be greeted with enthusiasm by the Iranians. The Bush administration also did not ignore Iran's restive youthful population, which seemingly opposed the clerics and had a favorable view of the United States and American-style democracy.

This view has been promoted by Michael Ledeen, neoconservative Fellow of the American Enterprise Institute and author of the book *The War Against the Terror Masters*.[42] He believes that a popular uprising in Iran is imminent, and advocates American support of it. Ledeen, with Iranian–American Rob Sobhani, created the Coalition for Democracy in Iran, which favors eventual reestablishment of the monarchy by restoring Reza Pahlavi, the son of the deposed shah. Ledeen has been identified by the Washington Post as one of only four political advisors to presidential advisor Karl Rove, who engineered George W. Bush's campaigns.

Restoration of a pro-American secular government in Iran was thought to be a great domestic political coup in the context of United States politics, giving the Bush administration the political success in the Middle East that eluded it in Iraq and Afghanistan. Restoration of Pahlavi rule was thought by Ledeen and other neoconservatives as a means to accomplish this. There were flaws in the plan, of course. Most Iranians didn't want a new Pahlavi ruler. They also remembered all too well the "restoration" of the Pahlavi monarchy in 1953, when the CIA toppled Prime Minister Mohammad Mossadeq, effectively colonizing their nation. Moreover, though many Iranians would welcome an opening to the West, they were tired of being insulted by Washington politicians. Establishing a truly pro-American government in Iran would be a long, long process after decades of these baseless accusations.

The Wisdom of the Wind

In the last chapter I pointed out that the United States had been tarred with the epithet the Great Satan. The appellation itself had less to do with American actions than with the need for the Iranian regime to attach a symbolic label to an enemy that would resonate with the Iranian public. Unfortunately for the United States, through several presidencies—both Democratic and Republican—the United States continued to act in a way that made it supremely easy for the Iranian religious regime to sustain this powerful negative characterization, to the detriment of American–Iranian relations.

In this chapter, I have tried to show how the Mad Mullah characterization of Iran continues to be substantiated in the American consciousness through the internal and external actions of the Tehran regime. However, just as Americans are selectively characterized by Iran, so is Iran selectively characterized by the United States. The Mad Mullah image is in effect a cocreation, with the United States choosing to see only those things that substantiate the image, and Iran continuing to fuel America's worst expectations through their behavior. Added to this is the investment both sides have in maintaining a feud. In a sense, Iran wants to be a thorn in the side of the United States, and the United States finds complaining about that thorn politically useful.

The ultimate harm in this standoff is that it constitutes a directionless policy for both sides. It is rarely a good idea to be blown around aimlessly by the winds of change when they come, but that is where America is heading with regard to Iran. The better course is to catch the wind and sail with it. In this case, it is not plotting to overthrow the Iranian government, but letting change take its own course in Iran. Whatever the misery suffered by the Iranian people, the resentment that an American-led coup would engender would eventually doom any government installed by Washington.

The way of the clerics has proved not to be the way of the people of their nation, who value independence and freedom perhaps even more than Americans. However they also value moral purity, and finding a way to ensure a balance between freedom and morality is the leitmotif of Iranian political life. This creates a highly nuanced political situation. The clerical leaders are both a source of purity and of discontent when they restrict freedoms that Iranians value. For U.S. officials merely looking at the clerics and deciding that their rule is inherently wrong and requiring replacement constitutes a foolish and uninformed course of action that, if anything, serves to solidify clerical power rather than erode it.

— 7 —

The Framework of U.S.-
Iranian Relations

Modernization and Development as an
Index of National Worth

Setting the Stage for Development

Before Iran and the United States can move toward coming to terms with each other, it is necessary to take a giant step backwards and focus on the large, dynamic patterns that have encompassed the relationship between the two states. It is too easy to focus on the slights and small insults of day-to-day politics. At the core of this framework of relationships is the drama of Iran's burning desire to resume a place among the powerful and respected nations of the world. For Iran, this is intrinsically connected with modernization and technological development. Iran is determined to achieve parity with the most prosperous nations on earth, but to do it entirely on its own terms. There is a very long history of symbolic development projects undertaken by Iran to demonstrate progress in this regard. For Reza Shah Pahlavi and his son, Mohammad Reza, infrastructural projects such as the development of railroads, modern roads, heavy industry—particularly iron and steel—and television and radio were hallmarks of Iran's "coming of age." The Iranian government even hired a public relations agency (involving Cynthia Helms, wife of former CIA director Richard Helms) to present this picture to the world. Under the Islamic Republic, this drive for symbolic projects to demonstrate Iranian skill and prowess continued unabated. Today, Iran has arguably the most developed computer industry in the Middle East, and continues to try and develop heavy industry, such as automobile and airplane manufacture. The development of Iran's nuclear industry is part and parcel of this thrust for demonstrable development. Contrary to American beliefs, it has little to do with making bombs, and almost everything to do with demonstrating Iran's arrival as an industrialized nation.

The great paradox for Iran is one that I have alluded to earlier in this discussion—the more Iran modernizes, the greater the danger to its spiritual core as a nation. In short, the greater the material gains to prove itself equal to the most advanced nations in the world, like the United States, the greater the sense of loss on the part of the population.

The United States seems from an Iranian standpoint, equally determined to only allow development to take place according to parameters set out in Washington—certainly never to the disadvantage of American economic, cultural, industrial or military institutions. Washington has frustrated this economic development again and again since the Revolution through economic sanctions, and direct threats to neighbor states who wish to collaborate and cooperate with Iran on development projects. Both Iran and the United States are stubborn in their goals and determined to a fault.

Iran has had a lot of experience resisting external powers trying to frustrate its ambitions and desires. Development in Iran is a longstanding drama played out on a vast stage that has at one time or another encompassed all of the great nations of the earth—the United States being only the most recent actor. This drama has been played against the background of struggle between international spheres of power and influence, all vying to mould Iran in their own image. Iranians are deeply aware of this, and equally cognizant of the strength of their own culture and society. The empire-like nations of the modern world: Russia, Britain, France, and the United States have been the principal foreign actors in the Iranian drama of development, but at times much smaller nations, such as Belgium, have also played a role.

The United States and Iran are both nations of great diversity. Both have some interesting similarities in their economic and ethnic composition. Agriculture dominated the past history of both nations; both have had to deal with adjustments between tribal and agricultural populations. However, here the similarities stop. The United States was never a monarchical society. It never had to deal with conquest of its territory, and it has a shallow cultural tradition. By contrast Iran had been a continuous monarchy until the Revolution;[1] it has been continually conquered throughout history, and it has an ancient intellectual and cultural tradition that predates almost every other civilization on earth. The result is an almost complete lack of understanding on the part of national leaders and ordinary citizens alike—in both nations—about each other's circumstances.

Internally, the great social and cultural forces working against each other in shaping the destiny of the modernizing Iranian nation have sewn the seeds of disorder among the Iranian people. Though one group or ideology may rise victorious for a period, the other rivalrous factions continue to have a life of their own, one that will not be snuffed out easily. The fall of the Pahlavi dynasty was but one act of the continuing drama. The rise of the Islamic Republic has been another. Iran is now on the verge of a third episode, as demographic and social change begin to create restiveness in the Iranian population; external forces, such as those generated by the United States exert pressure on the nation. It is well at this point for a waiting world to take a hard look at the patterns of the past in order to discern the shapes of things to come as they emerge from the wings.

Below, I attempt to put forth some highly generalized patterns governing economic and cultural sectors that have interacted with each other in Iranian society during the last two monarchical regimes: the Qajar and the Pahlavi, and the current Islamic Republic. The first set of patterns consists of the major social sectors playing a role in Iranian economic life, and their relationship to each other. I attempt to show here that: The relationship between central authority and the ulama, constituting the religious establishment; tribal groups and their leaders; peasant farmers and their landlords; and the bazaar have historically been tenuous at best. And yet, these are the sectors that had to be dealt with in the process of development by central authorities.

The second set of patterns concerns dimensions of human experience in dealing with the world at large. As already mentioned, a clear distinction is made in Iranian life between the internal as opposed to the external, and this distinction shapes one's experience of life to a great extent. In the realm of human interaction, I suggest that relations between individuals are highly idealized, and are divided into two spheres; unequal relations between superiors and inferiors, and equal relations between intimates. The ethics demanded in these spheres are clearly outlined in social life, and social harmony depends heavily on all fulfilling their obligations to them.

A general presumption in this discussion is that these patterns are both old and persistent. An examination of the Qajar period in Iran and the patterns established by its rulers for dealing with economic and cultural development shows this to be true. I argue here that many of the basic relationships between the throne and the people—especially in dealing with economic and technological advancement—were established during this period, continued on into the Pahlavi Era, and were transferred wholesale into the Islamic Republic.

In general, the difficulties with the shah's plans for development, as well as the difficulties faced by the rulers of the Islamic Republic are seen to lie in the increasing distance and estrangement of the nation's rulers from the basic patterns of Iranian culture. Paradoxically, both the shahs and the clerics thought they were directly in sync with Iranian culture. In fact, they embrace only a small part of the concerns of the ordinary Iranian citizen. As the ruling elite of Iran has grown further and further from the people, those rulers implemented policies that they thought were beneficial, but which only served to alienate the people from them. When the forces of the Revolution and those of contemporary protest put them to the test they found that they had few supporters.

It is likely too soon to be able to predict the course of the future. Iran's

Revolution is far from over. The individuals now in power may seem in many ways to be a totally new factor in Iranian history, but in truth, they are proving to be cut from the same cloth as their predecessors. Though it seems unlikely at this writing, they may still be able to provide some new directions for development, or they may be destroyed through their own incompetence.

It has been extremely difficult for officials in the United States to comprehend these patterns. Although Americans have a strong political and moral ideology of their own, it is problematic to try to factor the ideology of others into foreign policy. Administration after administration has blissfully ignored the cultural sensibilities of other peoples in formulating U.S. policy. The George W. Bush administration is no exception. With hubris and arrogance not previously seen in American history, Bush and his advisors have almost willfully failed to understand the cultural dynamics that have shaped the formation of the modern Iranian nation.

The Historic Sectors of Iranian Society

Mullahs, Monarchs, and Maldars

The proper relationship of religious to secular authority became an issue almost from the establishment of Twelver Shi'ism as the state religion in Iran. The Safavids (1501–1736 c.e.), who were largely responsible for the institutionalization of Shi'ism began, in fact, as a Sunni mystical sect; later they claimed direct descent from the Prophet through Musa al-Kazem, son of Ja'far al-Sadiq, the sixth Shi'a Imam. Shi'ism is generally acknowledged to have assumed a heavily nationalistic cast during this period, and persecution of Sunnis, Sufis, and non–Muslims seems to have been common. Indeed, it may well have been continual harassment of Sunni Afghans that prompted their destructive attacks in 1722, marking the effective end of the dynasty.[2]

During the Safavid Era, the Shi'a clergy had become concentrated in Iran, having been invited to settle there from the Levant and from Mesopotamia. They were incorporated into the state government and given important administrative and legal posts.[3]

As Safavid rule began to decline in the years following Shah Abbas (1588–1629), many of the religious leaders, who had acquired considerable power during this era, began to withdraw support from the corrupt and impious secular rulers, and urged the population to follow their guidance instead.[4]

Shi'ite doctrine during the Safavid period had grown toward increasing emphasis on the person of the twelfth Imam—the Mahdi, who would come at the Day of Judgment to "fill the earth with justice and equity as it is now filled with injustice and oppression."[5] In stressing man's need to be associated with the Mahdi as the only legitimate representative of God's law, a doctrine gradually was established which claimed that no temporal ruler had any authority over man. The only true authority was that of the Mahdi himself, or failing his presence on earth, that of the best representative of the Mahdi one could find.[6]

This was generally the wisest and most pious individual available, usually a mullah or mujtahid. The most popular mullahs thus accumulated enormous power as their followings grew, and served as a considerable challenge to the state.

Their personal wealth, control of *waqf*, bequest property, and the *khoms*, and *zakat*, charitable offerings, were paid directly to the ulama for distribution to worthy institutions, as I have mentioned in earlier chapters of this discussion.[7] Because much of this money was administered directly by the ulama, it gave them the opportunity to build virtual empires of their own. Keddie comments that the ulama leaders "often had what amounted to private armies, made up particularly of religious students, who could cause disturbances and terrorize the government, particularly when they were joined by popular crowds."[8]

In the late eighteenth and early nineteenth centuries, the principal mujtahids had moved in the face of the political unrest within Iran to the shrine cities of present-day Iraq: Kerbala, Kufa, Najaf, and Samarra, where the principal Shi'ite martyrs had been buried. These cities were, of course, located in the Ottoman Empire before World War I. Thus, the religious authorities were placed at a physical remove from the secular authority of the rulers of Iran—during the nineteenth century, the Qajars (1779–1924).[9]

Troublesome Tribes

The tribal population of Iran was estimated to constitute as much as half of the total population of the country during the first half of the nineteenth century. It was proportionately less by the end of the century, due to a large general population increase during this period.

Tribes have always proved troublesome for Iran's rulers. Tribal leaders generally insisted on maintaining a rough local autonomy for their own people. They had a system of self-governance and a sense of their own ethnic identity that precluded absorption into a central state system. One of the more disturbing aspects of their independence was the tacit acceptance of robbery as an honorable profession—so long as it was not committed within the tribe itself. Many villagers and even city dwellers came to fear tribal raids, especially during hard times.[10]

Tribal subsistence involved utilization of ecological niches that were unavailable for exploitation in any other way. Thus, tribesmen needed to be free to migrate along prescribed routes in order to support what was essentially a highly efficient meat and dairy industry. When left to pursue their own course, the tribes would migrate from summer to winter pasture in such a way that they would leave the lowlands before the grass was dried out by the heat of summer, and arrive in the highlands just as the snows had melted away to reveal the first grass of spring. The process was reversed in the fall. Because the time difference between the availability of grass at either end of the migration route left a gap of up to two months, the flocks had to be herded carefully up and down the mountain slopes so that they would never outrun their food supply.

This complicated ecological adaptive pattern required a tight, authoritarian form of leadership to make it work. It is not hard to see how coordinating the movements of several thousand families and several hundred thousand animals would necessitate a strong central figure.

The tribal khans and sheiks were formidable opponents when angered. Normally they were on good terms with the government, as long as they were left alone. Indeed, some eventually became co-opted into government service and left tribal life all together for the life of the city.

Nevertheless, tribal leaders rarely abandoned their power bases entirely, standing ready to challenge the government at any time they felt the encroachment of the throne.

Landlords and Peasants

A third, formidable section of the Iranian population consisted of peasant farmers, very few of whom actually owned the lands they farmed. Landlords, few of whom actually lived in the village or villages they owned, fostered a sharecropping system with their tenants. The system was generally based on a division of the crops with the tenants, on the basis of proportions of the five basic elements of agricultural production: land, water, human labor, animal labor, and seed. Under one of a number of formulas found throughout the country, for example, if the landlord provided three of these elements he would take three-fifths of the crop.

Some farmers had no land to farm and were employed for cash wages by other farmers, or by the landlord himself. These "khoshneshin" (literally, "he who sits well or comfortably") might also be engaged in other work, such as shop-keeping, artisanry, barbering, ritual practice, or building. From the nineteenth century on down to land reform in 1963, the life of these landless peasants did not differ drastically from sharecropping farmers, nor as a class were they much worse off.[11]

Agricultural life was very delicately balanced. Water was scarce in most areas of the country except for in the north and the northwest. Thus, farmers developed some of the most ingenious mechanical devices and social institutions for maximizing water, and cooperating in its distribution.

The *qanat* system was one of the most original methods for obtaining water ever invented by man. A long tunnel was made from a source of water near the base of a mountain or hill, dug through a series of vertical shafts spaced at frequent intervals. The slope of the land was calculated so that the water would emerge in a gentle flow from the source to the village where it was to be used. These qanats were often in excess of twenty-five miles long, and required considerable engineering skills to keep them maintained. Thus, villagers contributed extensive cooperative labor or cash to hire laborers to maintain the qanat. At times, the landlord would own the qanat outright, and would himself be responsible for its maintenance.[12]

Once water was obtained for the village, it needed to be allocated on an equitable basis. Throughout Iran, a remarkable system of cooperative labor, operating under various names, provided for the distribution of water to all agriculturalists, thus preserving the differentiated nature of the landholdings of each farmer. This system, here designated by one of its more common names, the *boneh* system, consisted of the division of the village into "irrigation groups," or *bonehs*. Each group was allocated a specific number of hours, as a proportion of the total irrigation cycle. Thus, if the village needed to water its crops (for example, wheat) on a ten-day cycle, then there might be twenty bonehs, each with twelve hours irrigation time. Each boneh would then be subdivided into shares in proportion to the land each man owned. In this way, land measures and water rights became inseparable. Indeed, farmers often measured their land according to the amount of water it took to irrigate it, instead of using surface measures.[13]

Not surprisingly, the boneh often turned into a cooperative labor group. Members of the same boneh would plow, sow, and reap together as well as irrigate. The system was efficient, tightly integrated, and superbly adapted to rural agriculture in Iranian villages.[14]

For the peasants, the landlord was a formidable figure in village life. He could be cruel and greedy. Often he treated villagers as chattel, either through his personal conduct, or through his representative in the village. Nevertheless, he had certain obligations vis-à-vis villagers, which he was required to fulfill. He was charged with correct distribution of the crops at the end of the season. Additionally, he had to provide for the welfare of his villagers in lean times. He would often provide clothing for peasants at the Iranian New Year, and he could be approached for special aid: medical treatment, a loan, support for building religious structures, schooling for a bright youngster, and other such needs.

It is probably accurate to say that the landlord was the principal link between villagers and the external world of the urban centers. He or she, for there were many female landlords, was responsible for the marketing of the crops, including any surplus that villagers might have. In the twentieth century, the landlord was the primary agent of technological change, importing new machinery and techniques whenever they became available.[15]

In the nineteenth century, landlords became more independent, and consolidated their control over the affairs of the rural countryside. Landowning became fashionable, and the large landowners became formidable rivals of the throne itself. Especially in the waning years of the century, many landowners controlled land and wealth, which rivaled that of the royal family. Many even maintained what amounted to their own private armies. Keddie notes that the taxation system under the Qajar shahs was also favorable to landlords.[16]

Landowning was in some ways the universal destiny of the wealthy. The clergy turned to it as a means of absorbing excess *waqf* funds, tribal leaders would settle out on huge parcels of land, sometimes adjoining summer or winter pastures, and urban merchants would look to rural agricultural land not only as a fine investment, but also as a pleasant retreat from city life. Even civil servants often came by land in less honorable ways; the government could encroach on private lands and confiscate them for "state purposes."

The Bazaar

Perhaps the most independent sector of Iranian society was the bazaar. As with other major sectors of society, bazaar merchants were used to tolerating the central government so long as it did not interfere too severely with their business dealings. The bazaar was operated on a guild system with rigid codes of financial and personal behavior. Financial dealings within the bazaar were based largely on personal connections and good faith. A man's business reputation depended on his personal conduct in dealing with others.

All of this contributed to making the bazaar the most conservative sector of society. The tight inner organization of the merchant class also led to resistance against the government whenever the prerogatives of the commercial sector were compromised.

The bazaar was, in the past, and continues to be today, the heart of the Iranian commercial world. It has its own banking practices, provisions for the transfer of goods and money, and an almost organic system of raising and lowering prices. Moreover, it has resisted government control in every way possible. Indeed, in the nineteenth century, the bazaar insisted on conducting its business using foreign coins (the Austrian Maria Theresa Thaler being favored) in order to avoid coming under the unwelcome yoke of the monetary system of the throne.[17] Lest one think that the bazaar may have over estimated its strength at times, it is sobering to remember that even up to the last months of the Pahlavi regime, Iran's second most important export, after oil, was carpets—exported through the bazaar.

The bazaar has never shaken one aspect of its mentality—an aspect that has been the bane of the Iranian central government for over a century. This is the fear of long-term, high-risk investment. For the bazaar, the best investment is that which provides a 100 percent return in a matter of days. In this atmosphere, innovation and change has a difficult time making any headway.

Checks and Balances

Thus, the nineteenth-century Iranian court maintained an extraordinarily tenuous hold on authority. The religious establishment was wealthy and powerful and fundamentally disapproved of it. Tribal leaders were not openly hostile, but would offer a severe challenge if provoked. Landlords were growing wealthier and more protective of their own prerogatives year by year, and the bazaar was conservative and isolated from the operations of government. Moreover, all of these traditional sectors were relatively financially independent, and as noted above, all had their own private paramilitary forces to counteract the government if need be.

It is in this context that the dynamics of development must be considered. If development is to be carried out in a systematic way, it is necessary that some means be established to reach out into all sectors of society. It should be clear that the government of the Qajar dynasty was supremely incapable of doing this; the troubles of that century and the present one can be laid partly to that inability.

The Basic Dimensions of Iranian Cultural Orientation

In previous chapters, particularly in Chapters 3 and 4, I have written extensively about the underlying principles of Iranian social and ideological life. I do not wish to repeat my arguments here, but since they play a major role in questions of development, I thought it useful to repeat some of the main points, especially for those reading the chapters out of order. Those who have already become familiar with these arguments may wish to skip this section.

As I have said, underlying all of Iranian social and ideological life are several major cultural principles. These principles serve as leitmotifs for public and private conduct. They are incorporated into both religious and secular philosophies of human interaction, and as such are extremely important in an understanding of a difficult process such as development.

These cultural principles, which serve as dimensions of orientation in all aspects of daily life, can be seen arranged in two large arenas of contrast. The first arena consists of a contrast between the internal and the external, as culturally defined. The second arena consists of a contrast between hierarchical ordering and equality, or unity. Within the dimension of hierarchical ordering, two polar positions emerge: superior, and inferior.

Although these principles exist in contrast with each other, they are seen most frequently in a state of dynamic tension—such as, in a kind of cosmic equilibrium. Each principle implies a state of affairs within society, in which the principle is in balance with its opposing principle. When affairs throw principles into disequilibria, social disturbance is the result.

Internal vs. External

The internal/external contrast found in many world societies,[18] is especially strong in Iranian ideology as I have mentioned often above. Because they are in a state of tension, the two dimensions continually threatened to destroy each other.

Of the two, the internal is by far the more positively valued, and in many ways the principal human spiritual struggle is seen to be the striving of the pure internal core to conquer the corrupt external periphery.

The internal is the locus of the purest aspects of human spirituality. It is also the principal focus for proper religious practice. Indeed, a common popular religious saying in Iran is: "Knowledge of Self is Knowledge of God." The internal is reflected in architecture in the anderun, the area of the household where the family convenes to the exclusion of outsiders. Iranians believe that they have an especially rich inner life, and concomitantly, that no one can really fully understand their inner core.

The external is the abode of the material world and all that it implies. Although man must live in the world, Iranians view the external world as constituting a potential danger for man's spiritual nature. Corruption comes from the external both as tangible attacks against man and his culture, and as seduction of man away from the core values of society and proper relations with men and higher spirituality. Desire for the external world and all in it is, in fact, given a name in philosophical and popular usage. It is called *nafs* and must be combated at all cost. Men occasionally fall into behavior patterns that indicate orientation to the external world: shrewdness, opportunism, obsequiousness, and hypocrisy. These behaviors are widely disapproved.

The internal/external distinction exists not only in the personal sphere, but in the political and historical consciousness of Iranians as well. Indeed, the struggle between the pure core of Iranian civilization and the external forces that threaten to destroy it is one of the principal popular idealizations of Iranian history.

As I pointed out in Chapter 3, for ordinary Iranians, the conquest of Iranian territory by the Greeks, Arabs, and Mongol hordes might well have happened yesterday. Foreign domination of the Iranian economy in the nineteenth century, culminating with the Anglo-Russian partition of the country into spheres of influence in 1907 was a continuation of this pattern of conquest, as was Allied occupation of the country during World War II, and the Soviet attempt to annex Azerbaijan and Kurdistan following the war.

Foreign domination has always been viewed as the greatest of insults to the Iranian nation, but popular wisdom has it that Iran has always risen from the ashes of domination and conquest to reestablish itself as a great civilization. Thus, the basic ability of the internal to conquer the external is verified in this Iranian popular view of world events.

In extreme situations of personal suffering or national need, the resources of this symbolic core can be marshaled for political action. Religious life in Iran idealizes sacrifice and martyrdom for the sake of core principles. Chief representative of those willing to be martyred, rather than to submit to external coercion was Imam Hossein, grandson of the prophet Mohammad. He was martyred on the plains of Kerbala near present-day Baghdad, rather than acquiesce to the demands of the Caliph of Damascus, Yazid, to acknowledge his right to leadership of the faithful.

The image of Imam Hossein continues to play a central role in popular religious life, in mourning ceremonies held throughout the year, where Iranians are encouraged not only to take him as an example of correct pious behavior, but to analogize his sufferings with their own.

Thus, a pattern is developed in Iran, which tends to view force and coercion from external sources negatively, to tend to blame external forces for any difficulties facing individuals or the nation as a whole, and to be willing to resist that which seems to emanate from a source external to Iranian core culture.

Hierarchy and Equality

Although hierarchical differentiation is a nearly universal feature of social life, there are few societies that take the obligations of hierarchical position as seriously as does Iranian society. Persons placed in a position of superiority should ideally rise to that position and retain it by fulfilling obligations to inferiors, which insures their support and respect. Inferiors, in turn, retain their ties to specific individuals in superior positions by reciprocal observance of obligations of their own.

In contrast to hierarchical orientation in Iranian society are ties of intimacy and equality between individuals. These ties involve mutual obligations of a severe and absolute nature, which often prove impossible or nearly impossible to fulfill.

The obligations incumbent on a superior in a hierarchical relationship prescribe that although demands may be made of inferiors, rewards and favors must also be granted. In general, the superior individual is bound to those in an inferior role by a concern for their general welfare, and a desire to provide them with opportunities for advancement, comfort, and benefits.

The tribal khan, the rural landlord, the religious sheik, the teacher, and the shah are all models of superior individuals who have the right to make almost unlimited demands on those bound to them in inferior roles, but who must also be unstinting in their concern for the welfare of those for whom they have charge. Any hint of exploitation on their part automatically voids the relationship.

Inferiors express their own demands through making petitions for things they need or desire, providing tribute and service to superiors as the balance of the bargain. The inferior person is, in fact, in an advantageous position with regard to the superior. If he is unable or unwilling to fulfill his obligations in the relationship, he has resort to his own inferiority as an excuse. Thus, in situations where power relationships are not defined, individuals will often jockey for the inferior position rather than the superior position as a means of "getting the lower hand" in the relationship.[19]

It should be emphasized that hierarchical relationships are accepted as the norm in life—no one is immune—even a minister is inferior compared to a national or spiritual leader. Even a street sweeper is superior to younger street sweepers. Moreover, status in this regard is relative, changing according to situation and circumstance. In this regard, there is no necessary stigma attached to being in an inferior position to another, unless that position is undeserved, or imposed on one against one's will. For this reason, both parties in the relationship respect each other. Indeed, lack of respect for one another is enough to bring about a breach in the relationship. Contempt on the part of the superior, or insubordination on the part of the inferior will cause a rupture.

As mentioned above, relations of intimacy and equality are very demanding and difficult to maintain in Iran. Reciprocity in such relationships should ideally be of an absolute nature. The parties involved should be willing to do anything at all for each other's benefit, and to share material and spiritual substance completely. The relationship is often never fully realized to the satisfaction of the parties involved. Indeed, many avoid even beginning a relationship that promises this sort of intimacy, for fear that they will be bitterly disappointed with its ultimate inadequacy. The most ideal form of this relationship is embodied in the Sufi notion of unity with the Absolute, also a theoretical goal, impossible except through long and arduous spiritual guidance.

Thus, in Iranian life, relationships tend toward hierarchy, where the roles and obligations between individuals are clearly set out. Breach or rupture occurs when individuals fail to fulfill their obligations to each other. When the obligations are carefully observed, however, harmony generally prevails.

The History of Modern Development in Iran

Economic development can arguably be said to have been more difficult to bring about in Iran than in any other nation in Asia. Iran never lost its integrity as a nation in the twentieth century, and yet it became almost entirely dependent on Western countries for the impetus for modernization during this period. Internal control of the country was very weak even under the Pahlavi regime, which also limited the power of the central government to act, or even to protect its own policy decisions when they met with resistance from the public at large.

In the twentieth century, the two great world wars combined with internal political strife to cripple the Iranian government at crucial junctures, throwing the nation even further into dependency on outside resources for development resources.

Finally, the reign of Mohammad Reza Pahlavi brought short-lived prosperity to some sectors of the nation. However, this prosperity could not be translated effectively into the infrastructural changes needed to transform Iran into the great world power desired by the throne. The pressures of wealth eventually began to erode the fabric of Iranian social structure. Influence of outside nations became essential to the continued survival of development programs, to the chagrin of the more traditional sectors of the population, and the throne began to exhibit the twin signs of megalomania and paranoia that should have warned the world that serious upheavals were likely to occur. Unfortunately, the nation was in the throes of revolution before these signs could be heeded.

The Qajar Period—Establishing the Pattern

The shahs of the Qajar Era were faced with increasing economic difficulties throughout the nineteenth century. As Iran came into greater contact with the Western world, the need for development of a transportation and communication infrastructure for the nation became imperative. A series of humiliating military defeats resulting in the loss of territory to Russia, and failure to establish sovereignty over Western Afghanistan under Fath Ali Shah (1797–1834) demonstrated the need for the state to provide better resources for the military. A new bureaucracy began to emerge—one that demanded cash wages rather than being content with what they could extort from the public in the exercise of their jobs.

Additionally, Iran began to feel pressure on its traditional manufacturing sectors from European industrial powers. Charles Issawi quotes British consul K.E. Abbot writing in the 1840s:

[In 1844] a memorial was presented to His Majesty the shah (then Mohammad Shah) by the traders and manufactures of Cashan [*sic*] praying for protection to their commerce which they represented as suffering in consequence of the introduction of European merchandize into their country. (In 1849) . . . The manufacturers have however rapidly declined for some time past in consequence of the trade with Europe which has gradually extended into every part of the kingdom to the detriment or ruin of many branches of native industry.[20]

Loss of income to the private sector through foreign competition was a serious matter for the throne as well, since the Qajar rulers, during the first half of the century, had little source of income other than taxation. They taxed with a vengeance, but despite their rapaciousness, they still fell short of the income they needed to maintain the state. An important new source of income was found in the sale of governmental posts, but this, too, did little to support the throne in an adequate way.

Foreign manufacture proved to be a double threat to Iran. If it eroded local industry, it also provided fatal attractions for the upper classes of the country. The aristocracy began to travel to Europe regularly, viewing how the upper classes lived. The Qajar shahs took the lead in the import of expensive toys and luxury goods. They took a highly superficial attitude toward the notion of modernization, feeling that mere importation of advanced technology and foreign goods would suffice to bring the nation up to European standards.

More seriously, they did not have the income to pay for this consumer-philosophy modernization program. The shortfalls in revenue became crucial during the reign of Naser ed-Din Shah (1848–96), who himself set a pattern for his successors by indulging in a ruinously expensive journey to Europe. This journey was planned by one of the most remarkable of Naser ed-Din's ministers, Hajji Mirza Hossein Sepah Salar, a man who had had extensive experience living abroad, and did all within his power to persuade the shah to transform his government into something resembling European rule. The journey to Europe was planned as a sort of royal "eye-opener," to provide the shah with direct experience of the modern world.

Naser ed-Din took well to modern ideas in at least one realm: the pursuit of new sources of income. Peter Avery in his book, *Modern Iran*, describes well the establishment of the pattern that was to persist for the rest of the century, in dealing with foreign financial interests:

> [Naser ed-Din] conceived a new plan for raising money and, incidentally, making himself more independent of his fickle subjects. He decided that if he could not take the offensive against foreigners (as in the disastrous attack on Herat), it might be possible to induce them to pay for his quiescence. But loans from foreign governments have strings attached to them, and it was not long before another scheme, that of selling concessions to foreign individuals, commended itself to him. Individuals were less powerful than governments. They paid readily for concessions the granting of which was both lucrative and gave the impression that the shah and his friends were anxious to see their country efficiently exploited. This indeed was a modern approach and showed how easily some of the more dubious ethics of the West had been absorbed.[21]

Naser ed-Din indeed learned his lesson well, and proceeded to sell numerous concessions to foreigners. The British, the Russians, the Belgians, the French, and many others obtained concessions for the development of mineral rights, the right to develop telegraphic communications (thus introducing the first extensive cadre of foreign technicians to the country), road building, railroads, and even the administration of Iranian customs. The throne squandered much of the funds thus obtained.

During the shah's celebrated European journey, the first significant religious opposition to the modernization schemes of the shah and Sepah Salar began to be felt. The clergy began to accuse the government of trying to make Iran like Europe, emulating Christendom. Their pressure was so great that the shah was compelled to issue an order prohibiting the Sepah Salar's reentry into Tehran.

There is no doubt that one of the principal bones of contention had to do with the largest concession ever offered to anyone. In 1873, Sepah Salar, faced with the problem of paying back enormous financial obligations to Russia, offered a general concession of enormous scope to the English Baron Julius de Reuter. This concession included the right to construct railways, work mines, and found a national bank. The nobility of Iran had learned that such concessions often meant enrichment for them as well, so they were all in favor. The clergy looked askance, but the "deal" would have probably gone through unabated had the Russians not expressed their displeasure with the deal, and had the shah not found the London financial community also unenthusiastic. The bank scheme was salvaged from the general concession, but the rest of the plan was cancelled on the shah's return to Tehran.[22]

The de Reuter concession affair in many ways epitomizes the pattern for development which was to be repeated again and again down to the present day. The nation was to be developed through concessions of one sort or another made to foreign interests. The upper classes of society, including the throne itself were to be partners in the plans, and reap great economic benefits there from, while the mass population of the country was largely left to be passively receptive to the schemes vested upon them. Religious leaders continued to play an important role in opposing these schemes. Their opposition was twofold: On the one hand, they opposed the gradual erosion of Iranian religion, customs and ideals at the hands of foreigners, on the other they resisted the massive growth in wealth and power experienced by the secular ruling classes at their expense. This opposition was a constant factor in Iranian political life throughout the latter part of the nineteenth century and the whole of the twentieth. It should also be noted that this period saw a general pan–Islamic movement opposed to the West, growing throughout the Muslim world under the charismatic reformer, Jamal ad-Din al-Afghani.

The Tobacco Rebellion of 1890–92 was perhaps the first important conflict in modern times involving all of the elements that characterized protest throughout the twentieth century. A British subject was granted the concession of a monopoly over all purchase, production, and sale of Iranian grown tobacco. This was too much for the public to take, and the ulama took the lead in stimulating public outcry. Nikki Keddie, the acknowledged expert on the history of the Tobacco Rebellion, describes the events thus:

> When foreigners arrived to buy up the tobacco crop in 1891, ulama-led protests developed in the major cities. The ulama had family and other ties to the merchants and guilds, and were largely dependent on popularity for their status. They were less vulnerable than others to government reprisal, and were seen as natural leaders. When a Shiraz mujtahid was expelled in 1891 for acts against the company, he went to Ottoman Iraq, where he first saw the Iranian born pan-Islamic and anti-Colonial activist, Jamal ad-Din al-Afghani, who had himself been expelled from Iran for propaganda against concessions to Westerners. The Shiraz mujtahid also saw in Iraq the leader of all the Shi'i ulama, Hajj Mirza Hasan Shirazi, and Afghani wrote a famous letter to Shirazi urging him to act. Major movements broke out in several cities; and in Tabriz the concession had to be suspended. Late in 1891 Shirazi issued a decree saying that the use of tobacco was against the will of the Twelfth Imam, and there followed a universal boycott of tobacco. Naser ed-Din was forced to cancel first the internal concession and then after new disturbances, the export concession. The ulama, united partly by telegraphic communication, saw the extent of their political power.[23]

The outlines of this rebellion point out that the public was beginning to feel that the leaders of the country were selling off national resources for personal profit. Disturbances continued until the Constitutional Revolution of 1905–11, which featured a similar unification of clergy and populace against the throne. These disturbances, it will be noted, did not prevent the granting of what proved in the twentieth century to be the most important concession of all—the right to develop all of Iran's oil resources, a concession granted to the British subject, William Knox D'Arcy in 1901. The resulting Anglo-Iranian oil company was indeed the basis for all subsequent industrialization in the country.

With the early concessions came foreign control, of course, and the British and the Russians were in the forefront of those nations anxious to control events in Iran to their own benefit. It is said that the government of the country was in reality controlled from the British and Russian embassies. The Anglo–Russian partition of the country into two spheres of influence, even in the throes of the constitutional revolution in 1907 constituted a grave insult to the Iranian people.[24]

Even as late as 1921, Dr. A. C. Millspaugh, appointed Administrator General of the Finances of Persia, reported: "It was intimated to me that Persian administrations were filled with Russian and British spies and that many if not most of the leading Persian officials put the interests of a foreign government ahead of the interests of their own country."[25]

The Reza Shah Period—Continuing the Pattern

The ascension of Reza Shah to the throne following World War II has been hailed by many as the beginning of a new era in Iranian history. In fact, many important structural changes took place within the central government of Iran, but Reza Shah established very little change in the basic structure of the traditional social sectors. If Reza Shah can be said to have had any policy at all with regard to these sectors, it was to destroy them when they resisted his schemes.

At least two new social forces appeared on the scene during the reign of Reza Shah. The army became strong, and took on an extremely powerful social profile. The bureaucracy increased to an enormous degree, and began to look for all the world like a European government with all its faults and inefficiency. The outer trappings of modern government could not entirely hide the basic Iranian patterns of social life, and despite many attempts to make the bureaucracy function like a modern efficient state system, personalism, favoritism, and individual connections continued to be dominant in day-to-day government functioning. Other new groups on the scene included cadres of professional men: doctors, lawyers, and engineers. Writers and artists also began to emerge, but in very small numbers. These new professionals constituted the core of an emergent bourgeoisie destined to first co-opt and then to replace the upper classes of the Qajar era.

Reza Shah can be said to have had as his major goal the modernization of Iran. Like his Qajar predecessors, however, he faced enormous difficulties in penetrating the traditional sectors of society. Tribal khans continued to resist acknowledgment of central authority. Therefore, Reza Shah countered their opposition by arresting the most defiant of the tribal leaders, and forcibly settling as many of the tribes as he could. Landlords continued to dominate the rural landscape. Because many were wealthy urban elites on whom he depended for power, Reza Shah was not able to penetrate their bastions of privilege in the countryside. In fact, he himself seized large tracts of lands and many villages, and became a considerable landlord in his own right. The bazaar benefited greatly from increased trade during this period, but foreign competition increased as well, and the merchants tended to remain suspicious of the shah.

Of all the traditional sectors, the clergy were probably the most disgruntled. One major objection concerned the considerable reforms instituted by

Reza Shah, which affected the status of women. Public education for women was begun, and women began to hold professional occupations for the first time. The most severe opposition to the policies of the shah from the clergy arose from his outlawing of the veil and the head-to-foot chador. Civil servants were required to appear for their paychecks with their unveiled wives, and gendarmes went through the streets tearing the illegal garments off of unsuspecting women. Clerics could perhaps have lived with some women not wearing the chador in public as a matter of choice, but to make it illegal seemed to be close to blasphemy. A riot in Mashhad against the new dress code, which also demanded Western dress for men, was cruelly put down by armed troops, who actually violated the sacred shrine of Imam Reza.

The religious establishment suffered other losses during Reza Shah's reign, in having almost all of their former legal and educational functions taken away from them. New schools and a new civil court system replaced the traditional religious courts and madrassahs.

Economic development projects during this period consisted largely of massive infrastructural construction projects. The most important of these was the trans–Iranian railway. The bazaar resisted investment in industrial manufacture—the start-up time was far too long and too expensive. Moreover, returns were unacceptably slow and far too low to satisfy the merchants who were used to quick returns and high profits. Thus, the government itself, bypassing the traditional economic institutions, undertook most industrial development during this period.

The principal theme of the Reza Shah period was centralization. Tehran became the center of all decision making, and former power bases in the provinces were not able to maintain themselves with any strength. With the judicial and educational systems centered in the secular government, the ulama were left with only limited power over the public. As mentioned, tribal groups were forcibly contained, and on occasion made to settle.

Thus, during the Reza Shah period, the government attempted to provide for modernization of the country, not by transforming the existing infrastructure of the nation, but rather through bypassing the traditional economic institutions of the nation. The new industrial sector was an overlay to the traditional economy, held almost entirely in government hands. Agriculture and animal husbandry remained almost unchanged, while new and much more powerful decision-making institutions arose in Tehran as the nation pushed forward toward increased centralization of power.

Like his predecessors, Reza Shah had a limited range of financial sources. Chief among these was heavy taxation. Consumer spending was also heavily controlled through restrictions on the import of consumer goods. Inflation was kept down through wage controls. Nevertheless, he was able to innovate on an old pattern, changing the old Qajar system of concessions into something new—industrialization with the state as partner. Although revenues from oil and other industries were small in the beginning, and used primarily for purchase of military equipment, these were the principal sources that his son would use as the linchpin in his own modernization program.

Mohammad Reza Shah—Closing the Pattern

Mohammad Reza Shah came to the throne at the forced abdication of his father (again at the hands of foreign powers) as a very young man. American officials viewed him as somewhat weak and irresolute at the time, but were willing to grant him the opportunity to prove himself. World War II was disruptive, but it also provided an opportunity for reform-minded national leaders to make a new beginning out from under the heavy autocratic hand of Reza Shah, who reportedly was so terrifying that his own ministers would physically tremble in his presence.

As mentioned above, prewar economic and development planning was extremely limited in scope. In 1946, a commission was appointed to prepare a development plan for the country. Again, in consultation with many foreign elements, the First Plan was launched in 1949 along with a new organization for its administration—the Sazeman-e Barnameh, or Plan Organization.

Political turmoil characterized this period in Iranian history as the newly powerful secular nationalists, the newly influential communist party, and the throne all continued to struggle for power. The prime ministry of Mohammad Mossadeq fell during this period, and conflicts with the British led to the cutting off of oil revenues. The coup, engineered by the CIA,[26] toppled Mossadeq from power and reinstated the shah as government strong man; this caused enormous disruption. The end result was the utter failure of the First Plan, which eventually only expended 16 percent of the 21 billion rials ($656 million) planned.[27]

The Second Plan extended from 1955–62, and was extremely loosely defined. It had the quality of a manifesto rather than a planning document, and provided no guidelines or priorities at all for planners to follow.[28]

It seems that, in fact, the principal priority for the government was to launch an investment program, rather than to plan carefully how to integrate its projects. The eventual investment of money thus tended to grandiose infrastructural schemes, many of which proved later to be non-cost-effective or useless. Although 26 percent of the money in the Second Plan was designated for agriculture, most was spent on dam construction or irrigation projects that benefited relatively few of the small farmers that dominated the agricultural sector.

Transportation received the largest share of the funds, and the road building thus undertaken was perhaps the area of the plan that had the greatest impact on the economy in the long run. "Social affairs" also received a large share of the funds (26 percent), but this turned out to be a residual category for spending, with little accounting of how the money was actually spent. Thus, the entire program (which in the end exceeded its original budget by almost some fourteen billion rials)[29] ended up by providing very few tangible benefits for the population as a whole.

The Third Plan was the first comprehensive development plan. The Economic Bureau of the Plan Organization, which benefited from some extremely well-trained young Iranian economists, determined that the earlier plans had suffered from: lack of coordination between the activities of various government agencies, and lack of a comprehensive view regarding the availability and use of resources in the whole economy.[30] The goal of the Third Plan was ostensibly to raise real GNP in the country by an annual rate of 6 percent per year, for a total growth of 35–40 percent for the entire duration of the Plan (1962–67). This goal reflected a simpleminded reading of the growth theories in economics fashionable at the time which promised "economic takeoff" if only GNP could be increased steadily over a long period.

The Plan took place concomitantly with the launching of the "White Revolution" of the shah, and its provisions meshed to a great degree with the new economic conditions brought about by the principal reform initiated in that movement—land reform. As landlords were divested of their property, there needed to be a new source for investment for them. The Third Plan provided for considerable funds for loans and technical assistance to private industry during this period. The private sector responded enthusiastically, and considerably exceeded the investment expected of them during the period.

Once again, however, the bulk of projects conceived during this period was large, new projects that were not planned to coordinate with existing economic sectors. The aim was to increase employment in the country as a whole, and due to an increase in industrial activity, this did occur. However, rather than increasing employment within traditional sectors, new sectors were created which tended to siphon off quality labor from existing pools—primarily the agricultural sector of the economy. This created the beginnings of the chain of urban migration that eventually led to the decline of agricultural production in the nation as a whole.

At this point, brief mention should be made of the Iranian land reform and its effects. Land reform was designed to be an enlightened program, which would return the title of lands to the farmers which cultivated them. It has also been noted that this program was forced on the shah as the price he would have to pay for good relations with the Kennedy administration in the United States, which was promoting such reforms as land reform throughout the world as a defense against communist penetration in third-world countries with repressive regimes.

Whatever his motives, the shah embraced the ideals of land reform with a vengeance. The entire program had many admirable goals, but it also had many flaws in its execution. Much has already been written about the difficulties of land reform.[31] In brief, the principal reasons for the ultimate failure of land reform to stimulate agricultural production stems from the following difficulties: The government failed to differentiate between sharecropping farmers and landless agricultural workers, who received no land. Once the landlords had been removed, these peasants had no source of cash wages. Therefore, they left the villages as soon as new employment opportunities presented themselves. This, in turn, left the landed peasants short of labor during times of year when labor-intensive activities were being undertaken: plowing, harvesting, winnowing, and so on.

Not all peasants were poor—especially those with outside funds, as from cultivating high profit crops, or from less legal activities, such as smuggling opium and other goods. When land became available, these representatives of the village bourgeoisie bought up all the land they could, and in cases where several absentee landlords had been involved previously, they sometimes ended up with greater holdings than the original owners.[32]

The cash support provided by landlords for maintenance of important water resources, canals, qanats, and so on, were removed, and reestablishing a system for cooperative payment for these functions was difficult.

The entire marketing system for agricultural crops was eliminated with the disapearance of the landlord; nothing replaced it, leaving peasant farmers at the mercy of produce brokers from the cities. These urban merchants would often buy a whole crop in advance of the growing season for much less than its actual value. The peasants, strapped for cash, would have no choice but to agree. Under these circumstances, they had no real incentive to work at producing better crops, or higher yields.

Young village men had for years adopted a pattern of leaving the village for a short period of their life before marriage to seek casual labor elsewhere. They would usually return, marry, and carry on agricultural production. New industry and construction, largely government-financed during this period, gave them better incentives never to return. Thus, after a period, villages consisted of nothing but old men, women, and young children.

Government price supports for wheat and other staples never kept pace with the increased costs of production. As agricultural labor was drawn away from the village, higher wages had to be paid to retain the few laborers that existed. This increased the total cost of production. By the mid-1970s it cost farmers about fourteen rials (then about 20¢) to produce a kilogram of wheat. The government paid only ten rials to purchace that same wheat. The results are obvious.

From the Third Plan onward, although great lip service was paid to designing agricultural development plans that would aid small farmers, massive irrigation projects and dams continued to dominate the construction side of planning. Farm cooperations and agribusiness schemes were then set up to better utilize the new irrigation resources. Rather than improve existing farming conditions for agriculturalists, farmers were often coerced into participating in these schemes, sometimes being forced to exchange title for their land for "shares" in a corporation. The farmers quite correctly wondered what kind of land reform it was that first gave them title to land, and then took it away from them again.

The Fourth Plan (1968–72) was designed to increase real GNP by 9 percent per year. In the end, it exceeded this by 2 percent, largely due to increased oil production. The Plan Organization had indeed learned a great deal from previous plans, and this plan was executed more efficiently. Nevertheless, the principal gains in the economy were made in the private and public industrial sectors. Although 1.2 million new jobs were created during this period, nearly 250,000 agricultural jobs were abandoned. The bazaar began to lose its centrality in the Iranian economy as industrialists took over.

Industrialization took on a particularly interesting turn during this period as foreign capital began to be made available to an unusual degree. Joint venture companies were established, involving Iranians and foreigners in "turnkey" operations. The foreign investor would essentially come in and deliver an entire construction plant, on a shared cost basis. Government officials and the royal family were prime partners in these ventures, because they provided the clout needed to avoid bureaucratic red tape. As these ventures began to achieve success, the nation experienced a boom.

The eventual source of *all* capital, however, was oil. Iran was not successful in achieving a significant increase in non-oil exports. Most of the new industries manufactured consumer goods for internal consumption. Thus, *both* the capital to *make* the goods and the capital to *buy* them came from oil.

There is no question that Iran achieved some real growth during the period of the Fourth Plan—the world began to take notice to an increasing degree. Nevertheless, the growth was enormously top-heavy. It was taking place among new classes of urban elites that had literally not existed twenty-five years previously. At the same time, traditional sectors of the economy were experiencing a decline. The country was again awash with foreigners, most of whom seemed to be prospering at the expense of Iran and Iranians. These individuals, to add insult to injury, seemed not to care much about Iran, nor to respect Iranians. Moreover, they were protected by the government to an extraordinary degree, allowed special privileges, and paid enormous wages in proportion to their Iranian counterparts.

The shah continued his father's policy of centralization. Land reform was one important measure for breaking the backs of the powerful landlords. Forcible settlement of the tribes continued with some extraordinarily bloody confrontations between army and tribesmen. The bazaar found itself saddled with new financial and banking regulations, as well as demands for stricter accounting procedures for purposes of taxation. Finally, the clerics had their last bastions of wealth and power removed during land reform, along with the landlords, as personal holdings and religious-bequest land, which had been in their keeping was placed under a government office in charge of a minister appointed by the throne.

The clergy had already suffered considerably from industrialization. Enrollments in religious schools had reached an all-time low. Few young men now aspired to religious life. Even if they completed a term of study at a traditional madresseh, they would often abandon their robes for an auto repair shop or factory. The government moved to fill the gap in support provided by the waqf lands and other sources of income that had been eliminated in this period by providing a regular subsidy to the clergy. But this was a stopgap effort at best. By 1974, many felt that the back of the religious leadership had effectively been broken, and that they no longer proved a political challenge to the throne.

Life in Iran was beginning to become increasingly frenetic and uncomfortable. The newly rich industrialists and professional classes, with their international values and social habits were looked at with deep suspicion by the mass of the population. In many ways these people did not seem to be Iranian at all. Their values fell into the realm of the "external"; they denied the basic spiritual qualities so central to Iranian culture. When they professed an acquaintance with poetry or mystical philosophy, their interest seemed faddish and hypocritical. The great writer Jalal al-e Ahmad was one of the principal critics of this growing class of individuals. His writings, including the powerful essay, *Gharbzadegi*, translated by Iranologist Giri Tikku as "Westoxication," often bitterly called into question the erosion of the Iranian spirit during the modernization process. He himself spent much time in the villages of the country, and wrote about rural people with much care and affection. Other writers, Gholam Hossein Sa'edi and Samad Behrangi among them, wrote in a similar manner of the core values of Iranian life, and criticized the government severely for selling out to superficialities, while actually causing harm to the core of the Iranian population. Modern poets took up the theme of alienation, and longed for some form of redemption. Clearly the price of modernization was a spiritual one, and it was very dear indeed. The government response was to harass and arrest these writers, and suppress their writings. Many of the more vocal died in mysterious ways.

The Coup de Grace—OPEC and After

Following the oil price increase of 1973, Iran began to reel out of control. Real growth continued unabated, but it continued to be spread only among the top echelons of society—people who had no real place within the traditional structure of the nation.

The shah finally achieved the elusive goal, pursued since the days of Naser ed-Din shah—financial independence from the population as a whole. In 1959, oil revenues contributed only 9.7 percent of Iran's total GNP. By 1974, the contribution had risen to 47 percent.[33] By some estimates, the government was receiving fully 80 percent of its revenues from oil. Since those in power were not elected, this gave them almost unlimited license in the exercise of their power.

For both the shah and his largely technocratic ministries, such power was very dangerous. It was almost as if Iran had turned into a private economic laboratory with mad scientists in charge. The prestige occupation in the land—after medicine—was engineering. In Iran, one even receives a social title, *mohandes* (literally, "geometrizer"), for engaging in this profession. Urban engineering, rural engineering, and planning engineering took their place in the land as technical specialties. At Pahlavi University in Shiraz, the sociology students petitioned to have their degree designated as one titled "social engineering."

Life in rural and urban areas became even more uncomfortable as the population was poked and prodded in interminable experiments to decrease inflation and increase productivity, and improve social indicators. It seemed at times that the statistics mattered far more than the people.

In the streets of Tehran, clogged with the new cars assembled in Iran since 1968, traffic flowed one-way for one week, and then were made to drive the other way the next. Parking regulations changed daily. The government legislated mandatory opening and closing hours for small businesses, then would change the hours for the next month. Birth control schemes were introduced without proper medical follow-up, causing many rural women to become sick without any idea what to do. Farmers were offered credit, then threatened for nonpayment of their debts when the credit schemes were suddenly withdrawn. This was clearly not progressive change, as has often been claimed in assessing the Pahlavi regime, but rather irresponsible and reckless experimentation.

By 1975, the increase in GNP topped 70 percent in real market prices, but inflation had begun to make itself felt at a rate exceeding 60 percent. In the next year, the inflation rate topped the growth rate, causing negative real growth of about 2 percent. Agricultural production, lagging nearly 1 percent behind the birth rate (2.3 percent vs. 3.2 percent) now went into real decline. The folly of tribal settlement came home to roost as millions of pounds of meat had to be imported from abroad to make up for the destruction of this traditional sector.[34]

Ordinary Iranians, particularly those on fixed incomes, or on rigidly limited government salaries were beginning to suffer mightily. Housing was rising at yearly increments exceeding 100 percent. Domestic food production, in severe decline, necessitated importing food. For the first time in recent history, Iranians were buying wheat abroad.[35]

The shah appointed Jamshid Amuzegar, his former oil minister, as prime minister. Amuzegar, a genuine technocrat, immediately moved to control inflation by cracking down on those few sectors of the economy in which the neglected bazaar had found a foothold: real estate, and the increasingly lucrative market in specialized produce: fruits, vegetables, nuts, eggs, and such. Draconian limitations were placed on the transfer of land, and severe price controls placed on produce—both regulations carring a penalty of a jail term if violated. The effects in the bazaar were immediate—merchants stopped paying back bank loans en masse and antigovernment propaganda began to surface.[36]

This gave the religious establishment their opening, and the revolutionary exhortations of Ayatollah Ruhollah Khomeini, who had opposed the course the government was taking in development actively since 1963 began to take hold throughout the population.

When the government moved to discredit Khomeini through a planted article in the daily paper *Ettela'at*, street riots began in the holy shrine city, Qom. The government confronted the rioters as they had in the past—with violence—but this time, counterprotests broke out throughout the nation. The clergy saw their opening, and once again, as in the past century, spearheaded the opposition.

Many Iranians wondered if they should oppose the throne. They were disturbed by developments in recent years, but had maintained hope that much of the difficulty would eventually pass as Iran became more prosperous. For these persons, the turning point was seeing young men and veiled women unarmed on the streets of Tehran and other cities, being gunned down by government troops. For Iranian citizens, this was the ultimate outrage—the sign that the throne had ceased having any respect for the population at all. The fragile bond that had obtained between shah and people had finally severed, and the rioting began.

At this point, the shah ceased to have any legitimacy as a leader for the population as a whole. It was only a matter of time before he was expelled.

The Crimes(?) of the Shah

In his last days in Iran, the shah was unusually depressed. He felt he had given his best for his country, but all had failed in the end.

Looking back on his regime, it is possible to see that many of the difficulties he faced were inherited from earlier generations. He, like his father and the Qajar rulers before them, had the difficulty of dealing with a diverse, unruly, and highly independent population. The desire to be able to rule without the need to curry public support had somehow been "built in" as a feature of kingship. When the shah finally achieved this elusive goal, he quickly discovered that even an absolute ruler needs to be in favor with the public at some level.

The shah had, in the end, failed to adhere to the duties of one in a superior position. He had, in the eyes of the public, shamelessly used the Iranian nation in a mounting game of aggrandizement. When they protested, he stood by while they were murdered. This was enough to disqualify him from a relationship which would guarantee the loyalty of the public.

Moreover, the shah seemed to be carrying out his plans for the nation with the collusion of foreign elements. This made the actions, in so far as they affected Iranians adversely, all the more severe. The fact that the principal influence of foreigners in Iran seemed to be to drive the population away from spiritual values and toward material desire only confirmed the formula that corruption comes from external sources. The shah's sanction and protection of these foreign elements only tended to confirm his collusion with anti–Iranian forces.

The traditional sectors of the economy may not have benefited from the reign of Reza Shah, but at least, with the exception of the ulama, and those tribes that defied the throne, their basic structure was left relatively unchanged. Land reform, industrialization, economic tinkering, and direct military force were all used by Mohammad Reza Shah as tools not just to modernize, but to destroy the infrastructure of existing institutions. The institutions that came to replace these older sectors, the professional classes and technocrats, seemed strange and bizarre to the mass of the population—ultimately unsupportable.

In the end, the shah may well have fallen prey to the kind of "Westoxication," described by Jalal al-e Ahmad in a particularly pernicious way. The goals of modernization were in the end, used by him to justify the use of extreme measures in an old struggle—the struggle between the Iranian monarchy and the rest of the population, with whom it had always enjoyed the most delicate of relationships.

The Postwar Period—Clerical "Beneficence"

The clerics, now in power for longer than Mohammad Reza Pahlavi, suffer from the opposite disease that afflicted the technocrats during the Pahlavi Era. They believe that they know a great deal about personal morality, and about traditional Iran and its values. However, they have proven to know very little about the modern world, and after nearly thirty years, have proved to be far less efficient at developing Iran than they first thought they would be.

Indeed, one cannot turn back the clock. Whether they were put there for the wrong reasons or not, the automobiles, the televisions, the chemical plants, the cargo ships, the oil rigs, and the mines now exist in Iran. Their owners have largely fled the country, but the facilities remain.

The regime of the Islamic republic adopted the only model they knew for the development of the nation—namely, charity. The clerics knew how to run orphanages and hospitals. They tended to treat industrial and rural development as an extension of these activities. Labeling the population as "*mostazefin*" (downtrodden), they proceeded to reframe such activities as rural electrification and the development of drinking water throughout the country as small-scale charity projects. The development effort was cast as a religious exercise—the *jihad-e sazandegi* or development jihad, using "jihad" in its correct meaning—"righteous struggle." The mechanism used is the establishment of *bonyad*s, or charitable foundations. From this base they carried out a wide range of these development projects.[37] The shrine of Imam Reza in Mashhad for example already owned virtually all of the land of that city, but subsequently purchased nearly all of the agricultural land in the surrounding countryside.[38] To some extent these projects were successful. Electricity, drinking water, and roads were extended to many rural areas that did not have them before, whether the provision of these utilities was cost-efficient or not.[39]

Agriculture has made a weak comeback since the revolution.[40] Wheat, which was exported in the 1950s, is again being produced in quantities enough to feed the nation. Meat is still in short supply at this writing, but somehow the situation feels as if it might resolve itself. The only systematic study of postrevolutionary agriculture in Iran[41] claims that bureaucratic inefficiency can be blamed for much of the inefficiency in restoring agriculture to Iran.[42]

Some of the greatest gains have been in health care and education. After a sharp rise in the birthrate following the Iran–Iraq war,[43] there was an equally precipitous drop in the birthrate, until today Iran has one of the lowest population growth rates in the Middle East—now estimated at 1.2 percent.[44] Some have attributed the drop in birthrate to the rise in educational opportunities for women. It is reported that in the year 2000, female literacy had increased to 70 percent and school enrollment for women was an astonishing 90 percent.[45]

Despite this good news on the health and education front, economic indicators remain poor. Unemployment is estimated to be as high as 50 percent among young people, despite educational gains.[46]

The country continues to be massively dependent on exported oil and gas. This unhealthy economic habit has not changed from the time of the shah. This fact alone has been the reason that U.S. economic sanctions have had little or no effect in creating political pressure on Iran. They have simply made it more difficult for Iran to diversify its economy. Extreme central planning has obviously not worked well in Iran. Neither have the simple growth philosophies of the old development plans: simple increase in GNP will not yield prosperity for all people. Finally, the scattered and disorganized attempts of the Islamic Republic at development proved long on goodwill and short on efficiency. The traditional sectors must clearly be developed from within, not assaulted from without if real change and development are to take place. Sadly, corruption remains a problem. Following the revolution, the clerical leaders have become fabulously wealthy.

Ali Akbar Hashemi-Rafsanjani, the former president and head of the Expediency Council, is now rumored to be one of the richest men in the world. His sons have cut deals all over Europe with Iran's oil supplies. Olav Fjell, the CEO of Statoil, the Danish state oil company, was forced to resign in September 2003, over shady dealings with Mehdi Hashemi-Rafsanjani, son of the former president.[47] If Ali Akbar Hashemi-Rafsanjani retains power after his unsuccessful presidential bid in 2005, Iranians can expect more of these sorts of questionable dealings.

It will require genuine wisdom to benefit from the lessons of the past. The clerical leaders of the fledgling Islamic Republic may continue to get caught in parochial power squabbles. Their ability to lead and hold power in the nation will definitely depend on their ability to keep their contract with the people, and protect their dignity and their welfare. The charitable model of development is good for public relations, but ultimately inefficient, and subject to fall prey to corrupting forces.

Throughout all of this, the continual struggle between external and internal political and economic forces, and external and internal personal forces, coupled with the Iranian acute sense of hieriarchy played out on a personal and international scale, figure prominently in every action that takes place. Americans, so frequently blinded by the seemingly exotic features of Iranian religious life, and unable to resist reacting to volleys of seemingly hostile political rhetoric and recalcitrance on the part of Iran's leaders, have a very hard time penetrating to the core of these cultural values. However, it is essential that all of these organizational structures be understood before progress can be made in Iranian-U.S. relations.

—— 8 ——

The Sins of the United States

Ongoing Rhetoric and Metaphor in the Image of the Great Satan

As treated earlier, the Great Satan is the negative image of the United States, which most Americans will retain in their minds from the Iranian Revolution and subsequent hostage crisis. Ayatollah Ruhollah Khomeini's epithet for the United States evokes an image so stark, ominous, and full of vitriol that it is difficult to look at it in a detached manner. As will be seen below, the image is an over-the-top characterization of American motives and action, bearing little relationship to reality. However, it becomes comprehensible when one views it in an Iranian cultural framework.

The use of the term Great Satan was in fact a brilliant rhetorical device used by Khomeini to great effect during the course of the hostage crisis. It immediately lunged to the core of Iranian dissatisfaction with the state of affairs during the final years of the Pahlavi Era, and concretized these feelings in a single, potent symbol. Analyzing the cultural underpinnings for this symbol is instructive both for understanding the revolution itself, and for understanding Iranian communication processes. The epithet has had extraordinary longevity, and is still being used, albeit less frequently today.[1] Americans were both deeply offended by the use of this term, and profoundly puzzled at its origin and usage.[2] Understanding this and other symbolic devices used by the Iranian government to vilify the United States is an important key to understanding why, after thirty years, images like this are still current. However, substantive Iranian complaints about the United States might be, the symbolic embodiment of those complaints are more powerful than the mere facts for an Iranian audience.

The skillful use of metaphor is a core feature of Iranian culture.[3] The careful turning of metaphorical phrases is one of the arts of great poetry, used to extraordinary advantage by the classic poets. By setting up equations of metaphors, the greatest writers could easily move their readers to great emotion. The great tenth-century poet, Rudaki, it is claimed, penned his famous verse, "Bu-ye Ju-ye Mulian" (The Fragrance of the Oxus River) at the request of the denizens of the city of Bukhara who wished him to persuade the Samanid Amir Nasr bin Ahmad to return to that city, which he had neglected for four years while enjoying himself in Herat. In part, Rudaki used the following simple but effective metaphors in his persuasive verse:

> Long live Bukhara! Be thou of good cheer!
> Joyous to you hastens our Amir!
> The Moon's the Prince, and Bukhara the sky;
> O Sky, the Moon shall light three by and by!
> Bukhara's the Mead, the Cypress he;
> Receive at last, O Mead, thy Cypress-tree!
>
> (after Edward Browne)[4]

Legend has it that on hearing this verse, the Amir jumped down from his throne and onto his horse without even putting on his riding boots, and rode straightaway to Bukhara.

The use of the Great Satan as a rhetorical device is not nearly so charming, but it was equally effective in mobilizing the Iranian population. For Americans, the reasons may seem incomprehensible; especially since the assessments of U.S. citizens of their own role in Iran are far more charitable than reflected in this image. Most felt that the U.S. government and industry had been working in Iran for the good of the Iranian people as well as for their own economic benefit. They felt that joint industrial ventures had provided for Iran's modernization and had increased the wealth of the population as a whole.

But as we have seen in earlier chapters by the assessment of the Iranian population, the relationship was exploitative, both economically and spiritually. More importantly, the significance of this spiritual crisis was not recognized by Western nations until Iran had actually passed the breaking point.

Thus, a highly complex, but very basic issue became concretized in the complex symbolic image of the Great Satan: the loss of the nation's spiritual core and the assignment of blame for the occurrence to the United States. The effectiveness of this symbolic equation is paradoxically not explained by reference to doctrinaire religion. The sense of despair coupled with anger toward America was widespread during and after the revolution, and not at all confined to people who followed the clergy. It was also experienced by members of the middle and upper classes, and even these relatively secularized individuals responded readily to the image of the Great Satan.

Dimensions of Cultural Orientation

Religious systems are not merely static arrangements of idealizations. They are dynamic, and occasionally make their dynamic nature explicit. Geertz's classic study of another Islamic society—that of Java—demonstrated the enormous distance that can separate the practice of religion from the demands of doctrine.[5] Such, too, is the case with Iran.

Throughout this book great emphasis has been placed on two large arenas of symbolic cultural contrast. The first arena of contrast, it will be remembered, consists of the opposition between the internal and the external as culturally defined. The second consists of a contrast between hierarchy and equality. Within the dimension of hierarchy, two polar positions emerge: superior and inferior.

Although these principles exist in contrast with each other, they are seen most frequently in a state of dynamic tension. Each principle implies a state of affairs within society in which it is in balance with its opposing principle. When affairs create a disequilibrium, widespread social disturbance is the result—such as in the case of the 1978–79 Revolution.

The contrast between internal and external is found in many world societies,[6] the shape taken in Iran is unique to Iranian culture.

The internal/external distinction is doubly potent in Iran, since it is also present in formal religious doctrine in Shi'a Islam. One of the hallmarks of Shi'ism is the distinction between exoteric (zaher) knowledge and esoteric (baten) knowledge.[7] Mohammad Hossein Tabataba'i, one of the great modern scholars of Shi'ism, makes it clear that the ability to understand the inner core of religious truth has a great deal to do with an individual's personal qualities: "[The Qur'an possesses] deeper and wider levels of meaning which only the spiritual elite who possess pure hearts can comprehend."[8]

Keddie, likewise shows how this doctrine was used to create a religious elite structure in the community of believers:

> there early arose the idea that in addition to the obvious, literal meaning of the scripture, there was a more profound, inner meaning open only to the initiate. Among the Shi'a sects the idea became common that this meaning had been handed over secretly by the Prophet to Ali, and by him to his descendents, in whatever line the particular sect happened to believe. . . . And the philosophers' approach to *zaher* and *baten* was also attuned to their intellectual and political position. According to them, the Qur'an contained crude religious notions for the masses, and at the same time had deliberate obscurities and ambiguities which would lead the philosophically minded to contemplate and to achieve a true rational understanding of religion.[9]

That the Great Satan might come to be located in the further reaches of the external in popular Shi'a belief systems is perhaps not surprising, given Iran's religious history. Even though there seems to be little question that present day Shi'ism involves synchretic incorporation of pre-Islamic belief systems, surprisingly little has been written on the exact nature of that syncretism.

Seyyed Hossein Nasr demonstrates how the Zoroastrian cosmology has been effectively taken over by Iranian-Islamic philosophers, geographers, and writers throughout the Safavid and Qajar periods in his, "Cosmographie en L'lran Pré-Islamique et Islamique."[10] Henri Corbin has likewise analyzed the influence of Mazdean concepts of time on Isma'ilism.[11]

The topic that seems to be most controversial in assessing Zoroastrian influences on Islam is predictably the question of dualism—the notion of the existence of matched forces of good and evil. This is, of course, incompatible with strict monotheistic doctrine. Gustav Von Grunebaum offers a remarkably astute set of observations concerning Ferdowsi's treatment of Iranian mythical history in the *Shahnameh* which suggest that the true incorporation of Zoroastrian dualism in popular Islam may have come through sources outside of strict orthodox commentary: "Without entering into theological disquisitions regarding the fundamental conflict between dualistic Zoroastrianism and monistic Islam, or regarding the individual tenets of the old religion, he allows mythical events to retain their significance in terms of the dualistic conflict between good and evil, Ormizd and Ahriman. . . . The fight of Good and Evil is real to (Ferdowsi), but as a Muslim he identifies the Good Principle, or Ormizd with Allah, the One, the Creator, and reduces the stature of Ahriman to that of a *div* or of the Koranic Iblis."[12]

Iblis is, of course, the Great Satan of the Qur'an—the *Shaitan al-Rajim*. In Qur'anic tradition, Iblis was the tempter of Adam, and likewise was cast out of God's grace for disobeying his command to bow down before Adam. Here the Qur'an makes a distinction in reference. In his fall he is referred to as Iblis, but as the tempter, he is called *al-Shaitan*.

In popular Islam it is in the role as tempter that the Great Satan is best known. His principal task is to draw men from the path of God, and into the path of sin and destruction. His connection with man is intimate, and the locus of his activities is predictably, the everyday, external world—the zaher. A. S. Tritton cites this tale in his article on the *Shaitan* for the first edition of the *Encyclopedia of Islam*: "(Shaitan) complained to God of the privileges granted to men and was thereupon given similar ones. Diviners were his prophets; tatoo marks, his sacred books; lies, his traditions; poetry, his religious reading; musical instruments, his muezzins; the market, his mosque; the baths, his home; his food was everything on which the name of God was not invoked; his drink, all intoxicating liquors; and the object of his hunting, women."[13]

In popular pre-Islamic belief in Iran, the locus of various of the many divs was outside of the nation of Iran. The great White Div mentioned in Chapter 5—the principal monster of Ferdowsi's epic *Shahnameh* and similar figures were located on the periphery of the civilized world.[14] This too is another kind of zaher—a place external to Iranian core civilization, and a likely mental locus for the figure of the Great Satan.

The internal/external distinction exists in the political and historical consciousness of Iranians as well. Indeed, as was pointed out above, the struggle between the pure core of Iranian civilization and the external forces that threaten to destroy it is one of the principal popular idealizations of Iranian history. As mentioned, the various ways in which the United States has interfered in Iranian life following the revolution are further symbolic demonstrations of this attack on Iran's spiritual core through outside interference.[15] To this end, idealized sacrifice and martyrdom become ideals pursued for the sake of core principles.[16]

The question of relative status and the obligations of different social positions is of crucial importance in Shi'a religious doctrine, and is, moreover intimately tied to the notion of inner purity. Those who achieve positions of superiority among men should ideally do so because of the superiority of their knowledge, understanding and character. Those who attain their position dishonestly or through the use of brute force are illegitimate. Within Islam, supreme authority comes only from God. This authority is transmitted to his representatives on earth. In Shi'a theology, this line of authority becomes invested in the Imamate; in Sunni doctrine in the Caliphate. Anything that disturbs the legitimate exercise of authority can, by the exercise of religious doctrine, be declared to constitute corruption. Failing the presence of the Imams among men, Shi'a theologians have argued since the seventeenth century that those individuals who are wisest, purest, and most knowledgeable in the law of God should be the legitimate leaders of society.

For virtually all present-day Shi'a theologians, the doctrine of *velayat-e faqih* or "regency of the chief jurisprudent" in place of the "hidden" twelfth Imam, the Mahdi, now the central feature of the constitution of the Islamic Republic, is a position that is theologically too extreme.[17] Nevertheless, most theologians would agree that it is at least the duty of religious leaders to admonish the people not to follow corrupt leaders, or to submit to corrupting forces. As superior individuals within the framework of Iranian society, to do less would be shirking both one's religious and one's social duties, for it would be tantamount to failure to protect and care for one's legitimate followers.

For their part, it is incumbent upon the faithful as part of the cardinal duties within Shi'a Islam to "promote the right and resist the wrong." However, it is to religious authority that one must appeal in order to understand the difference. Moreover, as mentioned above, since religion has both an exoteric and an esoteric aspect to it in Shi'ism, it is only superior individuals who can gain the interior knowledge that allows them to grasp at the truth at the core.

For those who would know the truth, appeal must be made to those superior individuals who have the knowledge necessary to provide guidance. Since Islam has no formal system of certification of knowledge, a person becomes known for his superior knowledge by virtue of his reputation alone. Advancement to the higher ranks of authority within the community are determined through consensus. In this manner, theoretically no person need accept another as his superior, except in so far as he himself is willing.

The "superior" that one follows is a *marja'-e taqlid* (*marjah al-taqlid* in Arabic), or leader worthy of being emulated. The relationship between this emulated superior and his followers is a symbiotic one of mutual support. The *marja'* is revered and supported by service and monetary gifts, and he in turn provides spiritual guidance and integration for the individual in religious life.

There has been a curious parallelism between religious and secular authority in Iran on this last point. The shah was, like a religious *marja'*, a superior who enjoyed a symbiotic relationship with his subjects. In return for service, respect, and support, the shahs were to provide rewards and care for Iranian citizens.

For this reason, many thoughtful Iranians in the middle and upper classes reflected that they themselves were largely to blame for the economic and social difficulties during the years of Pahlavi rule. Their own willingness to overlook political repression in striving for wealth, foreign goods, and an easy life was due to the dependency they had on the court, from which all wealth and opportunity ultimately flowed.

The traditional classes—especially those who had a strong spiritual life—rejected this assessment, for in the classical cultural formulation described earlier, the ultimate locus of corruption for Iranians could not be internal—it had to come from without. The U.S. stood out in relief in the minds of Iranians both because of its enormous presence and because of its naiveté concerning its own public image. U.S. government and business interests acted the role of the exploiter and corrupter in highly visible ways, making it easy for revolutionary leaders to adopt successfully the position that the United States was the cause of all the nation's woes.

As I have already stated, many individuals became wealthy in the ten years before the revolution, and things seemed to be booming—but in fact the economy was sick. Simple increases in the gross national product (GNP), only blinded the regime to the folly of its superficial planning,[18] and concealed the existence of an economic bubble. It also concealed the fact that the economy could not wean itself from dependency on oil. In 1974, the oil sector contributed 9.7 percent of the total GNP, by 1974 it contributed 47 percent.[19] By some estimates, the dependency had risen to 80 percent or more before the revolution.

All of this meant that the shah and his court gradually became independent of the public. In effect, they had so much independent income, they had no need of the continued spiritual support provided through public loyalty. The public felt this lack of regard during the nonconsultative development schemes that uprooted the public and showed them contempt. Strikes and protests showed not so much economic distress (although that was certainly part of the motivation for protest) as they did the social distress emanating from the broken "social contract" between the ruler and the people. Merchants and ordinary workers' strikes did little to faze the regime, but all workers were not indispensable. Given the regime's dependency on oil, when oil workers went on strike as a contribution to the revolution, the act was a definitive blow to the shah's regime.[20]

Throughout all of these events, the United States was symbolically linked to the shah and his government. Although the United States was anxious to appear to be a power superior to Iran; it never was equipped to play the role of an Iranian-style superior, who actually cared for, and supported those providing loyalty. Indeed, Americans could barely even communicate with Iranians except at the most superficial levels. No American ambassador since World War II spoke even minimal Persian, and few embassy activities indicated American appreciation for Iranian culture.[21] The 50,000 American workers were utterly remote from Iranian social life and culture[22] This was reflected in bitterness over the doctrine of extraterritoriality for Americans mentioned in Chapter 5.[23] In failing to fulfill the proper role of superior, while simultaneously claiming superior status, the United States inspired both anger and contempt. This treatment was undeserved from an American standpoint, but perfectly understandable when seen in an Iranian cultural frame.

Spiritual Damage

Iranians may have resented what they viewed as direct exploitation on the part of the United States, but the more profound effects of the American presence in Iran had to do with the changes it was bringing about in traditional patterns of Iranian life. The story of the decline of life in Tehran was duplicated throughout the nation, and provides a capsule picture of what forces were taking hold of the nation.

The society became consumed by the media, much to the chagrin of the traditional sectors, who looked askance at the mass importation of Western values and sexual laxity through cinema, radio, and television. The role of the mass media in Iran is discussed in detail in Chapter 11.

Jalal al-e Ahmad's *Gharbzadegi* (Westoxication) became a common phrase on everyone's lips as life became increasingly foreign for ordinary

Iranians—even those who themselves had been educated in the West, or were familiar with Western culture. The epithet bitterly called into question the erosion of the Iranian spirit during the modernization process.

These feelings were not limited to the cultural elite. As mentioned above, for the religious community the new social orientation was nothing short of directly sinful. Dancing, music, and especially the cinema were singled out for harsh attacks from the mosque and religious schools. In the smaller towns and villages where the religious climate was considerably more conservative than in the cities, residents would explain their ownership of a radio by asserting that they only listened to the news (and not the likes of popular singers Gugush and Dariush). Television was somehow considered less dangerous than the dark city movie houses, and even after the Revolution was declared to be a useful device by Ayatollah Khomeini, provided it was supervised properly by religious authorities (see Chapter 11).

Of perhaps greater concern to religious authorities than the physical devices, which seemed to be introducing corruption into social life, was the increasing emphasis of the state on the secularization of society. In all areas of daily living, religious guidance seemed to be ignored in public policy making. Some activities, such as gambling in several casinos around the country, and the manufacture and consumption of liquor were directly and indirectly supported by the state (as in state-run hotels). There seemed to be a clear attempt by the Pahlavi dynasty to somehow circumvent Islam in the definition of the Iranian state, and distinctly pre-Islamic themes were clearly seen in national festivals such as the 2,500-year celebration of the Iranian monarchy and the shah's own self-coronation. In all of these events the United States was seen as the inspiration, if not the direct instigator.

In 1976, the shah was persuaded to announce a change in the official Iranian calendar. The year would henceforth be reckoned not according to the Hegira of Mohammad, but rather to the supposed date of the establishment of the Achaemenian dynasty. This even caught the attention of the Zoroastrians, who could not fail to notice the similarity between their traditional calendar and the new official one, to the point where some speculated that the shah would reveal that he too was actually a Zoroastrian, and would soon declare Iran to be a Zoroastrian state once more.

As silly as these speculations were, the seeming pre-Islamic orientation of the state was viewed by the clergy as yet another attempt on the part of the throne to undermine religious institutions and morality. Some of the first actions taken by the new government of the Islamic Republic after the Revolution were to eliminate official glorification of the pre-Islamic empires in an excess of pentup recrimination for actions seen as repressing Islam in the Pahlavi era. Once again, the United States was seen as the source for this "anti-Islamic" set of actions. Indeed, Ayatollah Ali-Asghar Dastqeib of Shiraz is reported to have sent a group to destroy the monuments at Persepolis and Pasargade in the summer of 1979, an action supposedly thwarted by Shiraz's other religious leader, Ayatollah Majdeddin Mahallati.

Setting the Stage—The Fall of the Shah

I have already remarked on the fact that the Iranian regime was so divorced from the people that statistics mattered more than social sentiment.[24] The public, torn between inner spirituality and external desire for material gains felt themselves virtually rent asunder by their ruler's schemes.[25]

It was all too easy to interpret economic failure as spiritual failure, projecting the collapse of the economy onto the symbolic relationship between ruler and people. This was as much a failure for rural people as for urbanites. Sadly, many extremely functional traditional institutions, such as the rural bonih cooperative system[26]—qanat irrigation, and tribal meat production[27]—were destroyed in the name of Western-oriented, "American inspired" modernization, to the economic detriment of the nation. Iranian industry in the 1970s placed heavy emphasis on such "turnkey" assembly operations; many firms concentrated on consumer goods to the exclusion of the far more essential infrastructural development.[28] The subsidized development loans available to well-connected industrialists were a far cry from the rates offered by private moneylenders to small businessmen, which ranged from 20–50 percent.[29]

The financial pressures were indeed horrendous on the less-privileged classes. The rural population was dramatically impacted. Hundreds of thousands abandoned their land in an exodus to the shantytowns that sprung up around all the large cities of the land.[30] As the state ran short of cash in the years preceding the revolution, the state began to crack down on the payment of taxes. Eventually, ten thousand inspectors were sent to the bazaar to examine store accounts. Guild courts eventually imprisoned 8,000 merchants, exiled 23,000 from their hometowns and fined as many as 200,000 more.[31]

Against this backdrop, the clergy joined forces in an improbable alliance with leftist and nationalist oppositionists, who still remembered with bitterness the forcible ouster of Prime Minister Mohammad Mossadeq by a CIA-led coup in 1953.[32] In this way, old oppositionist forces, some of whom had been railing against the monarchy for decades, suddenly found a new level of public support as hundreds of thousands of citizens who had never had a direct reason for protesting—such as having been arrested or tortured by SAVAK—became disaffected with the shah, and by extension, his supporter, the U.S. government.

The American Role

The United States was slowly and inexorably dragged into this symbolic complex of protest unwittingly and unwillingly. Because the natural explanatory tendency in Iranian popular historical imagination was to search for an external cause for social ills, the ready association between the shah and the United States followed naturally. The public penchant for thinking in this manner was, moreover, exploited in a highly successful way by the opposition to the shah—particularly by the religious opposition.

The message was quite clear: the attackers clearly identified the United States with the domestic policies of the shah. Disapproved economic policies included Iran's partnership with American oil companies and turnkey industry specialists, financial development schemes that seemingly led to inflation, and innovations in traditional employment areas such as agriculture, where agribusiness was destroying production. Social policies in which the United States was implicated included the training and advising of the dreaded Iranian secret police, SAVAK, which had arrested, tortured, and executed thousands of dissidents since its establishment. SAVAK had increased its activities in the early seventies, and these attacks on U.S. personnel were undoubtedly related to this.

The impression of the Iranian man on the street is in sharp contrast with the realities of the difficulties in the complex relationships between the American and Iranian governments. The shah was not especially happy when U.S. officials attempted to make contact with his political opposition. Even the simplest efforts to gain some first-hand knowledge of the feelings of the mass population were difficult. William Sullivan, U.S. ambassador during the revolutionary period writes: "I recall one day in 1978 when . . . I was visiting the holy city of Mashhad. In an effort to gauge the temper of the populace I decided to visit the bazaar. By the time I arrived there, the police had cleared out everyone except the shopkeepers and store owners, who were surly at the interruption of their commerce. From every perspective, my effort to obtain an objective insight was a disaster."

Even in day-to-day policy matters, Sullivan faced much contradiction in information which he could not easily resolve: "[W]henever I felt I could not make a definitive conclusion I used to pass all the conflicting information along to Washington without attempting assessment. This meant that often the more dire assessments from the young consular officers in the provinces were in contrast with the more measured reports from political officers in Tehran, who were in touch with government officials. It also meant that, in retrospect, too great a burden was placed on the sophistication and judgment of those in Washington who were responsible for making policy decisions."[33]

The excesses of SAVAK under the shah have been given an enormous amount of publicity both inside and outside of Iran (see United States Congress 1976). There may have been less torture than either SAVAK or the opposition forces care to admit. For the latter, the more horrible the picture of SAVAK, the more justified their struggle against the shah became. For SAVAK itself, rumors about its omniscience and ruthlessness only helped it to maintain a curtain of fear over the nation.[34] With regard to the United States, the chief link with SAVAK was the CIA. The CIA helped set up SAVAK,[35] but it was also accused by opposition forces of training SAVAK agents in torture techniques. Thus the United States was indirectly accused of being the direct cause of the torture of Iranian revolutionaries. A fact not so much emphasized today is that SAVAK was reconstituted under the leadership of the Islamic Republic as an organization called SAVAMA, with many of the same agents. Opposition to the Islamic Republic claims that torture is still being used.

This did not stop a few elderly die-hards from continuing to blame Iran's troubles on the British. One retired army colonel, whom I know personally, in a letter to his nephew in the United States was quite clear about this: "You will learn soon enough that the crimes of the shah and his fall were both engineered by the English, who hope through creating confusion to get their hands on Iran once again. Though the world thinks they are harmless, I know them—they are only waiting for an opportunity" (dated June 10, 1980).[36]

There were brief high hopes on the part of disaffected Iranians that Jimmy Carter's human rights campaign—one of the strong emphases of his presidency, would result in pressure on the shah, but American national interest apparently trumped this effort.[37] The disappointment of the religious opposition with Carter has already been noted above.[38] What is intriguing is that in later years, American analysts in effect blamed Carter for fomenting the revolution by promulgating human rights, but abandoning his resolve.[39]

Because of antipathy to the British, the United States made things worse by replicating almost exactly the tactics the British had used for more than 100 years in their dealings with Iran. These included demands for extraterritoriality, strong-arm tactics in the oil markets, manipulation of internal politics, and a disdainful attitude toward Iran and Iranians.[40] In other words, the United States gave no counter-evidence that it should *not* be labeled as the Great Satan. Its sins and its shortcomings were manifest, and its disdain for Iranian civilization kept it from answering the charges leveled against it.

As a metaphor, the Great Satan is thus far more than a rhetorical device. It is a statement of moral order that actually is more precise in its identification of the spiritual characteristics, rights, and legitimate actions of the Islamic clergy than in its specification of the crimes of the United States. Because of its wide classificatory power, it serves as an orientation device as well. Having Khomeini and the Islamic Republic at one antipode of spiritual legitimacy and the Great Satan at the other has allowed leaders of the Islamic Republic to position their enemies within a symbolic universe, which is easily understood by all Iranians. As an individual opposes the rule of the Islamic Republic, he draws closer in his moral position to the antipode of the Great Satan. Even being in contact with that antipode can endanger one's position. It is far easier to consider executing a person who is considered in this context, since his opposition becomes a variety of blasphemy.

The United States, for its part, did little to prevent itself from being identified in this manner. The Great Satan did not come into being at a single stroke with the taking of the hostages. Its creation as a suitable metaphor was a slow and steady process created over the years as the United States, in myopic fashion, persisted in digging itself into a ready-made villain's role.

As all serious students of culture know, symbolic structures are not erased quickly. The United States has become part of the Iranian cultural cosmology for the time being. It will take a great deal of creative work, and a rhetorician of at least the skill of Ayatollah Khomeini is needed to eradicate the image of the United States as Great Satan from the Iranian moral universe.

America Lives Up to Its Reputation

Following the Iranian Revolution, the United States might have been able to recover a positive image in the eyes of the Iranian people. However, for unclear reasons, the U.S. government continued to act in a manner that has confirmed its role as villain in Iranian eyes down to this present writing.

Protecting the Shah

The first great sin on the part of the U.S. government was the admission of Mohammad Reza Shah Pahlavi to U.S. soil following the Revolution. The shah was ill with lymphatic cancer. He had traveled to Egypt, Morocco, The Bahamas, and Mexico before President Jimmy Carter allowed him to enter the United States on October 22, 1979, for medical treatment. The shah had hidden his disease from everyone for many years, and the Iranian population was suspicious. They feared that the United States was engaged in an act of deception, and planned to return the shah to power as in 1953 with Mohammad Mossadeq.[41] First, Iranian leaders demanded that the United States allow a team of Iranian doctors to inspect the shah to make sure he was truly ill. The United States refused. Two weeks later Iranian militants seized the U.S. embassy in Tehran and took more than fifty American embassy personnel hostage, demanding the extradition of the shah in return for their release. The United States refused extradition but the shah later left for Panama and then Cairo, where he was granted asylum by President Anwar as-Sadat. Pahlavi eventually died on July 27, 1980. Many Iranians, even as the shah was dying, still believed that the United States intended to stage a coup. The hostage crisis continued for 444 days, setting the stage for hostile relations between the United States and Iran for years to come. The hostages were only released after Ronald Reagan took the presidential oath of office in January 1981.

Helping Iraq

The hostage crisis led indirectly to the next reason for hostility between the United States and Iran. This was the conduct of the United States during the Iran–Iraq War, from 1980 to 1988.[42]

On September 22, 1980, Saddam Hussein of Iraq took advantage both of the continuing hostage crisis in Iran and the political disarray in Tehran to invade the southwestern province of Khuzestan. Saddam believed that Iran was weak, and would put up no resistance.[43] The war quickly escalated. The Iraqis were bogged down just fifty to seventy-five miles inside Iran's border, having been repulsed by the Iranians.

The United States was an open supporter of Iraq during the war. The Reagan administration provided intelligence to the Iraqis through the CIA.[44] Richard Sale writes:

> The CIA/Defence [sic] Intelligence Agency relation with Saddam intensified after the start of the Iran-Iraq war in September 1980. During the war, the CIA regularly sent a team to Saddam to deliver battlefield intelligence obtained from Saudi AWACS surveillance aircraft to aide the effectiveness of Iraq's armed forces, according to a former DIA official, part of a U.S. interagency intelligence group. . . . According to Darwish,[45] the CIA and DIA provided military assistance to Saddam's ferocious February 1988 assault on Iranian positions in the al-Fao peninsula by blinding Iranian radars for three days.[46]

These facts were not lost on Iranians. They blamed the United States for its support of Iraq both during and after the war. As late as January 2003, the Iranians were still fuming over this matter. Citing *New York Times* and *Los Angeles Times* reports, the Voice of the Islamic Republic of Iran broadcast: "The Bush and Reagan governments allowed [Iraq] to buy goods with double use, including nerve gas and anthrax bacteria in order to prevent Iran's victory in the war in any way. In November 1983, a U.S. State Department official informed the then State Secretary George Schultz of the daily use of chemical weapons by Iraq against Iran. But this issue was not important for the United States."[47]

In the above passage, the Iranian commentators are objecting primarily to the callousness with which the United States supported Iraq. This became a primary theme of the Iranian opposition to the United States during this period.

Shooting Down Iran Air Flight 655

Despite dismay at U.S. support for Iraq during the war, nothing was more damaging to the U.S. reputation in Iranian eyes than the shooting down of Iran Air flight 655 over the Persian Gulf. On July 4, 1988, the USS. Vincennes, patrolling in the Persian Gulf accidentally shot down the commercial Iran Air flight, an Airbus A300 commercial liner. The Iranians claimed that the Vincennes gave the pilot no warning.[48] Foreign minister Ali Akbar Velayati called this event "the most inhumane military attack in the history of civilian aviation . . . a barbaric massacre."[49]

Rather than apologizing, then Vice President George H. W. Bush gave a startlingly callous defense of the U.S. action before the United Nations: "Mr. President, the critical issue confronting this body is not the how and why of Iran Air 655. It is the continuing refusal of the government of the Islamic Republic of Iran to comply with Resolution 598,[50] to negotiate an end to the war with Iraq, and to cease its acts of aggression against neutral shipping in the Persian Gulf . . . by allowing a civilian airliner to fly into the area of an engagement between Iranian warships and U.S. forces in the gulf, Iran must bear a substantial measure of responsibility for what has happened."[51]

The United States has never apologized for this event, and it remains a bitter issue for Iranians.

Economic Sanctions

The United States has imposed economic sanctions on Iran for more than twenty years. Formal sanctions were initiated in 1984 and renewed in 1995.[52] As the only nation in the world imposing such sanctions on Iran, it remains to be seen what they are accomplishing. Morgan and others claim that the United States is attempting a form of behavior modification through its use of sanctions:

> The U.S. would like Iran to adopt principles of Western liberalism. Ideally, it would see Iran become a secular society that valued individualism and an open economy. At a minimum, the U.S. wants Iran to behave as a liberal state internationally by valuing sovereignty and stability over the support of ethnic, religious, and ideological brothers. As will be seen below, the U.S. ideal point is at .8 [on an index of liberal democratic rule]: it would most like to see Iran be like Canada. Iran, as will be shown below, is currently at about .3 and (understandably) would like to remain true to its own philosophical

principles. The dispute, then, is over how liberal Iran should be, and the U.S. has imposed sanctions with the intent of forcing Iran to move to the right on this dimension.[53]

However, Morgan and others conclude that by 1997 (the date of the conclusion of their study), that "[the study] suggested that sanctions would result in no change in Iranian policy, and time has shown that the sanctions have not been effective."[54] Thus, the United States has engaged in behavior vis-à-vis Iran, which is merely antagonistic without achieving any results. This only provided more fuel for the Iranian regime to vilify the United States.

The Axis of Evil

President George W. Bush characterized Iran in his 2002 State of the Union Speech as part of an Axis of Evil in the world, along with Iraq and North Korea. The epithet was shocking to Iranians, especially since Iran had been cooperating with the United States in its military action against the Taliban of Afghanistan up to that point. It seemed that Iran could never do anything that would garner a positive reaction from a U.S. administration. The surprising hostility shown in President Bush's remarks had the unsatisfactory result of strengthening the public position of the most conservative elements of the Iranian government, and undercutting the reformers—precisely the opposite effect that was desired by the Bush administration. This was a case of the United States condemning itself to further opprobrium from the Iranians by issuing too strong an invective.

Finally, following the occupation of Iraq in 2003, the United States began to flirt with the idea of a "regime change in Iran."

Iranian Foreign Minister Kamal Kharrazi traveled to Turkey in April 2003, shortly after the U.S. invasion of Iran. With Turkish officials, he discussed preserving Iraq's territorial integrity, but undoubtedly he also discussed a possible American incursion in Iran, according to his spokesman Hamid Reza Asefi.

Responding to a question on the recent threats raised by U.S. officials against Iran, Asefi said: "If you mean political, economic and cultural threats, I have to say that the country has faced such threats since the victory of the 1979 Islamic Revolution. We are not concerned about any U.S. military threat."

It is easy to see that he meant: "We are concerned about a U.S. military threat."

This was reinforced on the same day by Iran's army chief, Major General Mohammad Salimi, who called on the country's armed forces to prepare for any confrontation with "probable foreign threats."

Iranians also pressed U.K. Defense Minister Geoff Hoon with questions about possible military action against Iran. Hoon claimed that no such action was proposed by the United Kingdom. The assurances rang hollow, however, as it became clear that Hoon, Prime Minister Tony Blair, and Foreign Minister Jack Straw were unwilling to speak for the United States. Straw said uneasily that although there was "no case whatsoever for taking any action," it would "worry me if it were true" that Iran and Syria were being lined up by the United States.

It is not clear that the United States was really serious about invading Iran. In April 2003, there was reported dissension in the White House about moving into Iran. The office of Douglas Feith, Undersecretary of Defense for Policy, had prepared invasion plans for both Syria and Iran. However, they were never presented to the National Security Council or to the president. Moreover, then National Security Advisor Condoleezza Rice was reported to be opposed to any further military action in the Middle East.

However, the fact that Israeli Prime Minister Ariel Sharon, as well as Secretary of Defense Donald Rumsfeld and other Bush officials called for action against Iran did not make the Iranians feel safer. Moreover, Condoleezza Rice accused Iran of supporting "terrorists" two months after the tragedy of September 11. Finally, a *Los Angeles Times* poll in the first week of April 2003 found 50 percent of Americans favoring "military action" against Iran if it "continues to develop nuclear weapons."

It is certain that any strike against Iran would be enormously more complex than the present invasion of Iraq, and would likely be more than America could handle in a ground war. Iran is almost four times the size of Iraq, with a complex terrain involving some of the most formidable mountains and deserts in the world. The population is three times as large as that of Iraq, and Tehran, the capital, has more than twelve million people. The young Iranian population provides a potential fighting force of ten million males.

Given these statistics, the United States would need to spend hundreds of billions to pursue such a conflict, with gargantuan losses of American life and no guarantee of any success. For these reasons, it is highly unlikely that the United States would ever try to invade Iran, but the skittishness with which even the mildest threats of invasion are met in Tehran shows that the Iranian people have still not recovered from their historical angst about U.S. intentions in their nation, and they continue to see the United States as hostile, even if the image of the Great Satan has faded.

In the face of difficulties that the United States might face in actually launching military action against Iran, the Bush administration flirted with supporting others who might do the job. Chief among these was the son of the deposed shah. Also called Reza, the young Pahlavi was largely out of the public eye until after September 11, 2001, when he suddenly surfaced as a possible Iranian ruler in a reformed government. For Iranians inside the country, his long exile and connections with the former shah made him an unacceptable potential ruler for Iran, but he was extraordinarily popular with Iranians in exile in California and other parts of the United States, who flocked to his cause. He was actively supported by denizens of Washington's neoconservative American Enterprise Institute, and was frequently seen there in the company of Michael Ledeen, a fellow of the Institute, who was a confidant of President Bush's chief political Advisor Karl Rove.[55] The Bush administration also flirted with supporting the Mujaheddin-e Khalq (MEK) in their efforts to overthrow the Tehran government,[56] and supporting Mahmudali Chehregani, leader of an Azerbaijan separatist movement calling for a federated Iran.[57]

In Early 2005, the United States was once again saber rattling with veiled threats to launch a military attack against Iran. In February 2005, rumors of a military buildup in Herat, Afghanistan, near the Iranian eastern border, began to raise alarms, and United States drone aircraft conducting surveillance of Iranian nuclear sites were detected by Iranian citizens who thought they might be UFO aircraft.[58] Newly minted Secretary of State Condoleezza Rice refused to rule out military action.[59] On February 19, 2005, correspondent Mark Jensen reported that former U.S. Marine and UNSCOM weapons inspector, Scott Ritter, told an Olympia, Washington audience that: "President George W. Bush has received and signed off on orders for an aerial attack on Iran planned for June 2005. Its purported goal is the destruction of Iran's alleged program to develop nuclear weapons, but Ritter said neoconservatives in the administration also expected that the attack would set in motion a chain of events leading to regime change in the oil-rich nation of seventy million—a possibility Ritter regards with the greatest skepticism."[60]

In the next chapter, I will deal with even more accusations levied against Iran by the United States, but with some greater justification than the mere name calling evoked by the Axis of Evil epithet, or by the saber-rattling of government officials in George W. Bush's second term. Unfortunately for the United States all of the justifiable criticisms against Iran are obscured and discounted by America's persistence in playing a villain's role in Iranian cultural terms.

—— 9 ——

The Sins of Iran

Demon Iran

Just as Iran has demonized the United States since 1978–79 in the worst possible terms for Iranian culture, so has the United States characterized Iran in the worst possible terms for U.S. culture. In the preceding chapters, I have tried to show how the actions of the United States call to mind the core elements of Iranian culture—those things that make Iranians doubt themselves, their motives and their stability as a nation. U.S. actions hit a cultural nerve in Iran.

The vilification of Iran since the revolution of 1978–79, and particularly since the hostage crisis following the war has been a continual process in Washington. It is almost as if nothing Iranians could do would spare them from the invective of the U.S. government. In this chapter I look at some of the things that Iran has done—or is purported to have done—that have created this sense of enmity on the part of the United States. Five principal activities in Iran stand out as particularly galling for Washington politicians: The hostage crisis of 1979–81, Iran's purported support of terrorists and terrorism, the treatment of cultural and religious minorities in Iran, the treatment of women under the Islamic Republic, and Iran's development of nuclear power—possibly nuclear weapons.

All five of these actions are areas of extreme concern for the people of the United States. It is hard to escape the conclusion that the reason for this concern is because they represent central uncertainties in U.S. culture for United States citizens. Iran's actions touch nerves in the American consciousness. The hostage crisis was a source of humiliation for a nation not yet comfortable with its role as an international leader. Iran's purported support of terrorism is seen both as a threat to the United States itself, and to the United States' chief regional ally, Israel. Iran's supposed discriminatory and misogynistic social policies calls into question the United States' own recent social evolution in the treatment of women and ethnic minorities. Finally, Iran's purported development of nuclear power is a painful reminder of the United States' own struggle with nuclear energy, starting with the destruction of Hiroshima and Nagasaki at the end of World War II. No one makes a person—or a society—more angry than someone whose sins remind a people of their own weaknesses.

Iran's actions in these areas, if they truly are as represented by Washington officials, would more than justify President Bush's inclusion of Iran in an Axis of Evil, with Iraq and North Korea as outlined in his 2002 State of the Union Address.

However, of the five areas of concern, only one was a concrete, demonstrable, and proven act enacted with the responsibility of the state itself— the hostage crisis. The other four can be classified as tendencies, purported action, actions that are moot or irrelevant today, or the actions of subgroups within Iran, acting without state sanction. Nevertheless, all five are treated in public address as if they were all established fact and ongoing threats to the U.S. and the world. This concretization of rumored action was aided by President Bush's Axis of Evil rhetoric.

European experts almost immediately denounced President Bush's Axis of Evil epithet as inaccurate. European Union commissioner in change of external relations, Chris Patten, called it "absolutist and simplistic." French Foreign Minister Hubert Vedrine echoed these sentiments, saying: "Today we are threatened by a simplistic quality in U.S. policy that reduces all the problems of the world to the struggle against terrorism. It is not properly thought out."[1]

Looking at these areas of concern one by one may be helpful in seeing why the United States has expressed opposition to Iran in such harsh terms, but examining them carefully will reveal the extent to which this picture is accurate.

The Hostage Crisis

The Iranian hostage crisis may be one of the most devastating non-war-related events to have ever occurred between two nations. As mentioned above, the crisis—the occupation of the U.S. Embassy in Tehran, and the holding of embassy personnel as captives—was precipitated by the admission of the shah to the United States for medical treatment following the revolution. The perpetrators were "Students Following the Line of Imam Khomeini," who expected to occupy the embassy for only a few days. They actually held the hostages for 444 days.

During this time, the hostages were subjected to public humiliation. Blindfolded, they were marched before crowds of people shouting "Death to America." The American flag was frequently burned or trampled during these public showings. These actions were broadcast relentlessly to the public of the United States, creating anger and resentment. The ABC Network began a series of nightly reports called "America Held Hostage," counting off the number of days the hostages were in capture every night. Eventually this special broadcast became institutionalized as the news program *Nightline*.

Of course, the hostage taking was utterly illegal according to international law. The United States repeatedly called on the fledgling government of the Islamic Republic to do something to stop the hostage holding. However, Khomeini and his supporters did not have control over matters.[2] They were being challenged from both the left and the right as the groups bid for power in the fledgling republic. The very course of the revolution was at stake for Khomeini, who initially seemed ambiguous concerning the crisis. His astonishingly bold move to embrace the hostage taking, undercut his most severe critics. The right wing was outflanked by Khomeini's shrewd embracing and sanctioning of the hostage taking. In this way, Khomini regained control of the revolution.

The hostages thus became a tangible symbol of U.S. "imperialism" on Iranian territory. On the back of the hostage crisis, Khomeini was able to establish a new form of government—the Islamic Republic, to convince the Iranian public to ratify a new constitution that would consolidate power in the hands of the clerical establishment, and to reconstitute the Iranian parliament. In truth, as horrific as the spectacle of American hostages on parade was for the U.S. citizenry, they were exceedingly useful to the leaders of the Iranian revolution.[3] The hostage crisis became an industry for both Iran and the United States for two years.

For the United States the crisis was maddening. It completely destroyed the presidency of Jimmy Carter, who was not re-elected after his first term.[4] This ensured that Democrats would never be sympathetic with the Iranian regime. The Republican administrations of Presidents Reagan and Bush became equally unsympathetic, even though, arguably, the Iranians had aided Reagan's presidential campaign.[5] Thus both Republicans and Democrats developed a solid enmity toward Iran during this period.

The Iranian government and the hostage-takers seemingly broke every rule of diplomacy. There was no one of authority to talk to. In desperation, U.S. special forces made an abortive rescue attempt,[6] which further infuriated the Iranians. The Iranian government used the abortive rescue mission as further proof of American "plots" against the revolution, further solidifying their hold on political affairs in Iran, and hardening the rhetoric against the United States.

In truth, the more the Iranian government inveighed against the United States, the more dangerous it became for Iranian officials to negotiate with American officials. Letters that were sent through back channels to Iranian officials were brought, sealed, into public press conferences, then opened and read out loud on the spot to avoid any possibility that Iranian officials might be thought complicit with the Americans.

Eventually the hostage crisis was settled through the culturally appropriate method of mediation through a third party—Algeria.[7] The crisis was a net financial loss to Iran, as many of its assets in the United States remained frozen.[8] Following the hostage crisis, the United States continued to press claims against Iran in international legal bodies; investigations were held for more than a decade.[9]

Iran—Supporter of Terrorists and Terrorism

The United States first began to identify Iran as a supporter of terrorist activities in 1984 under the Reagan administration. The accusations have grown more strident from year to year, until recently the State Department described Iran as "the most active state sponsor of terrorism in 2002."[10] The State Department document claims that: "[Iran] provided Lebanese Hizbollah [*sic*] and Palestinian rejectionist groups—notably HAMAS, the Palestine Islamic Jihad, and the Popular Front for the Liberation of Palestine-General Command—with funding, safehaven, training, and weapons. Tehran also encouraged Hezbollah and the Palestinian rejectionist groups to coordinate their planning and to escalate their terrorist activities against Israel. Iran also provided support to extremist groups in Central Asia, Afghanistan, and Iraq—those with ties to al Qaeda; less was provided to the groups opposed to Israel."[11]

This accusation has been repeated so often that it is cited almost universally as fact. An example was a series of appearances and op-ed articles by the late Constantine Menges, a senior fellow at the conservative Hudson Institute, who had no previous association with the Middle East, being primarily a Latin American and Soviet specialist. He wrote in the *Washington Times*:

> Since 1979, oil-rich Iran under a clerical dictatorship has been the progenitor of Islamic terrorism directed against the United States, Israel and the governments of many Muslim countries such as Saudi Arabia and Bahrain. Spending hundreds of millions of dollars annually for propaganda and in support of terrorists such as Hamas, Islamic Jihad, Hezbollah and the Palestine Liberation Organization, Iran has been coresponsible for the deaths of thousands of innocent civilians, including more than 1,500 Americans. These attacks include the 1983 truck bombs in Lebanon that destroyed the U.S. Embassy and later killed 241 Marines in their barracks as well as the 1996 attack against U.S. personnel in Saudi Arabia.
>
> After September 11, 2001, Iran held a series of terrorist summits, in which it openly increased its budget for Hamas and other terrorist organizations, while also providing additional millions for the families of homicide bombers who would kill civilians. Iran also publicly

announced training for terrorists volunteering to strike in America, and for the destruction of civilian passenger aircraft with shoulder-fired missiles. Iran is complicit in the recent upsurge in violence against Israel; Iran's leaders have said that, when they have nuclear weapons, they will be ready to "annihilate" the Jewish state.[12]

All of this sounds both ominous and convincing, but none of these assertions are documented in any governmental or nongovernmental source. Menges simply spouts unsubstantiated accusations and rumor. His assertions are a textbook example of "truth by repetition." Despite his lack of Middle East credentials, and the fact that he is merely mouthing unsubstantiated or exaggerated claims from Iranian detractors in the State Department and Department of Defense, Menges was given extensive press play for this message.

Of all of these claims, the assertion of Iranian support for Hezbollah is verifiable, but it is important to understand what the nature of this support is, and the extent to which Iran is able to influence the actions of this Shi'ite Lebanese group. Moreover, it is important to take into consideration the kind of organization Hezbollah has become in recent years.

Iran had an undeniable interest in the fate of the Shi'ite coreligionists in Lebanon following the revolution of 1978–79. Like Iranians, the Shi'ite community was under oppression both from Sunnis and Maronites. Moreover, Palestinian refugees, settled in their midst without consultation with their community, both served as a drain on weak local economic resources, and drew fire from Israel. The Shi'ite felt helpless and frustrated. The successful revolution in Iran was enormously inspirational to them, and the Iranians were looking for ways to spread their revolution. The Iranian central government was weak and scattered after the revolution, and semi-independent charitable organizations, called *bonyads* (literally, "foundations"). Sponsored by individual Shi'ite clerics, the bonyads began to help the fledgling Hezbollah organization get off the ground.[13] This was not state support. Moreover, given the semi-independent corporate nature of Shi'ite clerics, especially in the early days of the revolution when internal power struggles were endemic, there was little the Khomeini government could do to curtail these operations. Moreover, Syria also had a strong role in the early establishment and sustenance of Hezbollah, and its role was far more practical and self-serving than that of Iran's. Indeed, Iranian ideologues could never have had entrée to southern Lebanon without Syria's cooperation.[14]

Now, after nearly two decades, the export of Iranian revolutionary ideology in this loose and uncontrolled manner may have succeeded too well. Whereas the bulk of the Iranian population has at least some doubts about their own government, Hezbollah maintains a stronger commitment to the symbolic legacy of the Iranian Revolution than do Iranians, according to

Daniel Byman, writing in *Foreign Affairs*. Byman also points out that: "[Iran] lacks the means to force a significant change in the [Hezbollah] movement and its goals. It has no real presence on the ground in Lebanon and a call to disarm or cease resistance would likely cause Hezbollah's leadership, or at least its most militant elements simply to sever ties with Tehran's leadership."[15] In short, although Iranian religionists were instrumental in aiding its establishment, Hezbollah has now taken on a life of its own. Even if all Iranian financial and logistic support were cut off, Hezbollah would not only continue, it would thrive. In short, Iran's support is not essential for Hezbollah to continue. Commentator Byman states flatly that if the United States is really serious about stopping Hezbollah, it would do better to attack Syria than Iran.[16]

Hezbollah has achieved stability and prominence by becoming as much a social welfare and political organization as a militant resistance organization. Dwight J. Simpson writing in 2004, reported that it had "twelve elected parliamentary members . . . [and] many Hezbollah members hold elected positions within local governments." The group had by that time built five hospitals and is building more. It operated twenty-five primarily secular schools, and provided subsidies to shopkeepers. The source for their money, Simpson reported, is zakat—the charitable "tithe" required of all Muslims.[17] The Shi'ite, having seen their coreligionists in Iraq succeed in initial elections in 2005, have hopes that they too will assume the power in Lebanon that accords with their status as the nation's largest community. As this happens, Hezbollah will cease to be a terrorist group and will gradually assume the role of a political organization. Its "terrorist" activities will be reframed as national defense, especially as they gain control of conventional military forces and weapons.[18]

The charitable operations of Hezbollah strengthens the likelihood that the money sent from Iran to Hezbollah is non-state-level financial support.[19] Moreover, branches of Iran's Islamic guard may have been operating in Lebanon without the full knowledge of the central government of Iran. Given the ambiguity and looseness of Iranian government control over support for Hezbollah, the U.S. government claims that Iran has an organized state-level support system for such activities are clearly purposely exaggerated. Further weakening American claims, starting in 2000, Iran began to systematically remove its forces from Lebanon. By April 2005, virtually all had been removed.[20]

Why would the United States repeat such unfounded assertions with such incessant regularity? One reason is that these assertions accord with the American mythic worldview that asserts that terrorism would be unable to exist without state support.[21] If a state is needed to support groups like Hamas and Hezbollah, then Iran is an ideal candidate, ergo it is assumed that the connection must exist! The concomitant claims of Iranian State support for extremist groups in Central Asia, Afghanistan, Iraq, and al

Qaeda are pure fantasy, but they do help the United States government support its own mythic view of the world.

According to the Council on Foreign Relations, a relatively neutral source, the U.S. government characterizes Iran's support of terrorism as follows: "Iran mostly backs Islamist groups, including the Lebanese Shiite militants of Hezbollah (which Iran helped found in the 1980s) and such Palestinian terrorist groups as Hamas and Palestinian Islamic Jihad. It was also reportedly involved in a Hezbollah-linked January 2002 attempt to smuggle a boatload of arms to the Palestinian Authority. Iran has given support to the Kurdistan Workers' Party, a Kurdish separatist movement in Turkey, and to other militant groups in the Persian Gulf region, Africa, and Central Asia."[22]

Beyond the waning support for Hezbollah noted above, there is no evidence whatever that Iran has been providing aid to the Kurdistan Workers' Party, nor that it was involved in the smuggling of arms to the Palestinian Authority. This final accusation is the most specious of all. Understanding why it was put forward, and why the U.S. government continued to use it as proof of Iranian involvement with terrorism involves more than just Iran and the United States. U.S.-Israeli relations also come into play. It is worth taking a closer look at this incident, since it seems typical of the manner in which the George W. Bush administration has justified their vilification of Iran as a supporter of terrorism.

The Karine-A *Incident*

"Iran's arms shipments and support for terror fuel the fire of conflict in the Middle East, and must stop," President Bush said in April 2002.[23] A few days before that, on the CBS news program *60 Minutes*, Israeli Prime Minister Ariel Sharon similarly accused Iran of aiding Yasser Arafat and the Palestinian Authority. The accusation had been repeated continually from January 2002 until April by one or another Israeli politician. However, this was never substantiated.

To Iranian specialists, the accusations of Bush and Sharon were completely absurd, precisely because of the conservatism of the Iranian government. Iranian conservative mullahs were publicly opposed to Arafat, because hardliners in Tehran opposed the Israeli-Palestinian peace process. Moreover, they view the entire Palestinian Authority with suspicion because they are secular, not religious in their orientation. The idea that Tehran's religious leaders would suddenly support Arafat seemed implausible. Moreover, Israel's inability or unwillingness to provide hard evidence of Iranian government involvement with the Palestinians makes the accusation doubly suspect.

Israel's principal accusation, and thus that of the U.S. government, is based on the January 3, 2002, incident of the *Karine-A*, a ship purchased in Lebanon and commandeered by Palestinian military officials. The boat was indeed loaded with eighty crates of weapons on the Iranian Persian Gulf island of Kish, an international free port where virtually anything is available for a price. It then sailed to Dubai, where other cargo was loaded, and preceded to the Suez Canal. Israeli intelligence intercepted it in the Red Sea and off-loaded the cargo.

Only the Israeli accusations of Iranian government involvement were in dispute, never the facts of the arms shipment. There is no prima facie reason to attribute the purchase to the Iranian government. Israeli intelligence reportedly showed "incontrovertible evidence" to American intelligence sources, who then informed the press that they believed it. The "evidence" was never made public. In fact, there were, and are today many plausible private purchasers of arms for Palestinians—wealthy Saudi Arabian businessmen, nongovernment conservative religious groups in Iran, and, of course, the expatriate Palestinian community.

Kish Island is an international bazaar in open waters, as accessible from the Arabian peninsula as from Iran. Moreover, after the January 3 incident there was no other indication of Iranian involvement with the Palestinians. Why, therefore, did Sharon repeat the accusation of continued interference from Tehran, and why did the Bush administration use this unsubstantiated accusation to reinforce the idea that Iran was a wholesale supporter of terrorism?[24]

One possible answer may have more to do with Israeli-American relations than with Iranian actions. After September 11, Israel became worried that the United States was warming up to the government of Iran, because of Iran's help given to American forces combating the Taliban in Afghanistan. Iran at that time was the one nation that not only expressed opposition to Israel itself, but also to the peace process that would bring Israel and the Palestinian authority into rapprochement. Any alliance between Washington and Tehran was therefore seen as a threat to Israeli security.

Thus, Israel had some very good reasons for wanting to mislead the United States about Iranian actions. Three possibilities arise if the Iranians were indeed not aiding the Palestinians. The first possibility is, Israel was lying to the United States about Iran, and Americans believed the lies. The second possibility is that the United States may have doubted Israeli accusations, but preferred to accept them to gain leverage over the Iranians. Finally, Washington may have been collaborating with Israel to condemn Palestinians, Iranians, and the Hezbollah middlemen who brokered the arms shipment. The first possibility is easy to accept. Israeli officials knew that Iran is deeply distrusted in Washington. The likelihood that Israel is providing disinformation to the United States about Iran is reinforced when it is remembered that Israeli intelligence tried to discredit Iran in another matter, by telling Washington that Iran was harboring al Qaeda members—

an accusation that proved to be patently false. In considering the second possibility, many in Washington have good reasons to choose to believe the Israeli information even if they doubt it. There are many in Washington who also view a thaw in relations between America and Iran with horror. Old officials from the hostage crisis years, such as former Undersecretary of Defense Richard Pearle, are deeply involved with the current administration. Their attitude is that even if Iran did not do this deed, it was the kind of thing they might do, and so the United States should condemn them for it anyway. One salutary effect would be to put Tehran on notice not to try anything funny, just in case they were thinking of it.

Finally, Israel and the United States may be collaborating knowingly in public chicanery. President Bush's inclusion of Iran in his Axis of Evil in the State of the Union address in January caused worldwide public outcry. Iran seemed to have done nothing to justify such a status. Sharon and Bush knew this, and to justify continued alienation of Iran, they have found a convenient accusation that Iran could not easily repudiate.

For Israel, a successful accusation of Iranian involvement with the Palestinians made it seem that the cause of the horrific violence in Israel originated outside the Israel/West Bank/Gaza region. If Iran could be seen as a prime cause of Palestinian violence, Israeli responsibility would be seemingly reduced. By reinforcing each other, Israel and America created a common enemy, and made the Palestinian opposition look like an extension of worldwide terrorism.

The world may never know the truth in the matter of the *Karine-A*, but the apparent effort by Israel and the United States to create a chimera out of Iran certainly served the broader purpose of deflecting blame for West Bank violence temporarily away from the Israelis.

Other "Terrorist" Support

The Council on Foreign Relations has listed several other examples of the U.S. government's evidence of Iran's support for terrorism: In November 1979, Iranian student revolutionaries widely thought to be linked to the Khomeini government occupied the American Embassy in Tehran. Iran held fifty-two Americans hostage for 444 days; observers say Iran had prior knowledge of Hezbollah attacks, such as the 1988 kidnapping and murder of Colonel William Higgins, a U.S. Marine involved in a U.N. observer mission in Lebanon, and the 1992 and 1994 bombings of Jewish cultural institutions in Argentina; Iran still has a price on the head of the Indian–born British novelist Salman Rushdie for what Iranian leaders call blasphemous writings about Islam in his 1989 novel *The Satanic Verses*; and U.S. officials say Iran supported and inspired the group behind the 1996 truck bombing of Al-Khobar Towers, a U.S. military residence in Saudi Arabia, which killed nineteen U.S. servicemen.[25]

An inspection of these accusations shows that the only accusation that is definitive is the hostage crisis. The others are unsubstantiated accusations, or not terrorist support at all. Ayatollah Khomeini's fatwa, issued against author Salman Rushdie was chilling, cruel, and likely not justified in Islamic law, but it was a fatwa—an opinion by a senior cleric. Islamic believers were free to follow it or not. It proved to be an embarrassment for the Islamic Republic, but after Khomeini died and was replaced as faqih by Ayatollah Ali Khamene'i, it was impossible to rescind it. Most people now believe Khomeini's *original* fatwa to be moot.

The accusation that Iran had prior knowledge of Hezbollah attacks in Lebanon cannot be proved, and in any case is no evidence for support of these specific terrorist acts. The bombing of the Al-Khobar Towers was carried out entirely by Saudi Arabian elements. No Iranians were ever tied to the acts, and the accusation that Iran somehow "inspired" the bombing is equally insubstantial.

The strongest argument for rejecting the idea that Iran was behind the Al-Khobar bombings is that Saudi dissident elements had a much more compelling set of reasons—reasons which were revealed when a second bombing occurred on May 12, 2003 that duplicated those earlier bombings. As in the *Karine-A* event, the crucial facts needed to understand the Saudi bombings have to do with internal Saudi Arabian politics and the role of the United States in them.

President Bush characterized the May 12 suicide bombing in Riyadh, Saudi Arabia, as being carried out by "killers whose only faith is hate."[26] In fact, the devastating attack was a calculated, political act that was probably not orchestrated by al Qaeda and not directed primarily against the United States.

Both the May 12, 2003, bombings, the Al-Khobar attacks, and an earlier 1995 attack were made against the same targets. These were the U.S. Armed Forces, and the Vinnell Corporation, a Fairfax, Virginia, company recently acquired by Northrop–Grumman that trains the 80,000-member Saudi Arabian National Guard under the supervision of the U.S. Army.

Why Vinnell? The Vinnell operation represented everything that was wrong with the U.S.-Saudi relationship in the eyes of antimonarchist revolutionaries. The corporation, which employs ex-military and CIA personnel, had close connections with a series of U.S. administrations, including the current one. It had a contractual relationship to train the Saudi Arabian National Guard since 1975. The corporation was instrumental in the American "Twin Pillars" strategy, whereby both the Saudi Arabian regime and the shah of Iran would serve as U.S. surrogates in the Gulf region to protect American interests against the possible incursion of the Soviet Union.

Even before the first Gulf War, when the United States established a formal military presence in Saudi Arabia, Vinnell was a "stealth" military presence in the kingdom. It was seen as a military colonizing force. The Saudi Arabian National Guard, by extension, was seen as a de facto American military force.[27]

Additionally, the Guard had the specific duty of protecting the Saudi Royal Family, which the revolutionaries saw as corrupt. Without the National Guard, the family would be weakened, perhaps to the point of dissolution.

Thus, since the Vinnell operation looked to revolutionaries like a body of U.S.-sponsored mercenaries shoring up the National Guard, and by extension, the royal family, striking the Vinnell operation was a logical strategy to damage the Saudi regime.

There was another reason for attacking Vinnell. The dissidents knew that the United States had agreed to withdraw the 5,000 troops stationed at the Saudi Arabian Prince Sultan Air Force Base. However, the withdrawal would not have covered the Vinnell contract employees, who presumably would have stayed in Saudi Arabia and keep propping up the regime. Since the revolutionaries wanted all Americans out of Saudi Arabia, they were looking to the ouster of this group as well as the troops based at the Prince Sultan base.

Furthermore, the compound that was bombed was a relatively easy target. It was not as heavily defended as an embassy or ministry.

The 1995 attack also involved Vinnell. The terrorists attacked the Saudi National Guard Headquarters, where the Guard was trained by Vinnell. The bomb killed six people and injured many more. Among the dead were five U.S. citizens, including two soldiers. Two Saudi opposition groups took responsibility for the blast: the Tigers of the Gulf and the Islamic Movement for Change. Both had previously criticized the ruling Saudi monarchy and U.S. military presence. The 1996 attack on the Al-Khobar Towers was also directed at the U.S. military, and at the support troops for the Saudi Armed forces, including the National Guard.

Not only was Iran not the likely perpetrator of these bombings, but the facts of the earlier attacks call into question the theory that the al Qaeda operation directed by Osama bin Laden was responsible for the May 12 bombing. Ali al-Ahmed, executive director of the Washington-based Saudi Institute for Development and Studies, said on the PBS news program *NewsHour* on May 13 that this was a "homegrown operation" that borrowed ideas from al Qaeda but was not directed by Osama bin Laden. Americans became used to thinking of al Qaeda as the primary terrorist opponent of the United States. The Bush administration encouraged a public view of al Qaeda as a highly organized group with omnipotent, worldwide reach. This led to a general view that every group espousing violent political change was an emanation of Osama bin Laden's machinations. The view is inaccurate. Insofar as it has a structure at all, al Qaeda is a group of loosely affiliated cells, many of which have no knowledge of the operations of the others.

Groups opposed to the Saudi regime have been in continual existence for decades, predating bin Laden's activities, and certainly predating the Iranian Revolution. As soon as their leaders are arrested or killed, they regroup and renew their attack. It is more likely that al Qaeda, a relatively new organization, sprung from these earlier groups, rather than the other way around.

The desire of the George W. Bush administration to link all attacks on U.S. facilities to a global terrorist network is the undoubted cause of the accusation that Iran was behind the Al-Khobar Towers bombing, and that al Qaeda was behind the more recent bombings. What remained was to link Iran to al Qaeda, and members of the Bush administration tried desperately to do just that. "Of course, they have senior al Qaeda in Iran, that's a fact," said Secretary of Defense Donald Rumsfeld at a Pentagon briefing on May 21, 2003.[28] He had not one scrap of evidence.

Given that the Wahhabi movement of Sunni Islam, to which Osama bin Laden is allied, considers Shi'ite to be tantamount to illegitimate religionists, calling on their followers to eschew social contact with them, it is not likely that there would be much desire on the part of Iranian officials to cooperate with al Qaeda. Another reason for lack of cooperation are the historic ties between al Qaeda and the Taliban of Afghanistan, whom the Iranian government strenuously opposed.

Currently, the United States is wedded to a bipolar, black-and-white view of the world. On one side are the United States and its friends. On the other are the dark forces of terrorism. So strong is this formulation, and so self-centered the American worldview, that Washington no longer seems able to entertain the thought that there might be revolutionary groups that have entirely local reasons for their actions. The tragic attacks might well have taken place if the United States had not had a presence in Saudi Arabia. However, the existence of a quasi-military command force in the form of the Vinnell Corporation virtually guaranteed that Americans would be caught in the cross fire of what was arguably a local revolutionary action.

Women in the Islamic Republic

In Europe and the United States there is a pervasive stereotype about women in the Islamic world. They are perceived as helpless victims of a patriarchal system that oppresses and enslaves them. This image is reinforced through superficial observations of female dress, and outdated stories of female treatment in Islamic nations. Perhaps no work reinforced this stereotype more poignantly than the first person account *Not Without My Daughter*. This movie, a sad story of an American woman who married an Iranian man from a conservative family, only to have him capture their daughter and prevent her from leaving the country with her mother, painted a cruel picture of Iranian life for Americans, particularly when it was turned into a major motion picture.[29] The author, Betty Mahmoody, undoubtedly suffered terribly through a harrowing experience, but it is also clear that she never informed herself before marriage about Islamic custody laws, in which children belong to the family of the father after a specified age. Most Iranians who have seen the movie acknowledge that there are families who fit Mahmoody's profile of her in-laws, but they point out that the vast majority of families are kind and loving.

Similarly, many of the events reported in the highly popular book, *Reading Lolita in Tehran* by Azar Nafisi are outdated for Iran today. Although the classroom exercise of the "reading of *Lolita*" that defines the book in its early chapters takes place in the mid-1990s, the bulk of Nafisi's observations of female repression date from the early 1980s—more than twenty years ago. Many of the conditions she describes for the conduct and treatment of women have been modified significantly today.

A somewhat updated picture of the situation of women *and* men in Iran is provided by Azadeh Moaveni in her memoir, *Lipstick Jihad: A Memoir of Growing Up Iranian in America and American in Iran*,[30] which dates from the late 1990s and early 2000s. Moaveni's couturier is an Iranian male, with whom she meets unchaperoned. He designs "modest" dress as high-fashion, telling her: "We'll do this cut like a toga, in two tones, so that when you walk the beige will peek out underneath. It'll be so elegant. So subtle. So modest."[31] Writing about the ski slopes north of Tehran, Moaveni points out that "The figure-obscuring bulk of a ski suit satisfied the dress code requirement, and a wool cap, with hair tucked beneath, stood in for the veil. So on any given winter day men and women skied down the slopes looking and acting as though they were in Colorado or Switzerland.[32]

Beyond matters of dress, Moaveni portrays women in all areas of employment and professional responsibility in Iran today. To be sure she documents the stratagems that both males and females must pursue to avoid increasingly lax scrutiny from religious authorities, but it is quite clear from her writing that the system is loosening considerably, and largely due to the incessant efforts of women and young professionals themselves.

The simple truth is that the stereotypes of Iranian women promulgated in the West are hopelessly out of date. They ignore the extraordinary efforts that women have made on their own behalf to improve their lives. These efforts range from simple choices in clothing to more dramatic life choices in family composition, education, and career.

It is of course true that women live under greater restrictions in personal conduct today than they did under the Pahlavi regime. Especially during the first years of the revolution, female conduct and dress was heavily regulated. Even today, women and men are strictly segregated when in public. In light of progress that has been made in women's rights in the United States today, these restrictions seem oppressive, and many Iranian women object to them. It is not the dress codes or segregation that the women object to, since many women are equally restricted in other Islamic nations. What angers many women is the fact that restrictive female conduct is obligatory and imposed by law. Of course, there are perhaps just as many women who always had observed the modest dress code as a matter of course, even under the Pahlavi regime. For these women, the strict laws of conduct are not oppressive, because they have always conducted themselves according to those codes.

The big difference separating women in today's Iran from the past is the considerable social and educational progress that women are making throughout the nation. Iranian women are part of a regional progressive trend for women. There is, in reality, a New Islamic Woman emerging in the Middle East and South Asia—an intelligent, empowered woman, staking out her goals in life, but consciously carried out within the framework of Islam. One successful female entrepreneur told me: "Islam doesn't prevent me from having a career; in fact, it makes me a better businessperson because it provides a framework of ethical behavior that I can use to persuade my suppliers and customers to deal fairly with me."

Although, as mentioned above, no place in the Islamic world today has been more stigmatized for its alleged poor treatment of women than Iran, the reality behind the scenes belies the superficial appearances one may encounter on the streets. I began to travel to Iran in the late 1990s for the first time in many years. The most surprising development for me was the clear impression that, contrary to American belief, women in the Islamic Republic were better off in many respects than they were under the Pahlavi regime.[33] Moreover, their condition has continued to improve.

Women have always had a strong role in Iranian life. Their prominent and often decisive participation in public political movements has been especially noteworthy. Brave and often ruthlessly pragmatic, women have been more than willing to take to the streets in a good public cause throughout modern Iranian history.[34]

The Islamic Republic has made a special point of emphasizing women's equality in education, employment, and politics as a matter of national pride. Although women have served in the Iranian legislature and as government ministers since the 1950s, there are more women in the current parliament than ever served under the Pahlavi regime.

The average marriage age for women has increased from eighteen years before the revolution to 23.9 years in 2004. Education for women is obligatory and universal. More than 75 percent of he nation is under 25 years of age, and for this population, literacy for both men and women is well over 90 percent even in rural areas.[35] Women actually constitute 60 percent of university enrollees, including fields such as engineering and medicine. As women's education has increased, Iran's population growth rate has fallen dramatically. It was 3.2 percent in 1986 and dropped to 1.2 percent in 2001. This is "one of the fastest drops ever recorded," according to Janet Larsen of the Earth Policy Institute. Larsen goes on to point out that "From 1986 to 2001, Iran's total fertility—the average number of children born to a woman in her lifetime—plummeted from seven to less than three. The United Nations projects that by 2010 total fertility will drop to two, which is replacement-level fertility."[36]

Female employment is the one area where women have suffered a decline since the years immediately preceding the revolution. However, the statistics are difficult to assess, since unemployment is extremely high for both men and women (30 percent). Under the current Islamic regime, virtually all professions are theoretically open to women. A class of female religious leaders has even emerged. They have attended religious training schools and have the title *mujtahedeh*, the female form of the word *mujtahed*, or "religious judge."

Virtually the sole limitation on female employment is that women must maintain modest dress or *hejab* in the workplace. Islam requires that both women *and* men adopt modest dress that does not inflame carnal desire. For men this means eschewing tight pants, shorts, short-sleeved shirts, and open collars. Iranians view women's hair as erotic, and so covering both the hair and the female form are the basic requirements of modesty. This precludes women from some physically active professions. In earlier years, revolutionary guards accosted women who violated the dress codes in public, including wearing makeup. Today these attacks are rare, although periodic backlashes by the Revolutionary Guard and the conservative judiciary are troubling. Such attacks can be violent and sudden, and all the more surprising because they are much rarer than in the years following the revolution.

It should be noted that many middle-aged women who had prominent positions under the government of the shah would disagree with the positive assessment of affairs I am providing here. Many of these women emigrated to the United States and to Europe where they remain somewhat out of touch with day-to-day developments in Iran itself. Many are nostalgic for the monarchy, and take the physical and social restrictions imposed on women as a matter of law to be a backward step in social life. They are aghast at accounts of violence or imprisonment imposed on women who do not meet these standards. Nevertheless, it is not so much the restrictions themselves, as the fact that they are not a matter of choice that is most disturbing to these women, and as I have already pointed out, these restrictions have not prevented women from getting an education, or in developing careers.

For many centuries, women in Iran have practiced modesty by wearing the *chador*, a semicircular piece of dark cloth that is wrapped expertly around the body and head, and gathered at the chin. This garment is both wonderfully convenient, since it affords a degree of privacy, allowing one to wear virtually anything underneath. But it is restricting, since it must be held shut with one hand (some women cleverly use their teeth in awkward moments).

Since the revolution, an alternate form of acceptable dress has emerged of the kind described above by Azadeh Moaveni's coutourier in *Lipstick Jihad*—a long dress with full-length opaque stockings, a long-sleeved coat, and a head scarf covering the hair. The dress has gradually evolved into a thin shoulder-to-ankle smock called a *manto* after the French word *manteau* ("overcoat"). The head scarf has been transformed into a hood modeled after a similar garment in North Africa called a *magna'eh*.

In adopting this dress, women have been wonderfully inventive. The manto, though dark in color, is often made of silk or other fine fabric, embroidered, finely tailored, with elegant closures. Women wear it over jeans or other Western fashions. The *magna'eh* may also be of satin and turned out in fashionable colors like eggplant or dark teal. In short, the Iranian women have made virtue out of necessity and created high fashion from their concealing garments. Moaveni even describes a runway fashion show to display these elegant garments.[37]

Many older westernized women decry any restrictions on their dress, but younger women who grew up in the Islamic Republic take it in stride. "I view it as a kind of work uniform," claimed one female journalist. "I'm far more concerned about press restrictions than about dress codes."

Indeed, the universal modest dress code may have helped women from conservative families. "Before the revolution, religious parents would not let their girls even go to school for fear they would be dishonored," said Parvaneh Rashidi, a Tehran schoolteacher. "Now they have no trouble letting their daughters go anywhere." Judging from the large number of women one sees today on the streets, in retail management, in offices, and on the university campuses, Ms. Rashidi appears to be more than correct in her assessment.

Iranian women may actually be in the vanguard in the Islamic world. As their progress becomes better known, they are sure to inspire others to pursue their dreams. The New Islamic Woman is a reality, and will undoubtedly be a force to reckon with in the future.

Treatment of Minorites

Iran is a pluralistic nation where people of numerous ethnic backgrounds, language groups, and religious traditions have lived in relative harmony.[38] The constitution of the Islamic Republic continues the tradition; minorities are specifically represented in the Iranian parliament. As originally enacted in 1979, Article 64 stated that the Zoroastrians would have one representative as would the Jews. The Assyrians and Chaldean Christians together would share one elected representative. The Armenians in the north and south of Iran each would have one elected representative. The Article also provided for additional representation every ten years if a given minority group increased by 150,000.[39]

Of the three sources of minority status—ethnicity, language and religion, it has been religious differences that have caused the greatest difficulty over the years.[40]

Armenians and Assyrians, among Christian groups are very ancient[41] Tribal peoples, some of who speak varieties of Turkic languages are also frequently cited as disadvantaged.[42] Among linguistic minorities are Arabs in the southwest province of Khuzistan and along the Persian Gulf littoral, Kurds in the West, Azerbaijanis in the Northwest, Turkomen in the North-east, and Baluchis in the Southeast.[43] All minority communities in Iran are bilingual in their native language and Persian.[44] Recently, the government has begun school instruction in minority languages, a sharp departure from the government of the Pahlavi era, which repressed non–Persian languages.[45] These ethnic groups retain their identity even when they emigrate to the United States or to other locations.[46]

The question of official persecution of these minorities is frequently cited as a "problem" in the West, and there is no question that there was difficulty in the early days of the revolution, particulary with the strong Jewish community—the largest non–Israeli Jewish community in the Middle East. However, the matter is complicated, because the Jewish community of Iran is of great antiquity. It has the distinction of being the most ancient in the world in continuous residence in one place, since Iranian Jews date from the removal from Babylon. The tomb of Queen Esther is located in ancient Ecbatan—modern day Hamadan. The community has continually thrived, and has played an extensive role in Iranian culture and history.[47] Judeo–Persian is acknowledged as the earliest form of modern Persian.[48]

Iranian Jews are fiercely chauvinistic about their Iranian culture. In some ways they are the most Iranian of all populations in the nation. Afshin Molavi, in his recent memoir, *Persian Pilgrimages: Journeys Across Iran*, interviewed a young Iranian Jewish man, Pooya, whose attitudes were typical:

> "It was not easy for us in the early days of the revolution," Pooya said. "We were not persecuted, of course, but we felt uneasy. You know what I mean, right?" He whispered the last sentence, looking around as he spoke. I knew what he meant. Ayatollah Khomeini, then the new leader of Iran, regularly cited the state of Israel and Jews as international conspirators in plots to destroy Iran. . . . "I was too young to remember much," Pooya said, "but I do remember a loud argument between my parents over my father's gold necklace with the Star of David on it. My mother told my father to stop wearing the necklace. She thought it might cause problems. My father, however,

refused to take off the necklace. He said that he was a proud patriot of Iran, and no Iranian government could ever tell him otherwise. He kept saying that he was an Iranian and very proud! He was yelling it loudly. My mother cried. She said that it would only be temporary, in case the new government checked for these things. But my father refused. In the end he turned out to be right. Nobody bothered him."[49]

There was initial persecution of Iranian Jews following the revolution. Seventeen have been executed since 1979, including Habib Alqanayan, a head of the Jewish community, who was executed in 1979. As a result, a large number of Iranian Jews did move to Israel and to the United States after the revolution, particularly to Los Angeles,[50] where they maintained their Iranian identity.[51]

The incident that has made Iranian Jews—and most of the world—most nervous, aside from the execution of Alqanayan, was the arrest of thirteen Iranian Jews in 1999 in the city of Shiraz. According to the Anti-Defamation League, "Those arrested included a rabbi, community leaders and a sixteen-year-old boy. Eleven of the arrested were from Shiraz, two from Isfahan. While the thirteen were not formally charged for well over a year, the Iranian Government accused them of spying for the 'Zionist regime' and 'world arrogance.'"[52] The trial was long and dramatic, and eventually ten of the defendants were sentenced to prison terms lasting from four to ten years.

However, this event was not exactly what it seemed on the surface. For one thing, not all those arrested were Jews—eight Muslims were also accused. Second, this was a local trial in Shiraz, out of the hands of the national officials. Then-President Khatami reportedly worked behind the scenes to secure the release of the prisoners. "The President called for a fair trial and has been quick to point out that eight Muslims are also accused in the case. Khatami publicly met with a Jewish member of parliament to discuss the trial, and government officials agreed to go over issues with a Human Rights Watch representative visiting Iran."[53] Although ten defendants were eventually sentenced, the judge in the case was unusually solicitous. According to Azadeh Moaveni writing for *Time* magazine: "In perhaps the most remarkable face of Iranian justice seen in many years, Judge Sadeq Nourani not only agreed to a meeting with Iran's chief rabbi, but paid the defendants an emotional visit in prison. When he handed out gifts ahead of [the] Jewish observance of Passover, some of the accused wept."[54]

Knowledgeable observers pointed out that the trials may have had far less to do with persecution of the Jewish community, and more to do with the struggle between hard-liners and reformers in the government. Reportedly the arrests and trial had been staged by zealous prosecutors trying to undermine President Khatami on behalf of the conservative clerics in advance of the presidential elections in 2001.[55] Khatami, as part of his re-election campaign had issued a large number of statements calling for the rule of law and religious tolerance. When Khatami was re-elected, and there was nothing to be gained by continuing the incarceration of these individuals, they were released. Five were released shortly after their sentencing in July 2001. Eventually all were released, the last five having been freed on February 19, 2003. The official announcement of the release was not issued until nearly two months after the event. Clearly the officials were trying as hard as possible to rectify an embarrassing situation in the quietest manner they could.

The most palpable persecution of any minority group in Iran is the persecution of the members of the Bahá'í faith. Seyyed Ali-Mohammed (1819–50) founded the new religion called Bahá'í in 1844. Ali-Mohammed was called the "Báb," which means "the gateway."[56] Bahá'í grew out of Islam in a manner similar to the way Christianty grew out of Judaism, and Islam out of both. The government, along with the conservative Islamic clergy attempted to suppress the Bahá'ís. Eventually 20,000 people were killed, including Ali-Mohammed himself in 1850. Mirza Husayn Bahá'u'lláh and his supporters continued the Bahá'í faith, having been designated by the faithful as the latest messenger from God to humankind. The Bahá'ís later came to Europe and the United States, and have a worldwide following of more than five million.

The Bahá'í community in Iran has been persecuted since its founding. It attracted the attention of the great British Persian literary scholar, Edward Granville Browne, who wrote extensively about the movement.[57] It is curious that the adherents of Bahá'í were originally largely converts from other religious minorities in Iran—Jews, Zoroastrians, a few Christians and approximately 25 percent Muslims. The community has long practiced religiously approved dissimulation (*taqiyeh*) as a means of protecting its members. This sanctioned use of concealment of one's faith was also practiced historically by Shi'a Muslims. In prerevolutionary times, Bahá'ís in Iran were regularly asked about their faith on government employment applications. They simply left that question blank, thus both announcing and failing to announce their confessional preference. If they had done otherwise, their applications would have been rejected.

Bahá'ís are persecuted in Iran for two reasons. They are seen as heretical because of their belief that the Báb and Bahá'u'lláh superceded the Prophet Mohammad. Second, as one Iranian acquaintance put it: "They are not a religion, they are a political movement created by the British to undermine Iran by undermining Shi'ism." Certainly, Edward Browne's fascination with the religion created an indelible association between Bahá'í and the British, in the sensibility of some Iranians during a period when British colonial domination of the region was the source of political unrest. In any case, this persecution has been continual since the founding of Bahá'í, and as regrettable as it is from the perspective of the outside world, does not have its origins in the post–Revolutionary government.

Nuclear Matters

President George W. Bush declared on June 25, 2003, that "we will not tolerate" a nuclear-armed Iran. Over subsequent months, as the U.S. occupation of Iraq became more problematic, the idea that Iran had a developed a nuclear weapons program became conventional wisdom in Washington. It was cited as a virtually proven fact. However, President Bush's words were empty. The evidence for a nuclear weapons program in Iran simply did not exist. On November 26, 2003 the International Atomic Energy Agency (IAEA) adopted a resolution that condemns Iran's eighteen-year cover-up of its nuclear program, but welcomed Iran's new openness and cooperation. The IAEA resolution was based on an earlier report released on November 10, which said there was "no evidence" of a covert arms program although it claimed that "the jury was still out" as to whether one existed.[58,59] The IAEA Resolution was passed, much to the chagrin of the Bush administration,[60] who tried to get Iran brought before the U.N. Security Council for violation of the Nuclear Non-Proliferation Treaty (NPT) to which it was a signatory. Sanctions by the Security Council would have resulted in international economic sanctions against Iran, something European nations were not willing to support.[61]

Crucial to the understanding of the nature of the nuclear power struggle between Iran and the United States is the realization that Iran's possible development of nuclear weaponry is not the principal issue. The United States has a long, unsuccessful record of trying to prevent nuclear weapons proliferation, but this effort has always been undertaken with the equally important goal of preserving the United States' own nuclear weapons superiority. The Nuclear Non-Proliferation Treaty to which Iran is a signatory was supposed to preserve rights to peaceful development of nuclear technology while preventing new weapons development. The NPT is one of the oldest active international treaties in the world. It was signed in 1968, and entered into force in 1970 well before the Iranian Revolution, the fall of the Soviet Union, or current concerns with terrorist activity in the world. At a special conference, a majority of the NPT signatories agreed to an indefinite extension of the treaty in 1995. Israel, India, and Pakistan are non-signatories, and North Korea withdrew from the treaty in 2003. The treaty does more than prevent new nuclear weapons development. It also requires the United States and other nations to reduce their nuclear weapons stockpiles. The George W. Bush administration hates the treaty because of these restrictions on the United States, and because it allows nations the United States does not like, such as Iran, to develop nuclear technology, which, it is claimed, could be "weaponized" in the future. In fact, the United States is in violation of the weapons reduction provision of the treaty, while accusing Iran of developing a weapons program. The crucial scientific fact upon which this accusation hinges is that the "enrichment" of uranium to make it suitable as a fuel for a nuclear power reactor is the first stage in making it suitable as a fissile material for a bomb.

Iran has been working toward developing the capacity for uranium enrichment since before the revolution. Progress in achieving this goal had been concealed from nuclear weapons inspectors until, in November 2004, Tehran signed a temporary agreement with Germany, France, and Britain to cease uranium enrichment and the IAEA issued Iran a clean bill of health, effectively avoiding Security Council intervention. The European powers hoped to persuade Iran to abandon uranium enrichment altogether in exchange for technology aid and economic concessions. The United States continued to press the Europeans to insist on pressing Iran to cease all nuclear development activity, while refusing to engage with Iran in any kind of direct negotiations. In April 2005, Iran finally lost patience and insisted that nothing would stop Iran from exercising its rights under the Nuclear Non-Proliferation Treaty, to which it is a signatory, to enrich uranium for peaceful purposes.

Iran in 2003 was building a 1,000-megawatt nuclear power plant in Bushehr with Russian help. The site was common knowledge. It had been under construction for more than three decades, since before the founding of the Islamic Republic. Two other nuclear research facilities, then under development, came to light in 2003: a uranium enrichment plant in the city of Natanz and a deuterium ("heavy-water") facility in the city of Arak. But this was in fact, irrelevant at the time of the accusations. The Arak and Natanz facilities, none of which were in operation, were not at issue. The only question of interest should have been whether these facilities offered a plausible route to the manufacture of plutonium-based nuclear bombs, and the short answer was: they do not. This was the conclusion of the IAEA.

The Bushehr plant was, at the time of the IAEA resolution, the only part of the argument that would in any way demonstrate that Iran was embarked on a nuclear weapons program, but it was, at the time, the part which could readily be analyzed. Accusations of Iranian intentions for the the Natanz and Arak facilities, presented as evidence by the Bush Administration, remained a patchwork of untestable, murky assertions from dubious sources, including the People's Mojahedeen (Mojaheddin-e Khalq, MEK or MKO), which, as already stated above, the United States identified as a terrorist organization. They asserted—or inferred—that there were centrifuges for enriching uranium (an alternative to fissile plutonium for bombs) or covert facilities for extracting plutonium.[62] Neither of these claims—nor Iran's denials, for that matter—were especially credible. The sources were either unidentified or emanated from the same channels which disseminated the stories about Iraq's nonconventional weapons. These same sources had targeted the Shifa Chemical Plant in Khartoum, bombed by the United States in 1998 under orders from the Bill Clinton administration, because it was rumored to have been producing chemical and biological weapons.[63]

The testable part of the claim—that the Bushehr reactor was a proliferation threat—was demonstrably false for several reasons, some technical, some institutional: the Iranian reactor yields the wrong kind of plutonium for making bombs; the spent fuel pins in the Iranian reactor would, in any case be too dangerous to handle for weapons manufacture; any attempt to divert fuel from the Iranian plant will be detectable; and the Russian partners in the Bushehr project have stipulated that the fuel pins must be returned, as has been their practice worldwide for other export reactors.

Just as there are many different kinds of nuclear reactors, there are different forms of plutonium, distinctions which are frequently never made in public discussions of nuclear proliferation.

There are two different kinds of reactors: heavy-water or graphite-moderated reactors; and pressurized, or "light-water" reactors (PWRs). The Dimona nuclear power plant in Israel is an example of the former.[64] The Bushehr plant is the latter.

The Israeli plant is ideal for yielding the desirable isotope of plutonium[65] necessary for making bombs. The Iranian plant will produce plutonium, but the wrong kind. It will produce the heavier isotopes: Pu240, Pu241 and Pu242—which actually detract from its use in bombs.

Crucial to extracting weapons-grade plutonium is the type of reactor and the mode in which it is operated. The Israeli-type plant can be refueled on "on line," without shutting down. Thus, high-grade plutonium can be obtained covertly and continuously. In the Iranian plant, the entire reactor will have to be shut down—a step which cannot be concealed—in order to permit the extraction of even a single fuel pin. In the Israeli reactor, the fuel is recycled every few weeks, or at most every couple of months. This maximizes the yield of the highest-quality weapons-grade plutonium. In the Iranian-type reactor, the core is exchanged only every thirty to forty months—the longer the fuel cycle, the better for the production of power.

For the Iranian reactor at Bushehr, any effort to divert fuel will be transparent because a shutdown will be immediately noticeable. In the Israeli plant, the procedure is clandestine and only sophisticated surveillance aircraft can detect the production of bomb-grade plutonium. No case of production of bomb-grade material from fuel from an Iranian-type plant has ever been reported.

Some Bush administration officials claim that Iran's nuclear energy program is unnecessary given its oil reserves, therefore it must exist for weapons production. Ex-CIA director James Woolsey claimed in an interview on the PBS program *Frontline*, on February 23, 2003: "There is no underlying [reason] for one of the greatest oil producers in the world to need to get into the nuclear [energy] business."[66]

That reasoning is essentially fallacious—nuclear power can make sense in a country with vast amounts of gas, particularly given the unusual circumstances in the Iranian hydrocarbons industry. There are needs for gas in Iran which command much higher priorities than power plants. First, more and more gas is vitally needed for reinjection into existing oil reservoirs (repressurizing). This is indispensable for maintaining oil output levels, as well as for increasing overall, long-term recovery of oil.

Second, gas is needed for growing domestic uses where it can free up oil for more profitable export—substitution and new uses such as bus and taxi fleets.

Third, gas exports—via pipelines to Turkey or in liquefied form to the Subcontinent—set an attractive minimum value for any available natural gas. In fact, Iran concluded a large contract with Sinopec, a major Chinese energy firm in November, 2004 for $100 billion for development of a major Chinese Gas Field and delivery of Liquified Natural Gas (LNG).

Fourth, the economics of gas production in Iran are almost backwards, certainly counterintuitive. Much of Iran's gas is "rich"—it contains valuable by-products (LPG and light condensates). However, since Iran abides by its negotiated OPEC production quotas, and since the quotas de facto recognize total output of both crude oil and gas-derived condensates, the rich gas actually displaces crude oil within the quota. That crude oil is cheaper to produce. Hence, the usual by-product credit, familiar elsewhere in the industry, is very much smaller than one might expect.[67]

Overall, therefore, as illustrated by more comprehensive financial analysis, it can reasonably be argued that gas in Iran has economic uses which are superior to power generation, in spite of Iran's much touted large gas reserves. The economic rationale is therefore plausible—the costs of gas versus nuclear power generation are sufficiently close that the choice is a standoff.[68]

The shah's original plan, articulated in the 1970s, foresaw a dozen or more nuclear reactors. The scheme then was pure chutzpah. In those years, natural gas was a waste by-product and was being flared—disposed of by being burned off in the fields. Today, given the costs versus values of gas, and given the reported bargain price for the Russian reactor, the economics of nuclear power, in an ostensibly gas-rich state such as Iran, are paradoxically plausible.

Even if Iran proves to have ambitions for developing nuclear weapons, any actual production is years, perhaps decades away. Moreover, Iran has fully acquiesced to the international inspections process. Iran is a signatory to the Nuclear Non-Proliferation Treaty (NPT). On June 22, 2003, the head of the Iranian Atomic Energy Organization, Gholam-Reza Aghazadeh, reiterated that all of Iran's nuclear facilities are open for inspections by the International Atomic Energy Agency (IAEA) in compliance with treaty guarantees. This served as a precursor to the IAEA Resolution of November 26, 2003, which announced the brokered deal, in which Iran agreed to an additional inspection protocol and voluntarily agreed to cease uranium enrichment procedures. In 2004, some additional research operations were discovered by the IAEA, leading to a "censure" of Iran for "insufficient co-operation" in the inspection process.

The nuclear question in Iran has always been a matter of national sovereignty rather than a desire for weapons domination. With a nuclear-armed Pakistan on the East, an unstable Iraq with 135,000 American troops on the West, Afghanistan with more American troops to the Northeast, the strange governments of Azerbaijan and Turkmenistan on the North, and the volatile Persian Gulf on the South, Iran has every reason to be nervous about its own defense. There is a national pride factor as well. Iran is a civilization with a 2,500-year continuous history. It feels that it should be the dominant power in the region.

Iranians hate being told what to do by people with whom they have no relationship. The suspicion on the part of Iranians has always been that the United States pressured the IAEA to issue censure declarations. This is seen by Iranians as an example of *ghodrat-talabi* or "power mongering." The term is used for people who try to exercise power without having the social license to do so. It is an extraordinarily negative trait in Iranian culture, and when it is detected, people resist it furiously, even to their own detriment. This explains why Iranians have seemed to withhold information from inspectors even when it was not in their interest to do so. As long as the United States keeps up this indirect pressure, the Iranians can be expected to continue to resist.

Whether Iran has substantive nuclear weapons ambitions is not knowable from credible sources. But references to the Bushehr power reactor, and the Natanz and Arak research facilities, and the other less verified research efforts, such as an abandoned facility in the Lavizan section of Tehran and Parchin, 19 miles southeast of Tehran, as evidence of such ambitions are at best disingenuous and uninformed, if not outright disinformation.

It should be noted that Iran's spiritual leader, Ayatollah Ali Khamene'i issued a fatwa—an authoritative opinion regarding nuclear power usage. This was cited prominently in a television interview with Hassan Rowhani, Secretary of Iran's Supreme National Security Council on February 8, 2005. A portion of the interview is cited below, translated by the U.S. government's Foreign Broadcast Information Service (FBIS) on February 9, 2005:

> according to the esteemed leader's [Ayatollah Seyyed Ali Khamene'i] fatwa [religious decree] which he announced at Friday prayers, the production, stockpiling and use of nuclear weapons is not allowed by Shari'ah [religious teachings]. As a result, when the country's leader, clearly states this fatwa during Friday prayer, there is no place for such a discussion. We think that when on the one hand we are members of the NPT, then we have given a legal guarantee that we are not pursuing nuclear weapons. When the Iranian leader issues such a

fatwa, then we have given a political, religious, and ideological guarantee that we are not pursuing the production of nuclear weapons. As long as we are a member of the safeguards treaty and are a signatory to the NPT Additional Protocol, we have also given the technical guarantee. So to sum up, we have given political, legal, technical and religious guarantees. These objective guarantees (words rendered in English) which the Europeans are after, can't be more than these four concrete guarantees. As a result, on the whole, we don't think that it will be in the interests of our country and national security to do such a thing (pursue the production of nuclear weapons).

On November 15, 2004, Iran concluded a treaty with Great Britain, France, and Germany in which Iran stated explicitly: "Iran reaffirms, in accordance with Article II of the NPT, it does not and will not seek to acquire nuclear weapons. It commits itself to full cooperation and transparency with the IAEA."[69]

As a final word on this matter at this writing, Mohammad Elbaradei, Chief United Nations Inspector, provided an interview to *Newsweek* magazine on February 7, 2005. In this interview he points out that at the time of the interview there was no evidence of Iranian nuclear weapons, including the Natanz, Arak, Lavizan, and Parchin sites. Moreover, U.S. accusations of Iran's noncooperation with the weapons inspectors were unfounded:

NEWSWEEK: The Bush administration is arguing that you are not tough enough on Iran.

ELBARADEI: It depends how you define soft. Eighteen months ago, Iran was a black box. Now we have a fairly good picture of what is happening in Iran. We understand how complex and extensive that program is. Through our tenacity, Iran's facilities that could produce fissile material are frozen. And we are still going everywhere we think we need to go to be sure there are no undeclared activities in Iran. Between our tenacious verification and the diplomatic process, I hope we will be able to get a package solution to the Iranian issue.

NEWSWEEK: U.S. experts say that Iran has cheated and lied and continues to do so.

ELBARADEI: If they are still cheating, we haven't seen any evidence of that. We report facts. When they cheated, we said so; when they are cooperating, we say so. We have been supervising their suspension of fuel-cycle activities. Recently, we got access to a partial military site.

NEWSWEEK: How can Iran justify its full nuclear-fuel cycle as part of a peaceful program?

ELBARADEI: They probably can make a technical justification. The argument they also make is that they have been isolated, so they have to be self-sufficient.

NEWSWEEK: There is talk of a U.S. strike against the Iranian nuclear program.

ELBARADEI: Talk about military activities at this stage is very unhelpful. I cannot see how a military solution can resolve the Iran issue.[70]

Footnote: Iran as the Author of the Second U.S.-Iraq Conflict

In the summer of 2004, a strange rumor began to surface as the United States' war in Iraq and the subsequent occupation began to unravel. Every justification presented by the Bush administration for the invasion of Iraq had been discredited. There were no "weapons of mass destruction" being readied by ruler Saddam Hussein. Iraq could not be tied to the terrible attack on the World Trade Center in New York and the Pentagon in Washington on September 11, 2001. Moreover, creating "freedom" for the Iraqis seemed an increasingly distant goal; interim Iraqi president, Iyad Allawi installed on June 28, 2004, immediately claimed the right to institute marshal law.

Ahmad Chalabi, an Iraqi exile who worked furiously lobbying the U.S. Department of Defense to make him the new Iraqi ruler, was bypassed in favor of Allawi. Chalabi was blamed for American failings, and fell from grace just as the new interim government was about to take power. However, many American officials had publicly supported Chalabi, and were embarrassed by these accusations.

What better solution for the Bush administration than to blame the entire problem on Iran? Rumors began to arise that Iran had purposely misled the United States by planting false information through Ahmad Chalabi, about such things as weapons of mass destruction in order to "trick" the United States into ridding the region of Saddam Hussein, their old enemy. Why? So Iran could infiltrate Iraq and take over the region. Since Iran had already been established for several decades as an all-purpose villain, this far-fetched story was widely promulgated and believed by many.

Conclusion—Things Are Seldom What They Seem

If Iran truly did all that the United States accused it of, there would be more than enough justification for the cultivation of a continued hostile attitude toward the Islamic Republic. On inspection, however, it seems that the principal impetus for U.S. enmity began with the hostage crisis of 1979–81, and relations never recovered. The subsequent accusations—state support of terrorists, mistreatment of women, development of nuclear weapons, and blame for the Iraq invasion break down when examined closely. The hostage crisis itself was a terrible episode in the relations between the two countries, and it may be that as long as the current regime is in power in Iran, they will suffer criticism and scrutiny from the United States.

The U.S. government—no matter which party is in power—would like to see a very different form of government in Tehran, and the leaders of the Islamic Republic know this. For this reason, accusations of current misdeeds on the part of Iranian officials coming out of Washington are viewed askance by Tehran.

The widespread claims of the mistreatment of women in Iran are largely based on the extremes of the immediate post–revolutionary period—statements which ignore the extraordinary self-empowerment of Iranian women—a development that has resulted in astonishing improvement in social, educational, and employment conditions for women since the Revolution.

It seems that the United States' desire to effect regime change in Iran is fueled by accusations of development of nuclear weaponry. If state development of "weapons of mass destruction" could be the justification for eliminating the government of Saddam Hussein in Iraq, it may have been the thinking among the neoconservative political philosophers of the George W. Bush administration that the "discovery" of a weapons program in Iran might serve as the justification for eliminating the clerical regime that the United States has found so inconvenient and unpleasant. The fact that there was scant justification for these accusations was seemingly irrelevant to the Bush administration.

The accusations continued during the June 2005 presidential elections in Iran. A short account of the mutual demonization between the United States and Iran at that time, witnessed just before this book went to press, is included at the end of Chapter 11.

—— 10 ——

The Birth of Postmodern Conflict
How Iranian Media Came of Age

Iran underwent more than a political revolution in 1978–79;[1] it underwent a revolution in communication as well. In a short period, Iran went from a society where communication rarely took place outside of the family and immediate community to one where international communication became routine. The Revolution was made possible by enhanced media. The post-Revolutionary period was guided by new media; the reform movement of Mohammad Khatami was likewise media-driven. In the years proceeding the Revolution, only the largest urban areas had electricity and phone service. A quarter-century after the revolution, Iran is awash in satellite dishes, Internet cafes, and cell phones.[2]

Iran regularly talks to the United States, though there are no regular diplomatic relations. The communication takes place through the media. A dance of indirect messages is continually passing back and forth between the United States and Iran, as both sides check out the online newspapers, satellite news broadcasts, blogs, and e-mail messages that pass continually between the two nations.[3]

Even though the media and its use *looks* the same for both Iran and the United States, it is worth asking whether the mass media are culturally defined institutions for each society, or do they belong to some neutral international sphere? This is not a frivolous question, for the mass media in the post–World War II years may be the first forms of human communication that are at once culture specific and pan-cultural. Some few years ago, television, the cinema, and even radio, were limited in their world distribution to a minority of the world's population in the industrialized spheres. Even the news media traditionally held their influence largely among literate peoples—yet another minority. Yet, in the words of Colin Cherry, "What distinguishes mass communication today from earlier modes is its universal application to all classes and conditions of people, its relevance to all, not only to a highly literate aristocracy."[4]

Still, studies of the media functioning within the context of traditional culture are rather rare, and exist on a somewhat anecdotal level,[5] except for those works which deal with the role of the mass media in national development or health care delivery programs.[6]

Mass media function in several distinct ways in the world today. Media which operate exclusively within the context of a particular nation fill a cultural space in society, and thereby acquire a distinct and unique cultural definition. This cultural space may have been occupied by some other institution or object at an earlier time, in which case newly developing mass media can be seen as supplanting or becoming merged with earlier existing phenomena. In some areas of the world this leads to the death of traditional information and entertainment channels in the face of television and radio. In other places, new media become a vehicle for the support of traditional cultural activities.

At times mass media, when introduced have produced revolutionary effects as they forge a new space for themselves in the management of time and energy of the population as a whole. Thus the media are cultural forces as well as cultural objects. They produce specific concrete effects in their operation, which cannot be easily predicted. Each case requires close analysis of the web of cultural meanings operative at any given moment in a society under study. In India and the United States, for example, newspapers have traditionally played an important investigative role in government, and can be credited on occasion with the rise and fall of political regimes. In other nations, newspapers are considered an adjunct of official politics, and serve primarily to support official policy, rather than serve as its adversary. In many nations, the media have become adjunct to the overall commercial activity of the nation, and are potent vehicles for advertising— so much so that they may depend on advertising revenues to keep their operations going. In other nations, the media are thought of primarily as educational or cultural resources, and as such eschew commercial ties. Clearly, in each case one can see that the medium has become imbued with a whole range of meanings and potentialities for action within one culture which it will not possess for another.

There is another way in which the media play a cultural role in today's world, which has not been at all well-documented.[7] Media can now be seen to be truly international in scope. Because of this, they often *overlap* cultural space. This is to say that media generated at one place may be received at other places where the effects are not calculated in advance by the originators. The oldest historical example of this is shortwave radio broadcasts. These have long been used for propaganda purposes, but their unintended effects on political and social developments within receiving nations are not easily seen in advance.

Yet another example of this kind of unintended effect is seen in the world-wide syndication of television programs. Although the United States is the leader in this area, European nations, Mexico, and Egypt also provide television comedies and dramas for a wide audience outside their country of origin. In all cases, the effects of these television productions over a long period of time have come to be questioned by social critics in the nations importing them. Indeed, if the exporting nations only realized how often these exported programs result in negative views of the country of export, they might look harder at the desirability of allowing this activity to continue unrestricted.[8]

Some areas of media are designed to be international in scope. International newspapers and news magazines, and the aforementioned shortwave radio broadcasts must be recognized as important forces in international political relations. In this case the danger lies in assuming the opposite—that these areas of publication and broadcasting are somehow above the concerns of international cultural and political relations because they are targeted for an international audience.

One way to test the functions of mass media as cultural institutions is to study them in a dynamic context. By observing how they function when society is under stress, it should be possible to see if they adhere to a characteristic cultural logic in their operations.

The Iranian Revolution offers an unprecedented opportunity to study the functions of the media institutions of a non-Western society during a period of rapid change. During the Iranian Revolution, the press, radio, and television all seemed to undergo a radical transformation. Yet, once the revolution had taken place, within six months, the media returned to its familiar, well-established cultural role in Iranian society.

Remarkably, the same can be said to be true of the role of international media in Iranian society. The one important innovation in Iranian public communication—the cassette tape as a media tool—continued to play its newfound role in the media communication as an opposition tool to the revolutionary government. Studying this phenomenon may help students of the media in their cultural setting understand some of the dynamics in society that preserve the cultural shape of media institutions.

The Mass Media under Pahlavi Rule

The Iranian media during the reign of both Mohammad Reza Pahlavi and his father, Reza Shah were largely kept in check by the central government, and compelled to reflect views which were approved by central authorities. Only during the period of the prime ministership of Mohammad Mossadeq (1951–53) was there any relaxation of this rule of rigid censorship. Radio and television, which began as private commercial operations, were taken over by the government in the 1960s, and likewise used to promote an officially accepted view of the state of affairs.

Newspapers, it was claimed by the government, were not heavily censored. But in fact, if anything untoward appeared in the morning papers, the editor would receive a call from the Ministry of Information before breakfast. If the offense was great, all of the copies of the paper would be confiscated from dealers by the government before they went on sale.

The principal control over newspapers and magazines, which were privately owned, lay in government licensing procedures. If a publication did not publish for a specific period of time, its license would automatically lapse. If the government found a given publication to be continually offensive, it would force suspension of publication through various coercive means, (electrical inspections, building code violations, restriction on purchase of newsprint, and so on) until the license lapsed of its own accord. In this way it could get rid of those magazines and newspapers that it didn't like, and still claim not to have directly ordered them to close.

Print publications tried to survive as best they could. They downplayed local news, gave prominent coverage of the royal family and their activities, and provided strong coverage of international affairs. It was often frustrating for Iranians to be confronted with a newspaper that contained hundreds of lines of print on government scandals in Europe and America, but nothing of the corruption that all knew to exist at home; they could only experience this through the rumor mill. The Ministry of Information often would boast that they needed to do very little in the way of monitoring the newspapers, since they practiced such excellent self-monitoring.

Publications in foreign languages were surprisingly prominent in Tehran. There were two English language daily papers; one in French, and one German language weekly. The license allowed these publications was somewhat greater than that allowed Persian language newspapers.

The effects of radio on the Iranian population were enormous during the postwar years. Expensive radio sets penetrated the villages throughout the country, and served as an important communication link for the vast, remote, separated, areas of the sparsely populated countryside. Radio was, at the same time a somewhat controversial device, largely because of extensive broadcasts of popular and classical music. Under orthodox Islam, listening to music is highly disapproved. There is vague justification for music prohibition based on a few *hadith* (doings and sayings of the prophet), but not the Qur'an, which says nothing about music. However the more philosophical basis for the prohibition rests on the theory that music provides the means for an individual to be transported to a plane of attention and consciousness which is somehow outside of the here and now of the mundane world. Thus, to listen to music is in some sense to deny reality. This can be construed as blasphemous, since a denial of reality is a denial of God's Creation. Moreover, much popular music is thought to be lascivious. Although urban clerics would sometimes take a somewhat lax view of this prohibition, in rural areas public opinion has been historically quite clear that music is an improper human diversion. Thus, in rural areas of Iran, individuals buying radios would often claim that they were buying them only to listen to the news or to sports, but not for music.[9]

Nevertheless, it is clear that radio was indeed a source for music listening throughout the country. Moreover, Radio Iran became an important cultural institution throughout the country, not for news, but precisely for its controversial music. Rural areas possessed their own folk music, of course. This music, played at weddings and other celebrations, was an important aspect of rural life. The urban music played on the radio worked its way slowly into the folk repertoire until many urban melodies had become "folkloricised." As the national appetite for popular music grew, fed by radio broadcasts, writers began to look to the country for inspiration. Thus, rural folk melodies became incorporated into urban music. The vital link between the two traditions—urban and rural—was chiefly radio. Radio was matched in its impact on Iranian life only by television, which hit the nation like a bomb in the late 1960s and early 1970s. Its effects were profound in every part of the nation. National Iranian Radio-Television (NIRT), headed by a dynamic relative of Empress Farah, Reza Qotbi, and provided with an almost unlimited budget embarked on a drive to bring television to every area of the nation by 1976.

The ambitiousness of this goal is only properly understood when one takes Iranian geography into consideration. The nation is almost uniquely vast and mountainous. Television signals, in order to penetrate the valleys and vault over the mountains of the country had to utilize special technology. The system finally adopted was a microwave system which worked fairly well, but required a great deal of maintenance. As the coverage of the national television network spread, the public demand for the service became greater and greater. Lack of electricity seemed to be no impediment. In even the most remote villages, the sound of portable kerosene or gasoline generators could be heard every evening as the population watched their favorite programs.

If radio was the means for urban culture to spread into rural areas of Iran, television became the Iranian villager's window on the world. The dark urban cinema, with its morally questionable fare was heavily condemned by conservative religionists, but somehow, television escaped opprobrium. Some of the most conservative clerics went so far as to announce that they personally didn't watch television—a signal to their adherents that they should follow this example—but most religious figures remained neutral, saying only that popular music programs with "naked" (that is, bareheaded, barearmed) women should be avoided by the pious.

National Iranian Radio–Television generally did a reasonable job with television production, but like most of the world's television systems, it could not fill its entire schedule with home-produced fare. Thus, American and European syndicated programs became common. U.S. television star

Lee Majors came to Iran in 1978 expecting to be able to rest and be anonymous for a short period when he was under some pressure in the United States. He was completely shocked to be mobbed by rabid fans who recognized him as the "Six Million Dollar Man," which was being shown every week on Iranian television at that time.

The cultural impact of television cannot be underestimated. The reality of the television screen was overwhelmingly impressive for many, creating a whole new set of images of modern life for traditional Iranians. In the smaller, more traditional towns, there was predictably a degree of confusion in the predictable conflict between traditional local values and the more sophisticated values being shown on the screen. Parviz Kimiavi, a prominent contemporary filmmaker, documented this poignantly in his film, *The Mongols* (1973), where the coming of television is likened to the Mongol invasion, which destroyed Iranian society during the twelfth century.[10]

The social life of small towns was likewise transformed by television. In the traditional coffeehouses, storytellers who once entertained patrons were replaced by the television set. Mealtimes were dominated, as in the United States, by the television programs, particularly the news, which coincided with the usual times for the noon and evening meals, for the majority of Iranians. Television slowly took on the familiar role of legitimizing device for much of the population. What one saw on television was not necessarily any truer than what one read in the papers or heard on the radio, but somehow seeing events directly made them more real for viewers.

National Iranian Radio–Television had a curious attitude toward its public mission. On the one hand, it was a purveyor of much that was foreign to Iranian culture, vulgar and low in quality. Nevertheless, it also saw as one of its missions the rescue and revival of Iranian traditional culture. To this end it spent enormous amounts of money on the assembly and training of traditional musicians. It supported playwrights, actors, and directors, and gave out large grants for the production of film (indeed, even *The Mongols*, mentioned above, was produced with money from NIRT). It also sponsored live festivals and concerts, such as the annual Festival of Arts in Shiraz. These festivals were taped for later broadcast, but their cost was far greater than if the events had been produced for television alone. The results of all of this activity were impressive. In the space of ten years, a whole new generation of young artists had been developed through the good offices of NIRT, and the quality of their work was generally quite high. Some began to refer to NIRT as a "second Ministry of Culture," and indeed, there was a great rivalry between the two bodies over authority and roles.

The Changing Functions of the Media in the Iranian Revolution

The revolutionary events of 1978–79 demonstrate just how mutable the cultural role of the media can be during times of social and political stress.

The news media, radio, and television all played a highly prominent role in the conduct of the revolution itself, leading many to comment that the Iranian Revolution may have been the first revolution conducted by the media. Because their original roles in society were so different, the revolution produced different effects in each of the media considered in this discussion.

The first social protests to really sting the government began in the summer and fall of 1978. At that time the newspapers were somewhat at a loss as to what they were to print. When a confrontation with thousands of people took place on the streets with government troops, the papers couldn't simply ignore the fact—there were too many eyewitnesses to such events. In the early days, some of the papers took to quoting foreign news sources, as if that would reduce the onus on them, but this was patently absurd. The BBC (about which see below) became one of the principal sources for print commentary. Some papers would print BBC reports, along with government denials as a means of getting the news before the public by whatever means, however obtuse. The government became highly upset at the increased freedom being exercised by the newspapers, but was at a loss as to how to handle the situation.

On August 27, 1978, Prime Minister Jamshid Amuzegar was removed from office, and Ja'afar Sharif-Emami, an old-timey Iranian politician took over. He was faced with an immediate crisis, as government troops clashed with demonstrators in Jaleh square in Tehran on September 7. Between 700 and 2000 people were killed, depending on whom one wanted to believe. In a bid to quiet the restive population, Sharif-Emami introduced a number of reforms, including allowing the press to state for the first time that there were indeed social problems in Iran. This so-called "spring of freedom" was seized upon immediately by the press. The difference between the newspapers of August and September 1978 was palpable.

The military was alarmed at the boldness of the newspapers, and insisted on reinstating censorship to prevent them from inflaming the population further. The newspapers, having gotten one guarantee of freedom, took an uncharacteristically brave position and went on strike rather than publish under renewed control. For two weeks in October the major daily papers in Tehran refused to publish, but Sharif-Emami was able to prevail over the military authorities and the newspapers once again began to write freely on events as they took place in the capital. The government was forced to accept this situation, noting sourly that the public was being misinformed by the international news media and the rumor mill anyway, and they might as well get the story straight from Iranian sources.[11]

Some citizens of Tehran wondered cynically how the newspapers, which had played such a subservient role for years, had suddenly become social revolutionaries. Nevertheless, for almost one year, until the fall of 1979, the newspapers experienced an almost unprecedented lack of regulation in their operations.

A second response to this newfound freedom was the revival of newspapers, which had been closed years earlier under the force of censorship of the shah. Marxist and other leftist publications, some dating from before World War II, were suddenly seen on every newsstand. The government itself tried to bring out one or two daily papers, which would present the standard official line, but these were quickly detected and avoided by the majority of the population.

This period of press freedom continued after the establishment of the Islamic Republic, until approximately July 1979 when the new government reinstated press censorship. Many of the editors and press executives who had survived the fall of the shah and had continued their press activities were arrested, harassed, or otherwise forced out of their posts. The newspaper *Ayandegan*, which had published for decades, was suspended following mob demonstrations inspired by Ayatollah Ruhollah Khomeini's statement, "I will no longer read *Ayandegan*." In 1980, a number of other publications supported by moderate secularist politicians were also forced to close.

By 1981, the press situation was once more almost entirely as it had been under the regime of the shah. Some leftist papers continued to be published in extremely mild versions as a kind of sop for the intellectual classes, but for all intents and purposes press censorship had been reimposed.

The national radio lacked the initial freedom of the newspapers during the course of the revolution. Indeed, Shahpour Bakhtiar, the last prime minister before the establishment of the Islamic Republic, despite his general support of press freedom in principle, declared that since the national media were arms of the government, they naturally could not be allowed to broadcast anti-government sentiments.

Nevertheless, from August 27, 1978, with the ascension of Ja'afar Sharif-Emami to the prime ministership, to the fall of Bakhtiar's government in February 1979, radio broadcasts were far freer than ever before in the history of Iranian broadcasting. The radio occasionally broadcast opposition statements, and tried to avoid contradicting the reports coming from foreign media during the period.

The Tehran-based FM radio station, Radio Tehran, played an interesting role for a few days, between the time of the return of Ayatollah Khomeini from his exile in Paris on January 31, 1979 and the fall of Shahpour Bakhtiar on February 11–12. If the general population of Iran held radio to be somewhat tainted as a medium, FM radio was the most suspect of all, since it leaned heavily toward the broadcast of foreign popular music, and western-style broadcast techniques. It was, moreover, aimed more at the middle and upper classes than the traditional population. On February 3, 1979, during these final few days of secular rule, Radio Tehran opened its phone lines, allowing Tehran citizens to express their opinions openly and without censorship. Not surprisingly, given the composition of the listening audience, many expressed their misgivings about the nature of the revolution, aiming disparaging comments at "ultraconservative" forces, and suggesting that the revolutionary forces may have been more to blame for the violence in the street than was the government. The station was forced to close on February 6 by the revolutionary supporters and then-striking radio employees.

The capture of National Iranian Radio–Television was one of the chief priorities of the revolutionary forces. Once the government of Shahpour Bakhtiar had resigned, the nation first heard the news over the radio waves. The first hint was given at the playing of a nationalist anthem, "Ey, Iran, Ey Marz-e Por Gohar" (O, Iran, O Borders Filled with Jewels), instead of the familiar "Surud-e Shah-en-Shahi" (Imperial Anthem), and the announcement by radio staff of the success of the revolution. The rest of the day was given over to the reading of revolutionary bulletins, and the playing of a whole spate of revolutionary songs and chants including one rousing march based on the Islamic call to prayer: "Allah-u akbar, la illa-he ila Allah" (God is great, there is no god but God), and the equally energetic "Khomeini, ey Imam!" (Khomeini, O Imam!). Among Western music used, a lush orchestral version of the then-popular song, "Born Free" was played ad nauseum under readings of revolutionary writings.

Radio also underwent a rapid transformation as the revolution proceeded. From the first month, popular music was entirely banned, but the most popular commercial singers quickly began to write and record revolutionary songs that were barely different in form from the former Iranian Top 40. The bulk of radio broadcasts were quickly given over to long ideological discussions, and sermons from religious leaders. One important function of Radio Tehran was to release invective against the United States and other Western nations during times of stress. It is not clear whether these epithets and accusations represented the thinking of Iranian officials, or merely the language of radio commentators, but they were certainly harsh.[12]

Nevertheless, even the most vicious and vituperative rhetoric becomes dull after long and steady exposure. This political commentary, combined with the sermons and ideological lectures were fairly wearisome for the general Iranian listening public, who offered some muted complaints, expressing the opinion that radio broadcasts should be diverting in some way. Despite these mutterings, this pattern of broadcast has continued largely unchanged until the present. Limited broadcasts of Iranian classical and folk music have been allowed from time to time and indeed, have increased, but the present regime is clearly uncomfortable with the official broadcast of musical programs, even if they seem to be on a high cultural plane.

Iranian radio, like so many other Iranian institutions, seems to have felt its way carefully, trying to develop itself into something that would properly reflect the institutions and ideology of the new Islamic Republic. It still suffers from public complaints that it is tedious and dull. However, at present there seems to be no difficulty among the traditional classes—who once wondered about the propriety of radio listening—to listen to everything broadcast these days.

Television underwent a series of changes similar to that of radio during the course of the revolution. There were, under the regime of the shah, three broadcast networks. The first and second networks had semiseparate management and production facilities. The third network was the "International Program," broadcast primarily in English, with some limited broadcasts in French and German. This third network actually replaced the U.S. Air Force Television Station in the early 1970s, which had broadcast primarily old American situation comedies and adventure/crime shows. The largest controversy during the fall of 1978 raged over the broadcast of television news. The news programs were of varying length during this period, ranging from fifteen minutes to as long as an hour and a half. After Prime Minister Ja'afar Sharif-Emami's "liberalization" of news broadcasts, the television networks began to take a more daring attitude toward all programming. One highlight of programming was the live broadcast of parliamentary debate. In this way, controversy in the country could be broadcast without subjecting the television executives to criticism. In November 1979, one extremely important broadcast may have been more influential than any other in cementing public opposition against the shah. Television news carried pictures of Iranian troops firing at University of Tehran students from outside the closed gates of the university. The students, holding hands, advanced in a line toward the gates, and were shown being gunned down. This documentary proof of the military's attacks on unarmed protesters delivered a violent shock to the population as a whole. The next day, the crowds in Tehran went on a rampage, burning banks and government buildings in all sections of the city.

As with radio, the television studios were captured almost as soon as the government fell. Television newscasters immediately began to reflect the new rhetoric, and began to provide readings of revolutionary literature interspersed with speeches from clerical leaders. On the day after the resignation of Bakhtiar, Ayatollah Ali Akbar Hashemi-Rafsanjani, later to be speaker of Iran's parliament and then president, went on the air to deliver an hour-long revolutionary sermon. The public was stunned into boredom and calls by the hundreds demanding to know who had allowed such a person to speak besieged the station.

Immediately after the revolution the question of the control of the airways became a political issue. The television and radio stations both carried official notices from all groups who had taken part in the revolution during the first two days. Then an official government order declared that no more official notices from leftist groups, the Mujaheddin-e Khalq (MEK) and the Fadayan-e Islam—later to come into more violent conflict with the Islamic authorities—were to be read over the air. The leftist groups were incensed. On February 14, just three days after the start of the new regime, an attempt was made to lay siege to the television studios. The announcer at the time made a quick appeal to the population at large to come and defend the studios, and people rushed from all parts of the city to battle the attackers. No official announcement was ever made as to the identity of the attackers, but many assume that the disgruntled leftist groups were responsible.

Television quickly developed its own brand of revolutionary broadcasting. There were even children's shows for the first few days featuring pictures of five-year-old schoolgirls holding machine guns. One such program had the announcer telling children about proper revolutionary attitudes against the background of a giant bloody handprint. Once again, the phone lines were clogged with parents expressing their horror at such programming. Children themselves were upset at the removal of their favorite cartoon programs. One schoolyard chant took the revolutionary slogan: *Esteghal, Azadi, Jomhuri-ye Islami!* (Independence, Freedom, Islamic Republic!) and converted it into: *Esteghl, Azadi, Palang-e Surati!* (Independence, Freedom, The Pink Panther!).

Television had a much harder time surviving as a pure conduit for ideology than radio. Some visually interesting programming eventually had to be planned. In the early days of the revolution, this consisted of "safe" programs dealing with nature and animal life. Interestingly, one American program survived the revolution. This was *Little House on the Prairie*, obviously espousing enough in the way of acceptable moral values to be broadcast without censure.

Eventually, the television networks began to demonstrate their ideological differences. The third "international" channel was immediately closed, and never reopened after the fall of Bakhtiar's government. The first channel developed as the primary reflector of government attitude. The second channel, which had originally been established as a more intellectual and artistic programming conduit, kept a secular flavor to it. Sadeq Ghotbzadeh, the first director of television under the revolution, retained a degree of influence with the second channel even after the first channel was totally controlled by religious leaders. Ghotbzadeh eventually leveled some sharp criticisms at the Islamic Republic leaders in a forum broadcast over the second channel, an action which caused him to be imprisoned briefly.[13]

The American hostage crisis, lasting from November 4, 1979 to January 12, 1981, and the war with Iraq, which commenced on October 3, 1980, provided excellent opportunities for Iranian television to generate hours of documentary coverage. Iranian technical crews, often trained in the United States, performed work of high quality, and their locally broadcast coverage of these events, if they have been preserved, will in the future provide an invaluable resource for students of the history of broadcasting.

Iranian television gradually has managed to stake out a role for itself providing some balance between entertainment and ideology. In general, programming which reflects the righteous struggle of the oppressed against illegitimate authority is highly favored. Feature films such as *Z, The Battle of Algiers*, and *The Seven Samurai* have been screened regularly on television, and are approved by government authorities. Some original programming has also been produced along the same lines. Nevertheless, television viewers still complain, decades after the revolution, quietly to each other about the dullness of the television fare. One man writing to relatives in the states complained, "We all go to bed early these days, since there is nothing to do in the city, and we fall asleep in front of the television anyway, when we have to listen to these endless sermons and political discussions."

The First New Medium—Tape Cassettes

One of the more remarkable aspects of the Iranian Revolution was the emergence of a new communication medium—the tape cassette—as a vital element in the political process leading to the revolution. Iran was in many ways unique in its adaptation to recording technology. The phonograph record had limited use among the upper classes up until the 1960s. Since phonograph records recorded mainly music, it is not surprising that the traditional religious classes found little use for them. For this reason, the introduction of tape cassettes—and more importantly the combination radio-cassette recorder—launched a boom in the recording industry, which totally bypassed the phonograph record. In Iran, most popular music by the 1970s was recorded directly on cassettes, appearing in no other form. Moreover, even the traditional classes who did not listen to popular music found the cassettes useful. They were used to record the sermons of famous preachers (who, on religious holidays were invited to speak in the larger mosques for considerable honoraria). Indeed, around the great shrines throughout the nation, cassette vendors selling the recorded sermons of well-known clerics were common even years before the revolution. The religious chants performed during the Shi'a months of mourning for Imam Hossein, Moharram and Safar, were also recorded extensively, even professionally, and listened to both for practice, and for enjoyment by the pious.

The chief benefit of the cassette was that anyone possessing a recorder could duplicate it easily. Some cassette stores carried no stocks at all, but only master tapes which were endlessly reduplicated for customers. Being portable as well, and easily hidden, the cassettes became the ideal medium for relaying revolutionary messages from government opposition leaders both at home and abroad. Radio signals could be jammed, and television appearances were out of the question for the opposition. Printed tracts and broadsides were not only easily confiscated because of their bulkiness in distribution, but another danger also lurked: printed messages could be counterfeited by government officials attempting to carry out policies of dis-creditization or disinformation. Thus a tract might be issued in the name of Ayatollah Khomeini, or one or the other leaders, but readers had no guarantee that the purported author of the statement was the true author. The tape cassette provided the opportunity for the listener to satisfy himself or herself that the message or directive was genuine. This feature was particularly important during the final months of 1978, when revolutionary leaders were calling on individuals throughout the nation to strike, or to engage in work stoppages.

Ironically, the tape cassettes which had been so useful during the revolution returned to present problems for the new revolutionary regime, once the Islamic Republic had been established. Popular music continued to be sold for some months from the cassette tape stores in all large cities throughout the nation until late in 1979. Finally, the government moved to close the stores and ban the sales of the music tapes, despite the loud protests of the dealers.

Exiled former prime ministers Shahpour Bakhtiar, and later in 1981, Abol-Hassan Bani-Sadr, both taking a page from the revolutionary handbook, taped exhortations to their followers inside Iran to resist the new Islamic Republic. These were circulated widely within Iran, and the authorities of the Islamic Republic had as little success in stopping them as had the shah's officials before the Revolution.

International Broadcast Media

During the course of the revolution and afterward, international media played a truly profound role. The Iranian Revolution may have been the first major political upheaval in the history of the world to have been enacted almost on the spot before the eyes and ears of the world. Moreover, the Iranian revolutionaries knew very well the value of international press coverage, and courted it at every possible opportunity.

The international press, radio, and television aided the revolution in several ways. First, it provided an additional channel of information for individuals within Iran, effectively frustrating all attempts on the part of the government to control information on breaking events.

The giant among foreign broadcasters in terms of its influence on the Iranian people was the British Broadcasting Corporation. The BBC was the principal source of information for the Iranian people about the revolution for most of 1978 and 1979. Its prestige as a source was so great that persons who had never owned a radio before purchased one solely in order to hear the BBC. Stores in the Tehran bazaar used this as a selling point, and would tune the radio to the BBC when customers made a purchase.

The BBC was far more than an information source, however. It also served as a conduit for revolutionary messages. Oftentimes the first news of an impending strike, or the latest announcement from revolutionary leaders would be heard over the BBC Persian service.

Correspondent Andrew Whitley, who served as the principal relayer of information to the BBC London studios from his apartment in Tehran, faced an unending stream of telephone calls from all parts of the country, telling him about clashes with military troops, strike actions, revolutionary deaths, and local political developments. Sometimes he had to take his telephone off the hook at night in order to get any sleep at all.

The government of the shah was livid at the BBC, and seemingly tried to jam its broadcasts in a halfhearted way several times. It was accused of fabricating stories, inciting the people to riot, and serving leftist factions. Paradoxically, after the establishment of the Islamic Republic, the BBC faced similar criticisms from the new regime, who did not care for its continued reporting of arrests and executions by Islamic judges and local justice committees.

A different kind of information was provided by Radio Moscow, which operated Persian language broadcasts on several levels. Official Radio Moscow maintained a somewhat neutral, but definitely anti-shah stand as the revolution progressed. The heavy propaganda was dealt out by a broadcasting station called the National Voice of Iran, operating from Baku in Soviet Azerbaijan just over Iran's northern border, but purporting to be originating from inside the country. The chief purpose of this station seemed to be to convince the Iranian population that the United States was behind all of the excesses of the shah's regime, and was continuing to plot against the Iranian people. During the period following the fall of the Bakhtiar government, this invective was particularly strong. In this period it was impossible to turn on a radio to either the AM or shortwave bands and not encounter these messages, as they were being broadcast on dozens of frequencies all over the radio dial.

It is worth noting that the United States had no Persian language broadcasts at all at this time. This was somewhat remarkable, since even nations such as Romania broadcast in Persian. In any case, "Voice of America" broadcasts in English were understood only by the middle and upper classes, who had little need to be disabused of the violent invective coming both from the USSR and Radio Iran.[14]

No matter what its political color, however, foreign media attention to the Iranian Revolution served another important purpose, in that it served to legitimize the revolution itself in the eyes of the world. If the press had been prevented from covering these events, the revolution might conceivably have been smothered in a bloodbath, such as was greatly desired by many of the shah's generals. As it was, the shah was conscious of not only his own image, but also the image of his nation, which he had hoped to make the equal of the European powers before the end of the century. As analyst Barry Rubin put it succinctly, "He did not want to be regarded in the world's eyes as another Idi Amin."[15]

Finally, the presence of the international media tended to render the revolution itself more acceptable to Iranians. In fact, the population became almost giddy with the orgy of media attention that they were receiving, leading to statements like that printed in *Kayhan* on the day after the fall of the Bakhtiar government: "The Iranian Revolution is one of the greatest events in the history of the world."[16]

Media coverage of Iran in the past had tended to be inadequate.[17] The *New York Times* maintained a Tehran bureau for a brief period in the mid 70s, but except for this, none of the major news reporting bureaus maintained anything much better than a system of stringers, usually Indian or Pakistani writers, who would do occasional day-to-day reporting. The usual coverage of Iran consisted of having a writer fly in from Beirut for a day or so, stay in the Hilton or Intercontinental, and interview upper-class, English-speaking Iranians.[18] Of course, truly spectacular events like the shah's self-coronation, or the 2,500-year celebration of the history of the Iranian monarchy received some media coverage, but in general, Iranians of all classes were inured to the idea that their nation was an unimportant backwater, about which the world cared very little.

The revolution changed all that, of course. Suddenly the focus of the world was on Iran, and the Iranians liked this very much. They exclaimed proudly, even in the midst of the gunfire on the streets: "Now we won't have to explain to people where our country is. We're on the map now," as one university student in Shiraz said, commenting on the international news teams filming a demonstration in which he was taking part.

The effect of international media on the American hostage crisis is a subject that has been covered at great length by media analysis.[19] In general, the crisis as a media event had an astounding affect on both the American and Iranian public. Much of the hoopla around the American embassy generated by anti-American demonstrators was clearly produced for the benefit of the television cameras. The American viewing public failed somehow to appreciate this fact, and was simply appalled at the seeming virulence of the anti-American attacks. The hostage crisis, like the revolution itself, was shoveled into American living rooms as a media event, and the resulting negative attitudes toward Iranians, even completely innocent ones, was seen in a dismal record of public attacks on Iranian students, expulsions of Iranians from colleges and jobs, and failures of Iranian-owned businesses from lack of patronage.[20]

At the time, the international media coverage served Iranian government purposes well. The attention provided by the world press, television, and radio helped the nation to accept the hostage crisis as something positive rather than something to be ashamed of. The result was increased support for the Islamic Republic and its policies. On the back of the hostage crisis, the clerical leaders of the new nation were able easily to win support for a highly controversial constitution, elect a slate of handpicked candidates to parliament, and set up a government which featured clerical leaders in top posts.

Once the hostages had been released, however, the international media became troublesome. Continued stories of arrests and long imprisonment of members of the political opposition to the clerical regime, reporting on economic difficulties throughout Iran, and the failure of the government to get Iranian industry operating again, led to government charges that the international media was engaged in a "Western plot to discredit the revolution," as one official in the Ministry of National Guidance charged.

One after another the major wire services were expelled from the country for "inaccurate reporting." By the end of 1981, only the French, Italian, Yugoslav, and Russian national news agencies were left among the European press. The Indian and Japanese press remained as well, but as one reporter from the large Tokyo daily paper, *Yomiyuri*, said in January 1982, "We have a staff in Tehran, but we don't dare write anything controversial. The Iranian ambassador in Tokyo combs the papers every day looking for some reason to expel us too."

Media and the Search for Cultural Purity

Few societies are as invested in a search for their own identity is as Iran. The historical, linguistic, religious, and ethnic diversity of the nation makes such a quest perhaps inevitable. This process is dynamic, of course, and Iranians are continually involved both with expansion and contraction of their cultural vision. This is a powerful theme that pervades two recent studies of modern Iranian cultural institutions Darius M. Rejali's *Torture and Modernity: Self, Society and State in Modern Iran*,[21] and Hamid Naficy's *The Making of Exile Cultures: Iranian Television in Los Angeles*.[22]

Darius M. Rejali makes it clear that torture in Iranian society is a deeply rooted cultural institution. The surprise for some Western readers is to see how remarkably spiritual the practice is both for the tortured and for the torturers. The common bond between torturer and tortured is the intense desire for the maintenance of purity. In the case of the torturer of whatever historical period, the use of torture ensures the integrity of the ideological cast of society. This is equally true in the nineteenth-century premodern Qajar regime, the modernist Pahlavi regime, and the post-Revolutionary Islamic regime. For the tortured, the process often becomes a way to manifest spiritual integrity through suffering. In this regard, the process of "carceral rationality"[23] plods forward to an inevitable horrific result.

Rejali's account makes for grisly reading. It is not pleasant to hear of prisoners forced to chant, "This is not a prison, it is a university/We are happy to be here," as they watch others die; or prison guards marrying, then raping and executing female prisoners in order not to be accused of killing virgins. However, these stories prove his point that the history of torture, like the history of sexuality, proceeds in a course independent from other social and political developments. Torture, like all other social institutions exists in a cultural context, and the drive to impose a vision of purity on others in an Iranian setting is a powerful rationalization for essentially inhumane treatment.

The Iranian exiles in Los Angeles are also involved in a search for personal and cultural purity—essential Iranian culture. As exiles, their essential Iranian-ness is lost to them, and the pain is acute. The search for a pure cultural core is difficult. Iran is a multiethnic, multireligious culture. Armenian and Assyrian Christians, Jews, Arabic- and Turkish-speaking Sunni Muslims identify along with Persian speaking Shi'a Muslims as Iranian citizens.

The odd postmodern discovery of identity through commercial television both defines and unifies this diverse community in a way that was perhaps never realized in Iran itself. Naficy's detailed account of the Los Angeles ethnic television industry—replete with reader surveys, tables, and program lists—may be the definitive study of a specific television audience. A profile of television programming for this million-person exile group (including Iranians outside of Los Angeles reached through satellite broadcasts) is able to make a point that could never easily be proven by researchers working in prerevolutionary Iran: that the Iranian community truly embodies diversity within cultural unity. To appeal to all who call themselves Iranian, the divisive elements must be downplayed in the public culture. In such a community, that which "counts" as Iranian must minimalize religious, linguistic, and ethnic differences. This is reinforced by the fact that much of the economic backing for the programming is from Iranian Jews and Armenians. After eliminating all that is controversial, a bare core of the symbolic trappings of civilization is left—music, poetry, discourse, and visual symbols. The exilic television industry takes these materials and "fetishizes" (in Naficy's terms) Iranian culture.

Torture, Television, and Iran's Interaction with the West

Neither the form of institutionalized torture as it developed in Iran over the past two centuries, nor the development of television as an Iranian public cultural medium arose in a cultural vacuum. Both are the result of Iran's interaction with Western culture, hearkening back to major Iranian critics of Westernization (notably the sociologist Jalal al-e Ahmad).

Institutionalized torture as presented by Rejali is seen as a tool emerging in direct response to the development of the modern Iranian state, which in turn was forged as a result of the direct challenges posed by the

Western world in the wake of the industrial revolution. The need to develop modern military and educational institutions, with disciplined soldiers and citizens loyal to the ideals of the state, necessitated the practice
of state purification through purging of oppositionist forces. To this end,
torture was seen as both a ritual and an instrumentality.

Often the resistance to the state on the part of the citizenry had to do
with aspects of the modernization process itself. At times the citizenry was
opposed to economic or political policy that allied the throne with foreign
powers. At other times the public was pushing a reluctant government
toward reforms inspired through knowledge of human rights' advances
elsewhere. This push-pull syndrome became a mode of interaction between
the government and the people that continued through three dynasties and
is pervasive in the Islamic Republic today. The ideological controversies
merely shifted, depending on what seemed to be a plausible threat to the
state at any given time, from democracy to secularism to communism to
Western dominance—all of which ultimately emanated from the West. Thus
both the practice of torture and the reasons for which torture was employed
resulted from the interaction between traditional Iranian culture and Western culture.

As cited above, television was introduced into Iran on a massive scale
during the final two decades of the Pahlavi dynasty. It was a particular interest of the shah and the empress as hallmark of a "modern society."
Thousands of middle- and upper-middle-class Iranians born after World
War II were involved with the development of television (and film) in Iran.
At the time of the Iranian Revolution, those individuals were under direct
attack by the Islamic regime as purveyors of corrupt Western culture. Many
fled to the United States, where they found they could make a living, as
Naficy shows, with the technical and administrative skills they had learned
in Iran. Moreover, the kinds of programs that brought them under attack
by the Islamic authorities—music, dance, romantic and mystic poetry, and
political discussion—were exactly the things the exile community was long-
ing to see. In this way, the continuance of Iranian culture in the West,
through a quintessential Western medium, was preordained even before the
Islamic Revolution, through the extensive process of Westernization undertaken by the government of the shah.

As Naficy shows,[24] a great irony in this pattern is the one set of television
broadcast programs showing in the United States today, which emanates
from Iran. It is called the *Aftab* (Sun) network. Like the American-based
programming, it eschews religion and other divisive topics and sticks to cultural themes—largely travel, literature, and history. It is produced by members of the same cohort of television professionals that engendered the Los
Angeles television producers and directors. Nevertheless, the *Aftab* programs show Iran today in a positive light—a direct contradiction to the pervasive view, among the Los Angeles Iranian community, that Iran had

deteriorated after the revolution. Some members of the émigré community in Los Angeles have periodically called for a boycott of this programming, but to no avail. *Aftab* remained nonpolitical and attracted both advertisers and viewers. Its presence has "led to the gradual crumbling of the barriers that fetishization had erected in the path of understanding the complexities of life both in Iran and in exile."[25]

One thing is certain, television and radio are now pervasive in Iran, and all attempts to limit their influence on the Iranian population by the current regime are vain exercises. Nevertheless, it would be naïve to believe that television and radio are culturally neutral media. In Iran, as in many societies, the media fulfill specific culturally determined functions. In Iran, these functions include allowing Iranians to talk to the world in general. This will be discussed more extensively in the section to follow.

Media in Iran—A Shifting Cultural Role

At the beginning of this discussion it was suggested that the media is first and foremost a cultural institution in any society. As such, full understanding of the nature of its functioning and the meaning it holds for the population as a whole, must be considered against the backdrop of the totality of other cultural institutions and social events in the society.

The role of the media on all levels during the Iranian Revolution of 1978–79 and after provides some extremely interesting insights into the nature of media functioning during periods of social stress. In looking at the Iranian case, it is impossible to avoid the conclusion that, although the media underwent a fundamental change in their orientation and operations from October 1978 to July 1979, the essential quality and nature of their operations after the revolution, under the Islamic republic, is functionally the same as it was under the regime of the shah, even though qualitatively it has changed considerably. Functionally, the press, radio, and television before the revolution were largely organs which supported the principal ideology of the state at the time—namely, Iranian nationalism as reflected in the institution of the monarchy and its extensions in the form of the Iranian government. Television and radio programming were largely dictated on the basis of the opinions of social and political leaders, who felt they were providing the society with cultural materials that would ultimately prove beneficial. In this regard, seemingly contradictory events, like the financial support of films which might even provide criticism of television itself—like *The Mongols*—were subsumed under the general principle: that the public must have the opportunity to be exposed to advanced forms of culture, such as modern film, and state communications' institutions have the duty to provide this exposure.

During the revolution, the media turned to almost total opposition of the ideology represented by the monarchy, as well as the monarchy itself.

The willingness to do this was accompanied by some genuinely courageous actions on the part of journalists and broadcast officials.

Nevertheless, once the Islamic Republic had been established, the media returned to its role of supporter of the dominant state ideology. This time, however, the dominant ideology was that of the Islamic Revolution. Censorship, newspaper closings, arrests, and intolerance of critical opinion proceeded in a fashion nearly identical to that of the government of the shah.

Newspapers, which used to be overwhelming in their sycophancy of the monarchy, are now replete in every issue, with repeated glowing references to the "revolutionary clergy." It is a crime to insult a clergyman at present, and press reporters have been arrested for doing this. The pictures of the shah on the front page of every issue were replaced with those of major religious/political figures. It is reported that individuals such as Ayatollah Hashemi-Rafsanjani complain to the newspapers when they are missing from the front page for several days running.

Much of the press activity following the revolution was carried out with a degree of public approval. At a public meeting just a few days following the resignation of Shahpour Bakhtiar, these sentiments were expressed in Tehran: "Whatever the leaders of the revolution do it is for a good reason, so one shouldn't question it." "No one should be allowed to express opinions that will hinder the progress of the Revolution." "Anyone who writes that television and radio are censored is obviously a supporter of the CIA and only wants to discredit the Revolution."[26]

Television and radio programming are likewise not geared to public tastes or desires any more than under the shah's regime. Formerly, the people got what was "good for them" in terms of culture and Westernized programming. Now they get what is "good for them" in terms of revolutionary ideology and religious values.

The foreign press, radio, and television were highly restricted in their operations under the shah, due in part to incompetence in the conduct of their operations. At present their operations are officially restricted. For better or worse, intentionally or not, their role in Iranian life occupies the same minimal space it did before the revolution. Revolutions are extraordinary times in any society. They constitute the kind of events which anthropologist Victor Turner designates as "social dramas."[27] A social drama constitutes a disruption in the fabric of society—a rupture that must eventually be healed. During the period of the rupture and the restoration process, however, the society enters a state which can be described as "liminal."

During this period, the normal rules of society are suspended, or, more often totally reversed. In the worlds of the song, the society enters the state of "The World Turned Upside Down."

In assessing the role of the media before, during, and after the Iranian revolution, we see that its changing functions constitute an almost perfect textbook illustration of the process of liminality and reversal during a social drama. The media reversed its functions for the short period of social disruption, but once the government had reestablished itself, the old cultural functions of the media were completely established once again, but in new ideological trappings.

The Reform Period and Its Media Reflex

The late 1990s and early 2000s marked the reform period led by President Mohammad Khatami. This was also marked by a dramatic increase in press activity, publishing, international television reception, Internet activity, and cell phone usage. With the dramatic gaps in Iran's demographics, it is no surprise that an electronic communication revolution would be underway in Iran. The predominantly youthful population, with more than 75 percent of the people below the age of twenty-five, was intensely interested in this new technology, and the more conservative elements in government were completely unable to withstand the pressure for its unfettered use.[28]

The United States, aware of the growing youth population and their fascination with music and all things electronic, launched Radio Farda, a radio service targeting this population with Iranian, American, and international pop music, interspersed with pro-American messages.[29] Now television programs are beamed to Iran from the United States. The television programs produced in Los Angeles that Hamid Naficy writes about are broadcast to Iran via satellite. The exile community, many of whom are anxiously awaiting a regime change in Iran, have used these broadcasts to advance their political agenda, to the chagrin of the clerics in Tehran.[30]

Nothing could be more significant than the astonishing growth of the Internet in Iran. Despite state controls, Iran experienced the largest increase in Internet usage in the Middle East from the year 2000 to 2004, according to the Web site Internet World Stats. Iran saw a 1,820 percent increase in this period. The Internet is now used by 7 percent of the population, or 4.8 million people.[31] The government has tried to restrict satellite dishes and other means of connecting to the World Wide Web, but to no avail. The youth of the country are completely aware of the outside world as a result of this Internet usage. They follow popular culture trends elsewhere in the world, download music and images, and, in general, bypass all attempts to circumscribe their knowledge. American scholars receive e-mail letters from Iranian students on a regular basis, who show remarkable sophistication and range of knowledge. One can buy Iranian carpets, music, books, fruit, and nuts and arrange travel to and from Iran over the Internet from any place on earth. South Korea announced on September 9, 2004, that it would provide 100,000 broadband lines to twenty Iranian cities, making high-speed Internet connections available throughout the country. This is clearly a communication technology that is here to stay.

The most dramatic development during the reform period was the rise of newspapers. Tehran has a range of publications from ultraconservative to liberal. During Khatami's presidency, the more liberal papers were regularly shut down by the judiciary. The executive branch, in the form of the Minister for National Guidance (*Ershad*) could not rescind the judicial orders, but he did regularly reissue licenses to publish. At times a paper would be shut down, and then reopen the next day under a different name. In 2000, before the presidential elections of 2001, the judiciary allowed some fourteen papers to reopen when the parliament, under urging by Khatami, threatened to launch a parliamentary investigation of the closings.[32]

News media eventually fused with Internet technology. Such Iranian Web sites as *The Iranian* (www.iranian.com), *Payvand* (www.payvand.com), and *IranMania* (www.iranmania.com) are accessible anywhere on the planet, and young Iranians regularly avail themselves of them. This means that the government cannot really prevent them from getting information about the United States, Iran, or any other part of the world. In a recent trip to Iran, I was astonished at how well-informed young people were. Most of their information came from Internet sources. Similarly, cellular phones are ubiquitous in Iran, and serve as an incredibly subversive communications tool. For young people it is a way for boys and girls to be "together" without forbidden physical contact. It is a means for political organization and an astonishingly effective way to carry out private conversations outside of the purview of curious relatives, neighbors, and friends.

Both cell phones and the Internet also give Iranians a way to practice a kind of public witnessing to the values of individual integrity and morality that characterize concern with core values (discussed elsewhere in this book). As Fariba Adelkhah states in her astute study, *Being Modern in Iran*,[33] to be modern in Iran is "to set oneself up as a moral being in a relatively precise context, according to ideas of self-reflexivity and in relation to a public space of a rational-legal type. It is impossible to stress strongly enough that Islam is not really a relevant parameter in this matter."[34]

Communication via cell phone and through the Internet allow for this kind of communication in a particularly effective manner. Out of the range of control of the Islamic state, but still within the framework of society, this is the perfect culturally based technology. The advent of SMS text messaging on cell phones has created new possibilities both for romantic encounters and for political protest. One message circulated widely by SMS text to protest the clamp down on reform candidates in the 2004 parliamentary elections was "We will not take part in the funeral for freedom."

The latest communication technology is the Iranian Web log or "blog." In early 2005 an estimated 75,000 Iranians were putting their everyday observations onto the Internet in blogs for the world to read—a trend that had started in 2003, corresponding with continued repression of reformist newspapers and other print media. Reformist President Khatami bragged that Persian was the third most pervasive language for blogging in the world. Many of these blogs proved surprisingly frank and open, addressing topics that were taboo for religious conservatives—both political and personal. The situation became so widespread that it worried the Iranian government, who instituted crackdowns on some of the most widely read, outspoken bloggers.[35] This resulted in a number of arrests.

One thing is certain. Now that Iran has entered the "modern" age, in terms of having all the means of communication available to the rest of the world, it is now a postmodern state, with all the cynicisms attendant to that state. Media-savvy, quick to consume, but quick to criticize and abandon that which they find less than high quality, Iran's young people are nobody's media fools.

— 11 —

Living with Iran
Resistance as Postmodern Discourse

Deceptive Hostility

The great paradox in U.S.-Iranian relations is that despite hostile rhetoric, the two nations have never broken their psychological ties to each other. More than a quarter of a century after the revolution of 1978–79 they are, in fact, growing closer together, even as they continue to rant and rail at each other. The paradox of the married couple who can only show their close emotional connection to each other by fighting is a metaphor for this situation.

Despite the trade sanctions imposed on Iran in 1987 and 1995 (eased somewhat in 2000), Iranian trade with the United States has increased steadily since the revolution. Iranian students still constitute a sizeable student group on American soil, a group which is even larger when one counts the children of Iranian émigrés. More than a million Iranians chose to emigrate to the United States (more than half of them to California). The Iranian armed forces, largely American-trained, are heavily dependent on U.S. military equipment. And the United States has maintained steady, mediated contacts with Iranian government officials. Washington is fully cognizant that Iran occupies one of the most strategic geographic locations in the world, and sits on some of the most valuable mineral resources anywhere.

In less concrete terms, Iranians and Americans really seem to like each other on a one-to-one basis. Of the thousands of Americans living in Iran during the revolution, not one was physically harmed. The American hostages in Iran were for the most part persons with extended previous contact with Iran. Their relative lack of bitterness at their captivity and unwillingness to condemn Iranians—even their captors—has puzzled and angered some Americans who have less direct experience with Iran.[1] The small number of American businessmen and reporters returning to Iran in recent years report that they have been treated with great hospitality and no violence whatsoever.

Given the natural basis for alliance and reasonable amounts of personal goodwill, how can we understand the enmity that prevents closer dealings between Washington and Tehran? The source of much misunderstanding in international relations lies in the failure of nations to understand the symbolic bases for both the actions and the discourse used to describe those actions by other nations. Iran and the United States are at loggerheads over just these symbolic matters, as has been shown earlier in this book.

It is not surprising that for both sides, political maneuvering has been clumsy and often abortive. Iran's government is something with which few modern Western leaders have understandably had any experience—a fundamentalist Islamic theocratic state.[2] Iran's leaders, though intelligent and savvy in dealing with domestic politics, are still learning about the world of international diplomacy. They are not international statesmen by training and are extremely naïve about the U.S. political system. To break the impasse it is necessary first for both sides to understand the bases for the discourse and actions of the other. In developing such understanding, the burden of action may fall on the United States to work both at understanding why Iranians are acting as they are, and attempting to provide them with clues for interpreting the logic of American actions.

Part of the confusion, as has been maintained throughout this book, lies in conflicting strategies of discourse in ongoing international relations, which both sides view as essential to their national identity. Iranians have, since the beginning of the revolution been engaged in symbolic discourse which emphasizes *resistance* as a means of establishing and maintaining revolutionary credentials and a correct moral posture on the international scene. The United States maintains discourse which emphasizes *accommodation* to achieve the same goals. Both sides react with vehemence when pressed to abandon their postures.

These two discourse postures come in conflict when accommodation, as pressed by the United States, is understood as compromise, or seen as co-optation by Iranians. Both accommodation and resistance are well-grounded in the historical past of both nations, and for this reason it is extremely difficult for either side to persuade the other to weaken their posture. For the United States this has been particularly difficult, since the Pahlavi rulers continually adapted to the American accommodation discourse, even when they were not cooperating with the United States.

There is also a paradox inherent in these postures. For the United States, the goal of accommodation is for Iran to recognize American superiority. For Iran, the goal of resistance is to force the United States to recognize Iran's right to be treated as an equal member of the international community.

Islamic Discourse

The West was comfortable with the former shah and his family in part because they came from a century-long tradition of rulers who based their governance on accommodation with the political and economic powers of the West. The Qajar rulers of the nineteenth and early twentieth centuries, as I have mentioned earlier, were in desperate need to modernize their armies and domestic economy. They therefore sold concessions to their European competitors for a wide variety of mineral and commercial rights, thus subordinating themselves and their nations to Western powers. The Pahlavi family followed this same path.

In the course of working with the West, the Iranian rulers developed a discourse style that Western powers could understand. A strong desire for accommodation with the West was paramount.[3] Moreover, ambitions for Iran were spoken of in terms which Westerners understood well: economic development, increasing democracy, regional defense, expanding international trade, and broadening economic opportunity. Mohammad Reza Pahlavi may have had good intentions for his nation, but his actions served to move Iran out of a traditional cultural framework and into a Western one. The bulk of the population was simply not prepared for this.

Iran's post-Revolutionary clerical leaders came from an entirely different tradition, which for nearly a century gained political strength from opposing Iran's secular rulers. Ayatollah Ruhollah Khomeini and his mentors were all closely associated with a long line of Islamic reform movements begun in the nineteenth century under the aegis of the charismatic leader mentioned at the beginning of this discussion: Jamal ad-Din al-Afghani.[4]

Al-Afghani was born in Iran in 1838/39 (1254 A.H.),[5] but first emerged as a public figure in Afghanistan[6]—hence the name by which he was known throughout the Islamic world. Beginning in 1870,[7] he began a career of preaching a message to Muslims everywhere: to rise up and join in establishing a revitalized unified Islamic faith, in order to resist the incursion of European colonial powers. Not absolving Muslims of the need to set their own house in order, al-Afghani called for a rigorous purification of religious belief and practice, and more important, a political reunion of all Muslims in defense of the faith. He was particularly concerned with the need to defend spiritual values against the incursion of materialism, which he viewed as coming primarily from Europe. The Islamic movement had two primary directions: judicial and religious reform, and political action. These were embodied in al-Afghani's most dynamic followers, Muhammad Abduh and Hasan al-Banna, each of whom represented a different dimension of the Islamic Reform Movement.

Sheikh Muhammad Abduh, a revered Islamic scholar, was a brilliant thinker engaged in purification and reform of the Islamic legal system. It is said that he reopened the "gate of interpretation" of Islamic legal codes, which had been "closed" for centuries. He believed sincerely that Islam, when rightly understood and interpreted, could provide complete answers to every requirement of modern life. He was extremely well-read and felt that with rigorous application of scholarly energy most of Western thought could be reconciled with Islamic doctrine without corrupting the doctrine.

Hasan al-Banna, founder of the Muslim Brotherhood in Egypt in the 1930s was primarily a political activist. Although deeply affected by the spirit of the Islamic reforms proposed by Abduh, al-Banna was less concerned with the reworking of Islamic law than with political action and the rigorous purification of doctrine. He believed fervently that Islam "has all" and need not borrow ideas from any foreign source. He saw Western thought and political institutions as antithetical to the Islamic world. To counter colonialist incursion, the proper response to the West would be a reunification of Muslims throughout the world. Al-Banna felt Islam must be militarily strong, and he advocated the establishment of an Islamic army consisting of young men imbued with the spirit of *jihad* (properly glossed not as "holy war" as is the penchant of the press, but rather "righteous struggle"). The Muslim Brotherhood remains a strong force in the Islamic world today, particularly in Egypt, Syria, and the Sudan.[8]

The goals of the continuing Islamic revolution in Iran parallel those of Mohammad Abduh and Hasan al-Banna. Ayatollah Khomeini, an aged man at the time of the Revolution, was well-acquainted with the thinking of all the major Islamic reformers of the twentieth century. Pre-Revolutionary Iran, as viewed by Khomeini, constituted an almost perfect textbook case within the framework of the ideology of the Muslim Brotherhood: a nation drawn away from the tenets and spiritual purity of Islam by the corrupting materialistic forces of the West. It is thus not surprising that the central symbolism of political discourse in the Islamic revolutionary regime revolves around the concept of resistance as a means of promoting religious purity.

Resistance in ideological terms, means noncompromise with forces of evil and corruption. This is a flexible concept, which has been applied by the clerics variously to the Pahlavi regime, the United States, the government of Saddam Hussein of Iraq, and occasionally to the Soviet Union, particularly in its dealings in Afghanistan. Resistance in Iran is reinforced by religious symbolism particular to Shi'a history—the story of the death of Imam Hossein, grandson of the Prophet Mohammad, as has been seen in earlier chapters of this book.

The major political events of the last decades—the Revolution, the holding of American hostages and the Iran–Iraq War—have all been played out as if they had taken place on the plains of Kerbala. The leitmotif for all of these struggles is the opposition between inner truth and external corruption. Ayatollah Ruhollah Khomeini and his followers, like Imam

Hossein before them, have steadfastly refused to allow themselves to be placed in a position where they could be accused of compromise with any external force, and the political power of the revolutionary government has derived largely from this central action—the refusal to compromise. Resistance in this case became the clearest outward expression of non-compromise. Thus, resistance to U.S. demands that Iran cease its "outlaw" behavior served to underscore the religious and moral purity of the stance of Ayatollah Khomeini and his followers. As the U.S. government demanded repeatedly that Iran yield unequivocally during the course of the hostage crisis, it did not realize that it was asking the revolutionary leaders to do the one thing they could not do and still retain the symbolic purity of the revolution.

The tenaciousness of Ayatollah Khomeini in pursuing the war with Iraq after Iraq had attacked Iran is another expression of resistance to compromise. Iraqi President Saddam Hussein was declared corrupt and likened to the persecutors of the martyrs of Kerbala. Kerbala's location in present-day Iraq strengthened this image, and Iranian soldiers were regularly inspired to battle through the invocation of the death of Imam Hossein.

Ayatollah Ruhollah Khomeini himself became an enormously complex living symbol within the context of the revolution. In him pious Iranians saw elements of Ali—the founder of religious principles, the treat teacher and warrior—combined with the attributes of Hossein—the warrior, the person who would not compromise, the opponent of evil external forces. Under this strong set of ideals, it is clear that for Khomeini and his sincerest followers, defeat and destruction are infinitely preferable to compromise. Americans have a great deal of difficulty understanding the beauty Iranians see in willingness to sacrifice oneself, rather than veer even slightly from one's ideals. While the West can accept martyrdom as a rational act, it is viewed for the most part as a last resort after all other means of resolving conflict have failed. Yet for Khomeini and his followers, martyrdom is the only correct act for a person convinced he or she is acting in the name of correct principles when confronted with a stronger force. In this way martyrdom holds a position in the range of strategies of confrontation of being *preferred* to all other actions, taking second place only to complete and utter victory.

For Khomeini and his followers, there is an implicit world model implied in their religious discourse. The ideal world is one in which personal morality and statecraft are united under a single Islamic religious code. There is tolerance for other religious beliefs, but, no doubt, about the ultimate correctness of Islamic law as the will of God, which men may ignore only at their peril. The compass of this philosophy is universal; divisions of language, race, or culture pose no impediment. Thus, secular states should atrophy and fade away, or be destroyed as a single world community comes into being.

As mentioned several times in this discussion, in "Twelver" Shi'a doctrine there were twelve Imams (including Ali and Hossein) who led the faith following the death of Mohammad. It is believed that the twelfth Imam, the Mahdi, disappeared into occultation and will return at the end of the world with Jesus, to judge mankind. Until that time, there can be no truly perfect government. The world must limp along, striving to achieve the best understanding of divine law possible, under the guidance of the most respected religious scholars of the day (such as Ayatollah Ruhollah Khomeini). Iran's religious leaders feel that as the only government presently combining religious and civil authority under Islamic law, they constitute the best government possible at this time.

A Functioning Government

Washington politicians have cultivated, among Americans, the impression that Iran is a "theocracy" with no democratic institutions. Ignorance grew as the conflict in Iraq escalated, and the Bush administration continuously looked to blame Iran for U.S. failures. Larry Diamond, a scholar at the Hoover Institution, who advised the Coalition Provisional Authority in Iraq (CPA), told the Inter Press Service that the Mahdi Army of young cleric Muqtada al-Sadr, and other Shi'a militias (which gave American forces a very hard time in Iraq) are being armed and financed by Iran with the aim of imposing "another Iranian-style theocracy."[9] Diamond's comments were reiterated by another Coalition Provisional Authority Advisor, Michael Rubin.[10] The story was echoed by influential *New York Times* conservative columnists William Safire and David Brooks, further compounding the misinformation.[11] The claim was simply untrue. No official body in Iran was supporting al-Sadr and the idea that al-Sadr could ever dream of imposing an "Iranian-style theocracy" was absurd, especially given his youth and lack of serious religious authority. Nevertheless, the impression that Iran has nothing even resembling democratic institutions makes the neoconservative claims more believable to many Americans, who know nothing of Iran and who are fearful of Islamic attacks on Western culture.

A particularly ignorant formulation of this proposition was put forward in 2004 by the Committee on the Present Danger (CPD), a group of prominent Washington politicians, "Dedicated to Winning the War on Terrorism" and to that end, dedicated to regime change in Iran. Their paper, "Iran—A New Approach," was published on December 20, 2004, and was authored by former Deputy Secretary of State and Ambassador to Hungary, Mark Palmer, with the assistance of former Secretary of State George Schultz.[12] The paper contains some sensible ideas, such as announcing America's willingness to open its embassy in Iran.

However, this "new approach" is based on a cataclysmically flawed premise that is all too reflective of the bare bones lack of knowledge of

Iranian internal politics characteristic of opinion leaders among U.S. politicians since the Revolution of 1978–79. Palmer chose to make the fulcrum of the policy paper a direct attack on Iranian "Supreme Leader," Ayatollah Ali Khamene'i, whom he characterized as a dictator, much in the mold of Saddam Hussein. The first sentence of the paper is a frontal attack: "Supreme Leader Ali Khamenei [*sic*] of Iran presents a fundamental threat to peace." He goes on to say that "[the Iranian people] want to free themselves from Khamenei's oppression."

This formulation and its underlying misperception are so wrong that one is hard pressed to know where to start a constructive criticism. The bottom line is that although governmental change in Iran will inevitably result in the removal of Khamene'i from power, the opposite is not true. Directly removing Khamene'i from power will not bring about Iranian regime change; indeed, it will strengthen the religious hard-liners.

Ayatollah Khamene'i is an important figure in the governmental and power dynamics of Iran, but he is only one actor in a very complex religious oligarchy with interlocking leadership roles with many checks and balances. He has important authority, but is in no way a dictator in the mold of Saddam Hussein.

To start, the term "Supreme Leader," used continually in the CPD policy paper, is a purely American construct never used by Iranians to address or refer to Khamene'i (the correct title is "faqih" or "jurisprudent"). The term *rahbar* simply meaning "leader," is sometimes used in referring to the faqih.

Second, one must remember that Khamene'i was recruited years ago after a near-futile search for a successor to Ayatollah Ruhollah Khomeini as detailed earlier in this book. He did not have the requisite religious credentials, and has had to have his profile inflated to meet the gravity of the job. He is definitely a conservative presence in the Iranian constitutional governance mechanism, and is occasionally obstructionist. However, he is actually more moderate than some of the extremist denizens of the Iranian Judiciary or of the oversight body, the Council of Guardians, who are the true seat of power in Iran today. Khamene'i bases his actions on consultation with the people who brought him to power. Few would attribute that virtue to Saddam Hussein—or to other notable world leaders.

In sum, Khamene'i is best seen as the front actor for a deeper and more diffuse body of religious conservatives who exercise subtle control over his actions and decisions. This distorted characterization of his role in the Iranian government in a prominent policy paper demonstrates how badly current policy makers need to begin Living with Iran by educating themselves about the true structure of the Iranian government and its functioning.

The same limited thinking applies to the continual reference to Iranian government as a "theocracy." The very appellation "theocracy" is in itself misleading and shows a poor understanding of the governmental structure that was set up following the Iranian Revolution of 1978–79. Moreover, contrary to neoconservative implications, such as that in the Committee on the Present Danger report above, the original government of the Islamic Republic of Iran was not "imposed" by anyone. It was established through an electoral process following the Iranian Revolution. Iranians may regret having ratified the constitution they did, but they follow its provisions assiduously. Every election in Iran in the last twenty years has been free, and has followed the prescribed electoral process to the letter. The problems that have arisen in the country are related to the fact that half of the institutions in the Iranian government are indirectly elected, and these institutions have veto power over the elected institutions. Furthermore, the army and the judiciary are both controlled by these indirectly elected bodies. However, this would not be a problem, except for the fact that those occupying positions in these nonelected bodies are by and large the most conservative religionists in Iran. Therefore, problems with government in Iran stem not from the system of government, but rather from the political bent of those that occupy positions of power in the government.

An accurate picture of Iranian electoral institutions helps in assessing both their strengths and weaknesses, and puts aside the notion that Iran is some kind of theocratic dictatorship. Consequently, I present here a sketch of the Iranian electoral procedure, the main governmental institutional bodies in Iran, and some of the underlying dynamics of political life in Iran today.

Theocracy

The Iranian form of government is unique. Although it is intrinsically bound up with Shi'a religious philosophy, to merely label it a "theocracy" is to miss both the characteristics that set it apart from other governmental institutions, and the characteristics that make it unlikely to be adopted anywhere else in the world.

Shi'a Islam differs from Sunni Islam in a number of historical and philosophical ways. One important difference is that Sunni Islam is organized into legal "schools." Shi'ism is dependent on individual personalities—marja-e-taqlid. There is no formal clergy in Islam. Anyone (male or female) can study theology, and technically any Muslim can lead prayer or offer religious opinions.[13] The Shi'a system is based on consensus. When a person is known for their knowledge and wisdom, they are a faqih, or "jurisprudent." A very prominent faqih is known as a mujtahed, or "practitioner of exegesis." Such people are trusted to interpret Islamic law. When such a person, due to his (or her) superior leadership qualities and knowledge, becomes a focal point for a following, and prominent religious persons endorse the views of that mujtahed, then the mujtahed becomes a marja'-e taqlid. Technically, a marja'-e taqlid is a "grand ayatollah" in common parlance.[14]

Ithna'Ashara Shi'ism, or Twelver Shi'ism, is the dominant doctrine in Iran. Its name derives from adherents' belief in twelve Imams, who were leaders of the faithful and direct descendants of the Prophet Mohammad. The twelfth Imam, Mohammad al-Mahdi, disappeared in infancy. He is said to be in "occultation" until the end of the world. In the meantime, adherents to the Twelver Shi'a doctrine are technically without a present leader.

Grand Ayatollah Ruhollah Khomeini, who at the time of the Iranian Revolution was the marja'-e taqlid with the largest number of followers in the Twelver Shi'a world, introduced a completely new doctrine: the velayat-e faqih or regency of the jurisprudent. According to this doctrine, the most prominent grand ayatollah would rule over the faithful in the absence of the twelfth Imam, thus becoming the faqih. Ayatollah Khomeini's doctrine was rejected by every other grand ayatollah. Traditionally, Shi'a spiritual leaders had eschewed temporal power, and many felt that Khomeini's innovation was heretical. Nevertheless, his charisma and leadership skills were sufficient to convince the Iranian electorate to ratify a constitution granting the nonelected faqih power over all aspects of government.

Iranian Governmental Structures

Once the *faqih* was in place, other governmental institutions flowed from this office. Initially, the faqih was intended to be a remote figure, intervening to resolve questions of government and national leadership only when other means failed. As the early years of the Islamic Republic devolved into internal factionalism between moderate and conservative factions, Khomeini found himself having to intervene more and more. Over time, the institutions of the Iranian state came to be distributed according to the schema indicated on the chart on the next page.

As shown in the chart, although the faqih controls directly or indirectly almost every aspect of government, the faqih is, himself, chosen by an Assembly of Experts, who are elected by the people.

The Electorate

Voting rates are typically high in Iran. In the parliamentary elections of 2000, around 70 percent of voters cast ballots. In the presidential election of 2001, voter participation was nearly 80 percent. In the 2004 parliamentary elections, the rate fell to just above 50 percent, despite a call on the part of reformers to boycott the elections. Participation in Tehran was around 30 percent, showing both the effect of the urban dwellers' disaffection, but also showing that rural voters continued to vote at high rates. The June 2005 presidential election had a voting rate of above 60 percent.

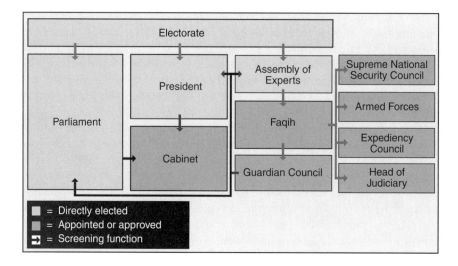

Of a total population of about sixty-five million, more than forty-six million people are eligible to vote and some eight million of these were born after the 1979 revolution; women and young people increasingly make up the majority of voters. The gap between male and female literacy has narrowed among the younger generation. Women now make up an estimated 60 percent of students enrolling in higher education, although the number of working women remains well below the number of men. Women have had the vote since 1963, and there are currently thirteen female members of the parliament. Youth and women were the main bloc of voters who brought reformist Mohammad Khatami to the presidency in 1997, and through their support, advocates of reform have also come to dominate the parliament. However, reformists have not had it all their own way in elections. Conservative candidates made a comeback—aided by low voter turnout in local council elections in March 2003. This was a harbinger of the February 2004 and June 2005 elections, where conservatives won decisively.

Indirectly Elected Bodies

It should be noted that although the following bodies are not directly elected by the general populace of Iran, they achieve their offices by constitutionally designated processes of indirect election or appointment. The tendency of the United States to speak disparagingly of these "unelected hands" was cited by Kenneth Pollack as one of the principal reasons for the failure of U.S. attempts to effect a rapprochement with Iran during the Clinton administration. In particular, one otherwise admirable attempt by Secretary of State Madeleine Albright on March 17, 1999, to improve relations through a general apology for past U.S. actions against Iran, was deemed to have failed because of the use of the phrase "unelected hands." Pollack, who was Director for Gulf Affairs at the National Security Council reports that Iran had recognized the Clinton administration gesture, and had wanted to give a positive response, but every time the writers of the official response formulated a draft "it came back from the Supreme Leader's office with orders to make it tougher because of the words 'unelected hands.' "[15]

Jurisprudent. The role of the jurisprudent, or faqih,[16] in the constitution is based on the ideas of Ayatollah Khomeini. The faqih, currently Ayatollah Ali Khamene'i, appoints the head of the judiciary, six of the members of the powerful Guardian Council, the commanders of all the armed forces, Friday prayer leaders, and the head of radio and television. He also confirms the election of the president. The faqih is chosen by the clerics who make up the Assembly of Experts. Tensions between the office of the leader and the office of the president have often been the source of political instability. These tensions increased since the election of President Mohammed Khatami—a reflection of the deeper tensions between religious rule and the democratic aspirations of most Iranians.

Armed Forces. The armed forces are made up of the Revolutionary Guard and the regular forces. The Revolutionary Guard was formed after the revolution to protect the new leaders and institutions and to fight those opposing the revolution; today it has a powerful presence in other institutions, and controls volunteer militias with branches in every town. The two bodies were once separate: the army under the control of the president, and the Revolutionary Guard under the control of the faqih. During the administration of President Hashemi-Rafsanjani, both bodies were placed under a joint general command under the direction of the faqih. Today, all leading army and Revolutionary Guard commanders are appointed by the faqih and are answerable only to him.[17]

Head of Judiciary. The Iranian judiciary has never been independent of political influence. Until early in the twentieth century it was controlled by the clergy, and after the revolution the Supreme Court revoked all previous laws that were deemed un-Islamic. New laws based on Shari'a law—derived from Islamic texts and teachings—were introduced soon after.

The judiciary ensures that the Islamic laws are enforced and defines legal policy. It also nominates the six lay members of the Guardian Council (see below). Ayatollah Mahmoud Hashemi Shahrudi is the current head of the judiciary, and is appointed by, and reports to, the faqih. As in the United States, different judges interpret the law according to their own judgments. In recent years, the hard-liners have used the judicial system to undermine reforms by imprisoning reformist personalities and journalists and by closing down reformist papers.

Expediency Council. The council is an advisory body for the leader, with ultimate adjudicative power in disputes over legislation between the parliament and the Guardian Council. The faqih appoints its members, who are prominent religious, social, and political figures. Its present chairman, former President Hashemi-Rafsanjani, turned it into an influential strategic planning and policy making body. Because it "mediates," it allowed Hashemi-Rafsanjani to actually initiate policy, since he could provide some guarantee that they will pass. As an example of its work, the Guardian Council demanded in June 2003 that the Majles rewrite certain provisions of its newly passed election law. The Majles refused, and the bill was referred to the Expediency Council. In effect, the Expediency Council then had the power to shape the bill as it saw fit.[18]

Elected Bodies

Assembly of Experts. The responsibilities of the Assembly of Experts are to appoint the faqih, monitor his performance and remove him if he is deemed incapable of fulfilling his duties. The assembly usually holds two sessions a year. Direct elections for the eighty-six members of the current assembly were last held in 1998. Only clerics can join the assembly and candidates for election are vetted by the Guardian Council. The assembly is dominated by conservatives, such as its chairman at this writing, Ayatollah Ali Meshkini. The key role is played by Deputy Chairman and former President Ali Akbar Hashemi-Rafsanjani, who also heads the Expediency Council.

President. The president is elected for four years and can serve no more than two consecutive terms. While most nations in the Middle East have continually elected leaders "for life," Iran, by contrast, has adhered strictly to presidential term limits. Nevertheless, former presidents have frequently been "recycled" into other leadership positions—the foremost being former President Ali Akbar Hashemi-Rafsanjani, who is Deputy Leader of the Assembly of Experts, and head of the Expediency Council. The constitution describes the president as the second-highest ranking official in the country. He is head of the executive branch of power and is responsible for ensuring the constitution is implemented. Presidential powers are limited by the members of indirectly elected bodies in Iran's power structure, most of whom are clerics, and by the authority of the faqih. It is the faqih, not the president, who controls the armed forces and makes decisions on security, defense and major foreign policy issues.

Mohammad Khatami was elected president in May 1997 with nearly 70 percent of the vote and reelected in June 2001 with over 77 percent. The Guardian Council frustrated most of his reforms, particularly in the areas of presidential power and electoral supervision, since they have veto power over all legislation. His failure to carry out reforms largely resulted in disaffection on the part of the voters in the parliamentary elections of 2004.

Parliament. The 296 members of the Majles, or parliament, are elected by popular vote every four years. The parliament has the power to introduce and pass laws, as well as to summon and impeach ministers or the president. However, all Majles bills have to be approved by the conservative Guardian Council. In February 2000, the sixth Majles was elected in free and fair elections. It was the first in which reformists gained a majority. However, the election of the seventh Majles in 2004 resulted in a predominantly conservative parliament, due largely to the fact that more than 2300 candidates were disqualified by the Guardian Council.

Council of Ministers. The Council of Ministers, as the Iranian presidential cabinet is called, are chosen by the president and approved by parliament, which can also impeach them. The cabinet is chaired by the president or first vice president, who is responsible for cabinet affairs. The faqih is closely involved in defense, security and foreign policy, and so his office also holds influence in decision making. Ministers responsible for cultural and social issues are heavily monitored by conservatives watching for any sign of deviation from their strict Islamic line. For example, during the past four years, as mentioned in the previous chapter, the Judiciary would close newspapers, and the ministry of culture would turn around and relicense them under a new name. This game was kept up for some time, to the frustration of the conservatives. It is assumed that under the new, more conservative Majles, these practices will stop.

Jointly Appointed Body

Guardian Council. The Guardian Council is the most influential political body in Iran. It is controlled by conservatives and consists of six theologians appointed by the faqih, and six jurists nominated by the judiciary and approved by parliament, thus creating a deep conservative bias under the present governmental structures. Members are elected for six years on a phased basis, so that half the membership changes every three years.

The Guardian Council has virtual veto power over every electoral candidate, and every piece of legislation that passes parliament, to make sure they conform to the constitution and Islamic law. It is this feature of government more than any other that has caused frustration throughout Iran. Reformists have tried to restrict the council's veto power without success. When they disqualified nearly a third of all candidates who had presented themselves for parliamentary elections more than 2,300 individuals, as mentioned above, they faced boycotts and resignations from sitting Majles members. This did not faze them. Only when Faqih Khamene'i called them in and pleaded with them to relax their hard line did they allow a few hundred candidates back on the ballot. Even so, as a result of their disqualifications, the elections were biased in favor of the conservatives.

The Elections

Over six thousand people presented themselves for election to parliament in February 2004. They were affiliated with dozens of parties, large and small. Despite the many parties, they were divided into conservative and reform camps. In response to the elimination of most of their candidates by the Guardian Council, the Militant Clerics Society—the principal reform group, of which President Khatami is a member—called for a boycott of the election, and withdrew its own candidates. Seven smaller reform parties could not mount enough candidates to contest the election. Of the 290 seats, approximately 130 were completely uncontested, resulting in a conservative victory.

A great deal was made of voter participation in this election. Since the last parliamentary and presidential elections had high voter turnouts (over 70 percent), it was thought that a low turnout would discredit the government. Turnout in rural areas and smaller towns and cities was heavy, whereas the residents of Tehran and other urban areas stayed away in large numbers. In Tehran, only 30 percent of the population voted, but the overall vote was around 50 percent. A number of races were not decided in the first round of polling. In districts where no candidate received more than 25 percent of the vote, runoff elections were held.

The reasons for the conservative victory are complex. It is an undisputed fact that despite the boycotts, a new parliament was elected, and with voter participation higher than is typical in the United States. Of course, the Guardian Council's role in eliminating many reform candidates ahead of time had a great deal to do with the reduced turnout and the overwhelming conservative victory. However, this does not completely explain why conservatives won.

Many voters who associated themselves with the reform movement were already displeased with the reform candidates for failing to make good on their promise to change things for the better, and were, as a result, philosophical about the takeover of the conservatives. Indeed, the Reformists' main failure has been their inability to connect with the average Iranian, the very ones who gave them 70 percent support in the 2000 elections. Moreover, the reformers, with their great progressive political ideas also espoused neoliberal economic reforms, such as making public schools self-supporting with "registration" fees, and eliminating subsidies on food and fuel and government services. They also failed to mobilize the popular support into any kind of effective political parties. These are the attributes that diminished their popularity.[19] Many Iranians simply want a better life for themselves and their families and feel that, perhaps with the parliament no longer expending its energy on internal political struggle, Iran will face better economic times. This is partly reflected in the emergence of one apparently conservative group that emerged in 2003, calling themselves the

"Coalition of Builders of Islamic Iran." They are technocrats with a conservative social view, but who reject "violence and force" to enforce Islamic regulations. Their spokesman, Gholam-Ali Hadad-Adel, declared that improving the economy was the country's top priority.

Despite the heavy hand of the Guardian Council, which many Americans might view as a non-democratic feature of the Iranian elections, the actual voting process seems to have been both free and fair. Typically, rigged elections return astonishingly high percentage figures in favor of current rulers. In Iran, although this time the conservatives won, they by no means took one hundred percent of the Majles seats. The example of Tehran is instructive. Despite widespread boycotts, of the eighty-three seats, forty-three were won by conservatives, twenty-one by reformists, seventeen were undecided and went to run-off elections because no one obtained the requisite twenty-five percent of the votes, and the other two seats were won by independents whose political views were not known.

In the runoff elections, held on May 7, 2004, for 57 seats, reformists did not improve their standing. The conservatives emerged with a two-thirds majority, leaving the reform movement in shambles. This was due in part to the small number of reformists running—approximately 20 of 114 total candidates.[20] I report on the June 2005 presidential election at the end of this chapter.

Reform?

What do the elections mean? It is difficult at this writing to predict with any certainty what is in store for Iran under this new parliament. A few guesses might be made, however. Reform cannot be turned back. The conservatives have been forced to relax their former draconian regulation of public morality. Hamid Dabashi claims that this is the inevitable consequence of Shi'ism itself. He claims that Shi'ism remains potent only when it is resisting oppression. When it is victorious it "easily collapses into the most ferocious form of tyranny of the most sacred severity the instant that it assumes power. Shi'ism has to be defeated in order to remain victorious."[21]

It does seem as though the draconian measures of the past are waning. The difficulties experienced by Azar Nafisi as a professional woman in the early 1980s[22] are no longer present to the same degree. Women must still adopt modest dress in public, but there are few squads of revolutionary guards throwing women in prison for showing too much hair, or breaking up wedding parties for playing popular music.[23] Iran is some distance from the broad range of freedom in public behavior that was prevalent under the shah, but definitely not as conservative as in the years immediately following the Revolution of 1978–79. It is important to remember, particularly with regard to public conduct of females, that a large proportion of the population always adopted modest dress, even under the shah.[24]

The conservative government favors, and will continue to develop, Iran's nuclear power capacity. As worrisome as this is, at this writing in 2005, Iran is nowhere near making a bomb, despite American fears to the contrary.[25] This is not to say that Iran will never have atomic weapons. In their "neighborhood" there are other states, such as Pakistan and India, with nuclear weapons. Iranians often note with a rueful cynicism that Americans tend to deal differently, and more respectfully, with nations that do have an atomic bomb.

It may also be difficult for the conservatives to curtail support of external Islamic groups such as Hezbollah in Lebanon. This has been one of the chief causes of hostility on the part of the United States.[26] The Coalition of Builders of Islamic Iran represent a vanguard of social conservative technocrats concentrating on industry and economy. They seem to be promulgating a kind of "China" model for Iran—promising consumer goods and improved living conditions, but eschewing relaxation of social processes. Their orientation is decidedly pragmatic, and their view may significantly shift the focus of the conservatives to more international concerns. It may not be too optimistic to look for a thaw in relations with the United States as these pragmatists begin to exercise power.

The passing of Ayatollah Khamene'i in a few years will be a watershed for Iran. No successor has been found for him, and the Khomeinist line he represents may die with him. The growing influence of Shi'a clerics in Iraq, who do not support the velayat-e faqih doctrine will hasten this likely development. Iran will continue to have conservative and liberal factions, but it is at this point that the form of government itself may change.

The driving source for this change will likely be women and youth. Today, approximately 60 percent of university students in Iran are women. Literacy for women under the age of twenty-five nearly equals that of men. As mentioned above, women are represented in every profession, and there are more women in the Majles than in the U.S. Congress. Seventy-five percent of the entire Iranian population is under twenty-five. They never saw the shah or Khomeini, and have no personal knowledge of the revolution. By 2010 they will constitute the majority of the voting population.

The elderly clerics will undoubtedly be supplanted as they pass from the scene. The next generation will be the one to effect change. They are the best educated Iranian population in history, and they have access to computers, satellite dishes, and every device of modern information technology. As a result, they are also exceptionally well informed about their own lives and about international affairs. They will come into political office sooner rather than later, and when they do, the reforms being clamored for will take place. The American neoconservative desire to destroy the current government will not bring about reform; it will set it back by unleashing social unrest. Iranians themselves have no desire for internal conflict. For the time being, they are able to work with their flawed governmental structures, despite the undercurrent of social unrest that will bring reform in time. Now, they make up about 40 percent of the voting population. As stated, by the next parliamentary election, they will be the majority, and then the world will see something very interesting happen in Iran.

Perhaps the most foolish idea circulated in Washington in the past few years is the notion that the United States could somehow engineer the "overthrow" of the Iranian government and the "establishment of a democracy" there. This idea has been promulgated incessantly in conservative think tanks, such as the American Enterprise Institute.[27] As one can see, although the government of the Islamic Republic has structural flaws that allow a group with a dominant ideology to gain a stranglehold over many areas of government, the system continues to work, albeit with a lot of creaks and groans. Iran is not a dictatorship like Iraq, and it is unclear whom the United States would "overthrow" if it wanted to foment revolution in Iran. Removing the faqih would do nothing at all. One would have to destroy several of the interlocking governmental bodies to have any effect. By that time, the population would be in revolt against the American backed usurpers.

Moreover, there are no good candidates for a replacement government. The public is disaffected with the Reformists, whom they believe betrayed them, or at least proved feckless. There is a small body of monarchists clamoring for the return of the son of the deposed shah, also named Reza Pahlavi, who is now living in the United States. However, he has no real support inside Iran. The Mujaheddin-e Khalq (MEK) have the support of some elements in Washington, since they were the source of information that tipped Washington off to Iranian nuclear power developments, but this group, which was supported and sheltered by Saddam Hussein, is openly hated in Iran. Additionally, they are an aging group. They would have no chance of ruling.

The Iranian population now also seems to have no stomach for revolution. They hover between apathy and vague hopes that the future will improve. Evolutionary change, therefore, seems to be the most plausible course. In many ways, the Iranian elections were quite normal. Having had several years to change things in Iran and failed, the Reformists were voted out of office. The same thing would have happened in the United States. The last elections were robust, and showed that they contained workable mechanisms. The Guardian Council notwithstanding, the electoral process is certain to be a lively, active, and moderately effective institution for the expression of Iran's public political will.

U.S. Symbolic Discourse

The United States has carried an uneasy symbolic burden since World War II. It has inherited all of the residual anger that the nations of Asia, Africa, and Latin America directed toward European powers in the nineteenth and early twentieth centuries. It has also chosen to assume all of the responsibilities those colonialist powers associated with their power: regulation of the world economy, international peacekeeping, and prevention of the spread of "evil."

In this final respect, U.S. leaders assume a moral posture surprisingly similar to that of the religious leaders of Iran. There is an important difference: evil for the United States is seen in secular, humanistic terms rather than in explicitly religious terms. The *summum bonum* for most American leaders is a pluralistic world of independent nation states, each fully democratic, which work internally to dignify the individual and protect his or her right to achieve success, happiness, and personal satisfaction through exercise of his or her own labor. These ideal states also work externally to promote balance and harmony with other states and to prevent hegemony and injustice. This was the vision promulgated by the "neoconservatives" in the administration of President George W. Bush, who hoped to impose this state of affairs on Iraq, Afghanistan, and eventually Iran, in hopes of "taming" the Middle East, and creating a safe environment for the continued existence of Israel.

Despite this somewhat monolithic vision, U.S. leaders see international politics as a continuing process. Nations, like individuals, must accommodate each other on the road to a harmonious and balanced future. Laws are imperfect and must be reviewed and modified continually. Thus, compromise, bargaining, and negotiation are necessary. Indeed, failure to show "good faith" in the process of negotiating differences is seen as unacceptable behavior. Such recalcitrance is justifiably met by persuasion, usually in the form of economic or military force.

As I argued in the early chapters of this book, the U.S. discourse on foreign policy, based as it is on the belief system that starts with the nation state as a given, breaks down quickly when the states of the world are given close scrutiny. One additional irony in this American world view is the further assumption that national leaders are empowered to act on behalf of their citizens—even when the states involved are not democracies. Negotiation is therefore generally carried out in a narrow framework involving a small number of elite leaders. A common tactic to gain leverage in negotiating difficult situations is to focus on co-opting or persuading these powerful individuals to accommodate, or at least to listen to, American wishes. Mohammad Reza Pahlavi used such tactics, as did Anwar Sadat.

It is hardly necessary to review the numerous international conflicts and disputes that the United States has justified by invoking these symbolic goals. But it is remarkable to remember that in the postwar era, no U.S. military operations anywhere have been undertaken in direct defense of United States territory. All have been undertaken to protect other nations from the incursion of forces that are undesirable from an American perspective. Ironically, the one military operation undertaken in retaliation to an attack on American facilities was the failed hostage-rescue mission in Iran. The invasion of Afghanistan following the attacks of September 11, 2001 was another, and the futile attempts of the Bush administration to tie this tragedy to Iran are noteworthy, as I will point discuss below.

The Clash of Discourse

It is a safe assumption that people—and nations—cannot be expected to shoot themselves in the foot on request, and yet this is just what U.S. and Iranian leaders have asked each other to do again and again since the Islamic Revolution of 1978–79. Whatever their personal feelings, political leaders of both nations are unable to engage in actions that directly violate the most sacred, symbolic political goals of their respective countries.

For Iranian leaders, this means they cannot appear to compromise, once a public moral position has been taken. They are unable to appear to accommodate individuals or nations that are seen as corrupting influences. American leaders are likewise unable to appear to back down in the face of recalcitrance and defiance of correct moral principles defined in American terms. It is at this point that both sides reach an impasse.

The holding of U.S. hostages in Iran in 1979–81 was just such an impasse. American officials attempted to negotiate the hostages' release, but in traditional fashion this meant seeking out a set of elite individuals to serve as "plumbers," who would supposedly "push a button" that would release the hostages. Similarly, in recent attempts to improve relations with Iran and secure Iranian cooperation in gaining the release of American hostages held in Lebanon (often labeled the Iran–Contra Affair), the United States aimed most of its efforts at finding individuals, so-called moderates, who would work on behalf of U.S. interests. In both cases Iranian officials were being asked to do things that would have amounted to political suicide, since close working contacts with the United States could be construed as accommodation to and compromise with an enemy. The Iranian officials in the hostage-taking incident were terrified of being tarred with such a brush. The eventual solution, reached after nearly a year, avoided this problem. Following the beginning of the conflict between Iran and Iraq in October 1980, responsibility for the handling of the hostage crisis passed exclusively into the hands of the State Department, led by Secretary of State Edmund Muskie. From then on, a mediated settlement was pursued. This allowed both sides to deal with each other on an equal basis while avoiding the pollution of direct contact. This eventually led to the hostages' release. The Iranian contacts were never identified; to this day no one knows who in Iran was responsible for their release. Had this approach been pursued earlier, the hostages would undoubtedly have been freed sooner.[28]

In attempting to improve relations with Iran a decade later, National Security Council operatives allowed themselves to be drawn naïvely into an Iranian political framework. In this context, the only way Iranians could approach Americans without being accused of compromise was for the Iranians to get the better of the Americans in a bargaining game. The Iranians quickly showed the superiority of their "bazaar" skills. The American officials provided millions of dollars worth of arms for Iran, and only two of six hostages were released. Relations between the two nations did not perceptibly improve, and one hoped-for result, a willingness on the part of Iran to negotiate a settlement to the Iran–Iraq war, was never even a remote possibility as the result of these contacts.

Iran miscalculated in dealing with the United States too, occasionally assuming that American leaders could be bypassed in a direct appeal to segments of the American population regarded by the Iranians as "downtrodden." During the hostage crisis, such an attempt was made by releasing two black hostages to demonstrate "solidarity with the oppressed black population of the United States." Iranian leaders also called on American politicians to fulfill impossible demands, such as abandoning support for Israel, as a precursor to improving relations with Tehran.

Iranian leaders' worst cultural miscalculation may have been in their adoption of a stonewall posture in almost every dealing with the United States, especially those dealings that promised to provide needed benefits for their country. While this is a common tactic in bazaar bargaining and in winning arguments with opponents in public, it is completely inappropriate with Americans, who need to know that negotiations have a chance of succeeding in order to have the heart to continue. Even in negotiations where Iranians have formally agreed to participate, such as in recent talks aimed at securing the release of Iranians' cash assets remaining in the United States, the process has often broken down when Iranian negotiators have walked out in pique, claiming American "bad faith" in the talks. While some of this is mere posturing, it is nevertheless counterproductive since it has prohibited Iran from receiving its own much-needed assets. One should remember that Iran actually received far less than it originally demanded in negotiations over the hostage release in 1981, largely because Tehran held up the bargaining process with impossible demands long after the hostages had become a political debit to them at home.

Similarly, as tension increased over Iran's development of nuclear energy, the stakes became so high for both the United States and Iran that neither side could retreat without losing honor (for Iran) or moral authority (for the United States). The result was an escalation that moved increasingly away from a solution rather than toward one.

The clerics may enjoy being tough with the United States and there may be clear political benefits at home in seeming to successfully defy a superpower, but Iran is squandering international goodwill through its behavior. This goodwill was needed as Iran began to rebuild after the end of the war with Iraq. The oil industry and other manufacturing facilities needed to be revived for Iran to have continuing income. International financing is a continuing need. American hostility to Iranian actions in areas mentioned in Chapter 9 led to economic sanctions, which were damaging, but not debilitating to Iran, since the United States was the only nation on earth observing them. Iran is not totally without friends—Japan and Germany are its major trading partners—but it will still be difficult for the Islamic Republic to rejoin international trade and commerce, given the standoff with the United States.

How NOT to Live with Iran—George W. Bush Attacks

More worrisome than sanctions was the possibility in 2004 that American ire would lead to violent attacks against Iran. The American hostility had been universal since 1978, coming both from the left and from the right. In the presidential election debates in 2004, both President George W. Bush and John Kerry articulated their intentions to continue a hard line against Tehran.

Hostility against Iran reached a peak in the fall of 2004. President George W. Bush was perpetually under fire for the debacles in the invasions of Iraq and Afghanistan. He also faced criticism for his administration's failings in preparing for and reacting to the tragic attacks against the World Trade Center in New York and the Pentagon in Washington by the al Qaeda organization on September 11, 2001. Consequently, the Bush administration adopted the old, tried and true ploy of muddying the waters to deflect negative press by blaming Iran for everything.

On July 17, 2004, President Bush stated that although the Central Intelligence Agency had found "no direct connection between Iran and the attacks of September 11. Nevertheless," he said, "we will continue to look and see if the Iranians were involved." What was he referring to? Some of the September 11 hijackers may have been allowed to travel through Iran in 1991 without having their passports stamped. This would have been a trivial event, if it happened at all. Once having made the accusation, the Bush administration never mentioned it again, presumably because there was no substance to it and no proof.

Accusations against Iran did not stop with implied involvement in the September 11 disaster. Resident analysts at the neoconservative, right wing American Enterprise Institute and other similar bodies tried to blame Iran for the faulty intelligence presented to justify the Iraq war by the Bush administration. The scenario was presented in the following way: Iran wanted the United States to remove its old enemy, Saddam Hussein. Iranian intelligence therefore supposedly worked through the Defense Department's discredited leader-in-waiting, Ahmad Chalabi, to provide false information to U.S. officials about weapons of mass destruction. This accusation was never documented.

As mentioned above in this chapter, Iran was also accused of supporting Iraqi firebrand cleric Muqtada al-Sadr and his al-Mahdi Army in their opposition to the U.S. occupation by neoconservative pundit, Michael Rubin, who had been an advisor to the U.S.-led Coalition Provisional Authority until summer 2004. Rubin's representation to the Department of Defense and to the public in the *National Observer*[29] a baroque set of connections between Iran and al-Sadr, tenuously based on family and personal relations led to press headlines on the order of "Iran supports al-Sadr rebellion!"

Such "guilt by accusation" constituted a longstanding practice on the part of Bush administration officials and their think tank surrogates. Because Iran was already demonized in the public mind, the administration hoped that any accusation against it would be treated as fact. And the process was cemented not by substantiating the accusation with facts, but by "truth by repetition" of the original charges.

President Bush's announcement that Iran should be investigated was followed by administration spokespersons casually mentioning in interviews and press conferences that Iran seemed to have been involved in killing Americans on September 11.

At one time it seemed that the administration was trumping up charges against Iran in advance of a military action against them—and at this writing, as mentioned above, it may still take place. However, this new round of Iran-bashing had another use—as a political ploy in an election year. The accusations against a demonized enemy, it seems clear, could help rouse the American electorate, and provide another demonstration of President Bush's resolve to resist evil in the world. They certainly had no effect on Iran, except to increase that country's hostility towards the United States.

The Bush administration was not able to keep this game up indefinitely. The Council on Foreign Relations issued a sober, thorough report on July 20 entitled "Iran: Time for a New Approach,"[30] that called the tension between the United States and Iran into question. The report recognized Iran as a "critical actor in the postwar evolution" of Afghanistan and Iraq, and as an "indispensable player in the world economy." It asserted that the United States and Iran have significant mutual interests that must be dealt with on a regular basis. And it advocated abandonment of the policy of estrangement, recommending "limited or selective engagement with the current Iranian government."[31]

The co-chairs of the report were Zbigniew Brzezinski, former National Security Advisor to President Carter, and Robert M. Gates, Director of the CIA from 1991–93. Neither of these men could be construed as doves or pro-Iranian sympathizers.

It would have been irresponsible of President Bush to ignore this report, but he did. It was clearly difficult for him to implement its recommendation of engagement while he and his supporters kept attacking the Islamic Republic of Iran with little justification. It is notable that even the flawed report of the Committee on the Present Danger, as well as Naval officer and professor at the navy war college Thomas P. M. Barnett and Kenneth Pollack, writers with close ties to the military and diplomatic establishments, endorse the proposal of strong diplomatic engagement with Iran—a policy that the Bush White House had absolutely refused to pursue up to early 2005.[32] One can only hope that the force of reason will prevail, and that American government officials will strive toward finding the common ground allowing development of a helpful and productive relationship with Iran. The world will be better for it.

The Discourse of Resistance

It is clear that the United States and Iran have had problems in two areas: in situations that allow moral posturing, and in situations where one nation makes unwarranted and unproven assumptions about the leaders of the other. Iran is not likely to abandon its ideological resistance to the West, nor is the United States likely to approve of revolutionary Islam very soon. However, it is important for both sides to understand that they are dealing with symbolic, rhetorical postures. Such postures need not inhibit the development of better concrete relations as measured in economic and cultural terms.

Americans barely understand Iranian leaders and what motivates them. Iranian leaders are just as naïve about American politics. Nevertheless, there is tremendous room for improved understanding if both sides will utilize the experience of the Americans and Iranians who do know the two systems well—who are, in essence, cultural mediators. Consultation with such individuals was woefully lacking during the Reagan administration—indeed, even former and current State Department officials with long experience in Iran were regularly ignored. Certainly the Iran-contra Affair would have been significantly tempered had the administration sought such consultation.

It is difficult to imagine how Iranian officials can be persuaded to pay more attention to American political sensibilities since they attach so little value to the American governmental system, but if relations in nongovernmental areas improve, they can be expected to become more sophisticated.

Improvement in nongovernmental relations is the real key to amelioration of overall U.S.-Iran relations, since in more benign areas of human endeavor it is possible to become acquainted with the symbolic discourse structures of the other party. Sincere efforts to improve nonmilitary trade should be a priority in this and subsequent administrations. The increase in trade since the revolution has been largely due to the efforts of persistent middlemen and brokers, and has come almost exclusively from the Iranian side. Attempts at reopening cultural exchange between the United

States and Iran, including exchanges of scholars, will also be helpful. At present, the U.S. Consular Service is actively preventing legitimate Iranian academics from coming to the United States, even for conferences and scholarly research. Iran has admitted very few American scholars since the revolution.

If even the small steps suggested above are taken, both nations will have begun a healthy recovery in their dealings with each other. One can hardly expect affairs to be as friendly as in the mid-1970s, when Iran was America's chief ally in the Islamic world, but Americans and Iranians will have some hope of restoring health to an ailing relationship.

Epilogue—The Presidential Elections of 2005

I had the good fortune to be in Iran for the June 2005 presidential election. The election of conservative Tehran mayor Mahmud Ahmadinejad as president was a surprise to the whole world. With a 7 percent share predicted in the pre-election polls, his stunning victory of over 60 percent was not foreseen by anyone. However, in this election, as in all matters involving Iran and the United States, both nations took the occasion to continue to demonize each other. Most particularly, Mr. Ahmadinejad had not even been declared the official winner of the election before he was attacked by the United States government and supporters of the Bush administration.

Neoconservatives in the United States were certain that Mr. Ahmadinejad's rival, former president Ayatollah Ali Akbar Hashemi-Rafsanjani, would win, denouncing his comeback as "due not to popular demand, but to machinations of mullahs"[33] even before the final voting began, thus producing the "Mad Mullah" image once again for the American public. Once Ahmadinejad had been declared the surprise victor, they began to denounce *him* as the candidate of *faqih* Ayatollah Ali Khamene'i, claiming that the election was fixed by the mullahs.[34] Clearly, Iran was to be demonized, whoever won.

True to form, the election was also loudly denounced by President George W. Bush while it was still underway. For their part, the media-savvy Iranian government leaders used President Bush's condemnation of the election as a spur to get voters to the polls, broadcasting his harsh words incessantly on television and radio. No one in Iran referred to the "Great Satan," since President Bush was doing an excellent job of presenting that image, but the implication was clear, and it was effective in motivating the Iranian people.

Then, the old tried-and-true wounds that embitter the United States and Iran toward each other were ritually torn open. On the day Mr. Ahmadinejad's victory was declared, the perpetual enemies of the Islamic Republic, the Mojaheddin-e Khalq (known by the acronyms MEK and MKO in the West) released an old photo purporting to show the newly-elected president with a blindfolded American hostage during the hostage crisis of 1979–81. The photo was immediately shot round the world, and the accusations that Mr. Ahmadinejad was a "hostage taker" flew fast and furious. Some of the former hostages thought they remembered him from their experience twenty-five years ago. Other accusations—that he had tortured or murdered dissidents—were also put forward.

However, it was all a lie. Sa'id Hajjarian, an aide to outgoing president Mohammad Khatami and one of the original planners of the hostage crisis, quickly verified that the man depicted in the photo was not Mr. Ahmadinejad, but rather Taqi Mohammadi, one of the young men involved in the hostage taking, who later joined the MEK, and died in prison. A second man also depicted in the photo died in the Iran–Iraq War. Mr. Hajjarian had spoken out against Mr. Ahmadinejad in the presidential election and had no reason to lend him undue support.[35] Even without Mr. Hajjarian's statement, a cursory inspection of the suspect photograph showed immediately that it was not Mr. Ahmadinejad.

Although Mr. Ahmadinejad *was* involved in the deliberations leading to the hostage taking, he felt that the Communists were a greater danger to the Revolution and favored an attack on the embassy of the Soviet Union. This would, of course, have been important for the MEK, since their philosophical inspiration was a blend of Marxism and Islamic thinking.

Aside from the MEK, at the time of the election there were a large number of people in the world interested in discrediting the Iranian government, even when they had to resort to outright lies or absurdly twisted logic. The MEK, who participated in the original Revolution twenty-seven years ago but were cut out of power six months later, still harbored fantasies of marching on Tehran and taking over the nation. They created a shadow government outside of Iran and maintained a coterie of aging troops massed near the Iranian border in Iraq, with the blessing of the United States. In an astonishingly effective political coup, they co-opted a number of American legislators who supported them with American taxpayer dollars in the years following the September 11, 2001 tragedy. Among these were Senator Rick Santorum of Pennsylvania, Senator Sam Brownback of Kansas, and Representative Ileana Ros-Lehtinen of Florida. The MEK somehow convinced these American officials that they would be able to bring "democracy" to Iran. The fact is that at the time of Mr. Ahmadinejad's election, the MEK was still on the U.S. government list of terrorist groups. This seemed not to faze Santorum, Brownback, or Ros-Lehtinen, who undoubtedly associated the Iranian government with terrorism in a broad sense, and naïvely looked on any group that would get rid of the clerical government as a blessing.

The neoconservatives—many of whom have been mentioned in this book, such as Ledeen, Pletka, and others like Richard Pearle, Patrick Clawson and Daniel Pipes, all Bush administration confidants–still harbored the hope that the United States would launch a military strike against Iran, largely driven by the conviction that Iran poses a danger to Israel. Discrediting Iran's new president was to be yet another reason put forward by the Bush administration, demonstrating why the government in Tehran would have to go.

What the neoconservatives and the MEK were trying to hide from the American people is that Mr. Ahmadinejad is, in fact, a departure from the Iranian regime of the past. Although a religious conservative, he is not a cleric, and he embraced key aspects of Iran's reformist agenda. As an anti-corruption candidate, he appealed to the Iranian electorate, who are sick of the nepotism and outright theft that had crept into twenty-seven years of clerical rule—liabilities that many saw embodied in Mr. Ahmadinejad's rival, Ayatollah Hashemi-Rafsanjani.

There may indeed have been a "fix" in the Iranian presidential election, as many people inside and outside Iran claimed. Time will tell. However, in my observation of the election, there is no doubt that Mr. Ahmadinejad had genuine support. Westerners, including Westernized Iranians, tend to ignore the traditional population in South Tehran and outside the capital in assessing the Iranian political climate. It is largely these more traditional people who elected Ahmadinejad.

Mr. Ahmadinejad represented a clear departure from recent leaders. Some Iranian commentators have already noted at the time of the election that, far from being a tool of the ruling clerics, he seems to represent a rejection of everything the public disliked about them.

First, he is not a cleric. The first president of the Islamic Republic, Abol-Hasan Bani-Sadr—also not a cleric—was quickly removed from office. The next three presidents, Khamene'i, Hashemi-Rafsanjani, and Khatami, were all mullahs. For Iranians who consider themselves good Muslims, but who are tired of clerical rule, Ahmadinejad's election was a fresh approach to leadership. Chief among these were those who supported the original Revolution of 1978–79 but who felt that clerical rule had deprived them of the economic benefits that were supposed to accrue to the *mostazefin* (downtrodden).

Second, Mr. Ahmadinejad presents credentials as a technocrat, a civil engineer with a Ph.D. who is deeply committed to Iran's progress in technology, medical science, and industry—including nuclear power. He demonstrated in his successful term as mayor that he had the expertise to lead the country in this direction, which was fervently desired by the population.

Third, he gives the appearance of being modest, honest, and pious. The majority of Iranians believed that the clergy had become corrupt in their leadership, enriching themselves and their families, becoming a new kind of royalty in Iran. Mr. Ahmadinejad represents the antithesis of this image.

Beyond that, like all the other candidates in the election, he could not ignore the eight-year-old Reform Movement. His early pronouncements dealt with the respect due to women as equal partners in society, the need for improvement in economic conditions for the poor, and advancement of education. These statements hardly sounded reactionary to the voters—they sounded just like the aspirations of Iran's reformists.

In one important way Mr. Ahmadinejad is like most of his countrymen: he is seen as a fierce nationalist. Utterly uninterested in kowtowing to the United States, he expresses a desire to make Iran, independently, a great economic and intellectual power. In this, he continues the aspirations of Iranians from the past—willing to remain estranged from America until the time when Iran is held in equal regard to the other nations of the world.

Time will tell whether Mr. Ahmadinejad finds the power to make good on his early pronouncements. He deserves a chance to show his mettle. Certainly his ascension to office should be greeted with cautious respect. The danger in attacking him before he even gets started in office is that he, and the Iranian government, may turn further inward, adopting a defensive, defiant posture to the world, continuing the cycle of mutual demonization that I have outlined in this book.

The United States should fervently hope that this does not happen. This is why at this writing, one hopes that the Bush administration can ignore the naysayers. With patience and care, Mr. Ahmadinejad, along with Iran's rising youth generation, can be brought productively into cooperation with the United States. But first, a quarter century of bitterness between the two nations must cease. Rejecting the slander against Mr. Ahmadinejad would be an excellent first step toward dismantling and burying forever the two poisonous images of this book: the Great Satan and of the Mad Mullah.

Notes

Preface

1. Mead 1972.
2. Much of this work was documented in the *The Study of Culture at a Distance*. A new edition of this work was issued in 2000. Mead and Métraux 2000.
3. Fallers 1974.
4. Cf. Comaroff and Comaroff 1999, 2001; Fergusson 1990, 2004; Fergusson and Gupta 2002; Foucault 1991.

Chapter 1: Discourse and Demonization

1. I borrow this term from Professor R. K. Ramazani in his insightful book *The United States and Iran*. Ramazam 1982. See also his *Revolutionary Iran*. Ramazani 1986. As well as Ramazani 1990, 1998, and James Bill's remarkable account of U.S.–Iranian relations, *The Eagle and the Lion*. Bill 1988a. See also Beeman 1986c, 1987.
2. In 1849–50 c.e./1266 a.h. (Keddie 1972b: 13–14).
3. He departed for India in 1857 c.e./1273 a.h, where he first became acquainted with Western scholarship. Keddie 1972b: 24ff..
4. Ibid., 35.
5. Cf. Gluckman 1955; Siegel and Beals 1960; Levine 1961; Dahrendorf 1968; Gluckman 1955; LeVine 1961; Dahrendorf 1968.
6. However, some possible analogous parallels include dealings with North Korea and a variety of other nations, the United States and Cuba, and Israel and a number of Arab states.
7. Nader 2001. See also Nader 1997, 2002: Chapter 3.
8. Nader 2001: B13; Nader 2002.
9. Nader 2002.
10. Cf. Beeman 1987.
11. Cf. Bateson et al. 1977; Beeman 1976b.
12. Cf. Chelkowski and Dabashi 1999.

13. Michael M. J. Fischer and Mehdi Abedi point out that the "rhetorics of contemporary politicized Islam both simply fear difference and block access to the ethics of *difference*. 1990: 153. Paradoxically, the same can be said about the United States with regard to Iran.

Chapter 2: American Myths

1. Gadamer 1975.
2. I have elaborated on the U.S. foreign policy myth at greater length in other publications. Beeman 1986a, 1986d.
3. Nowhere is the structure of this belief so clearly seen as in the composition of U.S. embassy staffs. There are always economic attaches and political attaches, but in no embassy in the world is there a single officer whose primary duty is to interpret cultural differences which could cause misunderstandings between nations. This lack is reflected in mistake after mistake in the conduct of U.S. diplomatic personnel everywhere—events I hardly need to detail for readers here.

In fairness, I must note that the United States is hardly alone among nations in having some unskillful diplomats and foreign policy advisors, or being unable to analyze cultural differences. I should further note that the sensitivity that *is* demonstrated by talented, diligent persons at the working levels of the foreign policy community is often obscured in the United States when recommendations and observations reach the White House, where action decisions are made by persons with minimal direct experience in dealing with the cultural realities of the non-Western world. As an anthropologist I cannot resist stating that I think the world could use many more anthropologically trained individuals in foreign policy positions everywhere to compensate for those who believe that money and guns are the only basis for international understanding.

4. Two of the planes crashed into the World Trade Center, one into the Pentagon. A fourth crashed into a field in Pennsylvania. It was widely assumed that the fourth plane was headed for another target in Washington, D.C., or toward the presidential retreat at Camp David.
5. Of course, as the world knows, if broad social movements prove to be important in terms of the United States' interpretation of the East–West struggle, then great significance is attached to them.
6. Given the United States' extraordinary economic and military resources compared to the developing world (especially in the immediate post–World War II decade), this "superpower" mentality was perhaps understandable, but increasing sophistication of the educated world population (many of whom were educated in the United States) has made this view seem naive and anachronistic.
7. James Bill 1988a and Marvin Zonis 1991 document this isolation extremely effectively.
8. Arjomand 1988a, 1988b; Hoveyda 2003.
9. Hoveyda 2003; Keddie and Matthee 2002; Sciolino 2000.
10. Esposito and Ramazani 2001.

Chapter 3: Middle Eastern Myths

1. Hoveyda 2003.
2. The account of the opposition between the internal (*bāten* or *batin*) and

the external (*zāher*) is somewhat simplified for the purposes of this discussion. See also Beeman 1986d for a much fuller discussion. It should be pointed out that Iran is by no means unique in maintaining a distinction between "inside" and "outside" dimensions in symbolic culture. Javanese and Japanese are two other cultural systems with this distinction, but the particular content of the two cultural arenas in those societies is very different from that of Iran. For additional discussion on this point see Beeman 1977, 1986d, 1988. Nikki Keddie points out that the *zāher* need not be identified merely as the locus of evil. It also can be seen as a zone which contains and excludes those evil forces which may attempt to intrude on the pure *baten*, which should not be open to outsiders. cf. Nikki Keddie, "Symbol and Sincerity in Islam," *Studia Islamica* 19. 1963:27–64.

3. The term *bātin* or *baten*, depending on the system of transliteration used, refers to the figurative and symbolic "inside." The term *andarun* usually refers to a physical interior space, most often the interior of the home where the nuclear family resides. The term *zāher* refers to the figurative and symbolic "outside." *Birun* refers to the physical exterior, and the *biruni* is the part of the home reserved for guests to the household.

4. Cf. Michael M. J. Fischer, *Iran: From Religious Dispute to Revolution*: 147–56, for an account of the meaning of the figures of Hossein and his father, Ali, in present-day politico-religious discourse. Fischer terms the cultural symbolic complex of Hossein and his death the "Karbala paradigm."

5. Cole and Keddie 1986; Fischer 2003; Fischer and Abedi 1990.

6. Sciolino 2000.

7. Cf. Bateson, Clinton, Kassarjian, Safavi, Soraya, 1977: 257–73.

8. Bateson et al. 1977: 269–70.

9. See Corbin 1973; Sarraf and Corbin 1991.

10. Adelkhah 2000: 33, 45.

11. This was, of course, the immediate cause of the capture and holding of U.S. embassy personnel for 444 days in 1979–81.

12. As Kenneth Pollack, former director for Gulf affairs at the National Security Council, asserts out in his recent book, *The Persian Puzzle: The Conflict between Iran and America*, "the Iranian version of events is flat-out wrong. By the 1970s, the United States was not the arbiter of Iran's fate. Indeed, the United States had allowed itself to be reduced to a subordinate position in the U.S.–Iranian relationship. To the extent that anyone was manipulating anyone, it was the shah who was manipulating the United States through his abilitiy to influence oil prices, his ability to determine where billions of petro-dollars would be spent, his monopoly over strategic freedom of action in the Gulf region, his lobbying and propaganda network in the United states, and his control over virtually all of the information the United States received from his country." Pollack 2004: 138. Similar conclusions about the weakness of American power in the waning days of the Pahlavi dynasty are reached by Bill 1988, Rubin 1980, and Zonis 1991. Although this is Pollack's opinion, it does demonstrate both the disparity between American and Iranian views of the revolution, and the need for Iranians to frame the revolution in terms of the existence of a symbolic outside enemy. As anthropologists know, symbolic constructions often prevail in public attitudes over any number of provable facts. It should be noted that Pollack is the author of a widely cited book-length justification for the 2003 inva-

sion of Iraq. Pollack 2002. His affinity for the "official" line of the Bush administration can hardly be gainsaid.

13. Only after the hostage negotiations had been taken over by a completely different group of U.S. government officials than had directed the operations for the previous year.

14. The arms-for-hostages negotiations in 1986–87 are a case in point. The need to reestablish relations with Iran was correctly recognized by the Reagan administration, but the means used to achieve this were naive. For example, American negotiators still did not recognize the danger they constituted for Iranian officials. The only way these officials could "deal" with the Americans and not risk the charge of collusion with an enemy by their political rivals was to best the United States in the deal. See Beeman 1981a.

15. A *fatwa* is an opinion, generally issued by a recognized religious leader, which Osama bin Laden is not. His *fatwa* was ratified by a cleric, but many consider it illegitimate as a decree incumbent on believers.

Chapter 4: Discourse and Rhetoric

1. Modarresi 1993, 2001.
2. Friedrich 1981, 1986a, 1986b, 1998; Friedrich and Dil 1979.
3. Grice 1989, 1991a, 1991b, 2001.
4. Gumperz 1971, 1982; Gumperz, Cook-Gumperz, Szymanski, 1999; Gumperz and Hymes 1972.
5. Gumperz and Hymes 1972; Hymes 1964, 1972, 1974a, 1974b, 1978, 1980, 1981, 1983, 1995, 2003; Hymes and Fought 1981; Hymes, Johnson and Sapir 1998; Hymes, National Institute of Education (U.S.) and University of Pennsylvania Graduate School of Education 1982; Ochs, Schegloff, and Thompson 1996; Sacks and Jefferson 1992.
6. Sacks and Jefferson 1989, 1992.
7. Schegloff 1968, 1972, 1980, 1982.
8. Hymes 1962, Hymes 1964.
9. Jakobson 1960.
10. Cf. Hymes 1970: 72.
11. Nunberg 2004: 52.
12. For Rushdie's book, *The Satanic Verses*, which Ayatollah Ruhollah Khomeini deemed blasphemous.
13. Ibid., 53.
14. Lakoff 1991.
15. Lakoff 2004.
16. Ibid., 69.
17. Reported by Agence France Press in a syndicated story. The *Pakistani Daily Dawn* is one source that reprinted the story on April 28, www.dawn.com/2004/04/28/int8.htm.
18. Lakoff 2004: 70–71.
19. Corsi 2005.
20. January 19, 2005. Cf. http://news.bbc.co.uk/1/hi/world/americas/4186241.stm.
21. Posted on the White House web site: www.whitehouse.gov/news/releases/2005/03/20050308-3.html.

22. Said 1979.
23. See Asdjodi 2001 and Keshavarz 2001.
24. Beeman 1986d.
25. Sciolino 2003.

Chapter 5: Images of the Great Satan

1. See Fischer and Abedi 1990: 195–97 for a refutation by a prominent theologian of the proposition that Shi'a Islam is just a rewriting of Zoroastrianism.

2. The word "div" is both the root for "devil" and "daeva," the name for the deities of South Asia. The modern applellation: diva, comes from this term. The Vedic term for demons is "asura." In the transformation between South Asian languages and Iranian languages, "s" becomes "h," yielding "ahura." Ahura Mazda is the name of the supreme deity in Zoroastrianism. The fact that div is a word indicating a good spirit in India and a bad spirit in Iran has often been cited as an indication of religious divisions among Indo–European peoples in antiquity.

3. Azar Nafisi documents this repeatedly in her memoir, *Reading Lolita in Tehran*: "The color of my head scarf or my father's tie were symbols of Western decadence and imperialist tendencies. Not wearing a beard, shaking hands with members of the opposite sex, clapping or whistling in public meetings were likewise considered Western and therefore decadent, part of the plot by imperialists to bring down our culture. Nafisi 2003: 26. In a classroom debate over the merits of *The Great Gatsby*, one of her conservative students sums up the matter nicely: "[T]he West is our enemy, it is the Great Satan, not because of its military might, not because of its economic power but because of . . . its sinister assault on the very roots of our culture. What our Imam calls cultural aggression." Ibid: 126. Kenneth Pollack 2004 continually refers to the United States as viewed by Iran as the Great Satan.

4. Rubin 1981.
5. Zonis 1991.
6. Sick 1985.
7. Bill 1988a, 1988b, 2001
8. Pollack 2004.
9. Ramazani 1982. Ramazani's later postrevolutionary works deal much more with the pattern of Iranian culture as they played out in the formation of the new state. Ramazani 1986, 1990, 1998.
10. Fischer 1980; Fischer and Abedi 1990.
11. Mottahedeh 1980, 1985.
12. Amini 2002; Downes 2002; Ganji 2002; Hooglund 2002; Hoveyda 2003; Kazemzadeh 2002; Keddie and Matthee 2002; Keddie and Richard 2003; Ruhollah Khomeini and Algar 2002; Rundle 2002; Tapper 1983a, 1983b, 2002; Vahdat 2002; Wright 2001.
13. Cf. Chapter 3, footnote 2 above.
14. Bateson et al. 1977.
15. Bateson et al. 1977: 269–70.
16. Iranians take inordinate pride in these facts, and justifiably. Persian accomplishments in poetry, literature, mathematics, art, and architecture are arguably unparalleled in the history of human culture.

17. Cf. Fischer 1980: 147–56, for an account of the meaning of the figures of Hossein and his father, Ali in present-day politico-religious discourse.

18. Beeman 1976a, 1986d, 2001a.

19. Curzon 1892: 15.

20. In a study carried out at Harvard University in 1972, James Prior (personal communication) maintained that the highest degree of correlation between vocabulary terms on a list of affective dimensions presented to Iranian students for matching was between *dust dashtan,* "to like, love," and *ehteram gozardan,* "to respect." Szalay 1979: 3–6, 7–16.

21. It is reported that the son of the former shah, Crown Prince Reza, counciled his high school companions to seek out the best foreign universities for their higher education "since," he reportedly said, "you will all have important positions in my government, and it is important that you get the best training possible." Likewise, the former shah was struck to the heart with grief by the fact that many of those who had betrayed him in the downfall of his regime were army officers whom he had known and trusted since they had gone to school together as boys.

22. For further discussion on superior-inferior and equality relationships, particularly as they relate to language usage, see Beeman 1976d, 1986d.

23. The source for the above figures is Vakil 1977. Similar data based on Iran's GDP are presented in: United Nations.

24. Cf. Rubin 1981: 136–38.

25. Haliburton later aquired Kellogg, Brown, and Root and continued operating in this fashion up to the present day. Dick Cheney became president of the corporation and continued its business practices until elected vice president in 2000. The "cost-plus" principle had by this time become an ingrained principle of Haliburton's business practices. Having been awarded a no-bid contract for supplying the U.S. military during the U.S. invasion of Iraq in 2003, the "cost-plus" principle resulted in hugely inflated costs during the invasion and in the reconstruction period. At this writing, Haliburton's business dealings are still under federal investigation.

26. Cf. Mottahedeh 1980: 25.

27. The Iranian parliament.

28. Ibid., 27.

29. Ibid., 28.

30. Ibid., 28–29.

31. Cf. Graham 1978: Chapter 11, for an extensive discussion of further aspects of cultural dilemmas created for Iranians by modernization.

32. Parviz Kimiavi's film, *The Mongols* (1973), burlesques the effects of the invasion of television in rural Iran by likening it to the Mongol invasions of the twelfth and thirteenth centuries. Ironically, the film was financed by National Iranian Radio–Television itself, and shown on television.

33. Cf. Naficy 1981.

34. Pace 1975: 43.

35. Cf. footnote 76 above.

36. Abrahamian 1980: 25. See also Keddie and Matthee 2002.

37. J. Kendell, "The Tehran Bazaar," *New York Times,* June 29, 1979. Cited in Abrahamian 1980: 25. Charles Kurzman's study of the Iranian revolution highlights the role of the bazaar in fomenting the revolution. As the core of the Iranian non-oil economy, and the center of religious life, there was hardly an institution

more essential for the promulgation of the forces that toppled the shah. Kurzman 2004.

38. The well-known Iranian secret police force SAVAK is an acronym for Sazeman-e Amniat va Ettela'at-e Keshvar (Organization (for) National Security and Intellegence).

39. Bill 1978/79: 329.

40. Interview in *Al Nahar Al-'Arabi wa al-Duwali*, December 24–30, l979. Cited in Rubin, *Paved with Good Intentions*: 195.

41. A hilarious illustration of mistrust of the British is seen in Iraj Pezeshkhzad's magnificent comic novel *My Uncle Napoleon*, which became an unprecedented success as an Iranian television series. Pezeshkhzad 1996.

42. United States. Congress. House. Committee on International Relations. Subcommittee on International Organizations. 1976: 56. Cited in Rubin, 1981: 137. The hearings were continued in 1977.

43. Khomeini 1979: 49.

44. Ibid., 15–16.

45. *Washington Post*, Novmber 18, 1979. Cited in Rubin 1981: 203.

46. Note James Davies now classic "J-Curve" theory to describe a revolution of rising expectations: "When a long period of rising expectations and gratifications is followed by a short period during which expectations continue to rise while gratifications fall off sharply, the probability of civil violence against the government rises rapidly." Davies 1978: 1357–58. See also Davies 1962, 1969, 1977. Cf. also Zabih 1979: 76.

Chapter 6: Images of the Mad Mullah

1. Mobasser 2003.

2. Keddie and Richard 1981, 2003.

3. Although there are a number of differences in religious practice, including the number of times for prayer (3 vs. 5), the attitude of the hands during prayer, the addition of a phrase acknowledging Ali as the "regent of God" in the creed of faith, and other matters that some conservative Sunnis find disturbing. cf. Cole, Fischer and Abedi 1990; Nakhash 2003a.

4. Abdo and Lyons 2003: 7, 9, 27–28; Al-Qazwini 1999; Halm and Brown 1997.

5. Material concerning celebration of Imam Hossein's martyrdom is very extensive. One excellent source is Chelkowski 1979. See also Fischer 1980, Fischer and Abedi 1990 on the "Karbala [sic] paradigm."

6. Keddie and Richard 1981.

7. Cf. Algar 1969, 1972. The official term is velayat-e faqih or regency of the jurisprudent

8. Lewis 2003a, 2003b; Hodgson 1980. Hodgson specifically discounts the widespread report that the assassins were given hashish to anesthetize them for their exploits. It should also be noted that the "assassins" were Isma'ili, not "Twelver" Shi'ites—the dominant sect in Iran.

9. See Sciolino 2000: 254–60.

10. Cf. Beeman 1983a, 1983b.

11. Arjomand 1980, 1988a, 1988b.

12. Arjomand 1988; Hooglund 1982; Keddie and Hooglund 1986; Keddie,

Hooglund, Woodrow Wilson International Center for Scholars and Middle East Institute, Washington, DC 1982.

13. Ansari 2000.

14. Ibid.: 81.

15. Abdo and Lyons 2003; Ansari 2000: 38, 44, 73, 76; Arjomand 1988b: 97–98.

16. Bayat-Philip 1980; Rahnama 2000; Yousefi 1995.

17. Abdo and Lyons 2003. The implementation of the velayat-e faqih doctrine was by no means a foregone conclusion. Ayatollah Taleghani was a fierce opponent of this innovation. Mohammad Mohaddessin reports: "Because the mullahs did not want to alienate Taleghani [sic] or his supporters, they did not incorporate the velayet-efaqih into the constitution until after Taleghani's death in September, 1979." Mohaddessin 1993: 163.

18. Arjomand 1988b: 117–18, 140–41, 154–57, 167.

19. Kazemipur and Rezaei 2003.

20. Pipes and Clawson 2003a, 2003b. Several U.S. Senators and Representatives actively support the MEK. Notable among them are Senators Sam Brownback (R-Kansas) and Rick Santorum (R-Pennsylvania); and Representative Ileana Ros-Lehtinen (R-Florida) who issued a letter in support of the MEK in November, 2002 claiming support from 150 Congressional colleagues for funding the MEK, but declining to name them (Dealey 2003). Rep. Ros-Lehtinen and Senator Santorum later introduced legislation in the 109th Congress (H-228, S-333) in 2005 calling for extension of economic sanctions against Iran, and funding for "at least one" opposition group to the current Iranian regime. It is fairly certain that given their support for the MEK that it is that organization that they plan to fund. Senator Brownback was successful in introducing a $3 million provision in the omnibus funding bill for the one hundred and eighth Congress in 2004 to fund activities supporting opposition to the Iranian government.

21. Mohaddessin 1993: 43. Mohaddessin has been a prominent member of the MEK.

22. Abdo and Lyons 2003: 30–31.

23. Ibid., 137.

24. One of the most valuable sections of Geneive Abdo and Johnathan Lyons' memoir *Answering Only To God* is their extensive treatment of Montazeri's life and his thought. 2003: 133–44. The couple interviewed Montazeri in his home.

25. Abdo and Lyons 2003: 139.

26. Middle East Review World of Information provides a recent report on Iran's economy as of this writing: "Real GNP grew by 5.0 percent in 2002, compared to 5.1 percent in 2001, and the country's trade surplus remained the same. However, inflation remained high at 17.3 percent, unemployment was 13.5 percent and structural problems persist in the Iranian economy, despite the efforts of the Third FYEDP. In fact, under Khatami average non-oil export growth is at its lowest rate since the 1979 revolution. Meanwhile, population growth and a lack of investment is swelling the number of jobless. Iran's first foreign investment law since the 1950s was passed in June 2002, to help open up the economy and reduce dependence on oil revenues. This raised hopes that Iran may finally reach its targets in 2003 and beyond."

External trade: "Shortages of foreign currency have produced a boom in counter (barter) trade, which obscures the extent of foreign trade; Iran is also understandably reluctant to declare the full extent of its oil traffic in the Gulf, but oil revenues are thought to exceed US $ fifteen billion per annum." Source: Quest Economics Database 2003.

27. Chen and Lin 1994.

28. *Economist* 1980, 1981.

29. Ansari 2000: 170.

30. Ibid., 174.

31. Ibid., 171–73.

32. Ibid., 106–8.

33. Forty women applied to run for president. None of them were approved. Farhi 2001.

34. Ayatollah al-Sistani is known by both the Arabic rendition of his name, Essayyid Ali al-Hossein al-Sistani, and the Persian rendition, Sayyid Ali Hosseini Sistani. In this writing I will use Ayatollah Ali al-Sistani, the appellation most commonly used in the United States press at this writing.

35. Baktiari and Vaziri 2003; Clawson 1998; Esposito and Ramazani 2001; Fairbanks 1998; Hunter 1998; Torkzahrani 1997; Baktiari and Vaziri 2003; Clawson 1998a, 1998b; Esposito 2001; Fairbanks 1998; Hunter 1998.

36. Buchta 1998; Hiro 1980, 1989.

37. Ansari 2000: 209–10.

38. Amuzegar 2003: 57.

39. Gerecht 2002a, 2002b.

40. See the FBI electronic wanted poster for al Adel. www.fbi.gov/mostwant/terrorists/teraladel.htm.

41. Gunaratna 2002. Gunaratna, a Sri Lankan with a penchant for exaggerating his own credentials, in an interview with *Playboy* magazine in the November 2002 issue (Froehlich 2002) claims that "Al Qaeda has gone beyond the ideological divide, which is unprecedented. In fact, the world's two most dangerous groups are Hezbollah and Al Qaeda, a Shia group and a Sunni group that now work together." Australian journalist Gary Hughes, in an exposé of Gunaratna's more egregious speculations quotes Martin Bright, home affairs editor of the British newspaper *The Observer*, and acknowledged expert on Islamic terrorism, who describes "the least reliable of the experts on bin Laden." Hughes continues, saying that Bright maintains that "Gunaratna is often used by the British authorities as an expert witness in the prosecution of Islamist terror suspects because they can rely on him to be apocalyptic." Hughes 2003.

42. Ledeen 2002.

Chapter 7: The Framework of U.S.-Iranian Relations

1. Although some would claim that the clerical regime in Post-Revolutionary Iran is a de facto continuation of the monarchy. Cf. Milani 1988, and Arjomand 1988b.

2. Michael M. J. Fischer 1980. See also Hodgson 1974: 22ff.

3. Ibid.

4. Keddie 1980a: 91–92.

5. Ibid.s: 86.

6. Keddie describes the doctrinal struggle that led to this formulation in the following way: "[T]he second half of the eighteenth century . . . saw developments of socio-political significance within Shi'ism. There was a doctrinal struggle between the Akhbaris, who thought that the Koran and Shi'i Traditions sufficed to guide believers, and the Mujtahidis or Usulis, who said that each believer must choose a living mujtahid whose dicta he was bound to follow. The Mujtahidis finally won, and this reinforced the power of the mujtahids, giving them a force unequalled in Sunni lands, where the ulama had no such power to interpret basic doctrine." Keddie 1980a: 92–3.

7. Indeed, even today most of the city of Mashhad is built on waqf land consecrated to the shrine of Imam Reza, the eighth Imam of Twelver Shi'ite who is buried there.

8. Keddie 1980a: 144.

9. It is fascinating how the seat of leadership in Shi'ism has shifted back and forth between Iran and Iraq over the years. In years when Iran was repressive, Shi'ite leaders sought refuge in Iraq. Under Saddam Hussein, leadership shifted to Qom and Mashhad in Iran. At this writing, following the U.S. invasion of Iraq, Shi'ite leaders, most of whom disagreed with Khomeini's philosophy of the Islamic Republic, have once again returned to Najaf, Kufa, and other Iraqi shrine cities.

10. Beck 1983a, 1983b, 1990; Garthwaite 1983; Gellner 1983; Strathern 1983; Tapper 1983b; Van Bruinessen 1983.

11. Cf. Hooglund 1973.

12. Bonine 1982; Lambton 1992.

13. Safi-Nezhad 1967, 1974; Hooglund 1973.

14. Ajami 1969; Beeman 1976c; Hooglund 1973, 1975, 1981, 1982; Lambton 1969a, 1969b, 1969c; Safi-Nezhad 1967, 1974.

15. Keddie 1972c; Lambton 1969a, 1969b, 1969c.

16. Keddie 1980a: 146.

17. Avery 1965: 81.

18. Cf. Geertz 1960, 1973 for Indonesian examples.

19. Cf. Beeman l976a, 1986a for a demonstration of the ways in which status jockeying in Iran is expressed in verbal behavior.

20. Issawi 1971: 258–59.

21. Avery 1965: 83.

22. Cf. Avery 1965: 88–90.

23. Keddie 1980a: 96.

24. Mohammad Djawad Scheikh-ol-Islami describes the Iranian reaction to the partition agreement thus:

In the first place, they regarded it as a formal agreement, giving effect to their country's partition and the fact that Persia had not been consulted at all about a treaty of such far-reaching consequences; this added fuel to their burning indignation. In the second place, they were engaged in a life-and-death struggle against an autocratic ruler whose words and pledges they had every reason not to trust. The shah was supported by the full weight of Russian diplomacy in Tehran. . . . Russia was absolutely determined to overthrow the newly acquired constitution for it gave promises of stability to the Persian State, which was contrary to the Persian Gulf policy. Persian constitutionalists had up to then, looked to Great Britain for moral and material support if and when the crisis came. Liberal England had entered into a formal agreement with Russia and had formally recognized for her, in the Persian Empire, a large sphere of influence which, incidentally, included Tehran, the capital of the country. Their feelings of fear, suspicion, and resentment were only too natural for, as Persians say, enemies are of three sorts: enemies, enemies of friends, and the friends of enemies. "Russia, the home of unbridled despotism, the ancient foe of liberty in all its forms, was regarded by the constitutionalists as their most deadly enemy and if England sought to make friends with her, how could she be regarded any longer as a trustworthy friend?" Browne 1910; Sheikh-ol-Islami 1965.

25. Millspaugh 1946: 34.
26. Kessler 1992: 50; 2003:90–1.
27. Daftary 1973: 180; Iran. Nukhust Vazir. 1972.
28. Daftary describes it thus: The objectives of the Second Plan were both general and vague, without any quantatative targets. The Plan aimed at: "increasing production, developing exports, preparing public necessities within the country, developing agriculture and industries, discovering and exporting mines and subterranean resources, improving and completing means of communication, improving public health, fulfilling any operations designed for the development of the country, raising the educational and living standard of the people, and improving living conditions" Government of Iran 1956: Article I. No more specific statement of the objectives is available. A glance at this list, which includes just about everything, reveals that it cannot be used as a guide to action. Daftary 1973: 183.
29. Arjomand 1988b.
30. Daftary 1973: 189.
31. Cf. Hooglund 1973, 1975, 1980; Lambton 1969a, 1969b, 1969c.
32. Cf. M. Hooglund 1980.
33. Vakil 1977: 716.
34. *Business Week* 1975.
35. *Business Week* 1977.
36. *Business Week* 1977.
37. Cf. Adelkhah 2000: 53–78.
38. Birch 2003.
39. Hooglund 2002.
40. Shakoori 2001.
41. Ibid.
42. Shakoori's work was appreciated as the first serious attempt at assessing the postrevolutionary agricultural situation, but it was thought to be methodologically weak by several reviewers. Nowshirvani, in a review of the book writes that it "confirms the dearth of sound scholarship on the subject." Nowshirvani 2002.
43. Aghajanian 1991, 1992.
44. Ladier-Fouladi 1997: 195–96; Larsen 2001, 2003. Ladier-Fouladi claims that the birthrate by 1997 was half of what it was in 1986. She attributes this largely to a fatwa or religious decree issued by Ayatollah Khomeini, which allowed birth control to be used provided that it caused no physical harm to the body of the woman, and that her husband agreed. Ladier-Fouladi 1997: 201.
45. Larsen 2001, 2003. Iran requires both men and women to attend classes on

modern birth control methods before obtaining a marriage license. This is also thought to have contributed to the dropping population growth rate.

46. Molavi 2003.

47. Business-Respect 2003.

Chapter 8: The Sins of the United States

1. Shirley 1998.

2. This is particularly the case when Americans travel to Iran and find themselves treated with extreme hospitality and genuine kindness. The contrast between this and the sloganeering and imagery of vilification is highly confusing. According to anthropologist, Victor Turner, it is natural to expect that the forces of evil and disorder should have their locus in the marginal areas of human society. Such areas are known as *liminal*, and a good deal of man's energy in ritual and ceremony is devoted to either preventing these corrupting forces from entering the core arenas of society, or expelling them once they make such an entrance. Clearly, if the equation between the United States and the Great Satan is believed, then many of the street demonstrations in Tehran that vilified the former can be easily understood as ritual purging of deeply felt forces of corruption. Cf. Turner 1967, 1969, 1974.

3. Michael M. J. Fischer documents this beautifully in his extended study of Persian poesis in political rhetoric, religion, and especially in modern media such as Iranian film. Fischer 2004.

4. Browne 1928: vol. 1.

5. Geertz 1960.

6. Cf. Geertz 1960, 1973.

7. Nasr 1967; Hodgson 1960.

8. Tabataba'i 1975.

9. Keddie 1963.

10. Nasr 1965; see also Nasr 1967.

11. Corbin 1957, 1973.

12. Von Grunebaum 1955: 171–72.

13. Tritton 1936: 286.

14. As mentioned earlier, the term "div" reflects the Indo–European root from which the word "devil" is derived.

15. Bahgat 2003; Bill 2001; Docherty, MacIntyre, Canadian Broadcasting Corporation, WGBH television station: Boston, Mass: PBS Home Video 2002; Dorman and Farhang 1987; Farhang 2003; Kinzer 2003; Marsh 2003; Schreer 2003.

16. Cf. Akhavi 1980, Fischer 1980, Keddie 1981a, 1981b.

17. Ahmadi and Ahmadi 1998, Jahanbakhsh 2001.

18. Cf. Daftary 1973.

19. Vakil 1977; United Nations 1978.

20. Kurzman 2004: 112–13.

21. The insensitivity and lack of language and cultural skills among U.S. embassy staff was widely attested. This changed somewhat following the revolution of 1978–79, but it was a case of too little, much too late. Sick 1985, 1989, 1991; Zonis 1991.

22. Cf. Rubin 1980: 136–38.

23. Mottahedeh 1980: 27–29.

24. Cf. Daftary 1973.

25. Cf. Goodell 1977; Hooglund, M. 1980; Weinbaum 1977.

26. Cf. Hooglund, E. 1975, 1981; Safi—Nezhad 1967, 1974, 1978.

27. Afshar—Naderi 1971, Beck 1980c.

28. Cf. Johnson 1980: 23.

29. Abrahamian 1980, 1982, 1999.

30. Kazemi 1980.

31. Kandell 1979.

32. Kessler 1992: 50, 2002, 2003: 90–1; Kinzer 2003; Roosevelt 1979.

33. See also Sullivan 1981, 1982.

34. Saikal 1980: 188–200.

35. Ibid., 55.

36. Personal communication—the individual declined to be identified. This feeling is very widely shared, however. See fn. 37, Chapter 5.

37. Bill 1978/79: 329.

38. Rubin 1980: 195.

39. Kurzman 2004: 17.

40. Cf. Keddie's work on this topic. Keddie and Richard 1981, 2003.

41. Kessler 1992: 50; Kessler 2003: 90–91.

42. The war was never officially concluded. A cease-fire was negotiated in 1988, which marked the conventional end of the war. Iraqi troops were not withdrawn from Iranian territory until 1990, and the last prisoners of war were exchanged in 2003.

43. Chubin and Tripp 1988; Tripp 2000: 233.

44. Evidently Saddam Hussein had a long history with the CIA. Richard Sale writes: "While many have thought that Saddam first became involved with U.S. intelligence agencies at the start of the September 1980 Iran–Iraq war, his first contacts with U.S. officials date back to 1959, when he was part of a CIA-authorized six-man squad tasked with assassinating then Iraqi Prime minister Gen. Abd al-Karim Qasim." Sale 2003: 17. Sale goes on to detail the Qasim assassination plot in great detail.

45. Adel Darwish, Middle East expert and coauthor of *Unholy Babylon.* Darwish and Alexander 1991.

46. Sale 2003: 20.

47. Voice of the Islamic Republic of Iran 2003.

48. Associated Press 1988; Foreign Minister Ali-Akbar Velayati presented the evidence before the United Nations on July 14, 1988.

49. Associated Press 1988.

50. Calling for a negotiated settlement of the war.

51. George H. W. Bush 1988. See also Bush and United States Dept. of State. Bureau of Public Affairs 1988; Raum 1988.

52. United States. Congress. House. Committee on International Relations. Subcommittee on International Economic Policy and Trade. 1995.

53. Morgan, Al-Sowayal, and Rhodes 1998.

54. Ibid.

55. Beeman 2003a, 2003b.

56. Pipes and Clawson 2003a, 2003b.

57. Ismailova 2003.

58. Linzer 2005.
59. FDCH-emedia (*Washington Post*) 2005.
60. Jensen 2005. See also Hersh 2005.

Chapter 9: The Sins of Iran

1. Kafala 2002.
2. Milani 1988.
3. Histories and accounts of the hostage crisis abound. Among some of the most interesting are first-person accounts by the hostages themselves, and by individuals involved in the seemingly endless and fruitless negotiations to obtain the hostages' release, such as Christopher, Kreisberg, and Council on Foreign Relations. 1985; Daugherty 2001; Engelmayer and Wagman 1981; Flaherty and United States. Congress. House. Committee on Banking Finance and Urban Affairs 1981; Jordan 1982; Laingen 1992; McFadden, Treaster and Carroll 1981; Ryan 1985; Scott 1984; Sick 1985, 1991; Vance and United States. Dept. of State. Office of Public Communication. Editorial Division. 1980; Wells 1985.
4. Zbigniew Brzezinski, National Security Advisor during the hostage crisis said in an interview in 1997, "I think the Iran hostage crisis was one of the two central reasons for Carter's political defeat in 1980, the other reason being domestic inflation." National Security Archive. 1997. Jordan 1982.
5. The so-called "October surprise" was an alleged "deal" between the Iranians and the Reagan-Bush campaign to purposely not release the American hostages until after the election in November 1980. This was alleged by a number of commentators, and eventually investigated by Congress. Honegger 1989; Parry 1993; Ross and Ross Film/Video Firm 1992; Sick 1991. United States. Congress. Senate. Committee on Foreign Relations. 1992.
6. Ryan 1985, United States. Joint Chiefs of Staff. Special Operations Review Group. 1980, United States. President 1977–81 and Carter 1980.
7. Algeria 1981, United States. Dept. of State. Bureau of Public Affairs. 1981.
8. Moses 1996, Stoessel and United States. Dept. of State. Office of Public Communication. Editorial Division. 1981, United States. Congress. House. Committee on Foreign Affairs. Subcommittee on Europe and the Middle East. United States. Congress. House. Committee on Foreign Affairs. Subcommittee on International Economic Policy and Trade. 1980.
9. Houghton 2001; Steele 1981; United States. Congress. House. Committee on Foreign Affairs. Subcommittee on Europe and the Middle East 1990; United States. Congress. House. Committee on Rules 1991a, b; United States. Congress. Senate. Committee on Foreign Relations 1992; United States. Congress. Senate. Committee on Foreign Relations. Subcommittee on Near Eastern and South Asian Affairs; 1992.
10. United States. Department of State. Office of the Coordinator for Counterterrorism 2003.
11. Ibid.
12. Menges 2003.
13. Harik 2004: 82–83. See also Vaziri 1992; Beeman 1986c.
14. Byman 2003: 60.
15. Ibid., 66.

16. Ibid.

17. Pasquini 2004: 56. Pasquini reports on a lecture by Simpson entitled "Hezbollah: the New Political/Military Model," held on June 17, 2004, at Dominican University of California in San Rafael. Simpson is professor of international relations at San Francisco State University.

18. Pasquini 2004: 57. Harik notes that Hezbollah is a force for social change, but that Washington's determiniation to eliminate it will remove this dynamic from Lebanon in the future. Harik 2004: 200–201.

19. Harik 2004; O'Ballance 1997. Both works emphasize the mix of private and institutional state support.

20. Wright 2005.

21. Beeman 1986e.

22. Council on Foreign Relations. 2003. Source for this material: United States. Department of State. 2001.

23. Bush 2002.

24. Kenneth Pollack deals with this incident by relying exclusively on the accounts of Israeli intelligence, and unproven assertions by members of the Bush administration who accept the Israeli conclusions with no independent verification. The best proof he can muster is the fact that "the U.S. government found the Israeli evidence to be 'compelling.'" Pollack 2004: 351.

25. Council on Foreign Relations. 2003.

26. May 13, 2003, in Indianapolis, IN.

27. Wellenson and Willenson 1975.

28. Iran's ambassador to the United Nations in New York, Javad Zarif, denied the allegations on the ABC television network's Sunday morning talk show, *This Week* on May 25: "Iran has been very active in capturing, arresting, preventing the entry of al Qaeda into Iran and once they enter Iran, in capturing them, arresting them and extraditing them to friendly governments. We have probably captured more al Qaeda people in the past fourteen months than any other country."

29. Mahmoody and Hoffer 1987.

30. Moaveni 2005.

31. Ibid.: 160.

32. Ibid.: 193.

34. This statement is, of course, both provocative and controversial. It depends entirely on what one defines as "better off." In this discussion I take advances in education, literacy, employment opportunities, health care, and family planning as prima facie evidence of an improved life. Those who claim that women's lives have been diminished under the revolution cite restrictions in public conduct, elimination of certain rights under law, and segregation of men and women in the public sphere. The public debate that attended my original publication of this statement has been published in a very interesting compendium. Keddie, Beeman, Mayer, Sick, Khonsari, Khajehpour, Partovi, Kurzman, Moghadam, Tohidi, Gharavi, and Asayesh 2001. There are literally hundreds of research publications dealing with the fascinating question of women in Iran. In this discussion I deal exclusively with U.S. impressions of the state of women, and the use to which these impressions have been put to demonize Iran.

34. Sarah F. D. Ansari and Martin 2001; Nikki R. Keddie and Baron 1991; Nashat 1983; Shahidian 2002; Azar Tabari and Yeganeh 1982.

35. According to senior demographer Sadreddin Beladi Mousavi of the Statistics Center of Iran (*Iran Daily* 2005).

36. Larsen 2001.

37. Moaveni 2005: 161–63.

38. Higgins 1984, Zenner 1961. Sanasarian 2000 takes a somewhat darker view. While acknowledging that religious minorities live relatively well, she feels they have been co-opted under the Islamic Republic.

39. It should be noted that not everyone is pleased with this arrangement. Some have criticized it as "religious apartheid," noting that separating the minorities means that they are not integrated into the overall political system—no Muslim politician need pay any attention to them (Mirfendereski 2001). See also Sanasarian 2000: 73–74.

40. Although other ethnic groups have frequently been described as outcaste or disadvantaged, including Jews as an ethnic group (Loeb 1977b), Kurds (Rubin 2003), Lurs (Amanolahi 1985), Gypsies (Amanolahi and Norbeck 1975).

41. Berberian 2001, Gregorian 1974.

42. Beck 1980, 1983a, 1983b, 1990, 2004; Bradburd 1989; Digard 1983; Garrod 1946; Gellner 1983; Kraus 1998; Kurup 1974; Shahshahani 1995; Tapper 1983a, 1983b.

43. Higgins 1984.

44. Nercissians 2001.

45. According to Article 15 of the Constitution of the Islamic Republic, the official and common language and script of the people of Iran is Persian. Official documents, correspondence and statements, as well as textbooks, "shall be written in this language and script. However, the use of local and ethnic languages in the press and mass media is allowed." The teaching of ethnic literature in the school, together with Persian language instruction, is also permitted. In truth, instruction in vernacular languages only began in the late 1990s, and is still spotty.

46. Bozorgmehr 1997.

47. Baba'i ibn Farhad 1990; Goldin 2003; Loeb 1977, 1983; Moreen 1987; Netzer 1997; Neusner 1983; Rappaport 1996; Sarshar 2002; Tabari 1991.

48. The literature on Judeo-Persian is quite extensive, beyond the scope of this work. Some principal references include Abrahamyan 1936; Asmussen 1973; Asmussen and Paper 1977; Lagarde 1970; Moreen 2000; Moreen and Baba'i ibn Lotf 1987; Netzer 1997; Paper 1973, 1976; Paper and Benayahu 1976; Shaked 1982.

49. Molavi 2002: 291–92.

50. By some estimates, 52,000 have left Iran since 1978–79. Anti-Defamation League 2003. See Moaveni 2000 for an account of the trial.

51. Bozorgmehr 1997; Nahai 1999.

52. Anti-Defamation League 2003.

53. Moaveni 2000.

54. Ibid.

55. Dinmore 2001.

56. Bab 1902, 1911; Nicolas 1905, 1933.

57. Browne 1984, 1987. See also Sanasarian 2000 for modern problems of Baha'is.

58. Marking a challenge to the Bush administration, however, is the fact that Iran's nuclear program is "being built not in the shadows but in plain sight, and just inside most of the rules designed to foil nuclear proliferation," *Wall Street Journal*: June 19, 2003.

59. Charbonneau 2003.

60. The *Washington Times*, in an editorial on November 28, 2003 reported: "Undersecretary of State for Arms Control John Bolton sharply criticized the refusal of Mr. ElBaradei and the IAEA to publicly tell the truth about what Tehran is actually up to: developing nuclear weapons. 'I must say that the report's assertion is simply impossible to believe,' Mr. Bolton said." (*Washington Times* 2003).

61. Charbonneau 2003.

62. Mendez 1998.

63. BBC Online 1998.

64. Information concerning the establishment of the Dimona plant can be found in the Eisenhower archives. A summary of the principal documents with links is located at www.gwu.edu/~nsarchiv/israel/documents/reveal/.

65. Pu 239.

66. The full transcript of Woolsey's interview is available at www.pbs.org/wgbh/pages/frontline/shows/tehran/interviews/woolsey.html.

67. Information for the above is abstracted from Stauffer 2003.

68. Stauffer 2003.

69. United Nations. International Atomic Energy Commission (IAEA) 2004: 3.

70. Weymouth 2005: 32–33.

Chapter 10: The Birth of Postmodern Conflict

1. Much of the material contained in this discussion derives from my personal experience. During the period from 1976–79 I was resident in Iran, and was present in Tehran, Shiraz, and other cities mentioned during key political events of the revolution. I served additionally as research advisor to the Festival of Arts Center, a branch of National Iranian Radio–Television from 1976–1978. I wish to thank here all of my Iranian colleagues for their help and support during those years.

2. Barraclough 2001; Bollag 2000.

3. Brown and Vincent 1995.

4. Cherry 1971: 57.

5. Cf. Carpenter 1974.

6. Peterson 2003; Schramm 1964; Schramm and Roberts 1971.

7. But see Cherry 1971: 166–205.

8. Note that as early as 1932, Dr. R. E. Hoffman, a missionary in Iran, wrote: "Our films are suggesting to the Persians that American life consists chiefly of cowpunching, rescuing abducted girls, gangster warfare, and walking like Charlie Chaplin." Rubin 1980: 269. Rubin notes that American television programs just before the revolution averaged 30.6 percent of broadcast time. Ibid. See also Prakke 1979 and Last 1955: 167–8 for examples from Indonesia.

9. It is noteworthy that Ayatollah Khomeini, during the revolution did not prohibit the playing of martial music and revolutionary songs. These, in contrast to the pop songs, did not in theory "transport individuals to a separate imaginary re-

ality," but were allowed precisely because they allowed individuals to "better concentrate on the reality at hand"—namely, the Revolution.

10. See Naficy 1979, 1981, 1992, 1999, 2000, 2001 for additional discussion of the effects of film and television on the Iranian public.

11. Part of the discontent of the newspapers was occasioned by Sharif-Emami's seemingly specific permission to write freely, given in a speech on October 4 to National Iranian Radio–Television. In this he said, "Why shouldn't we write about strikes? The people themselves know what is going on . . . if our radio doesn't broadcast it, the BBC will." Shortly after this, the attempt to re-impose censorship was made.

12. For further discussion of the role of Radio Iran in presenting anti-American rhetoric see Rubin. 1980: Ch. 9.

13. The Iranians had also learned of the effectiveness of press and television coverage by witnessing the extraordinary coverage on American television during and after the revolution. Some Americans later claimed that the U.S. press was instrumental in bringing about the "loss"of Iran. This stark proposition is rejected by Dorman and Farhang 1986: 229, but they do go on to point out that, "The American press, by informing and influencing the general as well as the attentive publics on world events, affects the substance of United States foreign policy." Ibid. The Iranians learned this particular lesson very well.

14. For a brief additional discussion of Radio Moscow's role in Iran, see Beeman 1981b.

15. Rubin 1980: 219.

16. *Kayhan*, February 12, 1979.

17. Although note Rubin's assessment: "By 1975, Iran was being better covered, receiving more attention than any other Third World country." Rubin 1980: 346. This may well have been the case, but it does not speak well for U.S. press coverage of the developing world in general.

18. Predictably, much of the coverage was biased toward the interests of the upper classes, the financial military and foreign policy communities, and the throne. See Dorman and Omeed 1979; Dorman and Farhang 1987; Behnam 1979; Said 1980, 1981 for critiques of U.S. coverage of Iranian affairs. Cooley 1981; Hershman and Griggs 1981; Mortimer 1981; and most importantly, Sciolino 2000, provide some general perspectives on problems conducting journalistic inquiry in the Middle East.

19. See Rubin 1980: 356–64; also Beeman 1980a, 1980c; Quint 1980.

20. Cf. Beeman 1980c.

21. Rejali 1994.

22. Naficy 1993.

23. Rajali 1994: 176.

24. Naficy 1993.

25. Ibid., 171.

26. February 17, 1979. University of Tehran campus public rally.

27. Turner 1974.

28. Barraclough 2000, 2001; Bollag 2000.

29. Gilgoff 2003.

30. Beeman 2003b.

31. www.internetworldstats.com/stats5.htm.

32. Deutsche Presse-Agentur 2000.

33. Adelkhah 2000; Kheradpir 1992.
34. Adelkhah 2000: 178.
35. Motlagh 2005.

Chapter 11: Living with Iran

1. See Daugherty 2001 for a darker memoir.
2. There is one other modern example: post–World War II North Yemen, also a Shi'ite state.
3. Reza Shah Pahlavi followed closely the secular, Western-oriented precepts of Kamal Attatürk, the founder of modern Turkey, whose somewhat draconian methods modernized Turkey, but also alienated Turks from their own pre-twentieth century cultural traditions.
4. See Keddie 1972b. For more information on the role of Iranian clerics in revolutionary activities before the revolution, see Algar 1969, 1972.
5. Nikki Keddie quotes al-Afghani's nephew as claiming that he was born in the month of Sha'ban in 1254 A.H., corresponding to October–November, 1838 C.E. She further reports that he was born in the village of Asadabad, near the city of Hamadan in northwestern Iran. Keddie 1972b: 10–11.
6. Keddie notes many confusing and contradictory claims about al-Afghani's arrival in Afghanistan, but concludes on the basis of documentary evidence that he arrived in late 1866. Keddie 1972b: 33.
7. Keddie 1972b: 62–4.
8. Cf. Ibrahim 1980, 1982; Keddie 1994 for more on the development of the Islamic brotherhood.
9. Jim Lobe, "IRAQ: Neo–Cons See Iran Behind Shiite Uprising," *Inter Press Service*, 9 April 2004. Lobe 2004.
10. Michael Rubin, "Sadr Signs," *National Review Online*, 7 April 2004. www.nationalreview.com/comment/rubin200404060834.asp. Rubin 2004a, 2004b.
11. William Safire, "Two Front Insurgency," *New York Times*, 7 April 2004, 19A (Safire 2004); David Brooks, "Take a Deep Breath," *New York Times*, 10 April 2004, 15A (Brooks 2004).
12. Committee on the Present Danger 2004.
13. I do not want to give the impression that there is no formal training in Shi'a Islam. There is a formal clergy based on status attained in real seminaries where the religious training is more rigorous than in most Protestant Christian seminaries in the United States. A mujtahid is one who has passed all the requirements in the study of Islamic theology, philosophy, ethics, and law and received an *ejazeh-e ijtehad*, or right to interpret law, from senior mujtahids upon the recommendation of his or her principal mentor. This is the religious equivalent of a secular Ph.D. Still, lack of these credentials does not prevent anyone from leading prayer, setting themselves up as a religious leader, or wearing religious garb. Thanks to Eric Hooglund for this note.
14. Juan Ricardo Cole, *Sacred Space and Holy War: The Politics, Culture and History of Shi'ite Islam*. London: I.B. Tauris, 2002; Coles 2002. Yitzhak Nakash, *The Shi'is of Iraq*. Princeton, NJ: Princeton University Press, 2003. Nakash 2003a, 2003b.
15. Pollack 2004: 341.

16. The term *faqih* derives from the Arabic term "fiqh"or "reason." Fiqh is a major subject in theological education, and a faqih is so designated because of a mastery of this branch of theology.

17. Eric Hooglund, one of the foremost experts on Iran and editor of *Critique* magazine, writes in a personal communication: "The military in Iran is NOT under the control of the conservatives, even though top commanders are appointed by the faqih. If it were, the conservatives long ago would have used it to stage a coup against the reformists. The military is divided ideologically; it is a conscript army/revolutionary guards/basij militia, with career officers who are very much divided in their political views/loyalties. This diversity of views among the security forces is, I believe, a main guarantor of Iran's democratic process, which is still in a developing and fragile state."

18. "Iran Parliament forwards bill on Press Law to Expediency Council," *Payvand Iran News*, 23 June 2003. www.payvand.com/news/03/jun/1129.html. Payvand Iran News 2003.

19. Thanks to Eric Hooglund for contributions to these firsthand observations (personal communication).

20. Muir 2004.

21. Dabashi 2000.

22. Nafisi 2003.

23. Hooglund writes: "It has been many years since any woman was arrested or even fined for showing too much hair in public; if this were happening, then half the women or more would be arrested, as even in small towns and villages many women wear headscarves well back of the forehead; and women in movies and TV shows of the past few years also reveal much head hair, which indicates how much the society has relaxed on this issue in the past few years. When I was in Iran in December 2003 and February 2004, chadors were worn by only about 20 percent of women in Tehran, less in Shiraz. The preferred garment in public is the headscarf and ankle-length coat, although younger women wear a tunic-like cover that is mid-thigh length over tight-fitting pants" (personal communication). See also William O. Beeman "Lifting the Islamic Women's Veil," Pacific News Service, February 27, 2001 (http://news.pacificnews.org/news/view_article.html?article_id=28989d9744 ad6346f57372e490d760e6) for similar views.

24. Nevertheless, parliament legalized first trimester abortions on April 12, 2005, when the fetus is unviable or the health of the mother is endangered. This is a distinct liberalization that is directly the result of a greater sensibility to women's rights.

25. William O. Beeman and Thomas Stauffer, "Is Iran Building Nukes? An Analysis (Parts 1 and 2)," *Pacific News Service* 2003. www.news.pacificnews. org/newsview_article.html?article_id=1b68abecee07b0cb8cf9ed0bc9de5954; www. news.pacificnews.org/news/view_article.html?article_id=7188562b68f4f8f71e7b57 ee599db3f5. Beeman and Stauffer 2003; William O. Beeman, "Shi'ites and the New Culture in Iraq," *Strategic Insights 3*, no. 5, 2004. www.ccc.nps.navy.mil/si/2004/ may/beemanMay04.asp. Beeman 2004.

26. William O. Beeman," Iran and the United States—Postmodern Culture Conflict in Action," *Anthropological Quarterly* 76 no.4, 2003: 671–91. Beeman 2003a.

27. Michael Leeden, "The Future of Iran," *National Review* Online, 9 July 2003.

(Ledeen 2003b); See also Ledeen 2003a, www.nationalreview.com/ledeen/ledeen 070903.asp.. Michael Leeden, "The Iranian Hand: Regime Change in Tehran is Necessary for Peace in Iraq," *The Wall Street Journal*, 16 April 2004. Online at www.opinionjournal.com/editorial/feature.html?id=110004959. Ledeen 2003.

28. Cf. Beeman 1981 1981a.

29. 8 April 2004. www.nationalreview.com/rubin/shrubin200404080818.asp. Rubin 2004a. See also zendran 2005 for an account of "Black Ops."

30. Gates, Brzezinski, and Maloney 2004.

31. Ibid., p. vii.

32. Barnett 2004; Pollack 2004; Pollack and Takeyh 2005.

33. Pletka, Danielle "Not Our Man in Iran," *New York Times*, June 16, 2005: A27, 1.

34. When it was uncertain whether Hashemi-Rafsanjani or Ahmadinejad would win, Michael Ledeen wrote: "Iran today reminds me very much of the death struggle between Hitler and the SA, the brown-shirted thugs who led the Nazi 'revolution.' At a certain point Hitler knew they were a potential threat to his rule, and they were violently purged." "Iran Votes, Again" National Review Online, June 24, 2005. www.nationalreview.com/ledeen/ledeen200506241725.asp. It is unclear whether Mr. Ledeen's reference to the SA applies to Mr. Hashemi-Rafsanjani or to Mr. Ahmadinejad. Presumably either would have served his rhetorical purpose.

35. Dareini, Ali Akbar, "Ex-Iranian Agent: Photo Not Ahmadinejad" AP story released July 2, 2005. www.santamariatimes.com/articles/2005/07/02/ap/headlines/ d8b3h4p00.txt

Comprehensive Bibliography

Abdo, Geneive, and Jonathan Lyons. 2003. *Answering Only to God: Faith and Freedom in Twenty-First-Century Iran*. New York: Henry Holt and Co.

Abrahamian, Ervand. 1980. "Structural Causes of the Iranian Revolution." *MERIP Reports* (87): 21–26.

———. 1982. *Iran Between Two Revolutions*. Princeton, NJ: Princeton University Press.

———. 1999. *Tortured Confessions: Prisons and Public Recantations in Modern Iran*. Berkeley: University of California Press.

Abrahamyan (Abrahamean), Ruben. 1936. *Dialectes des Israélites de Hamadan et d'ispahan et Dialecte de Baba Tahir*. Paris: Adrien-Maisonneuve.

Adelkhah, Fariba. 2000. *Being Modern in Iran*. The CERI Series in Comparative Politics and International Studies. New York: Columbia University Press in association with the Centre d'Etudes et de Recherches Internationales.

Afshar-Naderi, Nader. 1971. *The Settlement of Nomads and Its Social and Economic Implications*. Tehran: Institute for Social Studies and Research.

Aghajanian, A. 1991. "Population-Change in Iran, 1966–86—a Stalled Demographic-Transition." *Population and Development Review* 17 (4): 703–15.

———. 1992. "Status of Women and Fertility in Iran." *Journal of Comparative Family Studies* 23 (3): 361–74.

Ahmadi, Nader, and Fereshteh Ahmadi. 1998. *Iranian Islam: The Concept of the Individual*. New York: St. Martin's Press.

Ajami, Isma'il. 1969. *Sheshdangi*. Shiraz: Pahlavi University Press.

Akhavi, Shahrough. 1980. *Religion and Politics in Contemporary Iran: Clergy-State Relations in the Pahlavi Period*. Albany: State University of New York Press.

Algar, Hamid. 1969. *Religion and State in Iran, 1785–1906; the Role of the Ulama in the Qajar Period*. Berkeley: University of California Press.

———. 1972. "The Oppositional Role of the Ulema in Twentieth Century Iran." *Scholars, Saints and Sufis*. Nikki R. Keddie, ed. Berkeley: University of California Press.

Allway, Tony. 1978. "Shah's Efforts to End Unrest and Win over the Religious Community. New Premier Charged with Preparing Iran Poll." *Times of London*. August 28.

Al-Qazwini, Syed Moustafa. 1999. *Answers to: Common Questions About Shi'a Islam*. Elmhurst, NY: Tahrike Tarsile Quran.

Amanolahi, Sekandar. 1985. "Lurs of Iran." *Cultural Survival Quarterly* 9 (1): 65–69.

Amanolahi, Sekandar, and Edward Norbeck. 1975. "Luti, an Outcaste Group of Iran." *Rice University Studies* 61 (2): 1–12. Houston: William Marsh Rice University.

Amini, Aliriza. 2002. *Tarikh-e Ravabit-e Khariji-ye Iran Dar Dowran-e Pahlavi*. Tehran: Sada-yi Mu'asir.

Amuzegar, Jahangir. 2003. "Iran's Crumbling Revolution." *Foreign Affairs* 82 (1): 44–57.

Anderson, Benedict R. O'G. 1983. *Imagined Communities: Reflections on the Origin and Spread of Nationalism*. London: Verso.

Ansari, Ali M. 2000a. *Iran, Islam and Democracy: The Politics of Managing Change*. London; Washington, DC: Royal Institute of International Affairs; distributed worldwide by the Brookings Institution.

Ansari, S. 2000b. "Women, Work and Islamism: Ideology and Resistance in Iran." *Bulletin of the School of Oriental and African Studies. University of London* 63: 433–34.

Ansari, Sarah F.D., and Vanessa Martin. 2001. *Women, Religion and Culture in Iran*. Royal Asiatic Society Books. Richmond: Curzon.

Anti-Defamation League. 2003. "Backgrounder: The Trial of 13 Iranian Jews." www.adl.org/backgrounders/Iranian_Jews.asp.

Arjomand, Said Amir. 1980. "State and Khomeini's Islamic Order." *Iranian Studies* 13 (1): 147–64.

———. 1988a. *Authority and Political Culture in Shi'ism*. Suny Series in Near Eastern Studies. Albany: State University of New York Press.

———. 1988b. *The Turban for the Crown: The Islamic Revolution in Iran*. New York: Oxford University Press.

Asdjodi, Minoo. 2001. "A Comparison between *Ta'arof* in Persian and *Limao* in Chinese." *International Journal of the Sociology of Language* 148: 71–92.

Askari, Hossein, John T. Cummings, and Mehmet Izbudak. 1977. "Iran's Migration of Skilled Labor to the United States." *Iranian Studies* 10 (1): 3–35.

Asmussen, Jes Peter. 1973. *Studies in Judeo-Persian Literature*. Studia Post–Biblica, V. 24. Leiden: Brill.

Asmussen, Jes Peter, and Herbert H. Paper. 1977. *The Song of Songs in Judeo-Persian: Introduction, Texts, Glossary*. København: [Det Kongelige Danske Videnskabernes Selskab]: kommissionaer, Munksgaards Boghandel, Nørregade 6, 1165 K.

Associated Press. 1988. "No Warning to Downed Jet, Iran Claims." *Toronto Star*. July 15: ME2.

Avery, Peter. 1965. *Modern Iran*. New York: F. A. Praeger.

Bab, Ali Muhammad Shirazi, and Louis Alphonse Daniel Nicolas. 1902. *Le Livre des Sept Preuves de La Mission du Bab*. Paris: J. Maison-neuve.

———. 1911. *Le Béyan Persan*. Paris: P. Geuthner.

Baba'i ibn Farhad, and Vera Basch Moreen. 1990. *Iranian Jewry During the Afghan Invasion: The Kitab-i Sar Guzasht-i Kashan of Baba'i B. Farhad.* Freiburger Islamstudien; Bd. 14. Stuttgart: F. Steiner.

Bahgat, Gawdat. 2003. "Iran, the United States, and the War on Terrorism." *Studies in Conflict and Terrorism* 26: 93–104.

Baktiari, Bahman, and Haleh Vaziri. 2003. "Iran: Doubting Reform?" *Current History* 102: 36–9.

Banani, Amin. 1961. *The Modernization of Iran, 1921–1941.* Stanford: Stanford University Press.

Banuazizi, Ali, Myron Weiner, Joint Committee on the Near and Middle East, and Joint Committee on South Asia. 1986. *The State, Religion, and Ethnic Politics: Afghanistan, Iran, and Pakistan.* Syracuse, NY: Syracuse University Press.

Barnett, Thomas P. M. 2004. *The Pentagon's New Map: War and Peace in the Twenty-First Century.* New York: G.P. Putnam's Sons.

Barraclough, Steven. 2000. "Satellite Television in Asia: Winners and Losers." *Asian Affairs* 31 (3): 263.

———. 2001. "Satellite Television in Iran: Prohibition, Imitation and Reform." *Middle Eastern Studies* 37 (3): 25.

Bateson, Gregory. 1935. "Culture Contact and Schismogenesis." *Man* 35: 178–83.

———. 1942. "Social Planning and the Concept of 'Deutero-Learning' in Relation to the Democratic Way of Life." *Science, Philosophy and Religion, Second Symposium.* Lyman Bryson and Louis Finkelstein, eds. New York: Harper: 81–97.

———. 1955. "A Theory of Play and Fantasy." *Psychiatric Research Reports* (2): 39–51.

———. 1956. "The Message, 'This Is Play.'" *Transactions of the Second Conference on Group Processes.* New York: Josiah Macy Foundation: 145–242.

———. 1958. "The New Conceptual Frames for Behavioral Research." *Proceedings of the Sixth Annual Psychiatric Institute.* Princeton, NJ: The New Jersey Neuro-Psychiatric Institute: 54–71.

———. 1960. "Minimal Requirements for a Theory of Schizophrenia." *Archives of General Psychiatry* 2: 477–91.

———. 1961. "The Biosocial Integration of the Schizophrenic Family." *In Exploring the Base for Family Therapy.* Nathan W. Ackerman, Frances L. Beatman, and Sanform N. Sherman, eds. New York: Family Service Association: 116–22.

———. 1964. "Some Varieties of Pathogenic Organization." *Disorders of Communication, Volume 42, Research Publications.* New York: Association for Research in Nervous and Mental Disease: 270–83.

———. 1972. *Steps to an Ecology of Mind: Collected Essays in Anthropology, Psychiatry, Evolution, and Epistemology.* Northvale, NJ: Jason Aronson, Inc.

———. 1979. *Mind and Nature: A Necessary Unity.* New York: Dutton.

Bateson, Gregory, Don D. Jackson, Jay Haley, and John Weakland. 1956. "Toward a Theory of Schizophrenia." *Behavioral Science* 1: 251–64.

Bateson, Mary Catherine, Jerome W. Clinton, J. Barkev M. Kassarjian, Hossein Safavi, Mehdi Soraya. 1977. "Safa-yi Batin. A Study of the Interrelations of a Set of Iranian Ideal Character Types." *Psychological Dimensions of Near*

Eastern Studies. L. Carl Brown and Norman Itzkowitz, eds. Princeton, NJ: Darwin Press: 257–73.

Bayat-Philip, Mangol. 1980. "Shi'ism in Contemporary Iranian Politics: The Case of Ali Shari'ati." *Iran: Toward Modernity*. Sylvia Haim and Elie Kedourie, eds. London: Frank Cass.

BBC Online. 1998. "Clinton 'a Liar'—Sudanese Leader." BBC News. August 21, 1998. http://news.bbc.co.uk/1/hi/not_in_website/syndication/monitoring/155559.stm.

Bean, Susan S. 1978. *Symbolic and Pragmatic Semantics: A Kannada System of Address*. Chicago: University of Chicago Press.

Beck, Lois. 1980a. "Revolutionary Iran and Its Tribal Peoples." *MERIP Reports* (87): 14–20.

———. 1980b. "Tribe and State Revolutionary Iran: The Return of the Qashqa'i Khans." *Iranian Studies* 13 (1): 215–55.

———. 1980c. "Herd Owners and Hired Shepherds: The Qashqa'i of Iran." *Ethnology* 19 (3): 327–51.

———. 1980d. "Religious Lives of Muslim Women." In *Women in Contemporary Muslim Societies*. Jane I. Smith, ed. Lewisburg, PA: Bucknell University Press: 27–60.

———. 1981. "Economic Transformations among Qashqa'i Nomads 1962–1978." *Modern Iran. The Dialects of Continuity and Change*. Michael E. Bonine and Nikki Keddie, eds. Albany: SUNY Press: 99–122.

———. 1983a. "Iran and the Qashqai Tribal Confederacy." *The Conflict of Tribe and State in Iran and Afghanistan*. Richard Tapper, ed. London: Croom Helm: 284–313.

———. 1983b. "Revolutionary Iran and Its Tribal Peoples." *The Middle East*. New York: Monthly Review Press: 115–26.

———. 1986. *The Qashqa'i People of Southern Iran*. Photographs by Nikki Keddie; assisted by Brad Hanson. Los Angeles: UCLA Museum of Cultural History.

———. 1990. "Tribes and the State in Nineteenth- and Twentieth-Century Iran." *Tribe and State Formation in the Middle East*. Philip S. Khoury and Joseph Kostiner, eds. Berkeley: University of California Press: 185–225.

———. 1997. "Gender in the Muslim Middle East." *American Anthropologist* 99 (1): 155–57.

———. 2004. "Qashqa'i Women in Postrevolutionary Iran." *Women in Iran from 1800 to the Islamic Republic*. Lois Beck and Guity Nashat, eds. Urbana: University of Illinois Press: 240–78.

Beeman, William. 1971. Interaction Semantics: Preliminary Foundations for the Observational Study of Meaning. M.A.: University of Chicago.

———. 1976a. "Status, Style and Strategy in Iranian Interaction." *Anthropological Linguistics* 18 (7): 305–22.

———. 1976b. "What Is (Iranian) National Character." *Iranian Studies* 9 (1): 29–43.

———. 1976c. "You Can Take Music out of the Country, But. . . . : The Dynamics of Change in Iranian Musical Tradition." *Asian Music*: 7(2): 6–19.

———. 1976d. The Meaning of Stylistic Variation in Iranian Verbal Interaction. Ph.D.: University of Chicago.

———. 1977. "The Hows and Whys of Persian Style: A Pragmatic Approach." *Studies in Language Variation: Semantics, Syntax, Phonology, Pragmatics, Social Situations, Ethnographic Approaches. Papers from the Third Annual Colloquium on New Ways of Analyzing Variation, Georgetown University, 1974.* Ralph W. Fasold and Roger Shuy, eds. Washington, DC: Georgetown University Press: 269–82.

———. 1980a. "Martyrdom Vs. Intervention: The Cultural Logic Behind Iranian Resistance to American Military Intervention." *Leviathan* (fall): 2–8.

———. 1980b. "Exeunt Omnes?" In *Nation*, vol: 677.

———. 1980c. "Televised Display of Dead U.S. Airmen—a Horror Show for Iranians Too." *Boston Globe*. April 29.

———. 1981a. "How Not to Negotiate: Crossed Signals on the Hostages." *Nation* 23 (2): 42–44.

———. 1981b. "War of Words: Soviets Are Gaining." *Los Angeles Times*. February 4: A16.

———. 1981c. "Why Do They Laugh? An Interactional Approach to Humor in Traditional Iranian Improvisatory Theater." *Journal of American Folklore (JAF)*. 1981 (October December) 94 (374): 506–26.

———. 1982. *Culture, Performance and Communication in Iran.* Performance in Culture; No. 1. Tokyo, Japan: Institute for the Study of Languages and Cultures of Asia & Africa.

———. 1983a. "Images of the Great Satan: Representations of the United States in the Iranian Revolution." *Religion and Politics in Iran: Shi'ism from Quietism to Revolution.* Nikki R. Keddie, ed. New Haven, CT: Yale University Press: 191–218.

———. 1983b. "Religion and Development in Iran from the Qajar Era to the Islamic Revolution of 1978–1979." *Global Economics and Religion.* James Finn, ed. New Brunswick, NJ: Transaction Books: 73–104.

———. 1985. "Dimensions of Dysphoria: The View from Linguistic Anthropology." *Culture and Depression: Studies in the Anthropology and Cross Cultural Psychiatry of Affect and Disorder.* Comparative Studies of Health Systems and Medical Care. Arthur Kleinman, ed. Berkeley: University of California Press: 216–43.

———. 1986a. "Anthropology and the Myths of Foreign Policy." *Anthropology and Public Policy: A Dialogue. A Special Publication of the American Anthropological Association; No. 21.* Walter Rochs Goldschmidt, ed. Washington, DC: American Anthropological Association: 45–54.

———. 1986b. "Conflict and Belief in American Foreign Policy." *Peace and War: Cross-Cultural Perspectives.* Mary LeCron Foster and Robert A. Rubinstein, eds. New Brunswick, NJ: Transaction Books: 333–42.

———. 1986c. "Iran's Religious Regime: What Makes It Tick? Will It Ever Run Down?" *The Annals of the American Academy of Political and Social Science* 483 (January): 73–83.

———. 1986d. *Language, Status, and Power in Iran.* Advances in Semiotics. Bloomington: Indiana University Press.

———. 1986e. "Terrorism: Community Based or State Supported?" *American-Arab-Affairs.* pp. 29–36, Spring 1986.

———. 1987. "Living with Iran." *Ethics and International Affairs* 1: 85–96.

————. 1988. "Affectivity in Persian Language Use." *Culture, Medicine and Psychiatry* 12 (1): 9–30.

————. 1995. "The Iranian Revolution of 1978–1979." *The Oxford Encyclopedia of the Modern Islamic World*. John L. Esposito, ed. New York: Oxford University Press: 232–36.

————. 1996. "Torture, Television, and Iranian Culture." *American Anthropologist* 98 (4): 875–77.

————. 2001a. "Emotion and Sincerity in Persian Discourse: Accomplishing the Representation of Inner States." *International Journal of the Sociology of Language* (148): 31–57.

————. 2001b. "Lifting the Islamic Woman's Veil." Pacific News Service. February 27, 2001. http://news.pacificnews.org/news/view_article.html?article_id=28989d9744ad6346f57372e490d760e6.

————. 2001c. "Writing for the Crisis." In *Anthropology Today*, vol. 17, p. 1.

————. 2003a. "Iran and the United States-Postmodern Culture Conflict in Action." *Anthropological Quarterly* 76 (4): 671–91.

————. 2003b. "Nonconservative Guru Sets Sights on Iran." In *National Catholic Reporter*, vol. 39, p. 14: National Catholic Reporter Publishing Company.

————. 2004. "Shi'ite and the New Culture in Iraq." *Strategic Insights* 3 (5).

Beeman, William O., and Mark A. Peterson. 2001. "Situations and Interpretations: Explorations in Interpretive Practice." *Anthropological Quarterly* 74 (4): 159–62.

Beeman, William O., and Thomas A. Stauffer. 2003. "Is Iran Building Nukes? An Analysis (Parts 1 and 2)" Syndicated Article. *Pacific News Service*. http://news.pacificnews.org/newsview_article.html?article_id=1b68abecee07b0cb8cf9ed0bc9de5954; http://news.pacificnews.org/news/view_article.html?article_id=7188562b68f4f8f71e7b57ee599db3f5.

Behnam, M. Reza. 1979. "Misreading Iran through U.S. News Media." *Christian Science Monitor*.

————. 1986. *Cultural Foundations of Iranian Politics*. Salt Lake City: University of Utah Press.

Berberian, Houri. 2001. *Armenians and the Iranian Constitutional Revolution of 1905–1911: The Love for Freedom Has No Fatherland*. Boulder, CO: Westview Press.

Bill, James A. 1978/79. "Iran and the Crisis of '78." *Foreign Affairs* 57 (2): 323–42.

————. 1988a. *The Eagle and the Lion: The Tragedy of American-Iranian Relations*. New Haven, CT: Yale University Press.

————. 1988b. *The Shah, the Ayatollah, and the United States*. New York: Foreign Policy Association.

————. 2001. "The Politics of Hegemony: The United States and Iran." *Middle East Policy* 8 (3): 89–100.

Birch, Nicholas. 2003. "In Iran, Clerics' Wealth Draws Ire." *Christian Science Monitor*. August 20: 6.

Bollag, Burton. 2000. "20 Years after the Islamic Revolution, Iran's Campuses Begin to Loosen Up." in *Chronicle of Higher Education*, vol. 46, p. A52: Chronicle of Higher Education.

Bonine, Michael E. 1982. "From Ganat to Kort: Traditional Irrigation Terminology and Pracitces of Central Iran." *Journal of the British Institute of Persian Studies* 20: 145–59.

Bonine, Michael E., and Nikki R. Keddie. 1981a. *Continuity and Change in Modern Iran*. Albany: SUNY Press.

———. 1981b. *Modern Iran: The Dialectics of Continuity and Change*. Albany: SUNY Press.

Boyd, A. 1990. "*Review of The United States and Iran 1946–51—Goode, J.F.*" *World Today* 46 (2): 35–36.

Bozorgmehr, M. 1997. "Internal Ethnicity: Iranians in Los Angeles." *Sociological Perspectives* 40 (3): 387–408.

Bradburd, Daniel. 1989. "Producing Their Fates: Why Poor Basseri Settled but Poor Komachi and Yomut Did Not." *American Ethnologist* 16 (3): 502–17.

Brigot, André, Olivier Roy, and Institut français de polémologie. 1988. *The War in Afghanistan: An Account and Analysis of the Country, Its People, Soviet Intervention and the Resistance*. New York; London: Harvester Wheatsheaf.

Brooks, David. 2004. "Take a Deep Breath." *New York Times*. April 10, 2004: 15 (A).

Brown, L. C. 1990. "*Review of Neither East nor West—Iran, the Soviet-Union, and the United States. Keddie, N.R., Gasiorowski, M.J.*" *International History Review* 12 (4): 855–57.

Brown, W. J., and R. C. Vincent. 1995. "Trading Arms for Hostages—How the Government and Print Media Spin Portrayals of the United States Policy toward Iran." *Political Communication* 12 (1): 65–79.

Browne, Edward Granville. 1910. *The Persian Revolution of 1905–1909*. Cambridge: Cambridge University Press.

———. 1928. *Literary History of Persia*. Cambridge: Cambridge University Press.

———. 1984. *A Year Amongst the Persians: Impressions as to the Life, Character & Thought of the People of Persia, Received During Twelve Months' Residence in That Country in the Years 1887–1888*. Century Travellers. London; New York: Century; Hippocrene Books.

Browne, Edward Granville, and Abbas Amanat. 1995. *The Persian Revolution of 1905–1909*. New edition. Washington, DC: Mage Publishers.

Browne, Edward Granville, and Moojan Momen. 1987. *Selections from the Writings of E.G. Browne on the Babi and Baha'i Religions*. Oxford: G. Ronald.

Buchta, Wilfried. 1998. "Ein Haus Mit Vielen Herren: Divergierende Machtzentren in Der Islamischen Republik Iran." *Orient* 39: 41–84.

Busby, Robert. 1998. *Reagan and the Iran-Contra Affair: The Politics of Presidential Recovery*. New York: St. Martin's Press.

Bush, George. 2002a. "President to Send Secretary Powell to Middle East—White House Press Release." White House. www.whitehouse.gov/news/releases/2002/04/20020404-1.html.

Bush, George, and United States. Dept. of State. Bureau of Public Affairs. 1988. *The Persian Gulf Conflict and Iran Air 655*. Washington, DC: U.S. Dept. of State, Bureau of Public Affairs.

Bush, George W. 2002. "Radio Remarks to the People of Iran." In *Weekly Compilation of Presidential Documents*, vol. 38, p. 2188: Superintendent of Documents.

Business-Respect. 2003. "Statoil Ceo Resigns over Iran Corruption Probe." September 23. www.mallenbaker.net/csr/CSRfiles/page.php?Story_ID=1069.

Business Week. 1975. "Iran Rethinks Its Grandiose Goals." *Business Week* (November 17): 58, 63.

———. 1977. "Iran: The Shah Cools His Overheated Economy." *Business Week* (December 26): 46–47.

Byman, Daniel. 2003. "Should Hezbollah Be Next?" *Foreign Affairs* 82 (6): 54–66.

Cameron, George Glenn, Louis Lawrence Orlin, and Michigan University Department of Near Eastern Studies. 1976. *Michigan Oriental Studies in Honor of George G. Cameron.* Ann Arbor: Department of Near Eastern Studies, University of Michigan.

Caron, D. D. 1990. "The Nature of the Iran United States Claims Tribunal and the Evolving Structure of International Dispute Resolution." *American Journal of International Law* 84 (1): 104–56.

Carpenter, Edmund Snow. 1973. *Oh, What a Blow That Phantom Gave Me!* New York: Holt, Rinehart and Winston.

Charbonneau, Louis. 2003. "Iran to Escape U.N. Nuclear Rap." Reuters UK. November 26, 2003. www.reuters.co.uk/newsPackageArticle.jhtml?type=world News&storyID=409224&section=news.

Chelkowski, Peter J., editor. 1979. *Ta'ziyeh, Ritual and Drama in Iran.* New York University Studies in Near Eastern Civilization No. 7. New York: New York University Press.

Chelkowski, Peter J., and Hamid Dabashi. 1999. *Staging a Revolution: The Art of Persuasion in the Islamic Republic of Iran.* New York: New York University Press.

Chen, Y. H., and W. T. Lin. 1994. "Political Risk and Adjusted Present Value." *International Journal of Systems Science* 25 (12): 2207–20.

Cherry, Colin. 1971. *World Communication: Threat or Promise?* London: Wiley Interscience.

Christopher, Warren, Paul H. Kreisberg, and Council on Foreign Relations. 1985. *American Hostages in Iran: The Conduct of a Crisis.* New Haven, CT: Yale University Press.

Chubin, Shahram, and Charles Tripp. 1988. *Iran and Iraq at War.* London: I. B. Tauris.

Clawson, Patrick. 1998a. "The Continuing Logic of Dual Containment." *Survival* 40: 33–47.

———. 1998b. *Iran under Khatami: A Political, Economic, and Military Assessment.* Washington, DC: Washington Institute for Near East Policy.

Cole, Juan Ricardo. 2002. *Sacred Space and Holy War: The Politics, Culture and History of Shi'ite Islam.* London: I.B. Tauris.

Cole, Juan Ricardo, and Nikki R. Keddie. 1986. *Shi'ism and Social Protest.* New Haven: Yale University Press.

Coles, R. L. 2002. "Manifest Destiny Adapted for 1990s War Discourse: Mission and Destiny Intertwined." *Sociology of Religion* 63 (4): 403–26.

Comaroff, Jean, and John L. Comaroff. 2001. *Millennial Capitalism and the Culture of Neoliberalism.* Durham, NC: Duke University Press.

Comaroff, John L., and Jean Comaroff. 1999. *Civil Society and the Political Imag-*

ination in Africa: Critical Perspectives. Chicago: University of Chicago Press.

Committee on the Present Danger. 2004. "Iran—A New Approach." Committee on the Present Danger. December 20. www.fightingterror.org/newsroom/CPD_Iran_policy_paper.pdf.

Cooley, John K. 1981. "The News from the Mid-east: A Working Approach." *The Middle East Journal* 35 (4): 465–80.

Corbin, Henri. 1951. "Le Temps Cyclique Dans Le Mazdeisme Et Dans l'Ismailism." *Eranos Jahrbuch* XXI.

———. 1973. "Introduction." *Traité Des Compagnons-Chevaliers.* Henri Corbin, ed. Tehran/Paris: Départment d'Iranologie de l'Institut Franco-Iranien de Recherche, Librarie d'Amérique et d'Orient, Adrien-Maisonneuve.

Corina, Maurice. 1977. "Iran Imposes Barter Rules for Imports in Face of Declining Revenue from Oil." *Times of London.* January 17.

Council-on-Foreign-Relations. 2003. "Terrorism: Questions & Answers." www.terrorismanswers.com/sponsors/iran.html#Q3

Crittenden, Ann. 1977. "Businessmen Tell Troubles to Diplomats." *New York Times.* May 30: 23, 2.

Cumming, Bruce. 1977. "Harsh Action Brings Results." *Times of London.* September 26.

Curzon, George Nathaniel Curzon. 1892. *Persia and the Persian Question.* London; New York: Longmans Green & Co.

Dabashi, H., and A. Mack. 2000. "Arrested in Iran (Protest against the Recent Grave Violation of the Civil Rights of Seven Men and Women)." *New York Review of Books* 47 (10): 81.

Dabashi, Hamid. 1993. *Theology of Discontent: The Ideological Foundations of the Islamic Revolution in Iran.* New York: New York University Press.

———. 2000. "The End of Islamic Ideology." *Social Research* 67 (2): 475.

———. 2001. *Close Up: Iranian Cinema, Past, Present, and Future.* London; New York: Verso.

Daftary, Farhad. 1973. "Development Planning in Iran: A Historical Survey." *Iranian Studies* 6 (4): 176–228.

Dahrendorf, Ralf. 1968. *Essays in the Theory of Society.* London: Routledge & K. Paul.

Darwish, Adel, and Gregory Alexander. 1991. *Unholy Babylon: The Secret History of Saddam's War,* 1st U.S. edition. New York: St. Martin's Press.

Daugherty, William J. 2001a. "Behind the Intelligence Failure in Iran." *International Journal of Intelligence and Counterintelligence* 14: 449–84.

———. 2001b. *In the Shadow of the Ayatollah: A CIA Hostage in Iran.* Annapolis, MD: Naval Institute Press.

David, Charles Philippe, Nancy Ann Carrol, and Zachary A. Selden. 1993. *Foreign Policy Failure in the White House: Reappraising the Fall of the Shah and the Iran-Contra Affair.* Lanham, MD: University Press of America.

Davies, James C. 1962. "Toward a Theory of Revolution." *American Sociological Review* 27: 5–19.

———. 1969. "The J-Curve of Rising and Declining Satisfactions as a Cause of Some Great Revolutions and a Contained Rebellion." *The History of Violence in America, a Report to the National Commission on the Causes and*

Prevention of Violence. H. D. and T. R. Gurr Graham, eds. New York: Bantam: 690–730.

———. 1977. "The Priority of Human Needs and the Stages of Political Development." *Human Nature in Politics.* J. R. and J. W. Chapman Pennock, eds. New York: New York University Press: 157–96.

———. 1978. "The J-Curve Theory." *American Political Science Review* 72 (4): 1357–58.

Dealey, Sam. 2003. "Rep. Ros-Lehtinen Defends Iranian Group Labeled Terrorist Front for Saddam Hussein." *The Hill.* April 8. www.hillnews.com/news/040803/roslehtinen.aspx.

Deutsche Presse-Agentur. 2000. "Iran's Judiciary to Reopen Some Banned Reformist Dailies." http://web.lexis-nexis.com/universe/document?_m=ea1c706819648dd76c3dda9410885d97&_docnum=4&wchp=dGLbVlz-zSkVA&_md5=052bee46a633d4fb4c488a4a3fb43843.

Digard, Jean-Pierre. 1983. "On the Bakhtiari: Comments on 'Tribes, Confederation and the State.'" *The Conflict of Tribe and State in Iran and Afghanistan.* London: 331–36.

Dinmore, Guy. 2001. "Iran Jews' Appeal Blocked." *Financial Times* (January 24): 9.

Docherty, Neil, Linden MacIntyre, Canadian Broadcasting Corporation, WGBH and PBS Home Video. 2002. "Terror and Tehran." Alexandria, VA: PBS Home Video.

Dorman, William, and Ehsan Omid (pseud. for Mansour Farhang). 1979. "Reporting the Shah's Way." *Columbia Journalism Review* 17 (5): 27–33.

Dorman, William A., and Mansour Farhang. 1987. *The U.S. Press and Iran: Foreign Policy and the Journalism of Deference.* Berkeley: University of California Press.

Downes, Mark. 2002. *Iran's Unresolved Revolution.* Aldershot, Hants, UK; Burlington, VT: Ashgate.

Dumont, Louis. 1970. *Homo Hierarchicus: An Essay on the Caste System.* Chicago: University of Chicago Press.

Economist, The. 1980. "Bandar Khomeini; the World's Most Expensive Rubble." (November 22): 90.

———. 1981. "Japan-Iran Petrochemicals; Mitsui Moves to a Showdown." (May 2): 79 (U.S. Edition, p. 83).

———. 2003. "The Surreal World of Iranian Politics." (January 18): 5.

Ehlers, Eckart, and Grace E. Goodell. 1975. *Traditionelle Und Moderne Formen Der Landwirtschaft in Iran: Siedlung, Wirtschaft Und Agrarsozialstruktur Im Nèordlichen Khuzistan Seit Dem Ende Des 19. Jahrhunderts.* Marburger Geographische Schriften; Heft 64. Marburg, Lahn: Im Selbstverlag des Geographischen Institutes der Universitèat Marburg.

Ehteshami, Anoushiravan, and Manshour Varasteh. 1991. *Iran and the International Community.* London; New York: Routledge.

Emirbayer, Mustafa, and Jeff Goodwin. 1996. "Symbols, Positions, Objects: Toward a New Theory of Revolutions and Collective Action. Review of Debating Revolutions. Keddie, Nikki R." *History and Theory* 35 (3): 358–74.

Engelmayer, Sheldon D., and Robert J. Wagman. 1981. *Hostage.* Ottawa, IL: Caroline House Publishers.

Esposito, John L. 1998. *Islam and Politics*, 4th edition. Contemporary Issues in the Middle East. Syracuse, NY: Syracuse University Press.

Esposito, John L., and Natana J. DeLong-Bas. 2001. *Women in Muslim Family Law*, 2nd edition. Contemporary Issues in the Middle East. Syracuse, NY: Syracuse University Press.

Esposito, John L., and Rouhollah K. Ramazani, et al. 2001. *Iran at the Crossroads*. New York: Palgrave.

Esposito, John L., and John Obert Voll. 2001. *Makers of Contemporary Islam*. New York: Oxford University Press.

Fairbanks, S. C. 1998. "Theocracy Versus Democracy: Iran Considers Political Parties." *Middle East Journal* 52 (1): 17–31.

Fallers, Lloyd A. 1974. *The Social Anthropology of the Nation-State*. The Lewis Henry Morgan Lectures; 1971. Chicago: Aldine Publishing Company.

Farhang, M. 2003. "A Triangle of Realpolitik: Iran, Iraq and the United States." *Nation* 276 (10): 18–21.

Farhi, Farideh. 2001. *Political Paralysis: Iran's 2001 Election and the Future of Reform*. New York: Asia Society.

FDCH-emedia (*Washington Post*). 2005. "Transcript-Rice at Nato Headquarters." *The Washington Post*. February 9. www.washingtonpost.com/wp-dyn/arti cles/A10788-2005Feb9.html.

Ferguson, James. 1990. *The Anti-Politics Machine: "Development," Depoliticization, and Bureaucratic Power in Lesotho*. Cambridge, UK; New York: Cambridge University Press.

———. 2004. "Power Typographies." *A Companion to the Anthropology of Politics*. David Nugent and Joan Vincent, eds. Oxford: Blackwell: 383–99.

Ferguson, James, and Akhil Gupta. 2002. "Spatializing States: Toward an Ethnography of Neoliberal Governmentality." *American Ethnologist* 29 (4): 981–1002.

Fischer, Heinz Dietrich, and Stefan R. Melnik, eds. 1979. *Entertainment, a Cross-Cultural Examination*. New York: Hastings House.

Fischer, Michael M. J. 1980. *Iran: From Religious Dispute to Revolution*. Cambridge, MA: Harvard University Press.

———. 2003. *Iran: From Religious Dispute to Revolution*. Madison: University of Wisconsin Press.

———. 2004. *Mute Dreams, Blind Owls and Dispersed Knowledges: Persian Poesis in the Transnational Circuitry*. Durham, NC: Duke University Press.

Fischer, Michael M. J., and Mehdi Abedi. 1990. *Debating Muslims: Cultural Dialogues in Postmodernity and Tradition*. Madison: University of Wisconsin Press.

Flaherty, Michael P., and United States. Congress. House. Committee on Banking Finance and Urban Affairs. 1981. *Iran: The Financial Aspects of the Hostage Settlement Agreement*. Washington, DC: Government Printing Office.

Foreign Broadcast Information Service (FBIS). 2005. "Interview with Hasan Rowhani, Secretary of Iran's Supreme National Security Council." February 9, 2005. http://toolkit.dialog.com/intranet/cgi/present?STYLE=739318018& PRESENT=DB=985,AN=202850253,FM=9,SEARCH=MD.GenericSearch.

Foucault, Michel. 1991. "Governmentality." *The Foucault Effect: Studies in Governmentality*. Graham Burchell, Colin Gordon, and Peter Miller, eds. Chicago: University of Chicago Press: 87–104.

Fried, Amy. 1997. *Muffled Echoes: Oliver North and the Politics of Public Opinion*. New York: Columbia University Press.

Friedl, Erika. 1989. *Women of Deh Kol: Lives in an Iranian Village*. Washington, DC: Smithsonian Institution Press.

———. 1997. *Children of Deh Kol: Young Life in an Iranian Village*. Syracuse: Syracuse University Press.

Friedrich, Paul. 1981. *Agrarian Leadership and Violence in Mexico*. Chicago: University of Chicago.

———. 1986a. *The Language Parallax: Linguistic Relativism and Poetic Indeterminacy*. Austin: University of Texas Press.

———. 1986b. *The Princes of Naranja: An Essay in Anthrohistorical Method*. Austin: University of Texas Press.

———. 1998. *Music in Russian Poetry*. Middlebury Studies in Russian Language and Literature; Vol. 10. New York: Peter Lang.

Friedrich, Paul, and Anwar S. Dil. 1979. *Language, Context, and the Imagination: Essays*. Stanford, CA: Stanford University Press.

Froehlich, Leopold. 2002. "A Conversation with Rohan Gunaratna." *Playboy* 49 (11 [November]): 72–74, 147–50.

Gadamer, Hans Georg. 1975. *Truth and Method*. London: Sheed & Ward.

———. 1990. *Truth and Method*, 2nd rev. edition. New York: Crossroad.

Gage, Nicholas. 1978. "Iranian Opposition's Quandary: Coalition or Military Rule." *New York Times*. November 8: A–14.

Ganji, Manouchehr. 2002. *Defying the Iranian Revolution: From a Minister to the Shah to a Leader of Resistance*. Westport, CT: Praeger.

Garrod, Oliver. 1946. "The Qashqai Tribe of Fars." *Royal Central Asian journal*: 293–306.

Garthwaite, Gene R. 1983. "Tribes, Confederation and the State: An Historical Overview of the Bakhtiari and Iran." *The Conflict of Tribe and State in Iran and Afghanistan*. London: 314–30.

Gates, Robert M., Zbigniew Brzezinski, and Suzanne Maloney. 2004. *Iran: Time for a New Approach*. Washington, DC: Council on Foreign Relations.

Geertz, Clifford. 1960. *The Religion of Java*. Glencoe, IL: Free Press.

———. 1966. *Person, Time, and Conduct in Bali: An Essay in Cultural Analysis*. New Haven, CT: Yale University.

———. 1973. *The Interpretation of Cultures; Selected Essays*. New York: Basic Books.

Gellner, Ernest. 1983. "Tribal Society and Its Enemies." *The Conflict of Tribe and State in Iran and Afghanistan*. London: 436–48.

Gerecht, Reuel Marc. 2002a. "On to Iran! Checkmating the Clerics." *Weekly Standard* 7: 22–29.

———. 2002b. "Regime Change in Iran? Applying George W. Bush's 'Liberation Theology' to the Mullahs." *Weekly Standard* 7: 30–33.

Gilgoff, Dan. 2003. "Wolfman in Farsi?" *U.S. News & World Report* 134 (2 [January 20]): 28.

Gillespie, K. 1990. "United States Corporations and Iran at the Hague." *Middle East Journal* 44 (1): 18–36.

Gillespie, K., L. Riddle, E. Sayre, and D. Sturges. 1999. "Diaspora Interest in Homeland Investment." *Journal of International Business Studies* 30 (3): 623–34.

Gluckman, Max. 1955. *Custom and Conflict in Africa*. Oxford: Blackwell.

Göçek, Fatma Müge. 1998. *Political Cartoons in the Middle East.* Princeton, NJ: Markus Wiener Publishers.

Goldin, Farideh. 2003. *Wedding Song: Memoirs of an Iranian Jewish Woman.* Brandeis Series on Jewish Women. Hanover, NH: Brandeis University Press: Published by University Press of New England.

Goldsmith, David, and Steve Day. 1994. *John Poindexter St. & the Times of a Sign: a Folk History of the Iran-Contra Scandal.* New York: Sign Productions.

Good, Mary Jo DelVecchio. 1977. *Social Hierarchy and Social Change in a Provincial Iranian Town.* Cambridge, MA: Harvard University.

Goode, J. 1991. *"Review of Neither East nor West—Iran, the Soviet Union, and the United States. Keddie, N. R., Gasiorowski, M. J." Journal of American History* 78 (1): 402–3.

Goodell, Grace E. 1977. The Elementary Structures of Religious Life. Ph.D.: Columbia University.

———. 1986. *The Elementary Structures of Political Life: Rural Development in Pahlavi Iran.* New York: Oxford University Press.

Graham, Robert. 1978. *Iran, the Illusion of Power.* New York: St. Martin's Press.

Gregorian, Vartan. 1974. "Minorities of Isfahan: The Armenian Community of Isfahan 1587–1722." *Iranian Studies* 7: 652–80.

Grice, H. P. 1989. *Studies in the Way of Words.* Cambridge, MA: Harvard University Press.

———. 1991. *The Conception of Value.* New York: Clarendon Press; Oxford University Press.

———. 2001. *Aspects of Reason.* New York: Clarendon Press; Oxford University Press.

Gumperz, John Joseph. 1971. *Language in Social Groups.* Stanford, CA: Stanford University Press.

———. 1982. *Discourse Strategies.* New York: Cambridge University Press.

Gumperz, John Joseph, Jenny Cook-Gumperz, and Margaret H. Szymanski. 1999. "Collaborative Practices in Bilingual Cooperative Learning Classrooms." Santa Cruz, CA; Washington, DC: Center for Research on Education Diversity & Excellence; U.S. Dept. of Education, Office of Educational Research and Improvement, Educational Resources Information Center.

Gumperz, John Joseph, and Dell H. Hymes. 1972. *Directions in Sociolinguistics; the Ethnography of Communication.* New York: Holt, Rinehart and Winston.

Gunaratna, Rohan. 1993. *Indian Intervention in Sri Lanka: The Role of India's Intelligence Agencies.* Colombo: South Asian Network on Conflict Research.

———. 2002a. *Global Terror: Unearthing the Support Networks That Allow Terrorism to Survive and Succeed.* New York: New York University Press.

———. 2002b. *Inside Al Qaeda: Global Network of Terror.* New York: Columbia University Press.

Halliday, Fred. 1978. *Iran, Dictatorship and Development.* New York: Penguin.

Halm, Heinz, and Allison Brown. 1997. *Shi'a Islam: From Religion to Revolution.* Princeton Series on the Middle East. Princeton, NJ: Markus Wiener Publishers.

Hammam, Mona. 1981. "Review of 'Middle Eastern Muslim Women Speak' by Fernea, Elizabeth; Bazirgan, Basima; and 'Women in the Muslim World' by

Beck, Lois; Keddie, Nikki," "Women and Islam." *MERIP Reports* 95 (*Women and Work in the Middle East*): 28–30.

Hanassab, S., and R. Tidwell. 1996. "Sex Roles and Sexual Attitudes of Young Iranian Women: Implications for Cross-Cultural Counseling." *Social Behavior and Personality* 24 (2): 185–94.

Harik, Iliya F., and Denis Joseph Sullivan. 1992. *Privatization and Liberalization in the Middle East*. Indiana Series in Arab and Islamic Studies. Bloomington: Indiana University Press.

Harik, Judith P. 2004. *Hezbollah: The Changing Face of Terrorism*. London; New York: I.B. Tauris.

Hegland, Mary Elaine. 1983. "Ritual and Revolution in Iran." *Political Anthropology Yearbook* 2: 75–100.

———. 1990. "Women and the Iranian Revolution: A Village Case Study." *Dialectical Anthropology* 15 (2): 183–92.

———. 1992. "Wife Abuse and the Political System: A Middle Eastern Case Study." *Sanctions and Sanctuary: Cultural Perspectives on the Beating of Wives*: 203–18.

Hemmasi, Mohammad 1994. "Gender and Spatial Population Mobility in Iran." *Geoforum* 25 (2): 213–26.

Herrmann, R.K. 1991. "The Middle East and the New World Order—Rethinking United States Political Strategy after the Gulf War." *International Security* 16 (2): 42–75.

Hersh, Seymour. 2005. "The Coming Wars." *The New Yorker*. January 24 and 31. www.newyorker.com/fact/content/articles/050124fa_fact.

Hershman, Robert, and Henry L. Griggs Jr. 1981. "American Television News and the Middle East." *The Middle East Journal* 35 (4): 481–91.

Higgins, Patricia J. 1984. "Minority-State Relations in Contemporary Iran." *Iranian Studies* 17 (1): 37–71.

Hillman, Michael. 1981. "Language and Social Distinctions in Iran." *Modern Iran: The Dialectics of Continuity and Change*. Michael Bonine and Nikki Keddie, eds. Albany: SUNY Press.

Hinchman, James F., and United States. General Accounting Office. 1991. "Preliminary Inquiry into Alleged 1980 Negotiations to Delay Release of Iranian Hostages until after November Election. Statement for the Record of James F. Hinchman, General Counsel, before the Subcommittee on near Eastern and South Asian Affairs, Committee on Foreign Relations, United States Senate." Washington, DC: U.S. General Accounting Office.

Hiro, Dilip. 1980. "Rafsanjani's Central Role in the Upcoming Elections." Iran Mania. February 1, 1980. www.iranmania.com/news/currentaffairs/features/elections2000/articles/rafsanjani.asp.

———. 1989. *The Longest War: The Iran-Iraq Military Conflict*. London: Grafton.

Hobsbawm, Eric J. 1975. *The Crisis & the Outlook*. London: Birkbeck College Socialist Society; London Central Students Branch of the Communist Party.

Hodgson, Marshall G.S. 1974. *The Gunpowder Empires and Modern Times*. Chicago: University of Chicago Press.

———. 1980. *The Order of Assassins*. New York: AMS Press.

Hodgson, Marshall G. S. 1960. "Bataniya." *Encyclopedia of Islam*. 2nd edition.

Hoffman, Bruce, Rand Corporation, and United States. Office of the Under Secretary of Defense for Policy. 1990. *Recent Trends and Future Prospects of Iranian Sponsored International Terrorism*. Santa Monica, CA: Rand Corporation.

Hoffman, Paul. 1978. "However Slight, an Opposition Does Exist in Iran." *New York Times*. April 2, Section 4: 3, 5.

Honegger, Barbara. 1989. *October Surprise*. New York: Tudor Publishing Company.

Hooglund, Eric J. 1973. "The Khwushnishin Population of Iran." *Iranian Studies* 6 (4).

———. 1975. The Effects of the Land Reform Program on Rural Iran. Ph.D.: The Johns Hopkins University.

———. 1980. "Rural Participation in the Revolution." *MERIP Middle East Report*. Iran's Revolution: The Rural Dimension. No. 87 (May): 3–6.

———. 1981. "Rural Socioeconomic Organization in Transition: The Case of Iran's Bonehs." *Modern Iran: The Dialects of Continuity and Change*. Michael Bonine and Nikki Keddie, eds. Albany: SUNY Press: 191–210.

———. 1982. *Land and Revolution in Iran, 1960–1980*. Austin: University of Texas Press.

———, editor. 2002. *Twenty Years of Islamic Revolution: Political and Social Transition in Iran since 1979*, 1st edition. Contemporary Issues in the Middle East. Syracuse: Syracuse University Press.

Hooglund, Mary. 1980. "One Village in the Revolution." *MERIP Middle East Report*. Iran's Revolution: The Rural Dimension. No. 87 (May): 7–13.

Houghton, David Patrick. 2001. *U.S. Foreign Policy and the Iran Hostage Crisis*. Cambridge Studies in International Relations 75. Cambridge; New York: Cambridge University Press.

Hoveyda, Fereydoun. 2003. *The Shah and the Ayatollah: Iranian Mythology and Islamic Revolution*. National Committee on American Foreign Policy Study. Westport, CT: Praeger.

Howard, Jane Mary. 2002. *Inside Iran: Women's Lives*. Washington, DC: Mage Publishers.

Howe, Marvin. 1977. "Iranian Women Return to Veil in a Resurgence of Spirituality." *New York Times*. July 30: 4, 20.

Hughes, Gary. 2003. "Analyse This." *Melbourne Age*. July 20.

Hunter, Shireen T. 1985. *Internal Developments in Iran*. Significant Issues Series; V. 2, No. 3. Washington, DC: Center for Strategic and International Studies.

———. 1992. *Iran after Khomeini*. The Washington Papers, 156. New York: Praeger.

———. 1998. "Is Iranian Perestroika Possible without Fundamental Change?" *Washington Quarterly* 21: 23–41.

Hymes, Dell H. 1964. *Language in Culture and Society; a Reader in Linguistics and Anthropology*. New York: Harper & Row.

———. 1972. *Reinventing Anthropology*. New York: Pantheon Books.

———. 1974a. *Foundations in Sociolinguistics: An Ethnographic Approach*. Philadelphia: University of Pennsylvania Press.

———. 1974b. *Studies in the History of Linguistics: Traditions and Paradigms*. Bloomington: Indiana University Press.

———. 1978. *What Is Ethnography?* Austin, TX: Southwest Educational Development Laboratory.

———. 1980. *Language in Education: Ethnolinguistic Essays.* Washington, DC: Center for Applied Linguistics.

———. 1981. *"In Vain I Tried to Tell You": Essays in Native American Ethnopoetics.* Philadelphia: University of Pennsylvania Press.

———. 1983. *Essays in the History of Linguistic Anthropology.* Amsterdam; Philadelphia: J. Benjamins.

———. 1995. *Ethnography, Linguistics, Narrative Inequality: Toward an Understanding of Voice.* Critical Perspectives on Literacy and Education. London; Washington, DC: Taylor & Francis.

———. 2003. *Now I Know Only So Far: Essays in Ethnopoetics.* Lincoln: University of Nebraska Press.

Hymes, Dell H., and John G. Fought. 1981. *American Structuralism.* The Hague; New York: Mouton.

Hymes, Dell H., Frances Johnson, and Edward Sapir. 1998. *Reading Takelma Texts.* Bloomington, IN: Trickster Press.

Hymes, Dell H., National Institute of Education (U.S.), and University of Pennsylvania. Graduate School of Education. 1982. *Ethnolinguistic Study of Classroom Discourse: Final Report to the National Institute of Education.* Philadelphia: University of Pennsylvania Graduate School of Education.

Ibrahim, Saad Eddin. 1982. *The New Arab Social Order: A Study of the Social Impact of Oil Wealth.* Boulder, CO; London: Croom Helm.

Ibrahim, Yousef M. 1978. "Strife Cripples Iran's Economy." *New York Times.* November 28, 1978: D1, 2.

———. 1983a. "Burning Cause: A Rush to Martyrdom Gives Iran Advantage in War against Iraq." *Wall Street Journal* 202: 1+.

———. 1983b. "Iran Steps up Economic War on Iraq: Tehran Sells Cut-Rate Crude to Syria to Keep Big Iraqi Pipeline Closed." *Wall Street Journal* 201: 35.

———. 1983c. "New Mideast Risk: French-Iraqi Ties Get Ever Closer, Threaten to Widen War in Gulf: Paris Expands Its Arms Aid; Baghdad May Act to Halt Oil Shipments from Iran." *Wall Street Journal* 202: 1+.

———. 1984. "The Mideast War: Iraqis Scoff at Notion They Are on the Ropes in Conflict with Iran; Foes Appear Well-Matched in Power and Tenacity." *Wall Street Journal* 203: 1+.

Ibrahim, Youssef M., and Karen Elliott House. 1982. "Widening War: Ascendency of Iran in Conflict with Iraq Imperils Mideast Oil; Backed by Soviet Union, Teheran Renews Aim to Export Revolution [to Arab States]." *Wall Street Journal* 199: 1+.

Ibrahim, Youssef M., and David Ignatius. 1982. "Ominous Ripples from Iran's Victory [Probable Effects on the Balance of Power in the Persian Gulf]." *Wall Street Journal* 199: 35.

Iran Daily. 2005. "Marriage Age Up." Iran Daily. April 11. www.iran-daily.com/1384/2246/html/panorama.htm#53502

Iran. Nakhust Vazir. 1972. *Report of the Prime Minister on the State of the Iranian Economy 1347–50, Mar. 21, 1968–Mar. 20, 1972 and Government Programmes for the Year 1351, Mar. 21, 1972–Mar. 20, 1973.* Tehran: Central Bureau of the Budget Plan Organization.

Ismailova, Gulnara. 2003. "Iranian Azeri Leader Supports the Federalization of

Iran." Johns Hopkins University, School of Advanced International Studies. www.cacianalyst.org/view_article.php?articleid=1574.

Issawi, Charles Philip. 1971. *The Economic History of Iran, 1800–1914*. Chicago: University of Chicago Press.

Jahanbakhsh, Forough. 2001. *Islam, Democracy and Religious Modernism in Iran, 1953–2000: From Bazargan to Soroush*. Social, Economic, and Political Studies of the Middle East and Asia, V. 77. Leiden; Boston: Brill.

Jakobson, Roman. 1960. "Closing Statement: Linguistics and Poetics." *Style in Language*. Thomas Sebeok, ed. Cambridge, MA: MIT Press: 350–77.

Jenkins, Brian Michael, and Rand Corporation. 1990. *Getting the Hostages Out: Who Turns the Key?* Santa Monica, CA: Rand Corp.

Jensen, Mark. 2005. "Scott Ritter Says U.S. Plans June Attack on Iran, 'Cooked' Jan. 30 Iraqi Election Results." United for Peace of Pierce County. www.ufppc.org/content/view/2295/.

Jiri Press Ticker Service. 1980. "Koohyar Urges Start of Full-Scale Construction for Japan-Iran Complex Project." Jiri Press Ticker Service. June 25, 1980. www.lexis-nexis.com/.

Johnson, Gail Cook. 1980. *High-Level Manpower in Iran: From Hidden Conflict to Crisis*. New York: Praeger.

Jones, Sherry, Bill D. Moyers, Foster Wiley, Elizabeth Sams, WGBH and PBS Video. 1990. "High Crimes and Misdemeanors." Alexandria, VA: PBS Video.

Jordan, Hamilton. 1982. *Crisis: The Last Year of the Carter Presidency*. New York: Putnam.

Kafala, Tarik. 2002. "Analysis: Iran and the 'Axis of Evil'." British Broadcasting Corporation. http://news.bbc.co.uk/2/hi/middle_east/1814659.stm

Kandell, Jonathan. 1978a. "Iran Arrests Head of Secret Police, Other Officials and Businessmen." *New York Times*. November 8: A11.

———. 1978b. "Iran's Affluent, Indebted to Shah, Give Him Little Support in Crisis." *New York Times*. November 18: 1.

———. 1979. "The Tehran Bazaar." *New York Times*. July 1: 11.

Katz, M. N. 2003. "Losing Balance: Russian Foreign Policy toward Iraq and Iran." *Current History* 102 (666): 341–45.

Kazemi, Farhad. 1980. *Poverty and Revolution in Iran: The Migrant Poor, Urban Marginality, and Politics*. New York: New York University Press.

Kazemipur, Abdolmohammad, and Ali Rezaei. 2003. "Religious Life under Theocracy: The Case of Iran." *Journal for the Scientific Study of Religion* 42 (3): 347–61.

Kazemzadeh, Masoud. 2002. *Islamic Fundamentalism, Feminism, and Gender Inequality in Iran under Khomeini*. Lanham, MD: University Press of America.

Keddie, Nikki R. 1963. "Symbol and Sincerity in Islam." *Studia Islamica* 19: 27–64.

———. 1968. "The Iranian Village before and after Land Reform." *Journal of Contemporary History* 3 (3, The Middle East): 69–91.

———. 1972a. "Review of Religion and State in Iran 1785–1906: The Role of the Ulama in the Qajar Period by Algar, Hamid." *Journal of the American Oriental Society* 92 (1): 116–18.

———. 1972b. *Sayyid Jamal Ad-Din "Al-Afghani": A Political Biography*. Berkeley: University of California Press.

————. 1972c. "Stratification, Social Control, and Capitalism in Iranian Villages: Before and after Land Reform." *Rural politics and social change in the Middle East.* Richard Antoun, Richard Taft, and Iliya Harik, eds. Bloomington: Indiana University Press: 364–402.

————. 1980a. *Iran: Religion, Politics, and Society: Collected Essays.* London; Totowa, NJ: F. Cass, Biblio Distribution Centre.

————. 1980b. "Iran: Change in Islam; Islam and Change." *International Journal of Middle East Studies* 11 (4): 527–42.

————. 1981a. "Religion, Society and Revolution in Modern Iran." *Modern Iran: The Dialectics of Continuity and Change.* Michael Bonine and Nikki Keddie, eds. Albany: SUNY Press.

————. 1981b. "The Iranian Revolution and U.S. Policy." *SAIS-Review* 17 (1 [winter–spring]) 13–26.

————. 1994. "The Revolt of Islam, 1700 to 1993: Comparative Considerations and Relations to Imperialism." *Comparative Studies in Society and History* 36 (3): 463–87.

Keddie, Nikki R., and Beth Baron. 1991. *Women in Middle Eastern History: Shifting Boundaries in Sex and Gender.* New Haven, CT: Yale University Press.

Keddie, Nikki R., and Eric J. Hooglund. 1986. *The Iranian Revolution & the Islamic Republic,* New edition. Syracuse: Syracuse University Press.

Keddie, Nikki R., Eric J. Hooglund, Woodrow Wilson International Center for Scholars and Middle East Institute. 1982. *The Iranian Revolution and the Islamic Republic: Proceedings of a Conference.* Washington, DC: Middle East Institute in cooperation with Woodrow Wilson International Center for Scholars.

Keddie, Nikki R., and Rudolph P. Matthee. 2002. *Iran and the Surrounding World: Interactions in Culture and Cultural Politics.* Seattle: University of Washington Press.

Keddie, Nikki R., and Yann Richard. 1981. *Roots of Revolution: An Interpretive History of Modern Iran.* New Haven, CT: Yale University Press.

————. 2003. *Modern Iran: Roots and Results of Revolution.* New Haven, CT: Yale University Press.

Keddie, Nikki R., William O. Beeman, A. E. Mayer, Gary Sick, Mehdi Khonsari, B. Khajehpour, H. Partovi, C. Kurzman, F. E. Moghadam, N. Tohidi, N. Gharavi, and G. Asayesh. 2001. "Women in Iran: An Online Discussion." *Middle East Policy* 8 (4): 128–43.

Keshavarz, Mohammad Hossein. 2001. "The Role of Social Context, Intimacy, and Distance in the Choice of Forms of Address." *International Journal of the Sociology of Language* (148): 5–18.

Kessler, Ronald. 1992. *Inside the CIA: Revealing the Secrets of the World's Most Powerful Spy Agency.* New York: Pocket Books.

————. 2002. *The Bureau: The Secret History of the FBI.* New York: St. Martin's Press.

————. 2003. *The CIA at War: Inside the Secret Campaign against Terror.* New York: St. Martin's Press.

Kheradpir, A. T. 1992. "Review of 'Revolution Behind a Veil—Islamic Women of Iran' (in French) by Fariba Adelkhah." *Man* 27 (4): 893–94.

Khomeini, Ayatollah Ruhollah. 1979. *Islamic Government.* New York: Manor House.

Khomeini, Ruhollah, and Hamid Algar. 2002. *Islam and Revolution: The Writings and Declarations of Imam Khomeini*. The Kegan Paul Library of Central Asia. London; New York: Kegan Paul.

Kinzer, Stephen. 2003. *All the Shah's Men: An American Coup and the Roots of Middle East Terror*. Hoboken, NJ: John Wiley & Sons.

Kraus, W. 1998. "Contestable Identities: Tribal Structures in the Moroccan High Atlas." *Journal of the Royal Anthropological Institute* 4 (1): 1–22.

Kurup, A. M. 1974. "Sedentarization of Nomadic Tribes in Two Countries—Soviet Union and Iran." *West Bengal*. Cultural Research Institute. *Bulletin* 10: 16–20.

Kurzman, Charles. 2004. *The Unthinkable Revolution in Iran*. Cambridge, MA: Harvard University Press.

Ladier-Fouladi, Marie. 1997. "The Fertility Transition in Iran." *Population: An English Selection* 9: 191–213.

Lagarde, Paul de. 1970. *Persische Studien*. Osnabrèuck: O. Zeller.

Laingen, L. Bruce. 1992. *Yellow Ribbon: The Secret Journal of Bruce Laingen*. Washington: Brassey's (U.S.).

Lakoff, George. 1991. "Metaphor and War: The Metaphor System Used to Justify War in the Gulf." *Peace Research* 23: 25–32.

———. 2004. *Don't Think of an Elephant! Know Your Values and Frame the Debate: The Essential Guide for Progressives*. White River Junction, VT: Chelsea Green Publishing Company.

Lambton, A.K.S. 1992. "The 'Qanats' of Yazd." *Journal of the Royal Asiatic Society* 2 (1): 21–35.

———. 1953. *Landlord and Peasant in Persia; a Study of Land Tenure and Land Revenue Administration*. London, New York: Oxford University Press.

———. 1969a. "Land Reform and Rural Cooperative Societies in Persia. Part I." *Royal Central Asian Journal* 56 (June): 142–55.

———. 1969b. *Landlord and Peasant in Persia: A Study of Land Tenure and Land Revenue Administration*. London: Oxford University Press.

———. 1969c. *The Persian Land Reform, 1962–1966*. Oxford: Clarendon Press.

Landolt, H. 1999. "Henry Corbin, 1903–1978: Between Philosophy and Orientalism." *Journal of the American Oriental Society* 119 (3): 484–90.

Larsen, Janet. 2001. "Iran's Birth Rate Is Falling Fast." People and Planet. December 29. www.peopleandplanet.net/doc.php?id=1399

———. 2003. "Iran's Birth Rate Plummeting at Record Pace." American Humanist Association. In *Humanist* 63 (1): 4.

Last, Jef. 1955. *Bali in De Kentering*. Amsterdam: Bezige Bij.

Ledeen, Michael Arthur. 1992. *Superpower Dilemmas: The U.S. And the U.S.S.R. at Century's End*. New Brunswick: Transaction Publishers.

———. 2002. *The War against the Terror Masters: Why It Happened, Where We Are Now, How We'll Win*, 1st edition. New York: St. Martin's Press.

———. 2003a. "The Future of Iran." *National Review* Online. July 9, 2003. www.nationalreview.com/ledeen/ledeen070903.asp.

———. 2003b. "The Iranian Hand: Regime Change in Tehran Is Necessary for Peace in Iraq." *Wall Street Journal*. April 16, 2004: A14.

LeVine, Robert A. 1961. "Anthropology and the Study of Conflict: An Introduction." *Journal of Conflict Resolution* 5 (1, The Anthropology of Conflict): 3–15.

Lewis, Bernard. 2003a. *The Crisis of Islam: Holy War and Unholy Terror*, Modern Library edition. New York: Modern Library.

———. 2003b. *What Went Wrong? The Clash between Islam and Modernity in the Middle East*. New York: Perennial.

Linzer, Dafna. 2005. "U.S. Uses Drones to Probe Iran for Arms: Surveillance Flights Are Sent from Iraq." *The Washington Post*. February 13: A1.

Lobe, Jim. 2004. "Iraq: Neo-Cons See Iran Behind Shiite Uprising." Inter Press Service News Agency. April 9, 2004. www.ipsnews.net/interna.asp?idnews= 23249

Loeb, Laurence D. 1977a. "Creating Antiques for Fun and Profit: Encounters between Iranian Jewish Merchants and Touring Coreligionists." *Hosts and guests*: 185–92.

———. 1977b. *Outcaste: Jewish Life in Southern Iran*. Library of Anthropology. New York; London: Gordon and Breach.

———. 1982. "Prestige and Piety in the Iranian Synagogue." *Jewish Societies in the Middle East*: 285–97.

Looney, Robert E. 1973. *The Economic Development of Iran; a Recent Survey with Projections to 1981*. Praeger Special Studies in International Economics and Development. New York: Praeger.

Mackey, Sandra, and W. Scott Harrop. 1996. *The Iranians: Persia, Islam and the Soul of a Nation*. New York: Dutton.

Mahmoody, Betty, and William Hoffer. 1987. *Not without My Daughter*. New York: St. Martin's Press.

Marsh, S. 2003. "The United States, Iran and Operation 'Ajax': Inverting Interpretative Orthodoxy." *Middle Eastern Studies* 39 (3): 1–38.

Matthee, Rudi. 1991. "Career of Mohammed Beg, Grand Vizier of Shah 'Abbas Ii (R. 1642–1666)." *Iranian Studies* 24 (1): 17–36.

———. 1994. "Administrative Stability and Change in Late 17th Century Iran: The Case of Shaykh Ali Khan." in *International Journal of Middle East Studies*, vol. 26, p. 77: Cambridge University Press.

———. 2000a. "Between Venice and Surat: The Trade in Gold in Late Safavid Iran." In *Modern Asian Studies*, vol. 34, p. 223.

———. 2000b. "Merchants in Safavid Iran: Participants and Perceptions." In *Journal of Early Modern History*, vol. 4, p. 233: Brill Academic Publishers.

———. 2001. "Mint Consolidation and the Worsening of the Late Safavid Coinage: The Mint of Huwayza." In *Journal of the Economic & Social History of the Orient*, vol. 44, pp. 505–39: Brill Academic Publishers.

———. 2002. "Review of Safavid Government Institutions by Floor, Willem." *Middle East Journal* 56 (3): 541.

———. 2003. "Merchants, Mamluks, and Murder: The Political Economy of Trade in Eighteenth-Century Basra (Book)." In *Journal of Near Eastern Studies*, vol. 62, p. 317: University of Chicago Press.

———. 2005. *The Pursuit of Pleasure: Drugs and Stimulants in Iranian History, 1500–1900*. Princeton, NJ: Princeton University Press.

McFadden, Robert D., Joseph Treaster, and Maurice C. Carroll. 1981. *No Hiding*

Place: The New York Times inside Report on the Hostage Crisis. New York: Times Books.

Mead, Margaret. 1972. *Blackberry Winter; My Earlier Years*. New York: Morrow.

Mead, Margaret, and Rhoda Bubendey Métraux. 2000. *The Study of Culture at a Distance*. Margaret Mead—Researching Western Contemporary Cultures; V. 1. New York: Berghahn Books.

Mehran, Golnar. 1991. "The Creation of the New Muslim Woman: Female Education in the Islamic Republic of Iran." *Convergence* 24 (4): 42–52.

———. 1999. "Lifelong Learning: New Opportunities for Women in a Muslim Country (Iran)." *Comparative Education* 35 (2): 201–15.

Mendez, Robert. 1998. "Prospects for Change in Iran." *Congressional Record* (June 3, 1998): E1002–03.

Menges, Constantine. 2003. "Path to Mideast Peace Via Iran?" *Washington Times*. October 26: B03.

Milani, Mohsen M. 1988. *The Making of Iran's Islamic Revolution: From Monarchy to Islamic Republic*. Boulder, CO: Westview Press.

Millspaugh, Arthur Chester. 1946. *Americans in Persia*. Washington, DC: The Brookings Institution.

Mirfendereski, Guive. 2001. "Separating Minorities from the Rest of the Nation (Article 64)." The Iranian. www.iranian.com/GuiveMirfendereski/2001/May/Elections/index.html.

Moaddel, M. 1998. "Religion and Women: Islamic Modernism Versus Fundamentalism." *Journal for the Scientific Study of Religion* 37 (1): 108–30.

Moaveni, Azadeh. 2000. "Letter from Shiraz: Jews on Trial. An Iranian Spy Case Undermines an Ancient Minority and a Modern President." *Time Europe* 155 (16).

———. 2005. *Lipstick Jihad: A Memoir of Growing up Iranian in America and American in Iran*. New York: Public Affairs.

Mobasser, Nilou. 2003. "Mad Mullahs and Mullah Lites." In *Index on Censorship*, 32 (3): 10: Writers & Scholars International.

Modarresi, Yahya. 1993. "Linguistic Consequences of Some Sociopolitical Changes in Iran." *International Journal of the Sociology of Language* (100/101): 87–99.

———. 2001. "The Iranian Community in the United States and the Maintenance of Persian." *International Journal of the Sociology of Language* (148): 93–115.

Mohaddessin, Mohammad. 1993. *Islamic Fundamentalism: The New Global Threat*. Washington, DC: Seven Locks Press.

Molavi, Afshin. 2002. *Persian Pilgrimages: Journeys across Iran*. New York: Norton.

———. 2003. "Letter from Iran." In *Nation* 277 (11): 16. Nation Company, Inc.

Monshipouri, Mahmood. 1999. "Reform and the Human Rights Quandary: Islamists vs. Secularists." In *Journal of Church & State* 41 (3): 445: J. M. Dawson Institute of Church State Studies.

Moreen, Vera Basch. 2000. *In Queen Esther's Garden: An Anthology of Judeo-Persian Literature*. Yale Judaica Series; V. 30. New Haven, CT: Yale University Press.

Moreen, Vera Basch, and Baba'i ibn Lotf. 1987. *Iranian Jewry's Hour of Peril and Heroism: A Study of Baba'i Ibn Lotf's Chronicle, 1617–1662.* New York: American Academy for Jewish Research.

Morgan, T. Clifton, Dina Al-Sowayal, and Carl Rhodes. 1998. "United States Policy toward Iran: Can Sanctions Work?" Baker Institute, Rice University. www.rice.edu/projects/baker/Pubs/studies/uspti/uspti.html.

Mortimer, Edward. 1981. "Islam and the Western Journalist." *The Middle East Journal* 35 (4): 492–505.

Moses, Russell Leigh. 1996. *Freeing the Hostages: Reexamining U.S.–Iranian Negotiations and Soviet Policy, 1979–1981.* Pitt Series in Policy and Institutional Studies. Pittsburgh, PA: University of Pittsburgh Press.

Motlagh, Jason. 2005. "Words Are Weapons for Iranian Bloggers." United Press International/*The Washington Times.* February 17, 2005. www.washtimes. com/upi-breaking/20050214-050322-8970r.htm.

Mottahedeh, Roy P. 1980. "Iran's Foreign Devils." *Foreign Policy* 38 (spring 1980): 25+.

———. 1985. *The Mantle of the Prophet: Religion and Politics in Iran.* New York: Simon and Schuster.

Muir, Jim. 2004. "Analysis: Iran Voting Resumes." BBC. May 6. http://news.bbc.co. uk/1/hi/middle_east/3689331.htm.

Nader, Laura. 1997. "Controlling Processes." *Current Anthropology* 38 (5): 711–39.

———. 2001. "Harmony Coerced Is Freedom Denied." In *Chronicle of Higher Education* 47 (44): B13.

———. 2002. *The Life of the Law: Anthropological Projects.* Berkeley: University of California Press.

Nader, Laura, and Elisabetta Grande. 2002. "Current Illusions and Delusions About Conflict Management-in Africa and Elsewhere." *Law & Social Inquiry*, vol. 27 (3): 573: American Bar Foundation.

Naficy, Hamid. 1979. "Nonfiction Fiction: Documentaries on Iran." *Iranian Studies* 12 (3): 217–38.

———. 1981. "Film in Iran, a Brief Critical History." *Modern Iran: The Dialectics of Continuity and Change.* Michael E. Bonine and Nikki R. Keddie, eds. Albany: SUNY Press.

———. 1992. "Cultural Dynamics of Iranian Post-Revolutionary Film Periodicals." *Iranian Studies* 25 (3): 67–73.

———. 1993. *The Making of Exile Cultures: Iranian Television in Los Angeles.* Minneapolis: University of Minnesota Press.

———. 1999. *Home, Exile, Homeland: Film, Media, and the Politics of Place.* New York: Routledge.

———. 2000. "Veiled Voice and Vision in Iranian Cinema: The Evolution of Rakhshan Banietemad's Films." In *Social Research*, 67 (2):559–76.

———. 2001. *An Accented Cinema: Exilic and Diasporic Filmmaking.* Princeton, NJ: Princeton University Press.

Naficy, Hamid, and Teshome H. Gabriel. 1993. *Otherness and the Media: The Ethnography of the Imagined and the Imaged.* Studies in Film and Video. Chur, Switzerland; Langhorne, PA: Harwood Academic Publishers.

Nafisi, Azar. 2003. *Reading Lolita in Tehran: A Memoir in Books.* New York: Random House.

Nahai, Gina Barkhordar. 1999. *Moonlight on the Avenue of Faith*. New York: Harcourt Brace.

Nakash, Yitzhak. 2003a. *The Shi'is of Iraq*. Princeton, NJ: Princeton University Press.

———. 2003b. "The Shi'ites and the Future of Iraq." In *Foreign Affairs* 82 (4): 17–26.

Nashat, Guity. 1983. *Women and Revolution in Iran*. Boulder, CO: Westview Press.

Nasr, Sayyid Hossein. 1965. "Cosmographie En L'iran Pré-Islamique Et Islamique, Le Problème De La Continuité Dans La Civilization Iranienne." *Arabic and Islamic Studies in Honor of Hamilton A.R. Gibb*. George Makdisi, ed. Leiden: E.J. Brill: 507–24.

———. 1967. *Ideals and Realities of Islam*. New York: Praeger.

National Security Archive. 1997. "Interview with Dr Zbigniew Brzezinski (13/6/97)." National Security Archive: George Washington University. www.gwu.edu~nsarchiv/coldwar/interviews/episode-17/brzezinski1.html

Nercissians, Emilia. 2001. "Bilingualism and Disglossia: Patterns of Language Use by Ethnic Minorities in Tehran." *International Journal of the Sociology of Language* 148: 59–70.

Netzer, Amnon. 1997. *Padyavand*. Judeo-Iranian and Jewish Studies Series, No. 2. Costa Mesa, CA: Mazda Publishers.

Neusner, Jacob. 1983. "Jews in Iran." *Cambridge History of Iran* 3: 909–23.

Nicolas, Louis Alphonse Daniel. 1905. *Seyyáed Ali Mohammed Dit Le Bãab; Histoire*. Bibliotháeque De Critique Religieuse, 15–16. Paris: Dujarric.

———. 1933. *Qui Est Le Successeur Du Bab?* Paris: A. Maisonneuve.

Nowshirvani, Vahid. 2002. "Review of The State and Rural Development in Post–Revolutionary Iran by Ali Shakoori." *The Middle East Journal* 56 (2): 336–37.

Nunberg, Geoffrey. 2004. *Going Nucular: Language, Politics and Culture in Confrontational Times*. New York: Public Affairs.

O'Ballance, Edgar. 1997. *Islamic Fundamentalist Terrorism, 1979–1995: The Iranian Connection*. Washington Square, NY: New York University Press.

Ochs, Elinor, Emanuel A. Schegloff, and Sandra A. Thompson. 1996. *Interaction and Grammar*. Studies in Interactional Sociolinguistics 13. Cambridge; New York: Cambridge University Press.

Pace, Eric. 1975. "Oil Boom Spawns Disorder in Isfahan." *New York Times*. September 8: 43.

Paper, Herbert H. 1973. *Biblia Judaeo-Persica*, editio variorum (microfilm). Edition. [Ann Arbor].

———. 1976. *A Judeo-Persian Book of Job*. Jerusalem: Israel Academy of Sciences and Humanities.

Paper, Herbert H., and Meir Benayahu. 1976. *A Judeo-Persian Book of Job*. Jerusalem: Israel Academy of Sciences and Humanities.

Parry, Robert. 1993. *Trick or Treason: The October Surprise Mystery*. Lanham, MD: Sheridan Square Press.

Pasquini, Elaine. 2004. "Hezbollah May Have 'Bright Political Future' in Lebanon, Says Dwight J. Simpson." *Washington Report on Middle East Affairs* 23 (7): 56–57.

Paydarfar, A. A., and R. Moini. 1995. "Modernization Process and Fertility Change in Pre-Islamic and Post-Islamic Revolution of Iran—A Cross-Provincial

Analysis, 1966–1986." *Population Research and Policy Review* 14 (1): 71–90.

Payvand Iran News. 2003. "Parliament Forwards Bill on Press Law to Expediency Council." June 23, 2003. www.payvand.com/news/03/jun/1129.html

Pesaran, M. Hashem. 1976. *World Economic Prospects and the Iranian Economy*. Tehran Papers; No. 5. Tehran: Institute for International Political and Economic Studies.

Peterson, Mark Allan. 2003. *Anthropology and Mass Communication: Media and Myth in the New Millennium*. New York: Berghahn Books.

Pezeshkhzad, Iraj. 1996. *My Uncle Napoleon: A Novel (tr. Dick Davis)*. Washington, DC: Mage Publishers.

Pipes, Daniel, and Patrick Clawson. 2003a. "A Terrorist U.S. Ally?" *New York Post*. May 20. www.danielpipes.org/article/1100

———. 2003b. "Turn Up the Pressure on Iran." *The Jerusalem Post*. May 21. [reprint of 2003a]

Pollack, Kenneth M. 2003. "Securing the Gulf." *Foreign Affairs* 82 (4): 2–16.

———. 2004. *The Persian Puzzle: The Conflict between Iran and America*. New York: Random House.

Pollack, Kenneth M., and Roy Takeyh. 2005. "Taking on Tehran." *Foreign Affairs* 84 (2): 20–34.

Prakke, Hendricus Johannes. 1979. "The Socius Function of the Press." *Entertainment, a Cross-Cultural Examination*. Heinz Dietrich Fischer and Stefan R. Melnik, eds. New York: Hastings House: xxi, 330.

Price, David H. 1998. "Cold War Anthropology: Collaborators and Victims of the National Security State." In *Identities*, vol. 4, p. 389: Taylor & Francis Ltd.

Pullapilly, Cyriac K. 1980. *Islam in the Contemporary World*. Notre Dame, IN: Cross Roads Books.

Purhadi, Ibrahim Vaqfi, and Library of Congress. Near East Section. 1982. *Iran and the United States, 1979–1981: Three Years of Confrontation: A Selected List of References*. Mideast Directions; Med 82-1. Washington, DC: Near East Section African and Middle Eastern Division, Library of Congress.

Quest Economics Database. 2003. "Iran: Country Profile." London: Middle East Review World of Information, Janet Matthews Information Service.

Quint, Bert. 1980. "Dateline Tehran: There Was a Touch of Fear." *T.V. Guide* (April 5).

Rahnama, Ali. 2000. *An Islamic Utopian: A Political Biography of Ali Shariati*. London; New York: I.B. Tauris.

Ramazani, N. 1993a. "A Revolution Behind the Veil—Islamic Women in Iran (French) Adelkhah, F." *Middle East Journal* 47 (2): 336–37.

———. 1993b. "Women in Iran: The Revolutionary Ebb and Flow." *Middle East Journal* 47 (3): 409–28.

Ramazani, Rouhollah K. 1975. *Iran's Foreign Policy, 1941–1973; a Study of Foreign Policy in Modernizing Nations*. Charlottesville: University Press of Virginia.

———. 1982. *The United States and Iran: The Patterns of Influence*. Studies of Influence in International Relations. New York: Praeger.

———. 1986. *Revolutionary Iran: Challenge and Response in the Middle East*. Baltimore, MD: Johns Hopkins University Press.

————. 1990. *Iran's Revolution: The Search for Consensus*. Bloomington: Indiana University Press.

————. 1998. "The Shifting Premise of Iran's Foreign Policy: Towards a Democratic Peace?" *Middle East Journal* 52 (2): 177–87.

Rappaport, U. 1996. "The Jews and Their Neighbors During the Persian, Hellenistic and Roman Period." *Annales-Histoire Sciences Sociales* 51 (5): 955.

Raum, Tom. 1988a. "Bush Defends U.S. Right to Be in Persian Gulf. Vice President Takes Stand at UN." *Philadelphia Daily News (AP)*. July 14: 3.

————. 1988b. "Bush Defends U.S. Rights in Gulf." *Associated Press*.

Rejali, Darius M. 1994. *Torture & Modernity: Self, Society, and State in Modern Iran*. Institutional Structures of Feeling. Boulder, CO: Westview Press.

Rizun, Miron, editor. 1990. *Iran at the Crossroads: Global Relations in a Turbulent Decade*. Boulder, CO: Westview Press.

Roosevelt, Kermit. 1979. *Countercoup, the Struggle for the Control of Iran*. New York: McGraw-Hill.

Ross, Jay. 1978. "Shah's Development Drive Sparks Bitter Reaction: News Analysis." *Washington Post*. September 9, Section 1: A14.

Ross, Robert, and Ross Film/Video 1992. "Investigating the October Surprise (Segment of PBS Television Program *Frontline*)." Alexandria, VA: PBS Video.

Roy, Olivier. 1995. *Afghanistan: From Holy War to Civil War*. The Leon B. Poullada Memorial Lecture Series. Princeton, NJ: Darwin Press.

Rubin, Barry M. 1980. *Paved with Good Intentions: The American Experience and Iran*. New York: Oxford University Press.

————. 1981a. *Paved with Good Intentions: The American Experience and Iran*. Harmondsworth, Middlesex, UK; New York: Penguin.

Rubin, Michael. 2003a. "Are Kurds a Pariah Minority?" In *Social Research*, vol. 70 (1), 295–330.

————. 2003b. "Review of 'Twenty Year of Islamic Revolution, Edited by Eric J. Hoogland'." In *Middle East Quarterly*, 10 (1): 92.

————. 2004a. "Learning from Sadr: Listen to the Iraqis." National Review Online. April 8, 2004. www.nationalreview.com/rubin/rubin200404080818.asp

————. 2004b. "Sadr Signs." National Review Online. April 7, 2004. www.nationalreview.com/comment/rubin200404060834.asp.

Rundle, Christopher. 2002. *Reflections on the Iranian Revolution and Iranian-British Relations*. Durham, UK: University of Durham Centre for Middle Eastern and Islamic Studies.

Ryan, Paul B. 1985. *The Iranian Rescue Mission: Why It Failed*. Annapolis, MD: Naval Institute Press.

Sacks, Harvey, and Gail Jefferson. 1989. *Harvey Sacks Lectures, 1964–1965*. Dordrecht; Boston: Kluwer Academic Publishers.

————. 1992. *Lectures on Conversation*. Oxford, UK; Cambridge, MA: Blackwell.

Safi-Nezhad, Javad. 1967. *Taleb-Abad: Nemuneh-ye Jame'i Az Barrasi-ye Yek Deh (Taleb-Abad, an Example of Community, through the Investigation of a Village)*. Tehran: Institute for Social Studies and Research.

————. 1974. *Bonih, Nezam-ha-ye Towlid-e Zera'i-ye Jam'i Qabl Az Eslahat-e Arzi. (the Bonih, the Structure of Collective Agricultural Production before Land Reform)*. 2nd edition. Tehran: Tus Publications.

————. 1978. *Asnad-e Boneh*. Tehran: University of Tehran.

Safire, William. 2004. "Two Front Insurgency." *New York Times*. April 7: 19A.

Said, Edward W. 1979. *Orientalism*. New York: Vintage Books.

———. 1980. "Iran." *Columbia Journalism Review* 18 (6).

———. 1997. *Covering Islam: How the Media and the Experts Determine How We See the Rest of the World*, Rev. edition. New York: Vintage Books.

Saikal, Amin. 1980. *The Rise and Fall of the Shah*. Princeton, NJ: Princeton University Press.

Sale, Richard. 2003. "Saddam-CIA Links (1959–1990)." *Peace Research* 35 (1): 17–20.

Sanasarian, Eliz. 2000. *Religious Minorities in Iran*. Cambridge Middle East Studies 13. Cambridge: Cambridge University Press.

Sarraf, Murtaza, and Henry Corbin. 1991. *Rasayil-i Javanmardan: Mushtamil Bar Haft Futuvvatânamah*. Tehran: Intisharat-i Mu'in: Anjuman-i Iranshinasi-ye Faransah.

Sarshar, Houman. Editor. 2002. *Esther's Children: A Portrait of Iranian Jews*. Beverly Hills, CA.; Philadelphia: Center for Iranian Jewish Oral History, Jewish Publication Society.

Schegloff, Emanuel A. 1968. "Sequencing in Conversational Openings." *American Anthropologist* 70 (6): 1075–95.

———. 1972. "Notes on a Conversational Practice:Formulating Place." *Studies in Social Interaction*. David Sudnow, ed. New York: Free Press: 75–119.

———. 1980. "Preliminaries to Preliminaries: 'Can I Ask You a Question?'" *Sociological Inquiry* 50 (3–4): 104–52.

———. 1982. "Discourse as an Intellectual Accomplishment: Some Uses of 'Uh Huh' and Other Things That Come between Sentences." *Georgetown University Round Table on Language and Linguistics: Analyzing Discourse: Text and Talk*. Deborah Tannen, ed. Washington, DC: Georgetown University Press: 71–93.

Schramm, Wilbur Lang. 1964. *Mass Media and National Development; the Role of Information in the Developing Countries*. Stanford, CA: Stanford University Press.

Schramm, Wilbur Lang, and Donald F. Roberts, editors. 1971. *The Process and Effects of Mass Communication*, Rev. edition. Urbana: University of Illinois Press.

Schreer, B. 2003. "Who's Next? The United States, Iran and Preemptive Strikes." *Internationale Politik* 58 (6): 55–58.

Schulz, Ann. 1977. "Iran's New Industrial State." *Current History* 72 (423): 15, 18+.

Sciolino, Elaine. 1983. "Iran's Durable Revolution" *Foreign Affairs* 61 (3): 893–920.

———. 2000. *Persian Mirrors: The Elusive Face of Iran*. New York: Free Press.

———. 2003. "Iran Will Allow U.N. Inspections of Nuclear Sites." *New York Times*. October 22: 1+.

Scott, Charles W. 1984. *Pieces of the Game: The Human Drama of Americans Held Hostage in Iran*. Atlanta, GA: Peachtree Publishers.

Shahidian, Hammed. 2002. *Women in Iran*. Contributions in Women's Studies, No. 197. Westport, CT: Greenwood Press.

Shahshahani, Soheila. 1995. "Tribal Schools in Iran: Sedentarization through Education." *Nomadic Peoples* 36: 145–55.

Shaked, Shaul. 1982. *Irano-Judaica: Studies Relating to Jewish Contacts with Persian Culture Throughout the Ages.* Jerusalem: Ben-Zvi Institute for the Study of Jewish Communities in the East.

Shakoori, Ali. 2001. *The State and Rural Development in Post-Revolutionary Iran.* Houndmills, Basingstoke, Hampshire; New York: Palgrave.

Shariati, Ali. 1979a. *Ali Shariati's an Approach to the Understanding of Islam.* The Islamic Renaissance Series. Group One, Translation of the Works of Ali Shariati. Tehran: Shariati Foundation.

———. 1979b. *Ali Shariati's One Followed by an Eternity of Zeros.* The Islamic Renaissance Series. Group One, Translation of the Works of Ali Shariati. Tehran: Hoseiniyeh Ershad.

———. 1979c. *Ali Shariati's Red Shi'ism.* The Islamic Renaissance Series. Group One, Translation of the Works of Ali Shariati. Tehran: Shariati Foundation.

———. 1979d. *Ali Shariati's Yea Brother! That's the Way It Was.* Islamic Renaissance Series. Group One, Translation of the Works of Ali Shariati. Tehran: Shariati Foundation.

———. 1982. *Man and Islam: Lectures.* Mashhad, Iran: University of Mashhad Press.

Sheikh-ol-Islami, Mohammad Djawad. 1965. Iran's First Experience of Military Coup d'Etat in the Era of Her Constitutional Government. Ph.D.: Ruprecht-Karl University.

Shirley, Edward G. (pseudonym) 1998. "Good Mullah, Bad Mullah: Revolutionary Iran and the 'Great Satan'." *The Weekly Standard* 3 (January 19): 20–25.

Sick, Gary. 1985. *All Fall Down: America's Tragic Encounter with Iran.* New York: Random House.

———. 1989. "Review of Iran and the United States—A Cold War Case Study by Cottam, Richard W." *Middle East Journal* 43 (3): 515–15.

———. 1991. *October Surprise: America's Hostages in Iran and the Election of Ronald Reagan.* New York, Toronto: Times Books, Random House.

Siegel, Bernard J., and Alan R. Beals. 1960. "Conflict and Factionalist Dispute." *Journal of the Anthropological Institute of Great Britain and Ireland* 90 (1): 107–17.

Singh, K. R. 1980. *Iran, Quest for Security.* New Delhi: Vikas.

Souresrafil, Omid. 2001. *Revolution in Iran: The Transition to Democracy.* London: Pluto.

Sparhawk, Frank. 1980. "Iran's Modernization Failure and the Muslim Background." *The Humanist* 40 (2): 8–12.

Stauffer, Thomas R. 2003a. "The Cost of Middle East Conflict, 1956–2002: What the U.S. Has Spent." *Middle East Policy* 10 (1): 45–112.

———. 2003b. "The Costs to American Taxpayers of the Israeli-Palestinian Conflict: $3 Trillion." In *Washington Report on Middle East Affairs*, vol. 22 (5): 20–23.

———. 2003c. "Unlike Dimona, Iran's Bushehr Reactor Not Useful For Weapons-Grade Plutonium." *Washington Report on Middle East Affairs* 22 (7): 28–29.

Steele, Robert D., James P. Rutherfurd, and John Bassett Moore Society of International Law. 1981. *The Iran Crisis and International Law: Proceedings of the John Bassett Moore Society of International Law Symposium on Iran Held at the University of Virginia School of Law, October 31, November 1, 1980.* Charlottesville, VA: John Bassett Moore Society of International Law.

Stoessel, Walter J., and United States. Dept. of State. Office of Public Communication. Editorial Division. 1981. *Implementing Hostage Agreements: March 4, 1981.* Washington, DC: U.S. Dept. of State, Bureau of Public Affairs, Office of Public Communication, Editorial Division.

Strathern, Andrew J. 1983. "Tribe and State: Some Concluding Remarks." *The Conflict of Tribe and State in Iran and Afghanistan.* Richard Tapper, ed. London: Croom Helm: 449–53.

Sullivan, William H. 1981. *Mission to Iran.* New York: Norton.

———. 1982. "For Embattled Ambassadors in Strife-Torn Countries—No Single Irrefutable 'Truths'." *Pacific News Service.* February 17.

Szalay, Lorand B. 1979. *Iranian and American Perceptions and Cultural Frames of Reference: A Communication Lexicon for Cultural Understanding.* Washington, DC: Institute of Comparative Social & Cultural Studies.

Tabari, Azar, and William M. Brinner. 1991. *The Children of Israel.* Albany: SUNY Press.

Tabari, Azar, and Nahid Yeganeh. 1982. *In the Shadow of Islam: The Women's Movement in Iran.* London: Zed Press.

Tabataba'i, Muhammad Husayn. 1975. *Shiite Islam.* London: Allen and Unwin.

Taheri, Amir. 2002. "George Bush Et L 'Axe Du Mal'." *Politique-Internationale* (96 [summer]): 69–80.

Talmadge, Caitlin, editor. 2002. "An Axis of Evil?" (Forum) *Harvard Political Review* 29 (1 [spring]): 11–24.

Tapper, Richard. editor. 1983a. *The Conflict of Tribe and State in Iran and Afghanistan.* London; New York: Croom Helm; St. Martin's Press.

———. 1983b. "Introduction." *The Conflict of Tribe and State in Iran and Afghanistan. London.* Richard Tapper, ed. London; New York: Croom Helm; St. Martin's Press: 1–82.

———. 2002. *The New Iranian Cinema: Politics, Representation and Identity.* London; New York: I. B. Tauris Publishers.

Tikku, Girdhari L., and Gustave E. Von Grunebaum. 1971. *Islam and Its Cultural Divergence; Studies in Honor of Gustave E. Von Grunebaum.* Urbana: University of Illinois Press.

Torkzahrani, Moustafa. 1997. "Iran after Khatami: Civil Society and Foreign Policy." *Iranian Journal of International Affairs* 9: 499–512.

Tripp, Charles. 2000. *A History of Iraq.* Cambridge: Cambridge University Press.

Tritton, A. S. 1936. "Shaitan." *Encyclopedia of Islam.* Leiden: Brill.

Turner, Victor Witter. 1967. *The Forest of Symbols; Aspects of Ndembu Ritual.* Ithaca, NY: Cornell University Press.

———. 1969. *The Ritual Process: Structure and Anti-Structure.* The Lewis Henry Morgan Lectures, 1966. Chicago: Aldine Pub. Co.

———. 1974. *Dramas, Fields, and Metaphors; Symbolic Action in Human Society.* Ithaca, NY: Cornell University Press.

United Nations. Economic and Social Commision for Asia and the Pacific, Development Planning Division. 1978. "The Iranian Economy: Oil and Development in the First Half of the 1970's." *Economic Bulletin for Asia and the Pacific* 29 (2): 37–48.

United Nations. International Atomic Energy Commission (IAEA). 2004. "Communication Dated 26 November 2004 Received from the Permanent Representatives of France, Germany, the Islamic Republic of Iran and the United Kingdom Concerning the Agreement Signed in Paris on 15 November 2004." Information Circular 637. November 26.

United States. 1980. *An Act to Provide Certain Benefits to Individuals Held Hostage in Iran and to Similarly Situated Individuals, and for Other Purposes.* Washington, DC: U.S. G.P.O. Supt. of Docs. U.S. G.P.O. distributor.

———. 1987. *Joint Resolution to Support a Ceasefire in the Iran-Iraq War and a Negotiated Solution to the Conflict.* Washington, DC: Supt. of Docs. U.S. G.P.O. distributor.

United States. Central Intelligence Agency. Directorate of Intelligence. 1991. "Government Structure of the Islamic Republic of Iran: A Reference Aid." Washington, DC, Springfield, VA: Central Intelligence Agency Directorate of Intelligence; National Technical Information Service distributor.

United States. Central Intelligence Agency. Directorate of Intelligence. 1991. "Government Structure of the Islamic Republic of Iran," p. v. Washington, DC, Springfield, VA: The Directorate: Document Expediting (DOCEX) Project Exchange and Gift Division Library of Congress distributor; National Technical Information Service distributor.

———. 1994. *Government Structure of the Islamic Republic of Iran: A Reference Aid.* Washington, DC: The Agency.

United States. Congress. House. Committee on Appropriations. 1979. *Hearings by Joint Subcommittees on Department of Defense Appropriations for 1980: Hearings before Subcommittees of the Committee on Appropriations, House of Representatives, Ninety-Sixth Congress, First Session.* Washington, DC: U.S. Government Printing Office.

United States. Congress. House. Committee on Foreign Affairs. Subcommittee on International Operations. 1980. *Hostage Relief Act of 1980: Hearings and Markup before the Committee on Foreign Affairs and Its Subcommittee on International Operations, House of Representatives, Ninety-Sixth Congress, Second Session, on H.R. 7085, July 24, September 3 and 10, 1980.* Washington, DC: U.S. Government Printing Office.

United States. Congress. House. Committee on Foreign Affairs. 1980. *Special Central American Economic Assistance: Compensation for Hostages in Iran: International Conference on Cambodia: Hearing and Markup before the Committee on Foreign Affairs, House of Representatives, Ninety-Sixth Congress, First Session, on H.R. 5954, H. Con. Res. 219 and 221, November 27 and December 11, 1979.* Washington, DC: U.S. Government Printing Office.

United States. Congress. House. Committee on Foreign Affairs. Subcommittee on Europe and the Middle East. 1992. *Developments in Europe, February 1992: Hearing before the Subcommittee on Europe and the Middle East of the Committee on Foreign Affairs, House of Representatives, One Hundred Second Congress, Second Session, February 26, 1992.* Washington, DC: U.S. Government Printing Office.

United States. Congress. House. Committee on Foreign Affairs. Subcommittee on

Europe and the Middle East., and United States. Congress. House. Committee on Foreign Affairs. Subcommittee on International Economic Policy and Trade. 1980. *Iranian Asset Controls: Hearing before the Subcommittees on Europe and the Middle East and on International Economic Policy and Trade of the Committee on Foreign Affairs, House of Representatives, Ninety-Sixth Congress, Second Session, May 8, 1980.* Washington, DC: U.S. Government Printing Office.

United States. Congress. House. Committee on Foreign Affairs. Task Force to Investigate Certain Allegations Concerning the Holding of American Hostages by Iran in 1980. 1993. *Joint Report of the Task Force to Investigate Certain Allegations Concerning the Holding of American Hostages by Iran in 1980 ("October Surprise Task Force").* Washington, DC: U.S. Government Printing Office.

United States. Congress. House. Committee on Government Operations. Environment Energy and Natural Resources Subcommittee. 1981. *Effect of Iraqi-Iranian Conflict on U.S. Energy Policy: Hearing before a Subcommittee on the Committee on Government Operations, House of Representatives, Ninety-Sixth Congress, Second Session, September 30, 1980.* Washington, DC: U.S. Government Printing Office.

United States. Congress. House. Committee on International Relations. Subcommittee on International Economic Policy and Trade. 1995. *U.S. Sanctions on Iran: Next Steps: Hearing before the Subcommittee on International Economic Policy and Trade of the Committee on International Relations, House of Representatives, One Hundred Fourth Congress, First Session, May 2, 1995.* Washington, DC: U.S. Government Printing Office.

United States. Congress. House. Committee on International Relations. Subcommittee on International Organizations. 1976. *Human Rights in Iran: Hearings before the Subcommittee on International Organizations of the Committee on International Relations, House of Representatives, Ninety-Fourth Congress, Second Session, August 3 and September 8, 1976.* International Human Rights. Washington, DC: U.S. Government Printing Office.

United States. Congress. House, Committee on International Relations, Subcommittee on International Organizations. 1977. *Human Rights in Iran: Hearings before the Subcommittee on International Organizations of the Committee on International Relations, House of Representatives, Ninety-Fifth Congress, First Session* Hearings of October 26, 1977. Washington, DC: U.S. Government Printing Office.

United States. Congress. House. Committee on Post Office and Civil Service, United States. Congress. House. Committee on Foreign Affairs, and United States. Congress. House. Committee on Ways and Means. 1980. *Hostage Relief Act of 1980: Report (to Accompany H.R. 7085) (Including Cost Estimate of the Congressional Budget Office).* Washington, DC: U.S. Government Printing Office.

United States. Congress. House. Committee on Rules. 1991a. *Creating a Task Force to Investigate Allegations Concerning the Holding of Americans as Hostages by Iran: Report Together with Additional and Minority Views (to Accompany H. Res. 258) (Including Cost Estimate of the Congressional Budget Office).* Washington, DC: U.S. Government Printing Office.

————. 1991b. *Providing for the Consideration of House Resolution 258: Report (to Accompany H. Res. 303)*. Washington, DC: U.S. Government Printing Office.

United States. Congress. Joint Economic Committee. 1980. *Economic Consequences of the Revolution in Iran: A Compendium of Papers*. Washington, DC: U.S. Government Printing Office.

United States. Congress. Senate. Committee on Foreign Relations. 1992. *The "October Surprise" Allegations and the Circumstances Surrounding the Release of the American Hostages Held in Iran: Report of the Special Counsel to Senator Terry Sanford and Senator James M. Jeffords of the Committee on Foreign Relations, United States Senate*. S. Prt.; 102–25. Washington, DC: U.S. Government Printing Office.

United States. Congress. Senate. Committee on Foreign Relations. 1981. *The Situation in Iran: Hearing before the Committee on Foreign Relations, United States Senate, Ninety-Sixth Congress, Second Session, May 8, 1980*. Washington, DC: U.S. Government Printing Office.

————. 1984. *War in the Gulf: A Staff Report*. Washington, DC: U.S. Government Printing Office.

————. 1991. *Supplemental Funding: Report Together with Additional and Minority Views (to Accompany S. Res. 198)*. Washington, DC: U.S. Government Printing Office.

————. 1992. *The "October Surprise" Allegations and the Circumstances Surrounding the Release of the American Hostages Held in Iran: Report of the Special Counsel to Senator Terry Sanford and Senator James M. Jeffords of the Committee on Foreign Relations, United States Senate*. S. Prt.; 102–25. Washington, DC: U.S. Government Printing Office.

United States. Congress. Senate. Committee on Foreign Relations. Subcommittee on Near Eastern and South Asian Affairs. 1992a. *Whether the Senate Should Proceed to Investigate Circumstances Surrounding the Release of the American Hostages in 1980: Hearing before the Subcommittee on near Eastern and South Asian Affairs of the Committee on Foreign Relations, United States Senate, One Hundred Second Congress, First Session*. Washington, DC: U.S. Government Printing Office.

————. 1992b. *Whether the Senate Should Proceed to Investigate Circumstances Surrounding the Release of the American Hostages in 1980: Hearing before the Subcommittee on near Eastern and South Asian Affairs of the Committee on Foreign Relations, United States Senate, One Hundred Second Congress, First Session, November 21 and 22, 1991*. Washington, DC: U.S. Government Printing Office.

United States. Department of State. 2001. "Patterns of Global Terrorism 2000." United States Department of State. April. www.state.gove/s/ct/rls/pgtrpt/2000.

United States. Department of State. Office of the Coordinator for Counterterrorism. 2003. "Patterns of Global Terrorism—2002." United States Department of State. www.state.gov/s/ct/rls/pgtrpt/2002/html/19988.htm

United States. Dept. of Justice. Office of Legal Counsel. 1980. "Opinions of the Office of Legal Counsel of the United States Department of Justice," p.v. Washington, DC: U.S. Government Printing Office.

United States. Department of State. 2001. "Patterns of Global Terrorism 2000, 2001." April 2001. www.state.gov/s/ct/rls/pgtrpt/2000.

United States. Department of State. Bureau of Public Affairs. 1981. *Hostage Agreements Transmitted to Congress: March 12, 1981.* Washington, DC: U.S. Department of State, Bureau of Public Affairs.

United States. Department of State. Office of Public Communication. Editorial Division. 1980a. *U.S. Presses Hostage Case in World Court: March 1980.* Washington, DC: U.S. Dept. of State, Bureau of Public Affairs, Office of Public Communication, Editorial Division.

————. 1980b. *U.S. Presses Hostage Case in World Court: March 1980.* Washington, DC: U.S. Dept. of State, Bureau of Public Affairs, Office of Public Communication, Editorial Division.

United States. Joint Chiefs of Staff. Special Operations Review Group. 1980. *Rescue Mission Report.* Washington, DC: Joint Chiefs of Staff.

United States. President (1977–1981: Carter), Harold Brown, and United States. Dept. of State. Office of Public Communication. Editorial Division. 1980. *Hostage Rescue Attempt in Iran.* Washington, DC: Dept. of State, Bureau of Public Affairs, Office of Public Communication, Editorial Division.

United States. President (1977–1981: Carter), and Jimmy Carter. 1980a. *Further Prohibitions on Transactions with Iran: Message from the President of the United States Transmitting Notice That He Has Exercised His Authority under the International Emergency Economic Powers Act to Impose Further Prohibitions on Transactions with Iran, Pursuant to Section 204(B) of the Act.* Washington, DC: U.S. Government Printing Office.

————. 1980b. *Sanctions against Iran: Message from the President of the United States Transmitting Notice That He Has Exercised His Authority under the International Emergency Economic Powers Act to Take Certain Trade, Financial and Other Measures against Iran and Its Nationals, Pursuant to Section 204(B) of the Act.* Washington, DC: U.S. Government Printing Office.

————. 1980c. *Use of U.S. Armed Forces in Attempted Rescue of Hostages in Iran: Communication from the President of the United States Transmitting a Report on the Use of United States Armed Forces in an Attempt to Rescue the American Hostages Held in Iran, Pursuant to Section 4(a) of the War Powers Resolution of 1973 (Public Law 93–148).* Washington, DC: U.S. Government Printing Office.

United States. President (1977–1981: Carter), Jimmy Carter, and United States. Congress. House. Committee on Foreign Affairs. 1980. *Semiannual Report on Sanctions against Iran: Message from the President of the United States, Transmitting a Report on Actions Taken since April 17, 1980, and Changes in Previously-Reported Information, with Respect to Executive Orders 12170, 12205, and 12211, Pursuant to Section 204(C) of the International Emergency Economic Powers Act.* Washington, DC: U.S. Government Printing Office.

United States. President (1977–1981: Carter), and United States. Congress. House. Committee on Foreign Affairs. 1980. *Continuing the National Emergency with Respect to the Situation in Iran: Message from the President of the United States Transmitting a Notice Extending the National Emergency Declared on November 14, 1979, Pursuant to Section 202(D) of Public Law 94–412.* Washington, DC: U.S. Government Printing Office.

United States. Congress. House. Committee on International Relations. 1998.

Developments Concerning National Emergency with Iran: Communication from the President of the United States Transmitting a Report on Developments Concerning the National Emergency with Respect to Iran That Was Declared in Executive Order 12170 of November 14, 1979, Pursuant to 50 U.S.C. 1703(C). Washington, DC: U.S. Government Printing Office.

Vahdat, Farzin. 2002. *God and Juggernaut: Iran's Intellectual Encounter with Modernity*, 1st edition. Modern Intellectual and Political History of the Middle East. Syracuse: Syracuse University Press.

Vakil, Firouz. 1977. "Iran's Basic Macroeconomic Problems: A Twenty-year Horizon." *Economic Development and Cultural Change* 25 (2): 713–30.

Van Bruinessen, Martin. 1983. "Kurdish Tribes and the State of Iran: The Case of Simko's Revolt." *The Conflict of tribe and state in Iran and Afghanistan.* London: 364–400.

Vance, Cyrus R., and United States. Dept. of State. Office of Public Communication. Editorial Division. 1980. *Statement on Iran to Security Council: December 29, 1979*. Washington, DC: U.S. Dept. of State, Bureau of Public Affairs, Office of Public Communication, Editorial Division.

Vaziri, Haleh. 1992. "Iran's Involvement in Lebanon: Polarization and Radicalization of Militant Islamic Movements." *Journal of South Asian and Middle Eastern Studies* 16 (2 [winter]): 1–16.

Vicker, Ray. 1975. "For Average Iranian, Oil Revenues Bring a More Modern Life. They Lead to a Better Job and Maybe Even a Car; but State Has Its Woes." *Wall Street Journal*. August 4: 1ff.

———. 1977. "Growing Pains: Despite Its Oil Money, Iran's Economy Suffers from Many Shortages. It Lags in Utility Services, Skilled Workers; Waste and Inflation Also Hurt, But Port Bottlenecks Ease." *Wall Street Journal*. April 11: 1+.

———. 1978. "The Opposition in Iran." *Wall Street Journal*. August 3: 12.

Voice of the Islamic Republic of Iran. 2003. *Iran: Radio Commentary Criticizes U.S. Support for Iraq During Iran–Iraq War*. January 19, 2003 10:30 GMT. Iran. BBC Monitoring International Reports.

Von Grunebaum, Gustave E. 1961. *Islam; Essays in the Nature and Growth of a Cultural Tradition*, 2nd. edition. London: Routledge & Kegan Paul.

Washington Times. 2003. "Tehran's Stonewalling [Editorial]." *Washington Times*. (November 28): A24.

Watts, David. 1978. "Is the Shah Unifying Those Who Are against Him?" *The Times of London*. May 26.

Watzlawick, Paul. 1977. *How Real Is Real? Confusion, Disinformation, Communication*. New York: Vintage Books.

———. 1978. *The Language of Change: Elements of Therapeutic Communication*. New York: Basic Books.

Watzlawick, Paul, Janet Beavin Bavelas, and Don D. Jackson. 1967. *Pragmatics of Human Communication; a Study of Interactional Patterns, Pathologies, and Paradoxes*. New York: Norton.

Watzlawick, Paul, John H. Weakland, and Mental Research Institute. 1977. *The Interactional View: Studies at the Mental Research Institute, Palo Alto, 1965–1974*. New York: Norton.

Weinbaum, Marvin G. 1977. "Agricultural Policy and Development Politics in Iran." *Middle East Journal* 31 (4): 434–50.

Wellenson, K., and K. Willenson. 1975. "This Gun for Hire." *Newsweek* 85: 30+.

Wells, Tim. 1985. *444 Days: The Hostages Remember*. San Diego: Harcourt Brace Jovanovich.

Weymouth, Lally. 2005. "Strains with America." in *Newsweek* 145 (February 7): 31–33. www.msnbc.msn.com/id/6885158/site/newsweek/.

Wright, Robin. 2005. "Most of Iran's Troops in Lebanon Are out, Western Officials Say." *The Washington Post*. April 13: A10.

Wright, Robin B. 2001. *The Last Great Revolution*. New York: Random House.

Yapp, Malcolm E. 1991. "Cold War Rituals: Review of Neither East nor West—Iran, the Soviet Union, and the United States, edited by Keddie, Nikki R., and Gasiorowski, Mark J." *The Times Literary Supplement* 4588 (March 8): 7.

Yetiv, Steve A. 1998. "The Evolution of U.S.–Russian Rivalry and Cooperation in the Persian Gulf." *Journal of South Asian and Middle Eastern Studies* 21: 13–30.

Yousefi, Naghi. 1995. *Religion and Revolution in the Modern World: Ali Shari'ati's Islam and Persian Revolution*. University Press of America.

Zabih, Sepehr. 1979. *Iran's Revolutionary Upheaval: An Interpretive Essay*. San Francisco: Alchemy Books.

Zendran, Peter Khan 2005. "Black Ops Target Iran" *The Iranian* June 2.

Zenner, Walter P. 1961. "The Non-Muslin Minorities of Iran." *Harvard University*. Department of Anthropology. *Anthropology 213*. Seminar. Peoples and Cultures of the Middle East.

Zirinsky, M. P. 1992. "Review of United States Foreign Policy and the Shah—Building a Client State in Iran by Gasiorowski, Mark J." *Middle East Journal* 46 (2): 324–25.

Zonis, Marvin. 1991. *Majestic Failure: The Fall of the Shah*. Chicago: University of Chicago Press.

Index

About the Author

WILLIAM O. BEEMAN is Professor of Anthropology and Director of Middle East Studies at Brown University. He has lived and conducted research for over 30 years in all areas of the Middle East. He has served as a consultant to the U.S. State Department and the Department of Defense, and has testified before Congress on Middle Eastern affairs. He is the President-Elect of the Middle East Section of the American Anthropological Association (2005–2006) and will serve as President from autumn 2006 until 2008, then as Outgoing President from 2008 to 2009.

.